World Economic and Financial

Global Financial Stability Report

Market Developments and Issues

April 2004

International Monetary Fund
Washington DC

Production: IMF Multimedia Services Division
Cover: Phil Torsani
Photo: Padraic Hughes
Figures: Theodore F. Peters, Jr.
Typesetting: Choon Lee

ISBN 1-58906-328-7
ISSN 0258-7440

Price: US$49.00
(US$46.00 to full-time faculty members and
students at universities and colleges)

Please send orders to:
International Monetary Fund, Publication Services
700 19th Street, N.W., Washington, D.C. 20431, U.S.A.
Tel.: (202) 623-7430   Telefax: (202) 623-7201
E-mail: publications@imf.org
Internet:http://www.imf.org

recycled paper

CONTENTS

Boxes

Tables

Figures

The following symbols have been used throughout this volume:

... to indicate that data are not available;

— to indicate that the figure is zero or less than half the final digit shown, or that the item does not exist;

– between years or months (for example, 1997–99 or January–June) to indicate the years or months covered, including the beginning and ending years or months;

/ between years (for example, 1998/99) to indicate a fiscal or financial year.

"Billion" means a thousand million; "trillion" means a thousand billion.

"Basis points" refer to hundredths of 1 percentage point (for example, 25 basis points are equivalent to ¼ of 1 percentage point).

"n.a." means not applicable.

Minor discrepancies between constituent figures and totals are due to rounding.

As used in this volume the term "country" does not in all cases refer to a territorial entity that is a state as understood by international law and practice. As used here, the term also covers some territorial entities that are not states but for which statistical data are maintained on a separate and independent basis.

PREFACE

The *Global Financial Stability Report* (GFSR) assesses global financial market developments with the view to identifying potential systemic weaknesses. By calling attention to potential fault lines in the global financial system, the report seeks to play a role in preventing crises, thereby contributing to global financial stability and to the sustained economic growth of the IMF's member countries.

The report was prepared by the International Capital Markets Department, under the direction of the Counsellor and Director, Gerd Häusler. It is managed by an Editorial Committee comprising Hung Q. Tran (Chairman), W. Todd Groome, Donald J. Mathieson, and David J. Ordoobadi, and benefits from comments and suggestions from Axel Bertuch-Samuels, Peter Dattels, and Eliot Kalter. Other contributors to this issue are Francesc Balcells, Elie Canetti, Jorge Chan-Lau, Toni Gravelle, François Haas, Anna Ilyina, Janet Kong, Markus Krygier, William Lee, Gabrielle Lipworth, Chris Morris, Jürgen Odenius, Kazunari Ohashi, Li Lian Ong, Lars Pedersen, Magdalena Polan, Jorge Roldos, Calvin Schnure, Manmohan Singh, Rupert Thorne, and a staff team from the Monetary and Financial Systems Department (MFD) that included S. Kal Wajid, Udaibir Das, Nigel Davies, Gianni De Nicoló, and Kalin Tintchev. Martin Edmonds, Ivan Guerra, Silvia Iorgova, Anne Jansen, Oksana Khadarina, Yoon Sook Kim, Ned Rumpeltin, and Peter Tran provided research assistance. Caroline Bagworth, Jane Harris, Vera Jasenovec, Elsa Portaro, and Ramanjeet Singh provided expert word processing assistance. Jeff Hayden of the External Relations Department edited the manuscript and coordinated production of the publication.

This particular issue draws, in part, on a series of informal discussions with commercial and investment banks, securities firms, asset management companies, insurance companies, pension funds, stock and futures exchanges, and credit rating agencies in Brazil, Chile, China, Colombia, France, Germany, Hong Kong SAR, Hungary, Japan, Korea, Mexico, Poland, Russia, Singapore, South Africa, Switzerland, Thailand, the United Kingdom, and the United States. The report reflects information available up to March 8, 2004.

The report has benefited from comments and suggestions from staff in other IMF departments, as well as from Executive Directors following their discussions of the *Global Financial Stability Report* on March 26, 2004. However, the analysis and policy considerations are those of the contributing staff and should not be attributed to the Executive Directors, their national authorities, or the IMF.

Global financial vulnerabilities have subsided further since the September 2003 *Global Financial Stability Report* (GFSR). International financial markets have continued to improve, strengthening the balance sheets of financial institutions and other market participants. At present, financial markets seem to be enjoying a "sweet spot:" economic activity and corporate earnings have made a strong recovery, most noticeably in the United States but also in other parts of the world. At the same time, inflation remains quiescent, enabling the monetary authorities to maintain very low policy interest rates.

Emerging bond markets have benefited from the abundance of liquidity and the search for yield, as well as from the improved credit quality of many emerging market sovereign and corporate borrowers. As a result, the EMBI yield spread has declined to near record lows. Capital flows to emerging market countries have increased, and borrowing costs are much lower, compared with recent years. Including prefinancing done last year, many emerging market countries have secured a substantial portion of their 2004 external financing needs.

Overall, many market indicators suggest that the current benign financial conditions in mature and emerging markets will likely continue for the time being (Chapter II). The price consolidation in many equity and emerging bond markets since the beginning of the year is a welcome development to the extent that it reflects a degree of caution on the part of investors. But this outlook is not without risk. A closer look exposes some fault lines that could impinge on stability in financial markets some time down the road.

Risks

The main risk to the benign outlook for global financial markets is that such an outlook rests on a very fine balancing of opposing economic forces. Low inflation, sustained by rising productivity and substantial slack in the economy, should help to maintain low interest rates for some time and would limit the extent of any potential tightening in policy rates. Consequently, while expecting interest rates to rise eventually, markets have remained sanguine about the potential impact of such a rate increase on other asset markets. But this benign view has been tempered by global economic imbalances, which have focused market attention on the sustainability of the unprecedented gross and net capital flows into the United States. Such concerns contributed to a weakening of the U.S. dollar. In recent months, however, official inflows—largely reflecting foreign exchange market interventions by many Asian central banks—have increased substantially. In addition, private sector inflows—notably to U.S. equities and corporate bonds from European investors—have recovered. These developments have helped ensure a gradual and orderly adjustment of the dollar that, so far, has not noticeably affected most financial asset prices. At this time, market participants expect the orderly adjustment process to continue. If this delicate balance were to be impaired, leading to a reduction of the official and private inflows, the dollar could weaken more pronouncedly. At any sign of that risk materializing, foreign investors could demand a risk premium on dollar assets—including pushing bond yields higher and with more volatility than current market expectations. This would have a negative spillover effect on other asset markets, including pushing up yields in Europe and emerging markets. This adverse development could reverse the strengthening of financial institutions' balance sheets and create headwinds to the economic recovery. This may also expose remaining structural weaknesses in several emerging market countries, so far masked by buoyant market conditions.

Another facet of the delicate balance is whether the abundance of liquidity, which has been instrumental in bolstering investor confidence and valuations in most asset markets, could at some point become more of a problem. Now that economic activities and corporate earnings have recovered strongly, the continued abundance of liquidity and a lack of two-way interest rate risk could lead to a sense of complacency and intensify the search for yield, while neglecting risk factors. There have been anecdotal signs of "herding behavior" as investors move to risky assets that may not be familiar to them, but have performed well in the past year. This process could lead to an overvaluation of certain financial assets, particularly in small and illiquid markets such as many emerging markets. The longer this process persists, the greater the potential for disruptive corrections.

The risks facing emerging market countries themselves are also finely balanced and increasingly differentiated. As a group, emerging market countries have greatly improved their economic fundamentals: stronger growth with inflation still under control, current account surplus in the sixth consecutive year—meaning they continue to be net exporters of capital to the rest of the world—and substantial accumulation of foreign exchange reserves. These improvements have reduced their external vulnerability. However, the aggregate performance masks a widening gulf between countries that have made significant progress and those that have not. Among the former are countries enjoying credit upgrades, including to investment grades. Presently, more than 50 percent of the emerging bond market capitalization carries an investment grade, compared to less than 10

percent five years ago. Among the countries that have made lackluster progress are those whose level and currency-mismatched nature of public debt would make them vulnerable to a deterioration in the external financing environment. This vulnerability is all the more relevant since these countries have had a degree of yield spread compression comparable to that of the improving countries, given the abundance of liquidity mentioned earlier. In some emerging market countries, including some of those where elections are on the horizon, social and political instability pose potential risks to policy continuity.

More Attention Needed for Structural Issues in Major Financial Centers

Given the currently benign conjunctural situation, increased attention should be given to fundamental changes that could improve the resiliency of the international financial system to future shocks. One of the most important changes in recent years has been the transfer of risk—in particular credit risk—from the banking sector to the nonbanking sectors of the financial system and beyond. So far, this phenomenon seems to have strengthened the resiliency of the banking sector in the face of severe shocks, including record credit defaults in recent years. But it has also meant a transfer of credit risk from relatively more regulated institutions to relatively less regulated institutions, and from relatively more transparent institutions to relatively less transparent institutions.

The transfer of risk to nonbanking sectors has therefore raised several concerns: Where has the risk gone? Has risk been widely dispersed or concentrated? Are the recipients of risk able to manage the risk they have assumed? Given all the changes, is there the potential for regulatory arbitrage? Inconsistencies and gaps in regulation and supervision could create strong incentives and the temptation to exploit such shortcomings. Moreover, as many nonbanks have also begun to reduce their own risk profiles, ultimately these risks would have to be transferred to end users of the financial system. Consequently, households, corporates, and public sector entities could become exposed more and more directly to financial risks.

A series of analytical chapters in this and future issues of the GFSR will examine the implication of these changes for global financial stability. In this context, financial stability is defined broadly to encompass not just the avoidance of bank failures that threaten payment systems and cause disruptions in economic activities. From this broader perspective, financial stability encompasses the absence of large and persistent changes in financial market prices and flows that interfere with efficient financial intermediation. Examples of this include exaggerated declines in asset prices, high risk aversion for a prolonged period, and market structures that allow normal market volatility to turn into financial instability.

The series of chapters will also attempt to analyze whether, given the increased exposure of the household sector to financial market risks, the authorities in major financial centers could feel pressured to add liquidity to help prevent large and sustained declines in asset prices. A large and sustained asset price fall could have huge economic costs, including contributing to the risk of deflation—as illustrated by Japan's experience. Such high costs, and the natural inclination to avoid them, could make it harder for the authorities to accept a downward correction of financial markets. In fact, this perception could lead to a new form of moral hazard. Market participants might expect the bailouts of key asset markets "too important to fall," while traditionally they could have expected rescues only of financial institutions "too big to fail." As a result, market participants could become complacent and prepare to take on more risk than otherwise justified by fundamental developments. Ultimately, such behavior could contribute to more pronounced upswings in

certain asset markets, to be followed eventually by a correction that could be more prolonged and painful.

Beginning this series, Chapter III focuses on the transfer of risk from banking to nonbanking institutions, in this case to the insurance industry, and examines the key factors shaping the risk appetite and risk management culture of life insurance companies. These factors include market characteristics, regulations, accounting standards, and rating agencies. Chapter III of the September 2004 GFSR will look at similar issues in the pension fund sector.

Chapter IV surveys the growth and development of international and domestic institutional investors for emerging market securities and the impact of these developments on the stability of capital flows to emerging capital markets.

Reallocation of Credit Risk to the Insurance Sector: Impact on Financial Stability

The recent growth in credit derivatives as complex credit risk transfer instruments and the lack of transparency on such transactions have prompted concerns about where risk has migrated from the banking sector (see March 2002 GFSR). Since then, various official bodies and private sector organizations have undertaken work, including surveys of market participants, to shed more light on this issue. In gross terms, banks have conducted credit derivative transactions largely with other banks to achieve their desired exposures. The insurance sector is a net taker of credit risk (through these derivatives), but these net positions form a small part (generally 3 to 4 percent) of their asset portfolios. Even more, exposure to traditional credit instruments, broadly defined, has been part of insurers' investment portfolios for a long time, and substantial in volume. In recent years, there seems to be relatively stronger growth in the credit exposure of the insurance sector compared to the banking sector. The broader and ongoing reallocation of credit risk could have implications for financial stability.

The patterns and levels of involvement of insurers in credit instruments, however, have differed widely by countries and regions, driven mainly by traditional market characteristics and regulations. Overall, credit instruments, with their low volatility and known cash flows, have proven to be appropriate for insurers to match against their long-term liabilities. They also offer a yield pickup over government securities, but at much lower risk than equity holdings. Moreover, a well-developed credit market, including credit derivatives, coupled with appropriate risk-based capital and accounting regimes create strong incentives for insurers to build their credit risk management capability. National insurance sectors that have a larger exposure to credit instruments than equities have been more stable during periods of financial stresses, most notably during 2000–03.

Driven by this experience, many large insurers—mainly in Europe—have raised their capital, increased exposures to credit instruments relative to equities, and strengthened their risk management capabilities. Taken together, these developments are likely to reduce the kind of balance sheet pressures encountered by the insurance sector in recent years. At the same time, previous issues of the GFSR have highlighted the improved resilience of the banking sector against financial shocks. Consequently, the relative reallocation of credit risk between these two sectors appears to have enhanced financial stability. This has been achieved by exploiting the insurers' comparative advantage in holding credit instruments and—more importantly—by encouraging further development in risk management capabilities in the insurance sector. This assessment, however, is subject to two caveats. First, in recent years, many insurers have changed their products in ways that have begun to shorten the duration of their liabilities. At some point in the future, this would

raise questions about the comparative advantage of insurers in holding credit risk. Second, as insurers have taken steps to manage their balance sheet risk, they would transfer some of these risks elsewhere, and ultimately to the household sector. This evidently will have implications for financial stability, and will be examined in a future issue of the GFSR.

The Role of Institutional Investors in Emerging Securities Markets

Despite a series of crises in recent years, emerging stock and bond markets have made progress in their maturation process. Key to this process is the increasing role played by institutional investors, both international and domestic, in emerging markets (Chapter IV).

The strong risk-adjusted returns of emerging securities, especially sovereign bonds, have led many international institutional investors, such as pension funds and life insurance companies, to make a strategic allocation to the emerging market asset class, mainly for diversification purposes. This has helped to widen the pool of funds committed to investing in emerging markets. Since these are long-term buy-and-hold investors, this is likely to enhance the stability of capital flows to emerging markets. This development could counterbalance the more frequent trading activity of hedge funds and other opportunistic investors. However, since the assets under management of these international institutions are so big, relative to the market capitalization as well as to the annual flows into many emerging markets, a relatively small reallocation by these players can have a disproportionate impact on the concerned markets.

Pension funds and insurance companies usually farm out funds to asset managers specializing in emerging markets or to mutual funds. Naturally these dedicated mutual funds also receive inflows from retail investors. The growth of dedicated emerging market funds has been accompanied by an improvement in the knowledge of portfolio managers and the professionalism of investment decisions. It has also enabled these funds to invest in a broadly diversified portfolio of emerging markets. For retail investors, this would be a superior way to invest in emerging markets, compared with the recent experience of many retail investors in Europe and Japan. These retail investors, perhaps on the naïve assumption that sovereign borrowers do not default, had bought specific international sovereign bonds. Overall, the larger role of mutual funds—with more sophisticated portfolio managers—could contribute to more discriminating behavior in emerging markets, and streamline the debt-restructuring process in the unavoidable situation when one is needed.

Despite their positive contributions, mutual funds have to cope with other risks that could contribute to volatility and thus bear watching. First, emerging market asset managers are subject to frequent (usually quarterly) performance reviews by the pension funds or insurance companies that invest in them, and those whose performance falls below a certain threshold will be replaced. This review process could lead asset managers to avoid making investment decisions that differ too much from the benchmark index or the investment behavior of their peers—the risk of having a substantially different performance from the average is too great. This could consequently introduce another element of herding behavior. Second, mutual funds have to cope with redemption risk as retail investors can quickly move money from funds containing assets tainted with potential credit events or losses. Sudden and large redemptions could force fund managers to liquidate assets in more liquid markets, even though these assets or markets may have little in common with the source of the problem causing the redemption in the first place. This, of course, is one of the usual channels for financial contagion.

Many emerging market countries have reformed their pension systems, in the process fostering the growth of funded pension funds.

In addition, life insurance companies and mutual funds have grown in several countries. The assets under management of these institutional investors have probably reached a critical mass and will likely grow further in the foreseeable future. In addition to spurring the development of local capital markets, the domestic institutional investors have exerted some stabilizing influence in external emerging market bond markets. However, relative to the growth of these institutions, domestic capital markets have tended to develop more slowly in terms of market capitalization, liquidity, and variety of instruments. Echoing the discussion in Chapter III, one noticeable feature is the relative underdevelopment of corporate bond markets, including securities of long duration. As a consequence, a major challenge for many countries in the near future is the mismatch between the growth of domestic institutional investors and the relatively less developed domestic securities markets that do not have sufficient size, liquidity, and instruments to satisfy the needs of these institutions.

Moreover, prudent regulations strictly limiting the holding of various types of assets, especially foreign assets, could lead these institutions to focus their investments in certain traditional products. This could lead to a concentration of risk, including a buildup of sovereign debt or asset bubbles in domestic capital markets.

Policy Conclusions

While the adjustment of global imbalances will take time, the key challenge for the authorities in major financial centers is to maintain orderly market conditions that facilitate the smooth financing of global imbalances without taking away the pressure for their adjustment. Any global cooperative effort, designed to reduce economic imbalances in the medium term, would greatly reinforce the favorable market prospects.[1]

---

[1] See IMF's *World Economic Outlook*, April 2004.

Conversely, any sign of policy discord among the major countries could upset the balancing act, leading to a more disorderly adjustment. Moreover, the authorities need to carefully manage the transition from a low interest rate environment, designed to guard against the risk of deflation, to a more normal interest rate environment commensurate with much stronger growth. Besides the timing and extent of any policy move, a communication strategy is essential in guiding market expectations and in avoiding misunderstandings that could contribute to market volatility and overshooting. Market overreactions of 1994 could serve as useful reminders to the authorities. Regulators and supervisors in the financial sector also need to be alert to possible mispricing of risk, excessive buildup of leverage, or concentrated risk exposures.

In the meantime, all countries should take advantage of the benign financial market conditions to persevere in their reform efforts. Mature market countries need to finish reforms to strengthen their market foundations—the ongoing scandals in the mutual fund industry and in companies such as Parmalat show that complacency is not warranted. Emerging market countries need to take steps to reduce the level and vulnerability of their public debt and to further develop local capital markets.

This issue of the GFSR highlights structural developments in key institutional investors and identifies policy measures aimed at improving their ability to manage risk.

In the case of the insurance industry in mature market countries, the policy recommendations refer to further development of credit markets and to the role of regulatory and supervisory regimes, accounting standards, and rating agencies in shaping the risk taking of insurance companies. These measures should aim at encouraging insurance companies to strengthen their credit risk management capability.

- *Further development of credit markets.* Given the positive role of credit instruments—including credit derivatives—in the asset portfolio of insurance companies, authorities should seek to support and facilitate further developments of credit markets. The authorities can review and change relevant legal, tax, and other regulatory measures to make it convenient for issuers and investors to use credit instruments. Private sector initiatives, such as efforts by the International Swap and Derivatives Association to standardize credit derivatives contracts, are welcome as they can stimulate growth in the market.

- *Regulation and supervision.* As insurance regulators and supervisors pay more attention to financial safety and soundness issues, they should pursue a risk-based capital framework. Such a framework aligns more closely prudential requirements with underlying insurance risks and encourages improved risk management capability at insurers. There seems to be a welcome convergence toward such a risk-based capital regime, especially with the evolving Solvency II in the European Union and CP195 in the United Kingdom (see page 92 in Chapter III).[2]

- *Supervisory resources should be enhanced* so that supervisors have appropriate staff and skills to evaluate the risk management models they require of insurers.

- *There is a need for increased dialogue among supervisors* to share information and to deal with the global aspects of insurance companies' activities, particularly those of reinsurers.

- *Disclosure requirements need to be strengthened* to improve transparency in various sub-sectors of the industry (e.g., reinsurance)[3] and in the holding of and dealing in complex instruments (such as credit derivatives).

---

[2]Solvency II is the European Union's "Review of the Overall Financial Position of an Insurance Undertaking" (initiated in 1999). Consultation Paper 195 is the United Kingdom's "Enhanced Capital Requirements and Individual Capital Assessments for Life Insurers" (2003).

[3]Also recommended by the International Association of Insurance Supervisors' Task Force on Enhancing Disclosure and Transparency in the Reinsurance Sector.

- *Accounting standards.* It is important to ensure that financial and regulatory accounts provide an accurate reflection of an insurance company's financial position (see discussion on Fair Value Accounting on page 99 in Chapter III). Assets and liabilities should be measured on a similar (e.g., market value) basis, reflecting all risk exposures. However, point estimates in financial statements are probably not so useful as a comprehensive disclosure that could help market participants understand the true business reality of insurers. It is also appropriate to encourage convergence in the principles of financial accounting and regulatory reporting standards.

- *Rating agencies.* While rating agencies play an important role in disseminating credit information about companies to market participants, it would seem desirable to reduce the disproportionate reliance on rating agencies as *de facto* regulators for reinsurance companies. To achieve this objective, supervisory oversight for these insurers needs to be strengthened. In addition, greater transparency of business activities and financial positions would be useful.

In the case of the investor bases for emerging markets assets, several policy conclusions can be highlighted.

- To attract and maintain the interest of international institutional investors in their sovereign and corporate securities, *emerging market countries should continue to implement strong economic and structural policies* to enhance their growth potential and the resilience of their financial systems. They should also improve disclosure and transparency through, among other measures, subscription to the Special Data Dissemination Standard (SDDS) and regular communications with their investor bases—for example, through investor relations programs.

- *Emerging market countries also need to have a comprehensive plan to develop domestic securities markets,* taking into consideration the growth and needs of domestic institutional investors. These markets should have sufficient size, liquidity, and variety of instruments—especially bonds of long duration—to meet the need of domestic institutional investors. More technically, they should improve market infrastructure, including a liquid secondary market and a good clearing and settlement system potentially in conjunction with other countries. A more developed local securities market could also attract international institutional investors. This would be a superior way for emerging market countries to attract portfolio capital flows as the currency risk ("the original sin") is borne by international investors.

- Pension fund regulators need to *gradually loosen restrictions on foreign investments by local pension managers,* paying attention to the limitations of local markets and to the diversification benefits of international markets, while maintaining adequate "prudent man" regulations.

- There should also be a conscious effort to *gradually replace prescriptive regulations with risk-based capital regimes* that can encourage the development of risk management capability on the part of local insurers. These skills will serve them well when they begin to invest internationally.

- *Mutual funds need to provide adequate disclosure and education* to prospective retail investors so as to reduce redemption risk.

CHAPTER II

GLOBAL FINANCIAL MARKET DEVELOPMENTS

Exceptionally low short-term interest rates in the major financial centers contributed to resurgent economic growth and rising corporate earnings and to progress in strengthening corporate balance sheets, thus improving the fundamental economic outlook.[1] Policies pursued to stimulate economic growth also created powerful incentives for investors to venture further out along the risk spectrum and contributed to a recovery of asset valuations.

The combination of improved fundamentals and abundant liquidity buoyed global asset prices. Appetite for risk recovered and investor flows suggested an allocation away from relatively low-yielding assets in favor of riskier investments. Equity markets worldwide staged strong rallies in 2003, following three successive years of declines. In part reflecting the impact of this rally on investor sentiment, the level of volatility implied by options on European and U.S. equity markets fell. The complementary catalysts of improved credit quality and abundant liquidity also pushed credit spreads on mature and emerging market bonds to low levels, led by precipitous spread compression on high-yield bonds.

This combination created a very favorable external financing environment for emerging market borrowers in 2003 and early 2004. Gross and net issuance by emerging market countries recovered strongly in 2003. Bond issuance in January 2004 was exceptionally high. Many borrowers have appropriately taken advantage of the relatively low cost of capital and strong investor appetite to prefinance their borrowing needs and to undertake liability management operations aimed at improving the structure of their domestic and external debt.

These developments have helped to underpin a further improvement in the outlook for financial market stability since the last issue of the GFSR. Looking ahead, there are two sources of downside risk to the outlook.

- In a low interest rate environment, asset valuations may be pushed beyond levels justified by tangible improvements in fundamentals. Stimulus aimed at recovery may also encourage overvaluation.

- The large global external imbalances and the equally sizable flows they engender pose another potential source of market instability. Adverse developments in the currency markets could heighten investor risk aversion and spill over into other asset markets.

Low short-term interest rates and a steep yield curve provide powerful incentives to boost leverage, undertake carry trades, and seek yield by going out along the credit risk spectrum. There is a real risk of investor complacency in a low interest rate environment. An unanticipated spike in yields and volatility in the U.S. treasury market could also trigger a widening of credit spreads in mature and emerging markets and encourage an unwinding of carry trades and leveraged positions.

In this environment, policymakers and regulators must be vigilant for excessively leveraged or concentrated investor positions. Moreover, if asset valuations become based on excess liquidity rather than fundamentals, the withdrawal of monetary stimulus could trigger a widespread reassessment of asset valuations. To limit this risk, the transition to tightening needs to be carefully managed and clearly

---

[1]See the April 2004 *World Economic Outlook* for a detailed discussion of global macroeconomic prospects and issues.

communicated to markets. In this context, the removal of the assurance that interest rates would remain low "for a considerable period" in the January 28 statement of the Federal Open Market Committee provided a salutary reminder to investors of the need to avoid being unduly influenced by low interest rates in making investment decisions. This reminder bears repeating.

Ensuring an orderly reduction in global external imbalances is another key challenge and a second potential source of risk to financial markets. The April 2004 *World Economic Outlook* highlights the need for cooperative international policy action to address the sources of these imbalances. From a financial market perspective, the magnitude of the capital flows needed to finance the large U.S. external current account deficit, the large share of official flows in this financing, and the heavy tilt toward fixed-income investments as a destination for such flows are attracting considerable attention.

The possibility that investors could demand an increased risk premium for U.S. dollar-denominated assets in an environment of a rapid decline in the value of the dollar raises the risk of broad financial market turbulence. In this case, yields on U.S. treasury securities could be pushed significantly higher, under-cutting the valuation of riskier assets. Although the dollar is widely expected to trend further downward in 2004, there are so far no signs of a lack of willingness to hold dollar assets. Indeed, data through the end of 2003 suggest continued strong official inflows related to currency intervention and renewed private investor interest in U.S. corporate bonds and equities. Moreover, the implied volatility on dollar/yen and dollar/euro currency options remains subdued.

Emerging markets face risks stemming from a potential deterioration in the favorable external financing environment. An unexpect-edly sharp increase in underlying U.S. treas-ury yields would likely trigger a widening of credit spreads on emerging market bonds.

Emerging market borrowers would face higher borrowing costs, and underlying vul-nerabilities that had been masked by the very favorable external financing environment would be more starkly exposed. Countries with large levels of public debt and volatile debt structures would be most at risk. The risks to emerging markets are mitigated, how-ever, by improved global growth prospects, higher commodity prices, the resilience afforded by increased exchange rate flexibil-ity, increased foreign exchange reserves, and action taken to address potentially volatile debt structures.

This chapter analyzes key developments and risks in mature and emerging financial mar-kets, focusing in particular on the factors underlying the strong rebound in global asset prices in 2003 and on whether that rebound has pushed asset valuations to levels that are not fully justified by fundamental improve-ments in earnings growth and credit quality.

- The first section highlights developments and vulnerabilities in mature markets, including in particular the role of low short-term interest rates in influencing investor behavior, market expectations for short-term interest rates, developments in mature equity and corporate bond markets, and changing market sentiment toward the dollar. Given the potential for a more abrupt than antici-pated increase in interest rates, the current yield curve environment is compared with that prevailing in 1994, the time of the last mature government bond market sell-off.

- The second section analyzes spread develop-ments in the emerging bond market, with particular attention to the degree to which low short-term interest rates rather than fundamentals alone have contributed to the steep decline in yield spreads on emerging market bonds. This section also provides an update on financial market developments in EU accession countries following the set-backs of 2003.

- The third section reviews developments in gross and net portfolio and foreign direct

Figure 2.1. The Real Federal Funds Rate
(In percent)

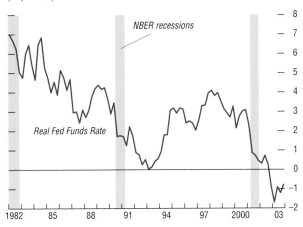

Sources: Bloomberg L.P.; National Bureau of Economic Research (NBER); and IMF staff estimates.

Figure 2.2. U.S. Nominal GDP and 10-Year Treasury Rates
(In percent)

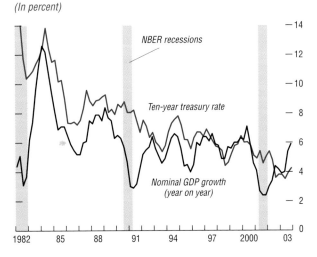

Sources: Bloomberg L.P.; National Bureau of Economic Research (NBER); and IMF staff estimates.

investment flows to emerging market countries, placing them in the context of developments in mature and emerging secondary markets. Steps taken to use the currently favorable financing environment to undertake liability management operations to improve the structure of domestic and external debt are highlighted.

- The fourth section applies financial soundness indicators to assess the vulnerabilities of selected emerging market banking systems.
- Finally, the discussion of risks in the main financial centers provided in the fifth section focuses on improvements in sectoral balance sheets, developments in the U.S. mortgage market, the factors underlying the recent proliferation of hedge funds, progress (and setbacks) in improving corporate governance standards, and key recent regulatory developments.
- Appendix I further explores the extent to which low short-term interest rates have compressed credit spreads on emerging market bonds to a point not fully justified by improvements in fundamental credit quality.
- Appendix II assesses recent initiatives to develop a regional bond market in Asia.

Developments and Vulnerabilities in Mature Markets

Yields in Major Government Bond Markets Remain Exceptionally Low

Interest rates in the United States and other major markets are low and will eventually need to rise. Indeed, in some countries, notably Australia and the United Kingdom, the tightening cycle has already begun. Speculation over the timing and magnitude of the U.S. tightening cycle has increased, with the dissipation of deflation fears in mid-2003 and subsequent mounting signs of economic recovery. The transition to tightening could have broad implications since abundant liquidity—and not just improved fundamentals—has played a major role in boosting asset prices and the near homogeneous compression of spreads observed in the mature and emerging markets. When risk-free rates rise, valuations in many markets could be pressured, and investors' appetite for risk tested.

With the Fed funds rate at a 45-year low of 1 percent, U.S. economic growth resurgent, and government bond issuance set to increase, the slope of the U.S. treasury yield curve has remained quite steep throughout 2003 and early 2004. The real Fed funds rate (deflated by the consumer price index) is negative. It is quite low by historical standards and given the stage in the economic cycle (Figure 2.1). Since short-term interest rates are a key building block for the valuation of other riskier assets, the maintenance of low short-term rates can have a pervasive effect on the price of other assets. As rates rise, asset valuations predicated on an unusually low level of risk-free rates could be called into question.

In the major government bond markets, low short-term rates and limited inflationary pressure have helped keep nominal yields along the maturity spectrum low by historical standards in most major markets. Yields on U.S. treasury securities remained negative in real terms in January 2004 for maturities of up to two years, as were yields on German Bunds with a tenor of one year or less.

The yield on 10-year U.S. treasury securities has in the past tended to move with nominal GDP growth during non-recessionary periods. While nominal GDP growth has recovered from the recent recession, 10-year U.S. treasury yields remain bound in a low range (Figure 2.2).

The real yields on inflation-indexed bonds in the euro area, the United Kingdom, and the United States have fallen to historically low levels (Figure 2.3). This decline largely reflects the influence of the low level of short-term rates on investor assessments of alternative investments. At the same time, market expectations for inflation in the euro area and the United States rose during 2003 (Figure 2.4).

Figure 2.3. Inflation-Indexed Bond Yields
(In percent)

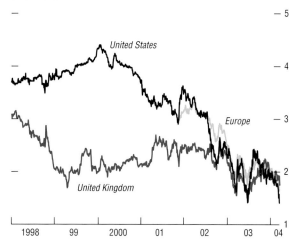

Sources: Bloomberg L.P.; and IMF staff estimates.

Figure 2.4. Long-Term Inflation Expectations
(In percent, 10-year nominal yields less inflation-indexed yields)

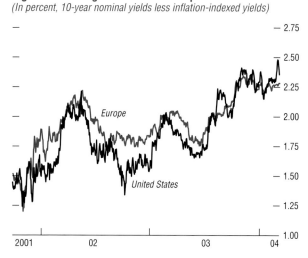

Sources: Bloomberg L.P.; and IMF staff estimates.

Figure 2.5. Inflation Expectations Less Current Inflation
(In percent)

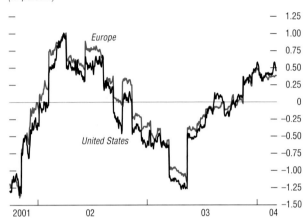

Sources: Bloomberg L.P.; and IMF staff estimates.

Figure 2.6. Three-Month LIBOR Futures Strip Curves
(In percent, as of March 2, 2004)

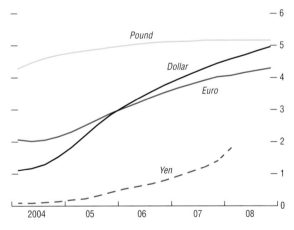

Sources: Bloomberg L.P.; and IMF staff estimates.

Throughout much of 2003, while deflation fears weighed on bond yields, the break-even inflation rates[2] in the euro area and the United States were below the actual inflation rate, suggesting that the market expected inflation to fall further (Figure 2.5). Since October 2003 however, the break-even inflation rate has risen and is now slightly above the actual inflation rate, suggesting markets now expect actual inflation to rise. While market-based measures of inflationary expectations can be distorted by market segmentation and by the smaller size and lower liquidity of the markets for inflation-protected securities compared with securities offering nominal yields, some market participants viewed these developments as a harbinger of upward pressure on yields.

Reflecting the steep slope of the U.S. treasury yield curve, short-term interest rate futures contracts are discounting an increase in U.S. dollar interest rates (Figure 2.6). Markets in the euro zone and the United Kingdom are also pricing in an increase in short-term rates, although not as rapid as that anticipated in the case of the United States. U.S. short-term interest rates are priced to exceed those in the euro area from 2005.

While global short-term interest rates are widely anticipated to increase from exceptionally low levels, this increase is presently not expected to be disruptive. Nevertheless, bond market volatility has remained high and investors could quickly revise their interest rate outlook, as they did during the 1994 sell-off of global fixed-income markets (Box 2.1). In 1994, policy rates in the United States rose much more rapidly than anticipated, resulting in a global government bond market sell-off.

---

[2]The spread between the real yield on inflation-indexed government bonds and their nominal counterparts provides an indicator of market expectations for average inflation over the life of the bonds being compared. The spread represents the break-even inflation rate that would make an investor indifferent to a conventional nominal bond and one linked to inflation.

Box 2.1. The Shift to Tightening: Parallels Between 1994 and 2004

Forward markets have priced in a gradual rise in U.S. short-term interest rates over the next years. Bond market volatility has remained elevated, however, reflecting uncertainty over the timing and extent of policy tightening. Investors could quickly revise their benign interest rate outlook, as they did prior to the sell-off in global fixed-income markets of 1994.

The Global Bond Market Rout of 1994

Prior to the sell-off in 1994, U.S. investors had built up sizable positions in Europe's bond markets, attempting to capture capital gains expected from the unwinding of financial market strain that followed the breakup of the European Exchange Rate Mechanism in 1992.[1] Entering 1994, financial markets anticipated monetary easing in Europe, driven by the uncertain recovery in Germany, subdued inflationary pressures, and high and rising unemployment. In the case of the United States, financial markets expected that a cyclical rebound would result in a gradual but steady increase in U.S. interest rates.

In the event, monetary easing in Europe fell short of expectations and markets were surprised by the pace of monetary tightening in the United States that began in February 1994. During the following 12 months, the Fed funds rate was doubled to 6 percent in the course of seven successive rate increases. The ensuing sell-off in the U.S. treasury bond market was exacerbated by attempts by leveraged U.S. investors to hedge their exposure to European bond markets. Bond market volatility and correlation rose, and 10-year U.S. treasury yields shot up by almost 250 basis points, peaking at 8 percent in November 1994. Short-term rates rose by more, triggering a marked flattening of the U.S. treasury yield curve. In the process, investors curtailed their borrowing at short-term rates and their exposure to longer-dated, higher-yielding assets. This de-leveraging was broad-based and resulted in a marked widening of

U.S. Treasury Market Yield Curve
(In percent)

As of January 3, 1994

As of January 2, 2004

1 month   3 month   6 month   2 year   5 year   10 year   30 year

Sources: Bloomberg L.P.; and IMF staff estimates.

emerging bond market yield spreads from 405 basis points at end-1993 to 800 basis points in mid-December, 1994, before the onset of the Tequila crisis.

Parallels with 1994

Just as in 1994, the outlook for interest rates in the United States was benign at the beginning of 2004. While inflation and nominal yields were substantially below those prevailing a decade ago, the shape of the yield curve at the beginning of 2004 was similar to that prevailing in 1994 (see the first Figure).

- The increase in short-term interest rates priced into futures markets at the beginning of 2004 was broadly comparable to the increase priced in a decade ago for shorter-dated contracts. However, for longer-dated contracts, the magnitudes of the interest rate increases expected at the beginning of 2004 exceeded those of 1994 (see second Figure).
- The U.S. treasury yield curve in 1994 and at the beginning of 2004 was extraordinarily steep (see the third Figure).
- The yield curve's unusual steepness provided strong incentives to seek leverage and build "carry trade" positions during both episodes. Such carry trades involve borrowing at low short-term interest rates to build positions in

[1]See, for example, Goldstein and Folkerts-Landau (1994).

Box 2.1 *(concluded)*

Implied Changes in Eurodollar Forwards Rate
(In basis points)

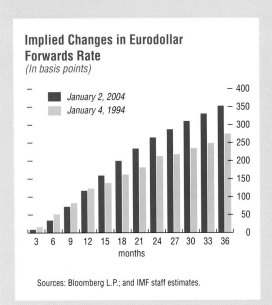

Sources: Bloomberg L.P.; and IMF staff estimates.

Excess 10-Year U.S. Treasury Yield Over Three-Month LIBOR

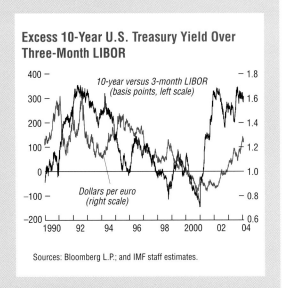

Sources: Bloomberg L.P.; and IMF staff estimates.

higher-yielding, longer-dated bonds. Abstracting from bond price movements, such positions yielded 3 percentage points on average during 2003, estimated as the differential between the yield on 10-year U.S. treasury bonds and three-month LIBOR (see the fourth Figure). This differential reached a 10-year high last year, underscoring the potential for volatility from an unwinding of carry trades in response to rising short-term rates and a flat-

U.S. Interest Rate Indicators

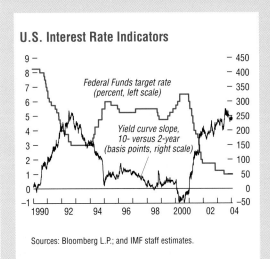

Sources: Bloomberg L.P.; and IMF staff estimates.

tening of the yield curve. In addition to carry trades, low short-term interest rates encourage investors to reach for yield in other ways, a factor that contributed to the marked compression in corporate credit spreads observed last year and a decade ago.

Divergences from 1994

While the phrase "it is different this time" is notorious for being a dangerous formulation in finance, no two market situations are ever identical. The similarities just described suggest that there is considerable scope for interest rate volatility and spillover to other markets, especially if market expectations shift from the gradual increase in rates currently discounted to a more abrupt pace of tightening and yield curve flattening. Current circumstances exhibit a number of major differences from those prevailing in 1994. However, some of these differences may as easily exacerbate as dampen volatility.

• Foreign holding of U.S. treasury securities reached an historic high at end-2003, accounting for 43 percent of the stock of marketable debt outstanding. Rising issuance was increasingly absorbed by demand from the foreign official sector, largely fueled by the proceeds of foreign exchange market intervention.

- Consequently, foreign official purchases had a discernible impact on yield developments. The stock of marketable debt securities rose by $370 billion during 2003. Private holdings—both foreign and domestic—increased by $209 billion, with the slack taken up by official purchases. While the Federal Reserve Bank increased its holdings by $37 billion, foreign official holdings increased by $130 billion. The latter absorbed about one-third of the net increase of the stock of marketable securities during this period. Consequently, foreign official holdings rose to an estimated 24 percent of the stock of marketable U.S. treasury securities outstanding.
- Real interest rates remained low by any standard in January 2004, much lower than real rates in 1994. Real interest rates, however, could come under pressure to rise, if demand for capital by the private or public sector were to exceed expectations.
- The macroeconomic backdrop for financial markets was substantially different at the beginning of 2004 from a decade ago. While the current recovery has been more forceful,

Selected U.S. Economic and Financial Indicators

	1993–94	2003–04
GDP growth[1]	3.8	6.1
Productivity[1]	1.8	5.2
Budget deficit (in percent of GDP)[2]	2.9	4.5
CPI (year-on-year percent change)[3]	2.7	1.9
Core CPI (year-on-year percent change)[3]	3.2	1.1
Fed Funds Rate[3]	3.0	1.0
Ten-year U.S. treasury yield[3]	5.8	4.2
Aa rated corporate bond spread (in basis points)[3]	51	48
B rated corporate bond spread (in basis points)[3,4]	407	357
EMBI/EMBI+ spread (in basis points)[3,5]	396	418

Sources: Bloomberg L.P.; and IMF, *World Economic Outlook.*
[1]Annualized second-half 1993 and 2003, respectively.
[2]FY1994 and FY2004, respectively.
[3]End-1993 and end-2003, respectively.
[4]End-1993 estimate using yield-to-worst convention.
[5]End-1993 EMBI, end-2003 EMBI+.

inflationary pressures are more subdued than in 1994, in part reflecting high productivity, softness in the labor market, and low capacity utilization. Consequently, pressure on yields to rise was limited in early 2004, notwithstanding the widening fiscal deficit and the need to boost issuance (see the Table).

In that episode, volatility and the correlation of global government bond markets rose sharply.

Bond and Equity Prices Surge

Corporate bond and equity market investment returns reflected an unusually vigorous credit cycle. With the first sign of global economic recovery, the value of claims on business in mature markets surged. A self-reinforcing improvement in valuations emerged as new high-yield credit and convertible financing for marginal borrowers again became available, sharply reducing the risk of business failure. Measures taken by corporations to cut costs, defer investment, and strengthen balance sheets amplified the positive impact of resurgent economic growth on earnings, cash flow, and credit quality. The cyclical rebound in asset prices was further accentuated by the low interest rate environment and a starting point of high risk aversion that had developed in 2002.

Credit spreads on corporate bonds narrowed sharply in 2003, led in particular by high-yield bonds (Figure 2.7). The return on high-yield bonds in Europe and the United States in 2003—of nearly 30 percent—exceeded equity returns in mature markets and were comparable to the return on emerging market bonds. These returns were fueled by improved credit quality and strong investor inflows into corporate bonds in a quest for yield.

Corporate bond markets were boosted by expectations of a continued decline in corporate default rates (Figure 2.8). Bond rating

Figure 2.7. United States and European Corporate Bond Spreads
(In basis points)

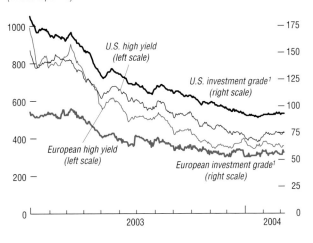

Sources: Merrill Lynch; and IMF staff estimates.
¹The average credit quality for the U.S. investment grade index is lower than that of the European index.

Figure 2.8. Corporate Default Rates
(In percent)

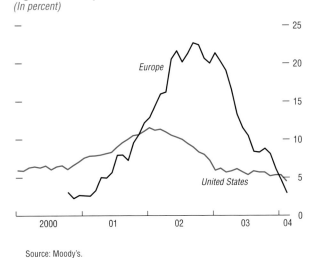

Source: Moody's.

downgrades of companies to below investment grade—which exclude them from some portfolios and cause significant loss in value for important investor groups—were also sharply lower. Reduced default risk and strong investor demand for high-yielding assets permitted a rebound in high-yield bond issuance by European and U.S. corporations in 2003.

Corporate bond valuations, for both investment grade and high-yield bonds, are high but not too far out of line compared with previous credit recoveries. Across a range of credit classes, spreads remain above those that prevailed during the last credit expansion of 1992–97 (Figure 2.9). Moreover, adjusting for the unusually low level of current risk-free rates, riskier yields appear attractive when measured as a proportion of the risk-free rate. This comparison is, of course, vulnerable to rising rates.

Global equity markets also staged a strong, broad-based rally in 2003, reversing three years of decline (Figure 2.10). As with the corporate bond market, the rebound in global share prices was largely in response to an improved outlook for corporate earnings and economic growth, progress in strengthening corporate balance sheets in the mature markets, and record low short-term interest rates in the major financial centers that helped to whet investor appetite for risk. Since the start of 2004, most major equity indices have experienced a period of consolidation as investors have shown renewed caution. Technology shares, in particular, have stabilized as investors have appropriately paused to await further signs of improving fundamentals. However, stocks in Japan have continued to rise.

Business earnings, a critical factor in equity valuations, have recovered. In the United States, for example, the operating earnings of firms in the S&P 500 index rose by 17 percent in 2003 from a year earlier. Earnings of U.S. firms in 2003 exceeded their previous peak in 2000, fully recovering from the recession. Earnings in Europe and Japan are recovering with a delay and remain below prior cyclical peaks.

In U.S. markets, aggregate analyst expectations of earnings drifted higher during the course of 2003, in contrast to sharp downward revisions in previous years. In Europe and Japan, earnings forecasts were also revised up strongly in 2003. The improving earnings outlook and strong rally in stock prices contributed to relatively subdued volatility expectations. The implied volatility of options on major equity markets fell over the course of the year (Figure 2.11). Earnings growth is expected to remain robust in 2004 in Europe, Japan, and the United States.

U.S. Dollar Depreciates as Deficits Rise

Markets see the U.S. dollar as facing pressure toward depreciation from a variety of sources. These include the need to sustain an unprecedented level of capital inflows to finance the external current account deficit and the high proportion of official inflows related to currency intervention. Markets do not appear overly concerned that the dollar's decline will either accelerate or have a disruptive impact on other asset markets. Should the expectations underpinning this outlook—notably continued strong foreign official inflows and a rebound in private flows—prove unfounded, the pressure on the dollar will intensify. A decline in demand for U.S. dollar assets could trigger an increase in bond yields.

The nominal depreciation of the U.S. dollar versus the other major currencies has been orderly, and options markets suggest that investors are not expecting sharp currency movements. The call for flexibility in last September's Group of Seven (G-7) communiqué caused the volatility implied by option contracts on the yen to rise temporarily (Figures 2.12 and 2.13). The February 2004 G-7 communiqué highlighting the undesirability of excess volatility helped to dampen volatility expectations. Nevertheless, the dollar has continued to decline and the volatility

Figure 2.9. U.S. Corporate Bond Spreads by Rating

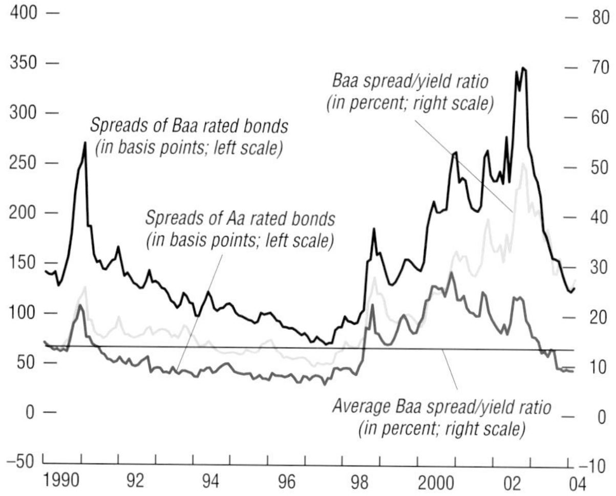

Sources: Lehman Brothers; and IMF staff estimates.

Figure 2.10. Selected Equity Market Performance
(January 1, 2000 = 100)

Sources: Bloomberg L.P.; and IMF staff estimates.

Figure 2.11. Implied Equity Market Option Volatility Indices
(In percent)

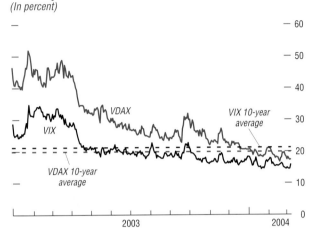

Sources: Bloomberg L.P.; and IMF staff estimates.

Figure 2.12. Yen Probability Density Function

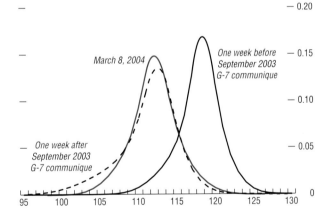

Sources: Bloomberg L.P.; Reuters, PLC; and IMF staff estimates.

implied on euro option contracts, while well within historical ranges, has risen (Figure 2.14). However, there is no strong directional tilt in the pricing of currency option contracts. The premium that investors are willing to pay for the right to sell dollars, over the equivalent right to buy dollars, has reverted to normal levels for both the euro and the yen.

While most market indicators now suggest a generally sanguine view of future currency movements, a few anomalies have emerged. These reflect market speculation of an eventual revaluation of Asian currencies. A marked rise in forward premiums on the yuan and the Hong Kong dollar in the second half of last year suggested that markets did not rule out a revaluation. Speculative inflows pushed the Hong Kong SAR interbank offered rate (HIBOR) well below LIBOR (Figure 2.15).

Official intervention by Asian central banks has remained strong. Japanese authorities intervened in increasing amounts in 2003 to prevent the yen from strengthening more rapidly. Foreign exchange reserves of the 11 major Asian central banks now approach $2 trillion, with no sign of a slowing in the trend (Figure 2.16).

Much of the reserves accumulated on account of currency market intervention has been invested in U.S. treasury and agency securities. These investments have helped underpin strong foreign portfolio flows into the United States and contributed to the substantial increase in the share of U.S. treasury and agency bonds held by foreigners (Figure 2.17). Private international investor flows into the U.S. equity and corporate bond markets rebounded with the recovery in U.S. corporate earnings and credit quality. So far, however, a substantial recovery of foreign direct investment into the United States, the dominant source of external financing during 1999–2000, appears unlikely. European corporations—major players in the past U.S. merger and acquisition boom—are not expected to have the interest or wherewithal to invest heavily in U.S. firms, notwithstanding the recent strengthening of the financial position of European firms.

Markets are not expecting a disorderly change in the value of the dollar versus the other G-3 currencies. Asian central banks are expected by the market to continue to intervene to stem the pace of appreciation. However, the effectiveness on market expectations of intervention could decline over time as the sustainability of high levels of intervention is questioned.

The importance of bonds as a destination for foreign inflows has so far been one of the factors helping to anchor longer-term U.S. treasury yields, notwithstanding the strong rebound in U.S. economic growth and the prospect of a substantial increase in U.S. treasury issuance. But the heavy tilt toward bonds in the composition of net foreign inflows carries risks. A spike in bond yields in the United States arising from an increased risk premium on U.S. dollar assets would be problematic given the role of low yields in supporting household consumption and in boosting the valuation of riskier assets. Turbulence in the U.S. treasury market could in particular also spill over to other fixed income markets, widening credit spreads from their current low levels. A rapid decline of the dollar in the context of slowing inflows would undermine the valuation of other assets and potentially contribute to broader market volatility.

Improved Fundamentals and the Quest for Yield Buoy Emerging Market Bonds

As in the case of mature corporate bond markets, emerging market credit spreads fell precipitously in 2003, with bonds at the low end of the credit risk spectrum leading the charge. The same factors that contributed to the compression of corporate bond spreads—improved fundamentals and the impact of abundant liquidity on investor behavior—underpinned a similarly impressive compression of spreads on emerging market bonds. However, valuations on emerging market

Figure 2.13. Euro Probability Density Function

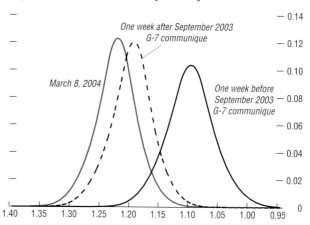

Sources: Bloomberg L.P.; Reuters, PLC; and IMF staff estimates.

Figure 2.14. Currency Volatilities
(In percent versus the U.S. dollar, 3 month)

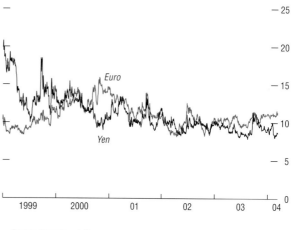

Source: Bloomberg L.P.

Figure 2.15. Hong Kong SAR: HIBOR Versus LIBOR
(In percent)

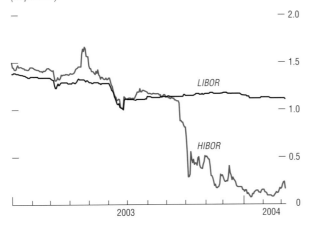

Sources: Bloomberg L.P.; and IMF staff estimates.

Figure 2.16. Foreign Exchange Reserves of Selected Asian Central Banks
(In billions of U.S. dollars)

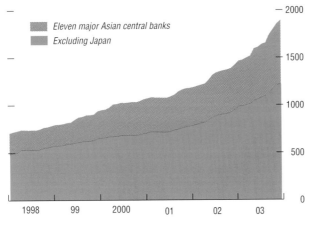

Sources: Bloomberg L.P.; and IMF staff estimates.

bonds, especially sub-investment grade bonds, appear vulnerable to an increase in underlying U.S. treasury yields.

Emerging market bonds posted impressive returns in 2003 (Figure 2.18). The highly accommodative monetary stance in the main industrialized countries contributed to a search for yield among investors that encouraged sizable new inflows into the secondary market for emerging market bonds. The inducement of low risk-free rates was complemented by expectations for strengthening fundamentals as a result of improved prospects for global growth, surging commodity prices, fiscal consolidation in some key countries, low inflation, increased foreign reserve holdings, and the earlier shift to floating exchange rates. This combination especially benefited high-yielding credits, whose spreads had been pushed to high levels in the environment of acute risk aversion of 2002. However, in early 2004, following a surge of new issuance, the prospect of a transition to tightening in the United States triggered a moderate correction. Emerging market bond spreads widened significantly in February as investors were reminded of the risk of being over-influenced by low short-term interest rates—instead of fundamentals—when making investment decisions. Moreover, investor discrimination seems to have increased during this period as the spreads on high-yielding Latin American credits widened more than those on lower-yielding Asian bonds.

The compression in emerging market bond spreads was mirrored by declines in implied default probabilities in the credit default swaps market (Figure 2.19).[3] The implied

[3]Credit default swaps are derivative contracts that insure the buyer of protection against the risk of default of a specified reference entity, such as a sovereign borrower. Following a contractually defined "credit event," the buyer of protection receives a payment intended to compensate for the loss stemming from that event. For a given assumed post-default recovery value, the implied probability of default can be estimated from the current market price of the protection.

default probabilities peaked in mid-2002, at the height of the Brazilian crisis. However, there were regional differences, with greater volatility in Latin America than elsewhere. Asian default probabilities remained low and stable.

Foreign investor interest in local emerging market investments has also risen. Foreign inflows are motivated in part by the high valuations on external emerging market bonds. In addition, the prospect that emerging equity markets will strongly benefit from resurgent global growth has attracted foreign flows into a number of emerging equity markets and helped underpin the strong rise in emerging market equity prices in 2003. Local bond markets attracted sizable inflows amid improving fundamentals, falling policy rates, and expectations for further currency appreciation in many of the larger markets, including Brazil, South Africa, and Turkey. Indeed, in some countries with debt denominated in or linked to foreign currencies, exchange rate appreciation has contributed at least temporarily to improved debt dynamics. However, financial market volatility increased in Hungary and Poland amid concerns that widening fiscal deficits would overburden monetary and exchange rate policy and potentially delay the adoption of the euro (Box 2.2).

There has been a noticeable improvement in credit quality among emerging market countries over the past several years. In 2003, there were a number of credit rating upgrades, notably Indonesia, Russia, South Africa, and Turkey. Moody's upgrade of Russia to Baa3 in 2003 resulted in over 50 percent of the asset class being investment grade. The credit quality of the EMBI Global—as calculated by the weighted average rating of its constituents—is now well anchored at double B compared with single B+ just two years ago (Figure 2.20).

While improved credit quality has undoubtedly contributed to the spread compression observed in 2003, favorable external financing conditions also played a significant role. The

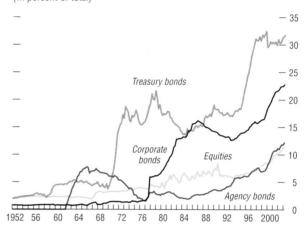

Figure 2.17. Foreign Ownership of U.S. Securities
(In percent of total)

Sources: U.S. Federal Reserve Flow of Funds Accounts; and IMF staff estimates.

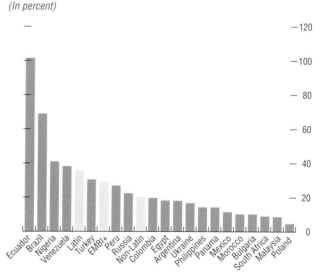

Figure 2.18. Returns During 2003 of the EMBI+ and Select Sub-Indices
(In percent)

Sources: J.P. Morgan Chase & Co.; and IMF staff estimates.

Figure 2.19. Default Probabilities Implied by Five-Year Credit Default Swap Spreads
(In percent, calculated as an average of 16 emerging market credit default swaps on senior debt and a 40% recovery rate)

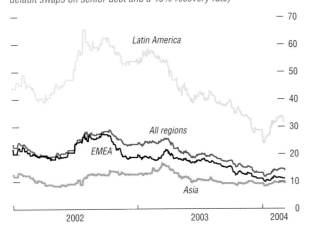

Sources: Bloomberg L.P.; and IMF staff estimates.

Figure 2.20. Emerging Market Average Credit Quality

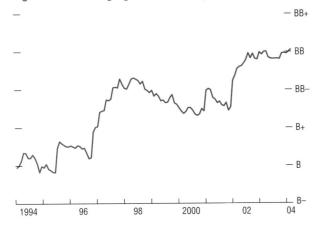

Sources: J.P. Morgan Chase & Co.; Moody's; Standard & Poor's; and IMF staff estimates.

broad-based nature of the rally, reduced discrimination among investors (as measured by the low dispersion of returns among credits), and the increase in cross-correlations among credits for most of last year point to a market being driven more by common factors including liquidity and market technicals, rather than individual country fundamentals (Figures 2.21 and 2.22). Likewise, the strong correlation between global risk indicators and emerging bond market spreads throughout most of 2003 suggests that performance of the latter was closely tied to increased global liquidity and risk appetite. Indeed, research suggests that low short-term interest rates have been a key determinant of emerging bond spreads since 2001 (Appendix I).

The strong emerging market performance of last year—three quarters of which was driven by spread compression with the balance accounted for by coupon payments—is unlikely to be repeated in 2004. The scope for further spread compression from already historically low levels is limited, and an increase in underlying U.S. treasury yields is widely anticipated. As a result, most analysts forecast low single-digit returns for the EMBI+.[4]

The prospect of lower returns in an environment of rising interest rates could deter new inflows, and even prompt a reallocation of assets away from emerging markets. In particular, an unexpected spike in U.S. treasury yields could lead to wider emerging market bond spreads and to a more pronounced reallocation by crossover investors from the asset class. Moreover, a disorderly adjustment in the major currency markets, particularly if accompanied by a spike in yields and volatility in mature debt markets, could raise investor risk aversion and contribute to a widening of spreads on emerging market bonds. Spreads on emerging market bonds at historically low

---

[4]Given a duration of 5½ years on the EMBI+ and a coupon of about 8 percent, a 1 percent increase in U.S. treasury yields would reduce returns to 2½ percent, even if spreads remain unchanged.

levels leave little buffer to absorb adverse developments.

The risks stemming from higher U.S. treasury yields were demonstrated in the summer of 2003 and again in January 2004. During June–August 2003, 10-year U.S. treasury yields rose by almost 150 basis points, triggering a sell-off in emerging bond markets. Spreads, however, were relatively stable. Analysts attributed this stability to the view that valuations remained relatively attractive at that point, and that the sell-off in the U.S. treasury market was largely due to technical considerations—convexity hedging by mortgage agencies—and an easing of deflationary fears, rather than a signal of tightening liquidity conditions. The situation was different in January 2004 when the change in language of the Federal Open Market Committee (FOMC) statement triggered an increase in emerging bond spreads. This spread widening was attributed by some to the partial unwinding of leveraged carry trades. To others, the abrupt widening of emerging market spreads was a reflection of stretched valuations that would be increasingly called into question in a rising interest rate environment. In addition, the record pace of new bond issuance in the first three weeks of January 2004 also temporarily weighed on the market.

For the present, however, a number of factors mitigate these risks. The global recovery has strengthened and broadened, and global commodity prices have risen strongly. The favorable external financing environment has enabled many countries to prefinance a significant part of their planned issuance. Many countries have also taken advantage of the favorable market conditions to improve their debt profiles by lowering borrowing costs, extending maturities, and reducing the share of debt indexed to short-term interest rates and foreign currencies. While many countries have used the inevitably temporary favorable external financing conditions prudently, others have loosened their fiscal stance and slackened the pace of adjustment. When the

Figure 2.21. Dispersion of Returns Within the EMBI+
(In percent)

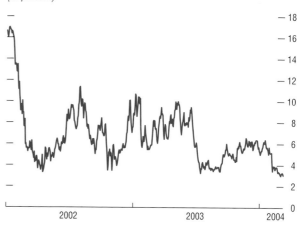

Sources: J.P. Morgan Chase & Co.; and IMF staff estimates.

Figure 2.22. Emerging Market Debt: Average Cross-Correlations

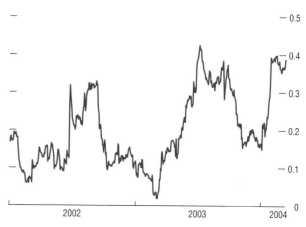

Sources: J.P. Morgan Chase & Co.; and IMF staff estimates.
Note: Thirty-day moving simple average across all pair-wise return correlations of 20 constituents included in the EMBI Global.

Box 2.2. Bond Market Convergence of EU Accession Countries: Recent Setbacks and Prospects

The September 2003 *Global Financial Stability Report* (GFSR) underscored the need for fiscal consolidation in Central Europe to mitigate the risks of exchange rate and interest rate volatility. While prospects of EU accession in May 2004 had spurred a secular broadening of the investor base, the dependence on portfolio inflows to finance large fiscal deficits had risen to unprecedented levels, most notably in Hungary and, to a lesser extent, in Poland. Fiscal laxity overburdened monetary and exchange rate policies in these countries. The June 2003 devaluation in Hungary reinforced concerns over an apparent subordination of inflation targeting to exchange rate considerations. Investor concerns that the timetable for euro adoption might slip—in part on account of warning signals that the Maastricht ceiling on general government debt could be breached in Hungary and Poland—were also emphasized in the September 2003 GFSR. Market developments in late 2003 have highlighted the risks associated with fiscal policy slippages and heavy reliance on foreign investor financing.

Recent Market Setbacks

In Hungary interest rate and exchange rate volatility surged in late 2003. Amid concerns over Hungary's widening twin deficits, foreign investors reduced their holdings of government securities—by an estimated €574 million—during the three-month period ending in November 2003. Faced with heightening pressure on the forint, the National Bank of Hungary raised its policy rate by 300 basis points to 12.5 percent in late November, following a 300 basis point rate hike in June. As a result, the yield of the five-year benchmark bond spiraled up to 11 percent in early December, widening its yield spread over Bunds to more than 700 basis points (see first and second Figures).

At the same time, investor concerns over the sustainability of fiscal policies in Poland rose. The widening of the general government deficit envisaged under the 2004 budget draft was widely seen as an indication that substantial fis-

cal reforms were unlikely ahead of Poland's parliamentary elections scheduled for 2005. Against this background, the yield spread of five-year benchmark bonds over Bunds widened substantially, temporarily reaching 400 basis points at the end of November 2003. Continuing the slide that began in mid-2001, the zloty depreciated to a new low of 4.80 zlotys per euro at the end of January 2004. Besides uncertainties about fiscal policy, investors attributed zloty weakness in part

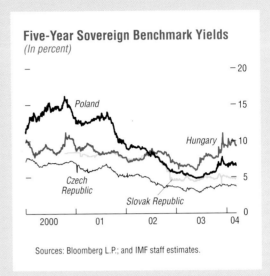

Five-Year Sovereign Benchmark Yields
(In percent)

Sources: Bloomberg L.P.; and IMF staff estimates.

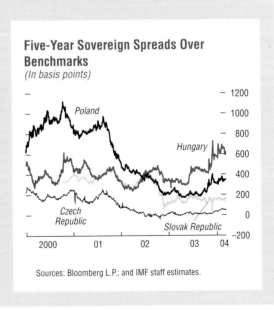

Five-Year Sovereign Spreads Over Benchmarks
(In basis points)

Sources: Bloomberg L.P.; and IMF staff estimates.

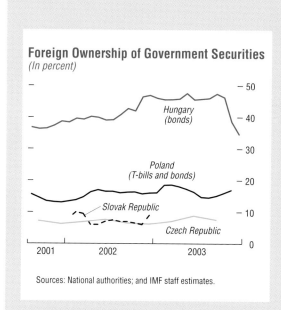

Foreign Ownership of Government Securities
(In percent)

Hungary (bonds)

Poland (T-bills and bonds)

Slovak Republic

Czech Republic

Sources: National authorities; and IMF staff estimates.

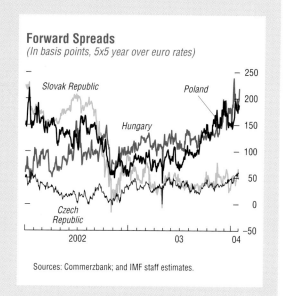

Forward Spreads
(In basis points, 5x5 year over euro rates)

Slovak Republic

Poland

Hungary

Czech Republic

Sources: Commerzbank; and IMF staff estimates.

to the perceived uncertainties over the course of monetary policy, following the appointment of a new monetary policy council in January.

The deteriorating investor sentiment toward Hungary and Poland, however, had only negligible repercussions for local markets in the Czech Republic and Slovak Republic. Fiscal reform measures aimed at almost halving their respective consolidated budget deficits by 2006—to 4 percent of GDP in the Czech Republic and 3 percent of GDP in the Slovak Republic—helped shelter these markets from the pressure experienced in the larger markets in Central Europe. The risk of a spillover was further mitigated by the relatively small foreign ownership of securities issued by the government of these countries (see the third Figure). Consequently, yield spreads over Bunds widened only marginally during 2003.

Policy Responses

Following substantial budget overruns in 2003, Hungary introduced further measures to reduce its fiscal deficit in January 2004. Earlier budget cuts—announced in June and December 2003—had proven insufficient to restore investor confidence. At the same time, the National Bank of Hungary abandoned its

focus on a narrow exchange rate fluctuation band and avoided any mention of explicit exchange rate targets. This was widely seen as an attempt to assuage investor concerns that inflation targeting had been subordinated to exchange rate considerations.

Measures to curtail Poland's widening budget deficit were adopted by the government in January 2004. As part of a medium-term fiscal strategy, the government agreed on expenditure cuts equivalent to almost 3 percent of GDP (29.4 billion zlotys) over the period of 2004–07. The minority government still needs to secure parliamentary approval of the necessary legislation. Recognizing the policy challenges lying ahead, the government extended its target for meeting the Maastricht criteria by two years to 2008–09, implying euro adoption in 2010 at the earliest.

Vulnerabilities and Market Outlook

Notwithstanding these initiatives, domestic government financing costs remained elevated in both Hungary and Poland in early 2004. Hungary's yield spread over Bunds was near a four-year high at the end of January, while that in Poland was near a two-year high. Investors emphasized that meeting the tightened fiscal targets was essential to mitigating the risk that

Box 2.2 *(concluded)*

foreign holdings of local securities could once more become a catalyst for interest rate and exchange rate volatility.

Forward markets underscored the risks of further slippages, while differentiating Hungary and Poland from the Czech Republic and the Slovak Republic. Five-year forward interest rates for Hungary and Poland have risen steadily, reaching about 200 basis points over comparable forward rates for the euro area by end-January, 2004 (see the fourth Figure). The elevated spread over forward rates in the euro area was widely seen as an indication that euro

membership was expected to be delayed beyond 2009 in the case of Hungary and Poland. In contrast, forward markets implied a high probability of euro area entry by the Czech Republic and Slovak Republic in five years' time.[1]

[1]Assuming a spread of 20 basis points over euro area rates upon euro area entry, forward rates at the end of January 2004 implied a probability of euro area entry by January 2009 of 88 percent for the Czech Republic; 30 percent for Hungary; 41 percent for Poland; and 92 percent for the Slovak Republic.

external financing environment becomes less favorable, underlying vulnerabilities veiled by the earlier ready access to financing are likely to become more apparent.

Surge in Issuance by Emerging Markets Meets Strong Investor Demand

Emerging market borrowers are benefiting from a very favorable external financing environment. Notwithstanding a marked increase in issuance levels, investor appetite still appears strong and the terms for new financing remain relatively attractive to borrowers. Gross financing raised by emerging markets in international capital markets rose in 2003 (Table 2.1 and Figure 2.23). Equity placements, which were facilitated by the strong rally in emerging stock markets, exceeded the levels of the previous two years by a wide margin. Bond issuance was also robust. Following the rebound in issuance in 2003 and the flurry of issues in January 2004, it is estimated that about 40 percent of emerging market sovereign bond issuance plans for 2004 had already been fulfilled. Syndicated loan commitments have been buoyed by a spate of deals in Europe, the Middle East, and Africa (EMEA), reflecting an uptick in corporate borrowing in Russia and lending in the Gulf.

Despite sizable amortizations in the bond and loan markets, net issuance levels recovered in 2003 (Figure 2.24). Net bond issuance, which was negligible in 2002, rebounded. Net flows associated with syndicated loans, which were negative in 2001 and 2002, also turned positive. In early 2004, issuance in the emerging bond and equity markets remained buoyant, and the near-term pipelines looked promising.

Bond Issuance

Bond issuance in 2003 exceeded levels witnessed over the last six years. After a slowdown in issuance during the summer owing to the spike in U.S. treasury yields, issuance was particularly heavy toward the end of the year and in early 2004 (Figure 2.25). Issuance was spurred by low yields and strong investor demand as borrowers sought to lock in low rates and extend maturities. Net issuance in 2003 ($35.3 billion), although significantly higher than 2002, was moderated by sizable amortization payments, however.

Among sovereigns, the increase in subinvestment grade issuance was noteworthy as it reflected the quest for yield that dominated yield spread developments in the secondary market. Sub-investment grade offerings were

Table 2.1. Emerging Market Financing

	2000	2001	2002	2003	2002 Q1	Q2	Q3	Q4	2003 Q1	Q2	Q3	Q4	Oct.	Nov.	Dec.	2004 Jan.	Feb.	Year-to-date[1]
								(In billions of U.S. dollars)										
Gross issuance by asset	216.4	162.1	135.6	195.2	37.0	32.9	32.1	33.6	34.9	45.3	52.9	62.0	24.9	13.7	23.4	22.8	8.1	31.0
Bonds	80.5	89.0	61.6	97.1	22.2	15.9	8.8	14.7	20.1	27.6	26.3	23.1	14.8	6.0	2.3	16.3	5.7	22.0
Equities	41.8	11.2	16.4	28.0	4.1	4.3	3.8	4.1	1.2	2.0	7.1	17.7	5.2	3.5	9.0	4.0	1.4	5.4
Loans	94.2	61.9	57.6	70.0	10.7	12.7	19.5	14.8	13.6	15.7	19.5	21.2	4.9	4.2	12.1	2.6	1.0	3.6
Gross issuance by region	216.4	162.1	135.6	195.2	37.0	32.9	32.1	33.6	34.9	45.3	52.9	62.0	24.9	13.7	23.4	22.8	8.1	31.0
Asia	85.9	67.5	53.9	81.8	13.3	11.9	14.1	14.6	12.9	15.5	22.9	30.5	13.7	5.4	11.4	7.0	5.6	12.7
Latin America	69.1	53.9	33.4	42.4	11.9	8.3	6.1	7.1	7.8	11.7	9.1	13.8	6.0	3.7	4.1	7.6	0.6	8.2
Europe, Middle East, Africa	61.4	40.8	48.3	71.0	11.9	12.7	11.9	11.8	14.3	18.1	21.0	17.7	5.1	4.6	7.9	8.2	2.0	10.2
Amortization by asset	114.3	148.0	129.3	124.2	27.5	35.6	31.1	35.1	22.1	34.3	29.6	38.2	9.1	10.5	18.6	9.2	10.5	n.a.
Bonds	52.2	60.0	59.8	61.8	12.6	18.0	14.5	14.7	10.5	17.5	15.6	18.2	3.4	5.6	9.2	5.1	8.1	n.a.
Loans	62.1	88.0	69.5	62.4	14.8	17.6	16.6	20.4	11.6	16.8	14.0	20.0	5.7	4.9	9.5	4.1	2.5	n.a.
Amortization by region	114.3	148.0	129.3	124.2	27.5	35.6	31.1	35.1	22.1	34.3	29.6	38.2	9.1	10.5	18.6	9.2	10.5	n.a.
Asia	57.1	66.5	56.2	49.4	12.3	14.9	13.7	15.3	8.3	12.0	14.5	14.7	2.6	3.8	8.2	6.0	4.4	n.a.
Latin America	32.3	45.9	41.2	40.8	8.3	11.5	10.5	10.9	7.6	10.1	8.0	15.1	4.4	3.4	7.3	1.2	4.6	n.a.
Europe, Middle East, Africa	24.9	35.5	31.9	33.9	6.9	9.2	6.9	8.9	6.2	12.2	7.1	8.4	2.1	3.2	3.1	2.0	1.6	n.a.
Net issuance by asset	102.2	14.2	6.4	71.0	9.6	-2.7	1.0	-1.5	12.9	11.0	23.3	23.8	15.7	3.3	4.8	-9.2	12.3	n.a.
Bonds	28.3	29.1	1.8	35.3	9.6	-2.1	-5.7	0.0	9.6	10.1	10.7	4.9	11.4	0.4	-6.8	-5.1	8.2	n.a.
Equities	41.8	11.2	16.4	28.0	4.1	4.3	3.8	4.1	1.2	2.0	7.1	17.7	5.2	3.5	9.0	0.0	4.0	n.a.
Loans	32.1	-26.1	-11.8	7.6	-4.1	-5.0	2.9	-5.6	2.0	-1.1	5.5	1.1	-0.9	-0.6	2.6	-4.1	0.1	n.a.
Net issuance by region	102.2	14.2	6.4	71.0	9.6	-2.7	1.0	-1.5	12.9	11.0	23.3	23.8	15.7	3.3	4.8	-9.2	12.3	n.a.
Asia	28.8	0.9	-2.3	32.4	1.0	-3.0	0.4	-0.7	4.6	3.6	8.4	15.8	11.1	1.5	3.2	-6.0	2.7	n.a.
Latin America	36.9	7.9	-7.8	1.5	3.6	-3.2	-4.4	-3.8	0.2	1.6	1.0	-1.3	1.6	0.3	-3.2	-1.2	3.0	n.a.
Europe, Middle East, Africa	36.5	5.3	16.4	37.1	5.0	3.5	5.0	3.0	8.1	5.9	13.9	9.2	3.0	1.4	4.8	-2.0	6.6	n.a.
Secondary Markets																		
Bonds																		
EMBI+ (spread in basis points)[2]	756	731	765	418	598	799	903	765	671	547	506	418	470	455	418	432	445	432
Merrill Lynch High Yield (spread in basis points)	871	734	802	368	623	809	890	802	696.1	554	482.6	368	415	401	368	360	381	386
Salomon Broad inv. Grade (spread in basis points)	89	78	62	45	69	73	75	62	55	51	57	45	50	48	45	44	43	41
U.S. 10 yr. Treasury yield (yield in percent)	5.12	5.051	3.816	4.248	5.396	4.799	3.596	3.816	3.798	3.515	3.939	4.248	4.295	4.334	4.248	4.134	3.973	3.77
								(In percent)										
Equity																		
Dow	-6.2	-7.1	-16.8	25.3	3.8	-11.2	-17.9	9.9	-4.2	12.4	3.2	12.7	5.7	-0.2	6.9	0.3	-3.1	-3.6
Nasdaq	-39.3	-21.1	-31.5	50.0	-5.4	-20.7	-19.9	13.9	0.4	21.0	10.1	12.1	8.1	1.5	2.2	3.1	-0.1	-0.3
MSCI Emerging Markets Free	-31.8	-4.9	-8.0	51.6	10.7	-9.0	-16.8	9.8	-6.8	22.2	13.5	17.3	8.3	1.0	7.1	3.3	0.0	-1.9
Asia	-42.5	4.2	-6.2	47.1	14.9	-6.3	-17.0	4.9	-9.3	21.4	14.9	16.3	10.1	-1.5	7.2	4.9	-0.3	1.6
Latin America	-18.4	-4.3	-24.8	67.1	7.1	-22.0	-24.7	19.6	-0.9	22.6	12.4	22.4	7.3	3.1	10.6	0.5	-0.1	0.0
Europe/Middle East	-23.4	-17.7	-9.1	62.7	0.2	-11.0	-6.5	9.1	-1.4	35.2	9.3	11.7	1.0	2.2	8.2	4.6	-0.7	-1.3

Sources: Bloomberg L.P.; Capital Data; J.P. Morgan Chase & Co.; Morgan Stanley Capital International; Salomon Smith Barney; and IMF staff estimates.

[1] Issuance data (net of U.S. trust facility issuance) are as of February 17, 2004 close-of-business London and secondary markets data are as of March 8, 2004, c.o.b. New York.

[2] On April 14, 2000 the EMBI+ was adjusted for the London Club agreement for Russia. This resulted in a one-off (131 basis point) decline in average measured spreads.

heavily oversubscribed and many were upsized, indicating strong investor demand. The market was also supported by strong cash flows of coupon and amortization payments, which increased the supply of funds available for reinvestment. By October, sovereigns, including Mexico, Brazil, and Poland, started to prefinance some of their 2004 funding needs.

Liability management was also an important feature in 2003. Many countries took advan-

Figure 2.23. Cumulative Gross Annual Issuance of Bonds, Loans, and Equity
(In billions of U.S. dollars)

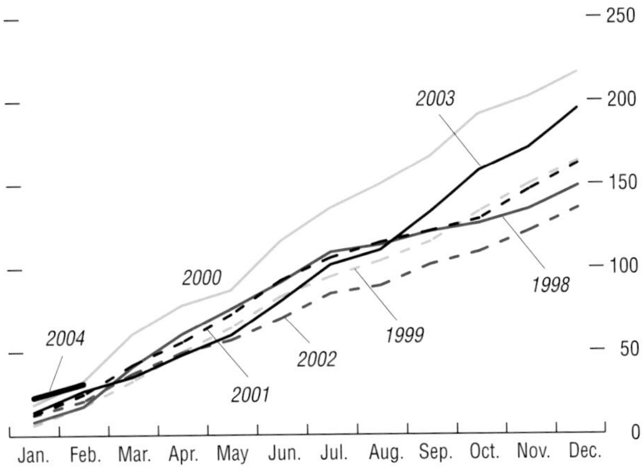

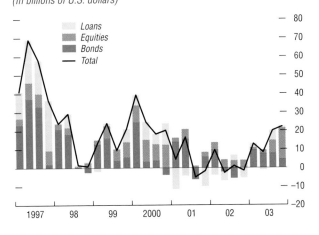

Source: Capital Data.
Note: 2004 data as of February 17.

Figure 2.24. Quarterly Net Issuance
(In billions of U.S. dollars)

Sources: Capital Data; and IMF staff estimates.

tage of the favorable external financing environment to improve the maturity profile of their debt and to release collateral. Mexico retired all its Brady bonds in an exchange. Panama, Poland, the Philippines, and Venezuela bought back some of their Brady bonds. On the domestic front, liability management activities included measures to address potentially volatile debt structures arising from short maturities and indexation to short-term interest rates and foreign currencies (Box 2.3).

Investor appetite also accommodated the issuance on a small scale of international bonds denominated in local currency. Uruguay issued 5.6 billion pesos of three-year inflation-linked bonds under New York law in October, its first foray into international bond markets since its 2002 debt exchange. While the issue was noteworthy given its currency denomination, the size of the issue was small, and secondary market liquidity quite limited as most investors appear to plan to hold the issue to maturity. Most investors were attracted to the deal by the prospect of a real appreciation of the peso. Others saw the opportunity to lock in relatively high real yields while the indexation to inflation would hedge out at least part of the accompanying currency risk. There appears to be some scope to increase the issuance of local currency debt internationally, and some large institutional investors have expressed a willingness to invest in such paper.

Corporate bond issuance rebounded in 2003, supported by an increase in global risk appetite and a search for yield as bond yields declined and spreads compressed across credit products (Figure 2.26). Latin American corporate issues were up nearly 150 percent from 2002, amid a plethora of deals from Mexico and Brazil. In Brazil, banks were the first to tap international markets, arbitraging between onshore and offshore rates, while nonfinancial corporates soon followed as investor sentiment turned unambiguously positive. Corporate issuance in EMEA was strong in early 2003, with Russian issuers particularly prominent, but supply tailed off in the latter part of the year in the aftermath of the corporate investigations starting in the summer. Issuance by Asian corporates gathered pace through the year as SARS-related concerns dissipated.

Dollar-denominated issuance picked up during the course of 2003. In the first half of 2003, over 25 percent of total issuance was euro-denominated, as the European investor base made its comeback after an 18-month absence following the Argentine default. However, amid an easing in access, cost considerations dominated funding decisions, so that the share of dollar-denominated issuance rose from to 87 percent in the second half of the year from roughly 70 percent in the first half.

Another salient development in 2003 was confirmation that the inclusion of collective action clauses (CACs) has developed into an industry standard for bonds issued under New York law. Investment grade credits blazed the trail at the outset of the year, followed by the sub-investment grade credits (Box 2.4). An exception, however, was the $1 billion global bond issued in October by China.

January 2004 witnessed a burst of activity in the primary debt market, following December's lull. Issuers rushed to market to take advantage of low borrowing costs and strong investor appetite. Inflows into the asset class by both institutional and retail investors were also supportive. The total volume of debt, the total number of issuers, and the weighted average maturity of issuance in January were all significantly higher than in previous years. On the sovereign side, Brazil, Turkey, and Venezuela came to market with 30-year deals. The long average maturities are particularly impressive given the number of corporate deals. Notably, two Brazilian corporates successfully sold 10-year paper, while one-third issued into the 30-year sector. More recently, however, the market has showed some signs of indigestion, exacerbated by the

Figure 2.25. Cumulative Gross Annual Issuance of Bonds
(In billions of U.S. dollars)

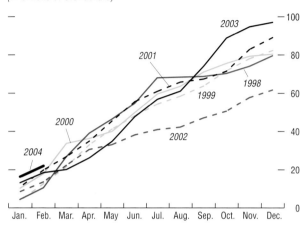

Source: Capital Data.
Note: 2004 data as of February 17.

Figure 2.26. Share of Bond Issues
(In percent)

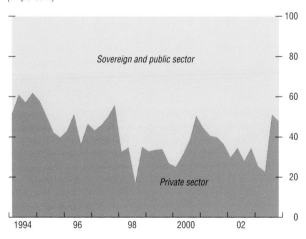

Source: Capital Data.

Box 2.3. Emerging Market Borrowers Improve Debt Structures: Case Studies

Past issues of the *Global Financial Stability Report* (GFSR) have highlighted the importance for emerging market borrowers of taking advantage of a favorable financing environment to improve the structure of their domestic and external obligations and to deepen local bond markets. Such measures are particularly important in countries with potentially volatile debt structures. Debt structures with short average maturities or a high share of outstanding debt linked to short-term interest rates or foreign currencies can be particularly problematic. Even countries with relatively stable debt structures have taken steps to deepen domestic financial markets and achieve a better debt profile. To illustrate these benefits, this box reviews the liability management operations of two large emerging market borrowers—Mexico and Brazil. Mexico, an investment grade credit, and Brazil, whose credit rating is sub-investment grade, have each taken steps to improve the profile of both their domestic and external debt while deepening their domestic bond markets.

Mexico: Recent Liability Management Operations

In an effort to reduce debt-service costs and to improve the financial conditions of future borrowing, Mexico undertook several liability management operations in 2003. These efforts have focused on prepaying debt obtained under less favorable market conditions, broadening its investor base, and diversifying its external financing sources. Since February 2003, the authorities have included collective action clauses in all dollar-denominated bonds issued under New York law.

In April 2003, Mexico prepaid $3.8 billion of outstanding dollar-denominated Brady Par Bonds, with maturity in December 2019. The bonds contained a call provision that gave Mexico the right to retire the bonds, and were guaranteed with principal and interest collateral. The resources to finance the operation were obtained from the federal government's liquidity position and from a one-year credit facility of $2 billion. Official estimates indicate the prepayment resulted in an external debt

reduction of $1.8 billion, generated an estimated net present savings of $327 million, and led to the release of collateral of $1.9 billion.

In June 2003, Mexico prepaid its remaining Brady Par Bonds denominated in Dutch guilders, German marks, Italian lira, and Swiss francs, which amounted to $1.3 billion. The bonds contained a call provision that gave Mexico the right to retire the bonds, and had an original expiration date of December 2019. The resources to finance the prepayment were obtained from the federal government's liquidity position. Official estimates suggest that the operation led to an external debt reduction of $1.3 billion, generated net present savings of $283 million, and led to the release of collateral of approximately $694 million.

After the buyback of the Brady Bonds, Mexico took steps to extend its investor base. On January 6, 2004, Mexico issued a $1 billion Global Floating Rate Note (FRN) with a five-year maturity, Mexico's first ever FRN. The bond has a floating interest rate in dollars of the three-month LIBOR rate plus 70 basis points. At the current level of LIBOR rates, the annualized financing cost of Mexico is 1.85 percent. The transaction put Mexico in touch with a new buyer base at a competitive cost, as 25 percent of the FRN was purchased by high-grade pension and bank funds and others that were not previously part of Mexico's traditional investor base.

Domestic debt management has aimed at increasing the average maturity of government debt, reducing refinancing risks for the federal government, and promoting the development of capital markets. During 2003, the stock of long-term fixed rate bonds with maturities between three and ten years increased significantly to around 50 percent of the outstanding stock in December 2003, while the stock of inflation-linked bonds decreased to around 10 percent (see first Figure). The amount auctioned of the 28-day Cetes was reduced, offset by increases in 91- and 182-day Cetes.

Favorable market conditions and increased investor confidence allowed Mexico to intro-

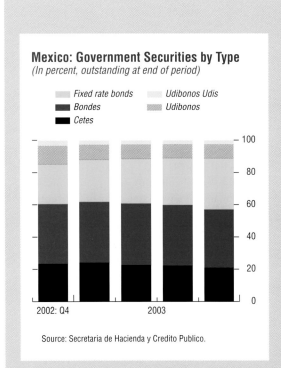

Mexico: Government Securities by Type
(In percent, outstanding at end of period)

Source: Secretaria de Hacienda y Credito Publico.

duce a new 20-year fixed-rate bond in October 2003. The bond should provide a long-dated government benchmark that facilitates the extension of corporate bond maturities in the local market. The increase in the auctioned amounts of long-term bonds and reduction in the amounts of shorter-term bonds should help increase liquidity in the secondary market and complement other recent efforts in this regard, including measures to improve the market-maker program, change the auction schedule, and reopen outstanding issues in primary auctions.

Brazil: Recent Liability Management Operations

After a 12-month hiatus, Brazil returned to international debt markets with a five-year $1 billion global bond in late April 2003 followed by a ten-year $1.25 billion global bond in June. The new bonds contained CACs, with a 85 percent threshold in the majority restructuring provision. All subsequent external issuance has contained similar provisions.

Brazil raised over $600 million through a debt swap augmented with new issuance at the end of July. The Republic offered bondholders to swap existing Par and Discount Bradies and the benchmark C-bond, for new sovereign debt maturing in 2011 and 2024. Nearly $1.3 billion of principal was exchanged, releasing approximately $490 million in collateral. Furthermore, $123 million was subsequently added in new issuance to the Global '11 for improved liquidity and additional financing, bringing the total issue size to $500 million. However, Brazil did not accept any offers for the C-bond as bondholders were unwilling to exchange out of the liquid benchmark bond for a longer-dated maturity during a period when U.S. treasury rates were under pressure. The exchange was essentially market-value neutral for bondholders.

Brazil completed external issuance for October 2003 and began pre-financing for 2004 with a $1.5 billion global bond with maturity in 2010. This brought total external issuance to $4.4 billion for the year or $3.9 billion, excluding the principal unlocked from the Brady swap. The favorable external environment continued into 2004 as Brazil was able to tap external debt markets in January with a 30-year $1.5 billion global bond at only 377 basis points above comparable U.S. treasuries.

In domestic markets, Brazil has made significant strides in reducing the amount of U.S. dollar-linked domestic debt while gradually improving the maturity profile. After rolling over 100 percent of principal on foreign exchange-linked debt during the first half of 2003, Brazil announced a policy to reduce the rollover rate beginning in June. The rollover rate fell quickly to 60 percent in July and has remained below 10 percent since October, allowing the withdrawal of some $6 billion in maturing principal as of end-January 2004 (see second Figure). As a result of this policy, and the steady appreciation of the currency throughout the year, the share of foreign exchange-linked debt (including foreign exchange swaps) in total domestic public sector debt has fallen from 37 percent in December 2002 to 22 percent at the end of 2003. The

Box 2.3 *(concluded)*

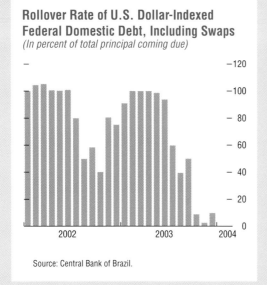

Rollover Rate of U.S. Dollar-Indexed Federal Domestic Debt, Including Swaps
(In percent of total principal coming due)

Source: Central Bank of Brazil.

withdrawal of foreign exchange-linked domestic debt has been primarily replaced by fixed-rate nominal coupon debt and inflation-indexed debt.

The maturity profile of domestic debt improved as Brazil sought to gradually lengthen the maturity of newly issued debt while simultaneously increasing average size and addressing gaps in the domestic yield curve. The average maturity of newly issued debt increased from a low of one year during the peak of market uncertainty in September of 2002 to three years in December 2003. As a result, the share of domestic debt maturing in the ensuing 12 months fell from 41 to 33 percent.

Brazil has also sought to strengthen domestic liability management practices by implementing new arrangements for primary and secondary dealers and expanding the domestic investor base. The aim of the new primary and secondary arrangements is to increase both liquidity and competition in domestic debt markets. The new arrangements will be bolstered by a new electronic trading platform on the Brazilian Mercantile and Futures Exchange in early 2004. The domestic investor base was expanded in late 2003 through the introduction of a Treasury Direct system, which allows direct access by individual accounts to Treasury auctions of domestic debt. Investor participation through this program has increased nearly fourfold since its introduction.

January 28 FOMC statement that temporarily reduced investor demand. Issuance slowed in February. However, almost 40 percent of expected sovereign issuance for 2004 had been completed by the end of January.

Equity Issuance

The surge in emerging market equity prices since April has triggered a sharp pickup in primary market activity, with the fourth quarter of 2003 far surpassing levels recorded prior to the bursting of the high-tech bubble (Figure 2.27). The distribution of issuance across regions differed starkly. After lying dormant for the better part of the year, Asia's equity market erupted with new stock issues from a wide array of companies in the final months of the year. Firms in China and Hong Kong SAR were particularly active, issuing $8 billion in the fourth quarter. The China Life IPO was noteworthy. At $3.46 billion, it was the largest IPO worldwide for 2003 and was 25 times oversubscribed. In Southeast Asia, Indonesian issuers were active, with stakes sold in Bank Mandiri, Bank Rakyat Indonesia, and PGN. Thailand's government successfully divested stakes in Krung Thai Bank and Thai Airways. By contrast, issuance in Latin America remained low, notwithstanding $540 million in issuance by Mexico's Cemex. New equity issuance was also limited in EMEA, where activity was dominated by the Central European telecom sector and a $300 million American Depository Receipt (ADR) issue by Russia's Norilsk Nickel. Amid ongoing inflows by international equity investors, there is no sign of the deal flow drying up. In particular, issuance by Asian companies continued at a fast pace in the first few weeks of the year, and several large deals are in the pipeline for the remainder of the year.

Syndicated Lending

Gross bank lending to emerging markets in 2003 exceeded levels of the previous two years. Net syndicated lending to the emerging markets was positive in 2003, marking a turn-around from the net contraction of the last two years (Figure 2.28). Amid ample global liquidity, borrowers eagerly refinanced, while international banks' appeared especially pre-pared to lend to Central and Eastern European borrowers and to the Middle East. Russian corporates were prominent borrowers in the fourth quarter, with a wide array of cor-porate facilities arranged on attractive terms prior to the unfolding of developments at Yukos. Market participants, however, reported that the extremely fine margins on some of the Central European credits, largely reflect-ing the abundance of liquidity in local mar-kets, drove some of the international banks further afield. Gulf states benefited from increased risk appetite by international banks, manifested in a rise in both project financing and lending to financial institutions. Latin America witnessed a pickup in loan volumes, primarily due to Mexican corporates.

Foreign Direct Investment

The declining trend in total private external financing for emerging market countries that had been in place since 1997 was reversed in 2003 (Figure 2.29). Foreign direct investment (FDI) to emerging market countries has been more resilient but has also declined in recent years, owing in large part to a sharp reduction in flows to Latin America and reduced privati-zations of state-owned assets in the service sec-tor. Nevertheless, FDI has remained the most

Figure 2.27. Cumulative Gross Annual Issuance of Equity
(In billions of U.S. dollars)

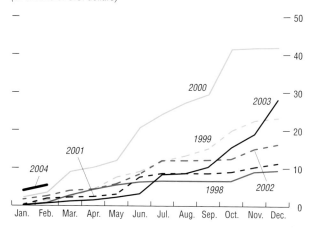

Source: Capital Data.
Note: 2004 data as of February 17.

Figure 2.28. Cumulative Gross Annual Issuance of Loans
(In billions of U.S. dollars)

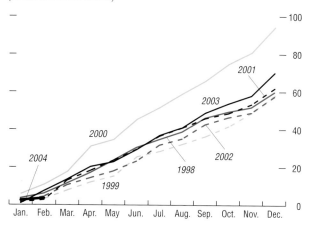

Source: Capital Data.
Note: 2004 data as of February 17.

Figure 2.29. Private Flows to Emerging Market Economies
(In billions of U.S. dollars)

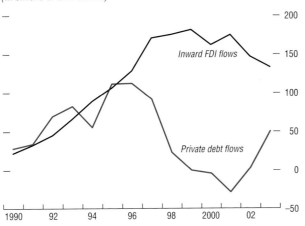

Source: World Bank, *Global Development Finance, 2004.*

Figure 2.30. Geographic Distribution of FDI Flows
(In percent of total)

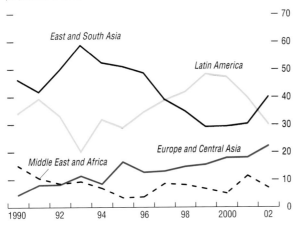

Source: World Bank, *Global Development Finance, 2004.*

important net source of private external capital for all regions.

Preliminary information indicates that FDI flows to emerging market countries continued to fall in 2003. However, the decline was smaller than in the previous year and largely reflected reduced FDI in Brazil and the EU accession countries. The outlook for FDI is expected to improve in 2004 with the strengthening growth prospects of the global economy.

In Latin America, FDI flows fell in 2003 by less than in the previous year with declines in Brazil (43 percent) and Mexico (15 percent) largely accounting for the regional drop (Figure 2.30). The decline in Brazil reflects, in part, the winding down of large-scale privatization in the telecommunication and energy sectors. FDI to Chile increased by over $1 billion reflecting the country's ongoing economic recovery and strong institutional base. FDI in Argentina appears to have stabilized at very low levels.

Asia increased its dominance as the main recipient of FDI to emerging market countries, with aggregate inflows increasing for the third year in a row. FDI to China continued to increase and now represents 86 percent of total FDI to emerging market countries in Asia. Elsewhere in Asia, FDI also increased in India (reflecting the easing of foreign investment restrictions in the automobile, private banking, and telecommunications sectors) and Thailand.

FDI flows to emerging Europe declined in 2003 reflecting a 50 percent decline to the EU accession countries (Czech Republic, Hungary, Poland, and Slovak Republic). FDI rose in Russia by almost 100 percent, mainly to the oil sector.

Results from a recently completed survey conducted by a working group of the Capital Markets Consultative Group (see CMCG, 2003) emphasized the importance of regional economic, structural, and institutional factors in influencing FDI prospects. The direct investors participating in that working group

Box 2.4. Collective Action Clauses: Update on Market Practice

An increasing number of emerging market countries have included collective action clauses (CACs) in their international sovereign bonds issued under New York law, where these clauses had not previously been the market standard. During the latter part of 2003 and early 2004, sovereign issues containing CACs grew to represent more than 70 percent of total volumes issued (see the Table).

In September 2003, Turkey included CACs in its bonds governed by New York law, followed shortly by Peru. These were the first two sub-investment grade countries that issued New York law bonds with CACs that included a voting threshold of 75 percent of outstanding principal for majority restructuring clauses. This represented a change in market practice with respect to previous non-investment grade issuers that had included higher voting thresholds (e.g., 85 percent in the case of Belize, Brazil, and Guatemala). Both issues were priced very tightly along the yield curve and there was no evidence of a yield premium as a result of the lower voting threshold.

In the latter part of 2003 and early 2004, Chile, Colombia, Costa Rica, Panama, the Philippines, Poland, and Venezuela also issued global bonds governed by New York law that included CACs. All issues were heavily oversubscribed and priced broadly along the yield

curve.[1] With respect to majority restructuring provisions, recent New York law bonds differ on the voting threshold for amending key terms. Chile, Colombia, Italy, Mexico, Panama, Peru, Poland, and Turkey used a 75 percent voting threshold while the issuances of Brazil and Venezuela relied upon a 85 percent voting threshold. Regarding majority enforcement provisions, all of the recent bond issues governed by New York law except Poland used a 25 percent threshold for acceleration.[2] However, they differ on the threshold for de-acceleration: in the case of Chile, Colombia, Mexico, Peru, and Venezuela, the threshold is set at more than 50 percent of outstanding principal while the issuances by Brazil, Italy, Panama, and Turkey included a $66\frac{2}{3}$ percent threshold for de-acceleration. All recent bond issues used a fiscal agency structure. In general, there was no evidence that the issue prices

[1] In the sole case of Colombia, prices were somewhat above the existing sovereign yield curve. However, market participants reported this was the result of high volumes of emerging market debt placed in the same week.
[2] The Polish bond allows each bondholder to accelerate its claim upon a payment default or declaration of moratorium by the sovereign issuer and does not provide for de-acceleration with respect to these events of default.

Emerging Market Sovereign Bond Issuance by Jurisdiction[1]

	2001				2002				2003				2004[2]
	Q1	Q2	Q3	Q4	Q1	Q2	Q3	Q4	Q1	Q2[3]	Q3	Q4	Q1
With collective action clauses[4]													
Number of issuance	14	10	2	10	6	5	2	4	9	31	10	5	15
of which: New York law		1							1	22	5	4	12
Volume of issuance	5.6	4.8	1.8	2.2	2.6	1.9	0.9	1.4	5.6	18.0	6.4	4.3	12.8
of which: New York law		1.5							1.0	12.8	3.6	4.0	9.1
Without collective action clauses[5]													
Number of issuance	16	17	6	18	17	12	5	10	14	4	7	7	2
Volume of issuance	6.7	8.5	3.8	6.1	11.6	6.4	3.3	4.4	8.1	2.5	3.5	4.2	1.5

Source: Capital Data.
[1] Number of issuance is in number. Volume of issuance is in billions of U.S. dollars.
[2] Data for 2004:Q1 are as of February 17, 2004.
[3] Includes issues of restructured bonds by Uruguay.
[4] English and Japanese laws, and New York law where relevant.
[5] German and New York laws.

included a premium for CACs, an opinion generally shared by private market participants who have lately been disregarding the inclusion of CACs in market reports on sovereign issues.

A number of international sovereign bonds were issued under English and Japanese law including CACs, as has been the practice in these markets. The emerging market issuers included Hungary, Poland, Slovak Republic, and Ukraine and mature market issuers included Austria and Sweden. Bond issues under German law continued to lack CACs, although legislative work aiming at the elimination of perceived legal risk in the usage of CACs under German law is underway. International bond issues under German law have been rare in the last three years, however, which may partly be due to lost or reduced market access of important traditional issuers.

reported that there was no large-scale withdrawal from Latin America and that the effect on FDI from the Argentina crisis was concentrated in the banking and utilities sectors.

The CMCG report also notes that FDI in emerging market countries is increasingly being undertaken to service domestic demand in the host country, which highlights the importance of large markets and promising growth prospects. Consequently, emerging market countries with good governance practices and improving infrastructure and institutions are likely to secure greater amounts of FDI.

Banking Sector Developments in Emerging Markets

The improved economic climate is supporting the recovery of banking systems in the major emerging market countries despite slow progress in fundamental restructuring. For the most part, banking systems in Asia continue to recover, although growing credit risk exposure to certain sectors, in conjunction with persistent balance sheet weaknesses, deserves close attention by the supervisors in a few countries. In Latin America, severe liquidity pressures on distressed banking systems are receding, but less-than-robust economic growth and political factors are exacerbating financial distress in some countries. Banking systems in emerging Europe have coped well with weak macroeconomic conditions and now stand to benefit from improved economic prospects. Nonetheless, fast credit growth in some countries needs to be closely monitored. The authorities are making efforts to address long-standing structural problems in the banking systems in some countries in Africa and the Middle East.

Capacity in emerging markets to absorb shocks from mismatches in the external asset-liability positions of banks has improved. Banks in emerging market countries now have on average a more balanced external position vis-à-vis BIS reporting banks than in 1997–98. Official reserves coverage of the banking systems' net liability positions has generally increased (Table 2.2). And supervisory and regulatory efforts have intensified, although significant improvement in effectiveness in this area will take time. The focus of regulations in several countries is shifting toward requirements for improved risk management by individual institutions. Regulatory authorities are also seeking to harness market discipline through greater disclosure and provision of accurate financial information to markets.

Asia

The financial systems of the major emerging market countries in Asia are being bolstered

Table 2.2. Individual Countries' Bank Net Asset/Liability Position vis-à-vis BIS Banks as a Ratio of Official Reserves[1]

	1997	1998	1999	2000	2001	2002	2003:Q2
Asia							
China	−0.1	0.0	0.1	0.3	0.2	0.2	0.1
Indonesia	−1.1	−0.3	−0.2	−0.2	−0.1	−0.1	0.0
Korea	−2.0	−0.5	−0.4	−0.2	−0.2	−0.2	−0.3
Malaysia	−0.6	−0.3	−0.3	−0.1	−0.2	−0.2	−0.3
Philippines	−0.5	−0.1	0.2	0.0	−0.2	−0.2	−0.2
Thailand	−2.2	−1.1	−0.5	−0.3	−0.1	−0.1	−0.1
Emerging Europe							
Czech Republic	0.0	0.0	0.3	0.3	0.5	0.1	0.0
Hungary	−0.4	−0.5	−0.3	−0.4	−0.3	−0.5	−0.6
Poland	0.5	0.2	0.2	0.2	0.3	0.1	0.1
Russia	−2.3	−3.9	−2.3	−0.1	0.1	0.4	0.3
Turkey	0.2	−0.3	−0.2	−0.3	0.0	0.1	−0.1
Ukraine	0.2	−0.3	−0.1	−0.1	0.0	0.3	0.4
Latin America							
Argentina	0.2	0.3	0.2	0.3	−0.5	−0.5	−0.4
Brazil	−0.3	−0.3	−0.3	−0.9	−0.7	−0.7	−0.3
Chile	0.3	0.4	0.6	0.5	0.5	0.3	0.3
Costa Rica	0.7	0.5	0.3	0.3	0.5	0.4	−0.2
Ecuador	−0.1	−0.4	0.0	0.3	0.6	1.5	0.9
El Salvador	0.3	0.1	0.0	−0.3	−0.3	−0.4	−0.2
Guatemala	0.1	−0.1	−0.1	0.2	0.1	0.3	0.2
Honduras	1.2	1.3	1.0	1.4	1.3	1.2	0.3
Mexico	0.0	0.1	0.3	0.5	0.6	0.4	0.4
Nicaragua	−0.6	−0.7	0.1	−0.3	−0.5	−0.5	−0.5
Uruguay	2.5	0.7	1.0	1.0	1.2	3.6	3.0
Venezuela	0.2	0.3	0.3	0.5	0.7	0.8	0.2
Middle East							
Egypt	0.8	0.7	0.7	0.8	0.7	0.8	0.9
Jordan	2.2	2.8	2.2	2.1	2.2	1.8	1.4
Lebanon	1.6	1.5	1.2	1.8	2.0	1.6	1.2
Morocco	0.6	0.7	0.5	0.5	0.3	0.3	0.2
Pakistan	−0.6	−0.7	−0.2	0.1	0.5	0.8	0.8
Tunisia	0.4	0.5	0.3	0.4	0.3	0.5	0.6
Sub-Saharan Africa							
Côte d'Ivoire	−0.4	0.4	0.4	−0.1	0.2	0.1	0.1
Ghana	0.7	0.8	0.4	1.0	0.7	0.7	0.6
Kenya	1.0	1.0	0.8	1.1	1.1	1.3	1.1
Nigeria	0.2	0.1	0.3	0.3	0.4	0.6	0.5
South Africa	−1.2	−1.3	−0.5	−0.3	−0.1	0.4	1.3
Zimbabwe	−2.5	−1.3	0.1	0.9	2.0	1.6	. . .

Sources: Bank for International Settlements; IMF, *International Financial Statistics;* and IMF staff estimates.

[1]A negative ratio indicates a net liability position (liabilities exceed assets).

by the economic recovery. Soundness indicators on average point to solid rates of return on assets and sustained improvement in capital adequacy and asset quality (Table 2.3). Bank ratings by private analysts and market valuation of bank stocks relative to overall stock indices also continue to improve (Figures 2.31 and 2.32).

In *India,* low interest rates have further boosted bank soundness and performance indicators as the authorities have adopted measures to contain credit risk, including legal and regulatory changes. The banking systems in *Thailand* and *Malaysia* are benefiting from restructuring and reforms. In *Korea,* the financial system has had to absorb the effects of the bankruptcy of the chaebol SKGlobal, an affiliate of SK, Korea's third largest chaebol, and substantial losses at some credit card companies—the latter prompting the authori-

Table 2.3. Selected Financial Soundness Indicators for Emerging Markets
(In percent)

	Return on Assets				Nonperforming Loans to Total Loans				Capital to Assets				Moody's Financial Strength Index[1]		
	2000	2001	2002	2003*	2000	2001	2002	2003*	2000	2001	2002	2003*	2001	2002	2003
Latin America															
Mean	0.7	0.6	0.3	0.9	9.3	9.1	8.6	10.5	10.9	10.9	10.5	11.1	27.8	19.7	18.7
Median	0.9	0.7	1.3	1.3	8.6	8.1	8.1	9.6	10.1	10.0	10.9	11.1	26.9	19.4	15.8
Standard deviation	1.6	2.2	3.4	1.3	6.7	6.6	5.2	6.9	2.1	2.4	4.2	2.9	12.2	17.0	18.7
Emerging Europe[2]															
Mean	0.7	0.2	1.4	1.6	12.0	12.4	10.0	8.8	10.8	11.6	11.3	10.1	29.2	28.9	29.8
Median	0.9	1.1	1.2	1.5	9.4	8.2	8.5	6.4	9.8	9.5	9.8	9.6	29.8	32.1	32.1
Standard deviation	1.1	2.9	0.8	0.5	8.8	9.4	6.5	7.3	4.3	5.9	5.1	2.6	12.9	13.6	13.3
Asia[3]															
Mean	0.6	0.7	0.7	0.9	16.5	14.6	13.4	12.1	7.3	7.6	8.1	9.9	25.9	26.7	27.5
Median	0.4	0.7	0.8	1.0	15.4	11.9	15.4	14.4	5.3	5.4	7.3	8.5	16.7	18.5	19.4
Standard deviation	1.4	0.9	0.4	0.3	8.6	9.3	8.6	7.0	4.6	4.5	4.2	4.4	25.4	24.0	23.5
Middle East															
Mean	1.1	1.0	1.1	. . .	16.3	16.4	15.4	. . .	8.5	8.6	8.7	. . .	29.8	28.6	28.6
Median	0.9	0.8	0.7	. . .	15.8	16.1	13.9	. . .	8.5	8.5	8.9	. . .	31.7	29.2	29.2
Standard deviation	0.6	0.7	0.7	. . .	6.4	6.0	6.9	. . .	3.1	2.9	2.8	. . .	8.9	9.6	9.6
Sub-Saharan Africa															
Mean	3.7	3.8	2.9	. . .	15.7	13.3	12.2	. . .	9.2	9.4	9.3	. . .	. . .	. . .	. . .
Median	3.2	3.3	2.3	. . .	14.6	11.7	8.9	. . .	9.1	9.1	9.4	. . .	. . .	. . .	. . .
Standard deviation	3.1	2.6	2.0	. . .	9.2	8.3	9.6	. . .	1.4	1.4	1.3	. . .	. . .	. . .	. . .

Sources: National authorities; EDSS; and IMF staff estimates.
Note (*): Data for 2003 is for various quarters and for a more limited sample.
[1]Constructed according to a numerical scale assigned to Moody's weighted average bank ratings by country. Zero indicates the lowest possible average rating and 100 indicates the highest possible average rating.
[2]Includes Central and Eastern Europe, Israel, Malta, and Turkey.
[3]Excluding Japan.

ties to announce steps to strengthen prudential supervision of credit card companies. While the banking system has remained stable, the urgency of enhancing reform of the insolvency regime and instituting tighter oversight of nonbank institutions has been brought into focus. The financial systems of *Hong Kong SAR* and *Singapore* have weathered the effects of SARS and are well positioned to take advantage of the region's economic recovery.

The process of bank restructuring in *Indonesia* has been completed and overall indicators of bank soundness continue to improve. Some concerns remain related to state-owned banks' lending growth, notwithstanding measures to strengthen the banking system, including careful monitoring. In the *Philippines,* banks' reported capital adequacy exceeds regulatory requirements and prof-

itability is improving somewhat. Asset quality, however, remains a problem and strategies are being devised to reinforce the capacity of the banking system to cope with shocks. In *China,* the recent capital injection into two large state-owned banks may represent an important step toward strengthening the banking system, provided restructuring plans, improved governance, and oversight of the two banks are promptly implemented (see Box 2.5).

Latin America

Although some aggregate indicators of banks' financial soundness for the region as a whole deteriorated further in 2003, the situation in countries recently in financial crisis has begun to stabilize. Moreover, banking soundness indicators have continued to slowly improve in the other countries in the region.

Financial conditions in *Argentina's* banking system stabilized during 2003, but credit growth remains marginal, while past policy-related losses have not been fully compensated and bank assets are concentrated in low-yielding government assets. Progress in restructuring the banking system in *Uruguay* has been limited.

Macroeconomic uncertainty, often coupled with political uncertainties, cloud the prospects for the banking system in several countries, including *Bolivia, Ecuador,* and *Paraguay,* where the ratio of nonperforming to total loans has continued to edge up without an offsetting increase in provisions. In the *Dominican Republic,* questions about the solvency of individual institutions have had a marked impact on market confidence.

By contrast, despite slow economic growth, banking sector performance has improved in *Brazil, Chile, Colombia,* and *Mexico.* Returns on assets have firmed and compare favorably with international norms, while excess provisioning and comfortable capitalization levels continue to provide a buffer against potential deterioration in credit quality.

Emerging Europe

Banking systems are enjoying improved rates of return and asset quality, and strong capital positions. This good performance is also reflected in private analysts' ratings of banks, which were on average raised in 2003 (Figure 2.31). After strengthening sharply in mid-2002, relative market valuations of bank stocks have receded somewhat, although they still stand above the average levels in the previous two years (Figure 2.32).

In *Turkey,* while the banking system has successfully coped with the effects of the Imar Bank scandal, the episode has again raised questions about the supervisory framework. In addition, a variety of structural issues—resolution of Pamukbank, sale of assets of

Figure 2.31. Moody's Financial Strength Index

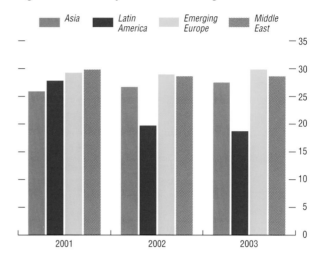

Sources: Moody's; and IMF staff estimates.

Figure 2.32. Emerging Market Countries: Banking Sector Market Valuation[1]
(February 1999 = 100)

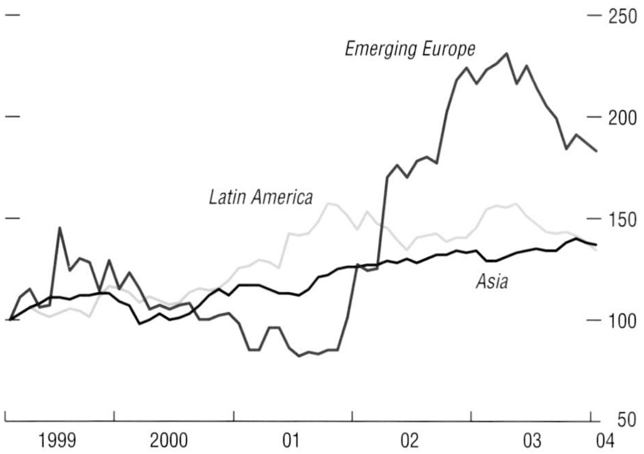

Sources: Datastream; and IMF staff estimates.
[1]Ratio of banking sector stock prices to total market stock prices, simple average.

Box 2.5. State Bank Recapitalization in China

On the basis of a decision by China's State Council, $45 billion (about 4 percent of GDP) of China's international reserves were used on December 30, 2003 to recapitalize two of China's four major state-owned commercial banks—the Bank of China and China Construction Bank. The capital injection was split equally between the two banks. The recapitalization was executed by the central bank (the People's Bank of China—PBC) transferring the funds from its international reserves holdings to a newly created holding company, owned by the State Administration of Foreign Exchange (SAFE), which was established to facilitate the recapitalization. The holding company exchanged the foreign currency assets (mostly in the form of U.S. treasury securities) that it received for equity positions in the two banks. The banks will retain these foreign currency assets in their original form.

The authorities have stated that the recapitalization is part of a broader overall reform strategy for these banks. As part of this strategy, they have suggested that additional steps will be taken, including (1) adopting stricter auditing requirements; (2) requiring the banks to move more quickly to fully meet provisioning requirements; and (3) boosting capital adequacy ratios to 8 percent, in line with international standards. If these steps are taken, the recapitalization may significantly improve the health of these two banks and that of the banking system as a whole, since these banks constitute about one-third of the assets of the banking system. However, to maximize the chances of a successful outcome, of immediate importance is the need to develop and begin implementing concrete restructuring plans for the two banks. In particular, substantial improvements in the internal operations and governance of the banks are required, accompanied by efforts to further improve oversight by the supervisory authorities.

---

other distressed banks, and privatization of state banks—are yet to be addressed adequately. Elsewhere in the region, risks have generally receded and banking systems maintain confidence and stability. Several countries, however, have experienced fairly rapid credit expansion, which warrants rigorous credit evaluations and close monitoring of credit quality.

Middle East and Africa

Banking systems in these regions are characterized by highly divergent financial performance and balance sheets.

Banks in the wealthy oil producing countries of the Middle East are generally strong and their positions strengthened further in 2003. In particular, the banking system in *Saudi Arabia* remains highly liquid, profitable, and well capitalized. The main risks stem from an economic slowdown and geopolitical uncertainties.

Elsewhere in the region banks continue to suffer from structural weaknesses that are being addressed. In *Egypt*, large public sector banks received a capital injection in early 2003 and efforts are under way to improve performance through changes in management. In *Morocco*, growing weaknesses in state-owned specialized banks are being addressed, while commercial banks generally have a strong capital base and prudent provisioning policies. Financial conditions in *Lebanon* have eased considerably, but asset quality and bank exposure to the sovereign, whose debt is very high, remain important issues. Bank restructuring and privatization efforts have also progressed in *Pakistan*, and banks' balance sheets have strengthened.

The financial system in *South Africa* has stabilized and undergone consolidation, following serious difficulties at some banks in 2001. The authorities are now turning to measures to broaden access to financial services for the population.

Structural Issues Should Be the Focus in Mature Markets

The relatively benign conditions in both mature and emerging markets described earlier have allowed further progress in reducing balance sheet vulnerabilities in mature markets. In large part, this represents the continuation of the trend reported in the September 2003 GFSR and earlier issues:

- *Corporate and household sectors have continued to build up liquidity.* In the United States in particular, strong corporate cash flow has reduced borrowing needs, while in Europe household savings continued to be directed into money market instruments.
- *Rising asset values have strengthened net worth across a wide range of sectors.* This is true not only for the corporate and household sectors but also for banks and for institutional investors such as insurance companies (discussed in detail in Chapter III).
- *Over the last six months, hedging activity in the U.S. mortgage market has become somewhat less of an influence on interest rate volatility.* As most borrowers who could refinance their mortgages have done so, refinancing levels are unlikely to rise to the peaks of 2003. However, the market has given increased attention recently to the possibility that, if 10-year yields fall much further, mortgage hedging activity could grow and thus accentuate the decline in yields.
- *Nevertheless, debt levels remain high in many sectors and remain a vulnerability if interest rates rise.* The stock of debt in Europe in particular continues to rise for both households and corporates. Although the debt service requirements are currently modest and many corporates and households (especially in the United States) have locked in low interest rates, rising interest rates would still increase the debt service burden.

During recovery points in a cycle it may be appropriate to focus on some of the longer-term topics of interest for financial stability:

- *The hedge fund industry has been growing rapidly and institutional investor participation has substantially increased.* Although leverage and counterparty exposures are better monitored (due in part to greater oversight by institutions), it would be helpful to have more consistent disclosure standards.
- *Corporate governance initiatives need to be pursued.* Although progress has been made in particular countries and multilaterally, the cases of Parmalat and of late trading and market timing in the U.S. mutual fund industry serve as a reminder that more can and should be done.
- *The Basel II Accord is due to be finalized by mid-2004.* It is likely to improve financial stability. However, some questions remain, particularly concerning its implementation.

This section discusses these issues in more detail.

Sectoral Balance Sheets

As the global economic recovery took hold and interest rates remained low, the balance sheets of household, corporate, and bank sectors strengthened over the course of 2003, extending the trend identified in the September 2003 GFSR. However, some fragilities and sources of potential vulnerabilities remain.

In most European countries and in the United States, buoyant housing and equity markets have contributed to the improvement in household balance sheets and increased net worth. Together with the low interest rate environment, this has led at the same time to a continuing growth in mortgage debt. Household balance sheets could thus prove sensitive to a turnaround in house prices, which could be triggered by a larger-than-expected rise in interest rates or disappointing income or employment growth. Consumer credit growth has been less strong and, in contrast to the United States, European consumer credit

Figure 2.33. United States: Household Net Worth
(In trillions of U.S. dollars)

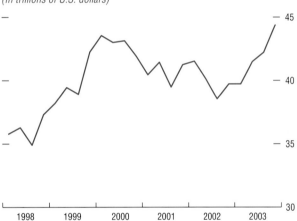

Source: Board of Governors of the Federal Reserve System, *Flow of Funds.*

growth has slowed, perhaps reflecting the lag in continental Europe's economic recovery.

Corporate balance sheet restructuring in the major mature markets progressed in 2003 as the economic recovery significantly strengthened cash flow. This factor, together with low interest rates, allowed corporates to lengthen debt maturities and reduce debt servicing costs. The degree of balance sheet improvement, however, differs between countries, largely reflecting the uneven pace of the global economic recovery. European nonfinancial corporations, for example, are still burdened by very high levels of debt and could be vulnerable to a rise in interest rates or a disappointing pace of recovery. In the United States, on the other hand, cash flow has been particularly strong. In Japan, rising profits have allowed corporates to reduce leverage.

Banks overall have benefited from improvements in the economic and financial background and in their own risk management. Strong mortgage lending in the United States and in many European countries has increased bank income. Simultaneously, the quality of their corporate credit portfolios benefited from the improved financial condition of borrowers. However, the current high exposure of banks to real estate, notably in Europe, represents a continuing risk. In Japan, progress is being made in reducing nonperforming loans but the large amount still outstanding and the slow restructuring of the stock of subperforming loans continue to leave bank balance sheets fragile.

Household Balance Sheets

UNITED STATES

The net worth of U.S. households increased 12 percent in 2003, due primarily to rising home and equity prices. These gains lifted household net worth above its previous peak in 2000 (Figure 2.33).

Household debt continued to expand throughout 2003. Although borrowing decelerated somewhat following the end of the mortgage refinancing boom in August 2003, mortgage debt during the second half of 2003 grew at an 11 percent annualized rate. Consumer credit has continued to grow at about a 5 percent annual rate.

Euro Area

In the euro area, consumer credit growth has slowed since late 2002. Despite rebounding in the fourth quarter of 2003, its 3 percent annual growth rate in 2003 remained below that for 2002. Mortgage borrowing has remained buoyant for several years, and it accelerated further in 2003 to an 8 percent growth rate. The 7 percent rise in house prices in 2003 also contributed to healthier household balance sheets. Euro area households continued to build liquidity during 2003, favoring short-term, low-risk instruments, although demand for money market funds and bank deposits slowed later in the year.

United Kingdom

Overall household borrowing in the United Kingdom remained strong at the end of 2003, with mortgage and consumer credit both growing at annual rates above 10 percent, despite slowing consumer borrowing over the course of the year. Past house price increases, on the other hand, may keep fueling mortgage borrowing in the coming months, despite the recent tightening of monetary policy. In the third quarter of 2003, mortgage equity withdrawal stood at 7 percent of disposable income, 2 percentage points above its level a year earlier (Figure 2.34). At the same time, U.K. households' debt-to-income ratio stood at 126 percent, compared to 119 percent in 2002 and 104 percent in 2000.

Japan

During the second and third quarters of 2003, the Japanese household sector's net worth improved, reflecting primarily valuation gains in equity holdings (Figure 2.35). Total financial assets rose by 2 percent during the same period.

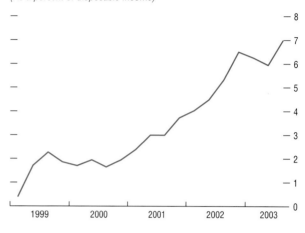

Figure 2.34. United Kingdom: Mortgage Equity Withdrawal
(As a percent of disposable income)

Source: Bank of England.

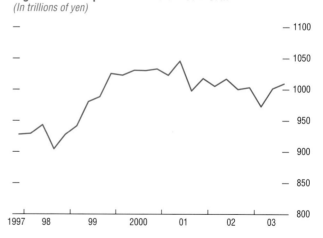

Figure 2.35. Japan: Household Net Worth
(In trillions of yen)

Source: Bank of Japan, *Flow of Funds*.

Figure 2.36. United States: Debt to Net Worth Ratio of Nonfinancial Corporations

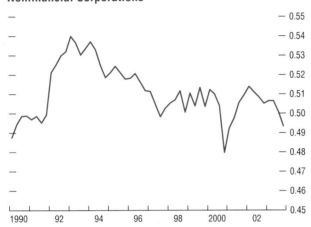

Source: Board of Governors of the Federal Reserve System, *Flow of Funds.*

Figure 2.37. United States: Financing Gap of Nonfinancial Corporations
(In billions of U.S. dollars)

Source: Board of Governors of the Federal Reserve System, *Flow of Funds.*

Corporate Balance Sheets

UNITED STATES

U.S. nonfinancial corporate balance sheets continued to improve. Net worth rose steadily in 2003 and leverage declined, as the ratio of debt to net worth dropped from its recent peak in 2002 of 51.4 percent to 49.3 percent by the end of 2003 (Figure 2.36). Corporate leverage is below the average since 1990, as improvements in net worth since the early 1990s have outpaced debt growth, but remains higher than earlier periods.

Nonfinancial corporate debt grew slowly in 2003, as surging cash flow eliminated the need to borrow for many firms. Corporate cash flow rose sharply by 21 percent over the course of 2003, and is now 35 percent above its pre-recession peak. Corporations had a surplus of cash flow over capital spending, despite the latter's double-digit growth rate in the third and fourth quarters, as the financing gap—the difference between these two amounts—was a record low and profit growth continued to be robust (Figure 2.37). Firms thus entered the new year with high liquidity. Strong cash flow also allowed corporations to reduce net bond issuance.

EURO AREA

In the euro area, nonfinancial corporations continued to limit their bank borrowing in recent months and increasingly turned to the securities market to restructure their balance sheets. As of November 2003, debt securities issuance by nonfinancial corporations was growing at 9 percent annually (Figure 2.38). Although cost-cutting efforts and asset disposals allowed some strengthening of nonfinancial corporate balance sheets in 2003, they remain burdened by relatively high levels of debt, with their debt/GDP remaining near 65 percent in the third quarter, a level last seen in the early 1980s.

UNITED KINGDOM

U.K. nonfinancial corporations' debt reached a historical high in the third quarter of 2003, rising to more than 75 percent of GDP, from 50 percent in the mid-1990s (Figure 2.39). However, balance sheet adjustment seems to be under way in the sector, aided by the financial surplus since mid-2001, and the progressive decline in the ratio of interest payments to gross operating surplus (18 percent in the third quarter of 2003, from 22 percent in 2000) as interest rates declined.

JAPAN

Continued profit growth allowed the Japanese corporate sector to further improve its balance sheet, including steady debt reduction during the second and third quarters of 2003 (Figure 2.40). Nevertheless, average debt levels remain high compared with other mature markets. Meanwhile, corporate pension funds returned assets that they had traditionally managed to the government pension fund. Under a prior arrangement, corporate pension funds could retain any surplus above target returns required by the government, but needed to compensate for any shortfalls from their own funds. The protracted period of poor stock market performance since 1990 and low interest rates have forced corporate pension schemes to continuously pay to the government compensation for losses, thus eroding their own funds. (The implications of global pension fund developments for financial stability will be the topic of a chapter in the September 2004 GFSR.)

Bank Balance Sheets

UNITED STATES

U.S. commercial banks posted strong earnings through the end of 2003, largely reflecting continued strong mortgage demand and a pickup in capital market activities among money-center banks. However, demand for business loans remained weak, and the volume of commercial and industrial loans fell further through the fourth quarter of 2003, although there are signs that demand for borrowing may improve in 2004 as economic activity strengthens.

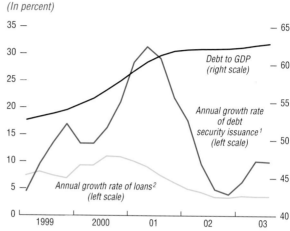

Figure 2.38. Euro Area: Nonfinancial Corporations—Financial Situation
(In percent)

Sources: European Central Bank; and IMF staff estimates.
[1]Data up to end-November 2003.
[2]From monetary and financial institutions.

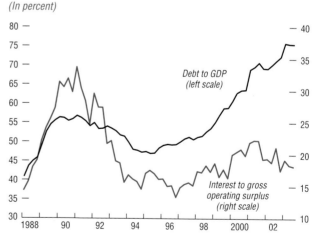

Figure 2.39. United Kingdom: Nonfinancial Corporations—Financial Situation
(In percent)

Source: United Kingdom, Office of National Statistics, *United Kingdom Economic Accounts*.

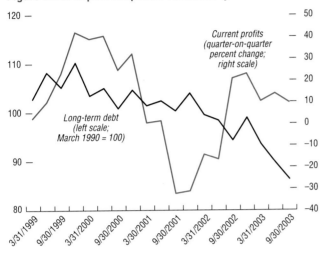

Figure 2.40. Japan: Corporate Profitability and Indebtedness

Source: Bank of Japan, *Flow of Funds.*

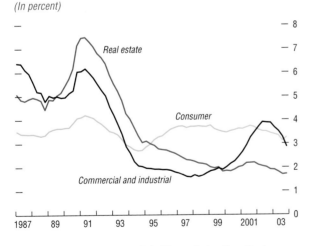

Figure 2.41. U.S. Commercial Banks: Delinquency Rates
(In percent)

Source: Board of Governors of the Federal Reserve System, *Flow of Funds.*

The credit quality of bank loan portfolios has continued to improve. Delinquency rates on commercial and industrial loans, which at their recent peak in early 2002 remained well below the levels of the previous recession, fell further throughout 2003 (Figure 2.41). Delinquencies on real estate loans are at an extremely low 1.7 percent. The credit quality of consumer loans has also improved somewhat, but delinquency rates are only slightly below their peak in late 2001.

EUROPE

Banks in the European Union appear to have contained loan losses reasonably well compared with previous economic slowdowns. Banks were helped by the ongoing low interest rate environment and continued improvement in bank credit risk management. Indeed, after two years of increases, provisioning seems to have declined during 2003, as corporate asset quality has stabilized.

The credit quality of European banking groups improved in 2003. Among the 20 largest European banking groups, Fitch took nine positive and only four negative rating actions in 2003, with most positive rating actions taken toward the end of the year. By contrast, it took three positive and eight negative rating actions in the second half of 2002.

Exposure to real estate remains significant. Mortgage lending now represents on average two-thirds of total bank lending to households and up to 35 percent of total loans to the nonfinancial private sector. European Union banks' exposure to the construction and real estate sectors comprised 36 percent of banks' own funds at the end of 2002, up from 33 percent a year earlier.

Overall, the profitability of large European Union banks increased in 2003, but part of this improvement came from nonrecurring items such as cost cutting, elimination of non-core activities, and declining loan-loss provisions. Banks' capacity to use one-off factors to offset another episode of weakened activity is accordingly diminished. This could potentially lead some European Union banks to raise fresh capital.

JAPAN

Japanese banks' balance sheets have improved significantly through the six-month period ended September 30, 2003. A strengthening economic recovery and a rising equity market supported bank profitability. In addition, Japanese banks reduced nonperforming loans by 10.5 percent during the six months ending September 2003, particularly among the major banks. A recovery in corporate profitability and some progress in corporate restructuring reduced new nonperforming loans, while banks accelerated write-offs. Major bank and supervisory officials are increasingly confident of achieving the supervisory requirement of halving the nonperforming loan ratio by March 2005. However, reductions in nonperforming loans by regional banks have lagged the major banks. During the first half of FY2003, regional banks reduced their nonperforming loans by only 5 percent, compared to major banks' 14 percent, and regional banks now account for 44 percent of total nonperforming loans in the Japanese banking system.

The nationalization of Ashikaga Bank, the eleventh largest regional bank, in December 2003, drove home the magnitude of the nonperforming loans problem of regional banks. The government took tough action in the case of Ashikaga and, unlike the previous Resona Bank case in which the government bailed out shareholders in full, it assessed the bank to be insolvent and wiped out shareholders' equity in Ashikaga (the first such occasion for a regional bank). The market initially reacted to the news favorably, and some industry observers thought it provided a precedent for future bank failures. However, many observers have since interpreted the Ashikaga case as an isolated and special situation. The Japanese Financial Services Agency (FSA) is currently considering legislation to establish a new framework for temporary injections of public funds into solvent banks, in order to strengthen their operations. Under the proposed new scheme, public funds would be injected, accompanied by management reforms, without eliminating shareholders' stakes.

While welcoming the improvement in balance sheets, private sector observers point to several remaining risks in the Japanese banking system. The stock of subperforming (but not yet nonperforming) loans in the banking system stands at 10 percent of GDP. These credits benefit from the current low interest rate environment, but their restructuring remains slow.[5]

Mortgage Markets

Refinancing of mortgages by borrowers fell abruptly last summer as mortgage interest rates reversed part of their earlier decline. Accordingly, mortgage hedging activity in the United States has been sharply lower since the third quarter of 2003. As such, there has been no repetition of the events seen last July and August and discussed in the September 2003 GFSR, when strains from the mortgage market apparently added to volatility in other fixed-income markets. However, recent falls in long-term yields have led to some increase in refinancing activity. A further fall in treasury yields could be amplified as investors in mortgage-backed securities (MBSs) adjust their hedges to offset their changed convexity risk. There have been further calls for regulatory changes for the U.S. government-sponsored housing enterprises (GSEs), Fannie Mae and Freddie Mac. Freddie Mac's accounting problems remain unresolved, and have led to a

---

[5]The Industrial Revitalization Corporation of Japan, a government agency mandated to rehabilitate distressed corporates in cooperation with banks, has so far received only 12 candidates since its inception in April 2003 because of a lack of demand by banks to use the facility.

tightening of the regulatory requirements on it. Meanwhile, the European mortgage-related securities market is growing rapidly, although it remains much smaller than in the United States.

U.S. Mortgage Markets

There have to date been no further amplifying pressures on U.S. bond market volatility from mortgage hedging since last summer, as mortgage refinancing activity has slowed. The Mortgage Bankers Association's index of refinancing volumes peaked in May 2003, well above previous high points, but fell abruptly during the third quarter as long-term interest rates rose. Refinancing levels have risen in 2004 as long-term interest rates gradually declined toward the levels of March and April 2003, but to date the pace of refinancing is no more than half of the average level in the first half of 2003 (Figure 2.42). Thus, up to now, the adjustments to hedges required by investors in mortgages and mortgage-backed securities (including the GSEs) so as to match changes in the expected duration of their mortgage-related assets have been much smaller than last summer. (The duration of mortgage-related assets depends heavily on the likely future tendency of borrowers to prepay their mortgages. See the September 2003 GFSR for a detailed discussion of mortgage hedging and market volatility.)

The fall in 10-year U.S. treasury yields to below 3.8 percent following the February employment report on March 5, 2004, sparked market speculation that interest rates were close to a point requiring further MBS convexity hedging, which in this case would amplify the downward move in yields rather than the upward move last summer. The degree of hedging depends on the coupon structure of outstanding mortgages, which has changed significantly, as a large fraction of higher-coupon mortgages were refinanced during 2002–03. In May 2003, for example, about 75 percent of the MBSs securitized by Fannie Mae (which reflect the distribution of

Figure 2.42. United States: Mortgage Market and Hedging

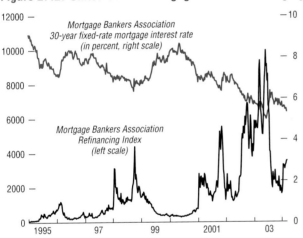

Source: Bloomberg L.P.

coupons on the underlying mortgages) had coupon rates of 6 percent or more, and these mortgages were the most frequently prepaid. By February 2004, however, the amount outstanding of these higher-rate MBSs had fallen by more than $250 billion, and they now represent only 40 percent of the total market. The remaining 60 percent of MBSs have coupons of 5.5 percent or less. With the interest rate for new 30-year mortgages falling to 5.3 percent on March 5, mortgage rates are back at a level where future changes will strongly affect MBS investors' expectations of future prepayment levels and hence their immediate hedging needs.

While there is some risk of amplified interest rate volatility in the future, MBS investors are better equipped to manage the risks involved than in earlier periods, such as 1994. Longer-term treasury returns in the third quarter of 2003 were, by some measures, the most volatile since 1986, as the previous steady reduction in yields reversed direction sharply (Figure 2.43). While mortgage hedging activity contributed to volatility in the short term, improved sophistication of risk management over the years helped to avoid the insolvencies among MBS investors that occurred in 1994. In particular, improvements in risk measurement of structured products and the use of a greater variety of hedging instruments helped investors to manage the risks arising from the mortgage market, which has grown at a 9 percent annual rate over the last decade.[6]

Despite calmer conditions in the mortgage market, the U.S. mortgage agencies have remained in the public eye. Freddie Mac, which announced in January 2003 that it would restate earnings and capital for prior

[6]In 1994, many pools of MBSs were repackaged into Collateralized Mortgage Obligations with some tranches having very unusual payment patterns and interest rate elasticities so complex that it was difficult or impossible to predict how they would behave under volatile market conditions. Many investors did little or no hedging of the prepayment option risk embedded in the instruments.

Figure 2.43. United States: Government Bond Index, Three-Month Return Volatility
(In percent)

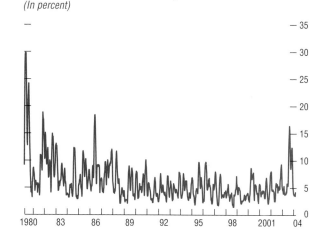

Source: Datastream.

Figure 2.44. United States: Agency Duration Gaps

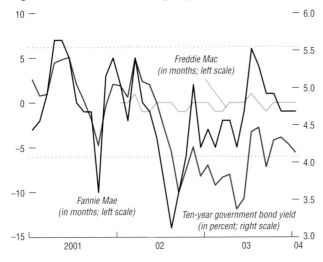

Sources: Fannie Mae; Freddie Mac; and Bloomberg L.P.
Note: The horizontal dotted lines show the boundaries of a six-month duration range.

years, has published restated financial statements for the years 2000 to 2002, but has not yet been able to complete its accounts for 2003. As previously predicted by Freddie Mac, the 2000–2002 accounts increased regulatory core capital, while also creating greater income volatility (see the September 2003 GFSR). In January 2004, the agencies' regulator, the Office of Federal Housing Enterprise Oversight (OFHEO), imposed a 30 percent capital surcharge on Freddie Mac until the accounting irregularities are resolved and placed additional restrictions on its ability to buy back shares or increase dividends. Freddie Mac already has sufficient surplus capital to meet the surcharge without raising fresh capital, but it may limit Freddie's ability to grow in the near term. Freddie Mac says that the accounting changes themselves, once they are implemented, will raise its capital levels, thus helping relax a capital constraint should the surcharge be longer lasting. Meanwhile, OFHEO is also conducting a special examination of accounting policies and practices at Fannie Mae, and has raised concerns about extensive reliance on manual systems.

Fannie Mae continues to keep the duration gap between its assets and liabilities in a narrower range, since being required to do so by OFHEO in November 2002. Although it continues to run a larger duration gap than Freddie Mac, it has kept the gap within a six-month duration range (Figure 2.44). The gap is very closely correlated from month to month with movements in treasury yields, suggesting a policy of not fully adjusting the hedge for movements in interest rates, and thus avoiding some of the hedging costs of continual full adjustment.

Senior U.S. officials recently made public statements calling for regulatory changes regarding the GSEs. Gregory Mankiw, chairman of the Council of Economic Advisers, called for legislation to reform the supervision of the GSEs, such as increasing the authority of the GSEs' regulator, including additional powers to set both risk-based and minimum capital standards, and removing some of the special privileges enjoyed by the GSEs that help convey the implicit guarantee of the federal government. In addition, in testimony before the Congress, Federal Reserve Board Chairman Alan Greenspan called for a stronger regulator (on a par with banking regulators) and for limits on the size of the GSEs' own debt as a proportion of the amount of debt they securitize, so as to limit their systemic impact while enhancing the liquidity of the securitization market.

We support moves such as these to strengthen regulation and to restrain the growth of the GSEs' portfolios, as well as to improve transparency and address the implicit government guarantee.

Mortgage and Securitization Markets in Europe

The market for European mortgage-related securities is much smaller than in the United States, but growing. Over $4 trillion of loans have been securitized in the United States, while European MBSs have grown to €310 billion and covered bonds (many of which are mortgage-related, as described below) to €1.5 trillion.[7] The remainder of this section reviews the European mortgage markets and the True Sale Initiative aimed at facilitating the development of securitization markets in Germany.

The variety of national taxation, property, and consumer protection frameworks helps to explain the differing structures of housing markets in Europe, and has contributed to the slow integration of the European securitization and, to a lesser extent, covered bond markets. However, these markets have grown rapidly in recent years, particularly with the adoption of the euro, and have benefited from growing demand for credit by some institutional investors (see Chapter III) and in

the short run by the search for yield in a low interest rate environment. According to the European Mortgage Association, the size of the covered bond market is around 18 percent of the total euro-denominated bond market (Figures 2.45 and 2.46).

In some European countries, the legal framework for the issuance of mortgage bonds has been enhanced. In Germany, amendments to the Mortgage Bank Act strengthened the position of Pfandbriefe creditors, including an overcollateralization requirement and better protection in case of bankruptcy of the issuer. Similarly, in Spain, a new insolvency law, expected to be effective in September 2004, would clarify the existing framework of legal prioritization, reinforcing the position of Cedula holders. Sweden recently introduced regulations that allow collateralization of mortgage bonds by a designated pool of assets. HBOS Treasury Services made the first U.K. issue of covered bonds, perhaps opening the door to the development of a new mortgage product in that country.

The European securitization market reached a record level of new issuance in 2003 (above €200 billion, up 30 percent from the previous year).[8] Four countries (the United Kingdom, Spain, the Netherlands, and Italy) represented 75 percent of the issuance volume (Figure 2.47). Overall, the fastest-growing component of the securitization market appears to be retail mortgages, believed to represent close to 60 percent of total issuance volume.

Initiatives have been proposed recently aimed at fostering further integration of the European securitization markets. Among them is a proposal by a small group of European banks for a European Mortgage Finance Agency to be created, modeled on

---

[7]Covered bonds are debt securities issued by credit institutions specifically backed by a pool of either mortgage assets or public sector assets, which remain on the balance sheet of the issuer. Pfandbriefe in Germany, Obligations Foncières in France, and Cedulas in Spain all belong to this class of fixed-income securities.

[8]The estimate of securitization issuance given here is larger than the estimate made by the European Commission, mostly because it includes currencies of issuance other than the euro, such as the U.S. dollar and sterling.

Figure 2.45. Euro Area: Jumbo Covered Bonds, November 2003

(Total amounts outstanding: €540 billion)

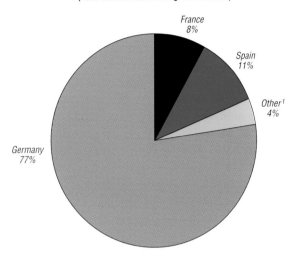

France
8%

Spain
11%

Other¹
4%

Germany
77%

Source: CDC-ixis.
¹Includes Austria, Luxembourg, and United Kingdom.

Figure 2.46. Euro-Denominated Bond Market: Gross Issuance Volumes, 2003¹
(In billions of euros)

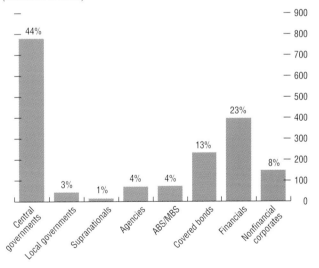

44%

3%

1%

4%

4%

13%

23%

8%

Central governments

Local governments

Supranationals

Agencies

ABS/MBS

Covered bonds

Financials

Nonfinancial corporates

Source: EU Commission.
¹Percentages refer to shares of total issuance volume.

the U.S. agencies. According to its sponsors, such an agency would help create a homogeneous single European market for mortgage-backed securities. Some suggest that this would increase market liquidity and facilitate the introduction of longer-term, fixed-rate mortgages. Others (echoing the debate on the U.S. market mentioned above) are concerned that implicit public sector guarantees would distort competition, and may encourage excessive lending in a sector that is already experiencing significant growth.

In July 2003, 13 banks launched the True Sale Initiative to help foster the development of a cash securitization market in Germany, where synthetic securitizations have been the norm in recent years.[9] The securitizations, at least initially focused on small- and medium-sized enterprise loans, would provide banks with a balance sheet management tool and diversify their funding sources. The project has been spearheaded by KfW, the German industrial development bank.

In summary, structural initiatives in individual European countries have been helpful in developing the mortgage-related and asset-backed markets, and there has been some convergence between different national markets. It is welcome that public sector guarantees have not been needed. Investor demand has grown rapidly, but the liquidity of these markets may be constrained in the future and the benefits to investors of diversification not fully realized, unless the legal and regulatory frameworks converge further.

Hedge Funds

The hedge fund industry has gone through significant growth and structural changes in recent years. Driven by increased institutional investor participation and related market discipline, transparency in the industry has

[9]Cash securitization involves the pooling of actual claims on various borrowers, whereas synthetic securitizations involve pools of derivative exposures.

improved. In addition, the use of leverage and counterparty exposures seem to be better monitored today. In general, hedge funds may have a positive effect on market stability, but macro-strategy and similarly styled funds active in smaller, less liquid markets may continue to present stability concerns. In general, better and more consistent disclosure standards for leverage, liquidity, and asset valuation would be helpful.

Assets under management within the global hedge fund industry have grown substantially, by $100 billion–$150 billion since early 2000, to above $700 billion by most current estimates.[10] U.S.-based hedge funds represent the bulk of the industry, with assets under management estimated at approximately $600 billion. Asian and European funds have also grown substantially, and are estimated to have $30 billion to $40 billion, and $75 billion to $100 billion assets under management, respectively. The growth primarily reflects a broadening of the investor base, which today includes more institutional investors, such as pension funds and insurance companies, and, in many markets, more retail investors.

The increasing popularity of hedge funds can be attributed to a variety of factors. The decline in bond yields and falling equity markets from 2000 to early 2003 have led investors to search for alternative investments, often seeking absolute performance and less correlation to broader markets. This is especially true of institutional investors. The performance of individual hedge funds is believed to result largely from the skill or strategy of the specific asset manager, with less influence from general market trends. As such, the popularity of so-called "alternative investment management" has grown significantly in recent years.

The structure of the hedge fund industry has also changed, with many more strategies

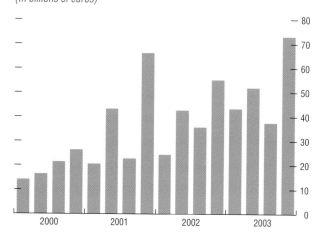

Figure 2.47. European Securitization, Quarterly Issuance[1]
(In billions of euros)

Sources: European Securitization Forum; Deutsche Bank; and IMF staff estimates.
[1]ABS and MBS issues placed in European markets with underlying collateral from Europe.

---

[10]A recent survey by Greenwich Associates estimated the size of the industry at $745 billion at the end of 2003.

Table 2.4. Performance of Selected Hedge Fund Strategies[1]

(In percent)

	2001	2002	2003
Emerging markets	5.8	7.4	28.8
Event driven	11.5	0.2	20.0
Of which:			
Distressed debts	. . .	−0.7	25.1
Risk arbitrage	. . .	−3.5	9.0
Global macro	18.4	14.7	18.0
Long/short equity	−3.7	−1.6	17.3
Convertible arbitrage	14.6	4.1	12.9
Fixed income arbitrage	8.0	5.8	8.0
Equity market neutral	9.3	7.4	7.1
Dedicated short bias	−3.6	18.1	−32.6
CSFB/Tremont Hedge Fund Index	4.4	3.0	15.4

Source: CSFB/Tremont.
[1]Based on CSFB/Tremont hedge fund database, methodology, and classification.

available to investors today. The industry is increasingly composed of small- and medium-size funds, implementing a variety of investment strategies (Table 2.4).[11] In recent years we have also seen the development of new vehicles, "funds of hedge funds," which allow investors to obtain a more diversified hedge fund exposure within a single investment product. Funds of funds are believed to be the fastest-growing segment of the industry and, according to market sources, account for approximately $200 billion in assets under management. As the institutional investor base grows, many investors prefer a fund of funds, in order to benefit from the manager's ability to create diversified portfolios and to monitor investments. Globally, insurance companies and pension funds are reported to have grown to about 7 and 8 percent, respectively, of the client base of funds of funds. High net worth investors account for about 70 percent of such investment activity, with most of these investments directed by professional advisors (family offices and private banks).

The rapid growth of the hedge fund industry has refocused official attention on financial stability issues. Hedge funds operate with a significantly higher degree of flexibility than other market participants. For example, they apply more leverage, depart from traditional diversification and liquidity requirements, and impose greater constraints on investors (who often accept only limited disclosure and liquidity).[12] The diversity of hedge fund styles and strategies and the limited information available on their investment and risk management practices make it difficult to assess the impact of hedge funds on financial stability. This lack of transparency has created its own pressure for more information, particularly regarding the use of leverage.

As a whole, hedge funds may contribute positively to the functioning of financial markets. It is generally agreed that hedge funds contribute to better pricing information, enhance market liquidity, and actively arbitrage price discrepancies between financial assets. Moreover, concerns related to investor herd behavior would seem no more true for, or even less applicable to, hedge funds than other investors, given that many hedge fund strategies seek to exploit market inefficiencies.

Macro-strategy funds, which take global positions on mature and emerging markets based on analysis of a wide range of factors, such as economic policies, interest rates or exchange rates, and aggressive trend-following trading strategies, may present a

---

[11]According to market estimates, less than 20 percent of hedge funds have assets under management above $100 million.

[12]Measuring use of leverage is difficult. Market sources estimate that close to 75 percent of hedge funds use leverage on an ongoing basis. The magnitude of leverage appears, however, to be limited overall (a ratio of 2 to 1 for the industry as a whole, and often less if provided by prime brokers). Furthermore, the use of leverage appears to differ significantly from one strategy to another; for example, most global macro funds leverage their portfolios by more than 2 to 1, but nearly half of the funds specializing in distressed securities do not leverage at all, according to Van Hedge Fund Advisors International Inc.

different profile. Global macro-strategies have become popular again in 2003; however, they represent a small part of the industry. Their investment style, often including higher turnover and more leverage, may contribute to amplifying market volatility. Of course, any destabilizing impact of such strategies will significantly depend on the structure of the markets in which they are executed. Smaller and more closed markets that lack liquidity and depth will be more prone to financial instability from such hedge fund activity.

The growth of institutional investor participation and the development of funds of funds have contributed to significantly greater market discipline. Because they impose a more rigorous investment process and stricter reporting requirements, institutional investors have greatly improved market discipline, directly and via funds of hedge funds. Moreover, industry representatives have proposed codes of practice and governance guidelines, addressing issues such as asset valuation and risk management.

Credit institutions and prime brokers are central to the function of the industry, particularly as providers of leverage.[13] As such, these institutions have a key role to play in monitoring their hedge fund clients (e.g., developing market standards and improving public sector understanding, including through existing regulatory reports). Since the Long-Term Capital Management crisis, the degree of leverage seems more closely managed, counterparties demand more balance sheet information, and many hedge funds are transparent with prime brokers and other service providers. However, information tends to be reported bilaterally to investors and counterparties, rather than in a more systematic manner. The question remains, therefore, from a financial stability standpoint, whether such market discipline is a sufficient substitute for regulation.

The trend toward greater retail participation has led policymakers in certain countries to adopt or consider new regulatory approaches. Traditionally, retail access to hedge funds has been restricted. But recently, regulations in various countries have been adopted to allow greater retail participation. For example, funds of funds have been made available to retail investors in France, Germany, Ireland, and Italy. Eligibility requirements for investors in these funds are generally lower than the "accredited investor" or similar standards in the United States. In the United Kingdom, the FSA has decided to maintain regulations preventing the sale of hedge funds to retail investors, and in the United States, the SEC has embarked on a similar discussion, again primarily focused on protecting retail investors.

IMF staff will continue to monitor closely hedge fund developments as the industry and its regulatory structure evolve.

Corporate Governance

Corporate Governance for Complex Corporate Structures: The Parmalat Case

After being shaken by the bankruptcies of Enron and WorldCom, investor confidence in recent years has been bolstered by continued progress in addressing weaknesses in accounting, auditing, and corporate governance. Although the size of the Enron and WorldCom losses were large ($19 billion and $40 billion, respectively), financial stability problems did not arise. This reflected the diversification of exposure through the markets, including the use of credit derivatives by some to reduce concentrations of credit risk, notwithstanding operational questions about the credit derivatives markets that surfaced at

---

[13]Prime brokers provide a wide range of services to hedge funds, including the financing, execution and back office support for transactions and positions, and securities borrowing and lending. Due to these functions, they monitor daily the leverage, liquidity, and other risk factors of their fund clients.

the time.[14] While no reforms can eliminate fraud or mismanagement, there is a need to strengthen the institutions and frameworks that are meant to guard against it. Legislation has been enacted to improve oversight on corporate management by strengthening corporate governance, disclosure, and accountability (e.g., the Sarbanes-Oxley Act, the European Union's Financial Services Action Plan (FSAP), and reforms to the Corporate Law of Japan). More recently, there has been important follow-through in implementing these initiatives. Notable examples include the creation of the Public Company Accounting Oversight Board (PCAOB) and the implementation of the part of the European Union's FSAP concerning Company Law and Corporate Governance.[15] Further work is also under way in many jurisdictions.

The Parmalat scandal, involving false billings and the creation of fictitious assets among its offshore subsidiaries, illustrates the need to ensure accounting, auditing, and corporate governance practices are consistent with legislative, regulatory, and supervisory principles and can be effectively applied to various local corporate structures. Parmalat was a large, closely held, family-controlled business with a complex corporate structure operating in multiple jurisdictions, which posed challenges for auditing and corporate governance as well as for implementation of adequate management checks and balances. This case raises general questions concerning corporate governance, the degree to which rating agencies and investors can provide adequate market discipline, and the role of financial auditors, regulators, and supervisors. Because Parmalat operated under Europe's principles-based accounting system, this episode shows that both principles-based and rules-based (as in the United States) accounting and regulatory systems can be vulnerable to fraudulent activities. Parmalat also illustrates the importance of effective accounting and auditing practices that would adequately disclose the activities of complex ownership and capital structures, especially the importance of coordination among multiple auditors.

The credit markets handled smoothly the news in early December that Parmalat's investors and auditors had begun to question Parmalat's ability to repay €150 million in debt due December 15, 2003. The spread on Parmalat's credit default swaps (CDS) began to rise rapidly as the company's credit ratings fell from investment grade to default (Figure 2.48).[16]

Traders reported that buyers of credit protection for Parmalat debt rushed to settle several billion euros of outstanding credit derivative contracts. While most of these contracts were settled without dispute, some of the expiring contracts raised questions about what constituted a credit event. Some argued that Parmalat's actions in the weeks leading up to its bankruptcy filing constituted steps "in furtherance of" bankruptcy. The clause was part of the 1999 ISDA definition of bankruptcy but was dropped under pressure from investors, and this question should arise much less in the future.

The Parmalat bankruptcy will likely have more impact among structured portfolio products, such as collateralized debt obliga-

---

[14]The March 2002 GFSR discussed the operation of the over-the-counter (OTC) credit derivative markets after the Enron crisis emerged and implications for strengthening financial oversight, market discipline, disclosure, corporate governance, and auditing.

[15]PCAOB was created by the post-Enron legislation (the Sarbanes-Oxley Act) to oversee auditors of public companies and is empowered with broad scope for creating accounting and auditing rules, and investigative and enforcement powers.

[16]Parmalat had a long-term debt rating of BBB- since 1999, until it was downgraded to B+ on December 9, and ultimately to D on December 22.

tions (CDOs), than in the cash market.[17] As Parmalat was an investment-grade company in a sector traditionally with little debt outstanding, many CDOs included Parmalat to provide diversification. Nevertheless, individual CDOs contained relatively small Parmalat exposure, ranging from 0.2 to 5 percent, with the average approximately 1 percent. According to Moody's, the largest exposure to Parmalat is among European investment-grade synthetic CDOs, and the aggregate exposure is €602 million. Because CDOs are sold in tranches of different credit quality, it is likely that the purchasers of the junior (riskier) portions would have suffered most of the losses. Nevertheless, market analysts have noted that CDOs with even 1 percent exposure to Parmalat may find that the AAA-rated tranches could be downgraded if Parmalat defaults. Rating agencies have also reminded investors that individual corporate defaults can affect synthetic CDOs, because the reference CDOs tend to have widely overlapping portfolios. Moreover, monoline insurers, who provide credit guarantees to financial instruments, including CDOs, will have to make payment as a result of the Parmalat default.

Although many questions remain to be answered concerning the Parmalat case, the following are a few of the preliminary lessons that can be drawn:

- Complex ownership and capital structures may require additional reforms to provide adequate corporate governance, transparency, and disclosure.
- Rating agencies may have to adapt their assessment procedures to adequately monitor complex ownership structures with global operations and relatively more sophisticated treasury operations compared to industry norms.
- Investors should not become complacent in their due diligence, particularly concern-

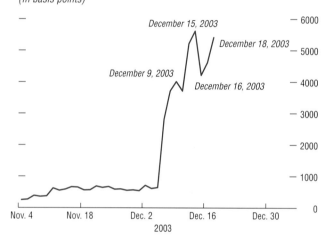

Figure 2.48. Parmalat: Credit Default Swap Spread
(In basis points)

Source: CreditTrade.

---

[17]Parmalat was reported to be the fourth most active name among the reference entities in the underlying securities for CDOs.

ing auditing and corporate governance issues.

- There is a case for more public oversight of auditing practices.
- Strengthening national securities regulators should help improve supervision and move toward the goal of reciprocal acceptance of regulation and supervision standards.

Proposed Strengthening of OECD Principles of Corporate Governance

Earlier corporate bankruptcies spurred the international community to address corporate governance failures. OECD members have been working to revise their Principles of Corporate Governance and draft revisions were posted on the OECD website on January 12, 2004. The following are some of the more notable proposed revisions: (1) to allow shareholders to question not only the Board but also directly the external auditor; (2) to allow shareholders the opportunity to review board members' remuneration and to decide equity-related pay (the principles stress the need for remuneration to be consistent with a company's long-term interests); (3) to encourage greater involvement of institutional shareholders in corporate governance; (4) to have auditors accountable to shareholders in addition to the board of directors; (5) to develop policies to manage potential conflicts of interest among analysts, brokers, rating agencies, and other market participants; and (6) to require the board of directors to uphold high ethical standards and to commit themselves to their responsibilities as directors.

The proposed tightening of the principles of corporate governance is welcome. Still, there is room for encouraging further transparency and disclosure. For example, the

principles should encourage whistle-blowers to reveal unethical or illegal practices not just to the company board (as proposed) but, if the issue is not dealt with there, to minority shareholders, creditors, and other stakeholders. More generally, protecting the rights of minority shareholders through the dissemination of information would also help encourage investment and improve transparency.

In strengthening the principles of corporate governance, it is important to not unduly stifle management's discretion and ability to make business decisions. Qualified individuals must not be unduly discouraged from serving as directors for fear of shareholder lawsuits, for instance.

Corporate Governance and Financial Institutions

Financial institutions have been a particular focus of the corporate governance debate. For example, the New York Stock Exchange has separated the functions of CEO and Chairman of the Board in order to reduce actual or perceived conflicts of interest. Most recently, there have been prosecutions of some U.S. mutual funds. The investigations of inappropriate trading practices were initiated by the New York Attorney General and have led to charges against mutual funds, hedge funds, and other financial institutions and their executives involving "late trading" (which is illegal) and "market timing" (which is contrary to declared mutual fund policies).[18] Subsequent investigations were conducted abroad, including by regulators in France, Germany, Switzerland, and the United Kingdom, but have not found evidence of additional wrongdoing. More recently, a group of mutual funds was fined for overcharging on commissions.

[18]"Late trading" is an illegal practice that involves trading mutual funds shares at the closing price after the market has closed, and puts the customer in a position to profit from any price-relevant information that has emerged after the close. "Market timing" involves holding funds for only a short period of time—most funds do not allow shareholders to make frequent trades based on market timing strategies because it could take advantage of the fact that fund prices are not continuously updated. The opportunity for profits is greatest among funds investing in foreign shares, where differences in time zones can be exploited for short-term arbitrage gains.

There has been no sign of outflows from the mutual fund industry as a whole, even as the list of mutual funds involved in corporate governance issues has grown. Recent data indicate that net inflows to equity mutual funds overall have in fact increased, while there have been flows out of funds involved in the scandals and into other mutual funds (Figure 2.49). Some of those individual funds that were implicated in the scandal, but are perceived to have taken prompt and strong remedial measures, have seen renewed inflows, which suggests that the potential erosion of investor confidence in the mutual fund industry in general can be limited by similar actions by other funds.

Update on Basel II Developments

The Basel Committee on Banking Supervision continues its work to revise the international accord on bank capital (Basel II). The work aims (in part) to incorporate improved bank risk management systems and more closely align regulatory capital standards with banks' economic capital modeling processes. Recent discussions have focused on issues such as the treatment of expected and unexpected credit losses (including accounting treatment), and credit risk mitigation techniques, as well as a variety of implementation topics. In January 2004, the Committee reported significant progress on some of these issues. In that report, the Committee emphasized, through the supervisory review process (Pillar II), the importance of maintaining appropriate capital buffers beyond the minimum capital requirement (Pillar I). A variety of such supervisory (Pillar II) and implementation issues remain outstanding, including coordination between home and host supervisors. Finalization of Basel II is tentatively planned for mid-2004.

From the point of view of financial stability, the work on Basel II has brought renewed focus on a few key capital markets-related issues:

Figure 2.49. U.S.-Based Equity Mutual Funds: Weekly Net Flows
(In billions of U.S. dollars; four-week moving average)

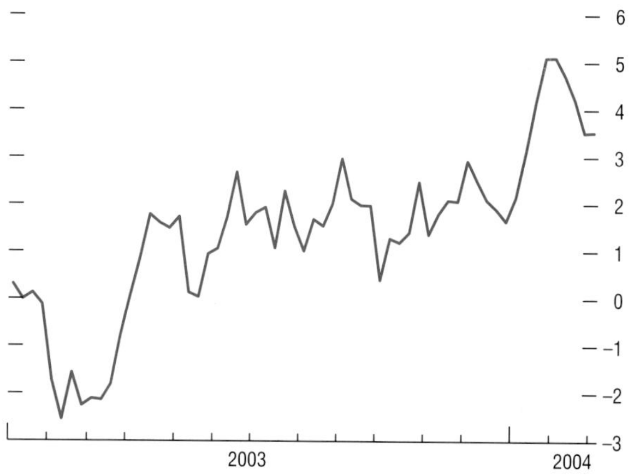

Source: AMG Data Services.

- How can the potential procyclical effects of a closer dependence of capital requirements on credit evaluation be mitigated?
- Do the proposed rules better achieve a level playing field, with minimum distortions stemming from regulatory incentives?
- With the ever increasing reliance on "appropriate supervision" under Pillar II, do national supervisory authorities have sufficient resources?

A closer dependence of capital requirements on credit risk evaluation implies some degree of procyclicality. This has several components, including the built-in procyclicality stemming from rising risk weightings as credit quality falls, and the behavior of banks' excess capital over the economic cycle. Basel II could be calibrated to provide banks with incentives to estimate the underlying risk parameters through the cycle and thereby reduce potential procyclical behavior. There has been a healthy dialogue between some of the larger banks and the Committee in this regard, but some degree of procyclicality is likely to persist in a risk-based capital regime.

Leveling the playing field has remained an elusive goal, but such issues are unlikely to overly concern capital market participants. A level playing field has long been a goal of the Basel principles; however, the "menu approach" allows much national discretion and complicates uniform application. One important example in Basel II is the measurement of operational risks, given that it can represent a relatively large share of the overall capital requirement, and any attempt to employ a uniform measure is difficult. Such issues have existed since Basel I, and some degree of national discretion seems appropriate. Nevertheless, the market can be expected to continue to scrutinize the use of supervisory discretion, and thereby differentiate among banks and banking systems, impacting relative costs of capital.

Basel II should improve financial stability; however, the real test will be the final adoption and implementation. Basel II tries to strike a balance between specific regulatory standards and general supervisory principles. More than under Basel I, Pillar II of Basel II makes clear the key role of supervision, as opposed to regulation and mere written standards. We support this emphasis, and mature market participants have long recognized the importance of supervision relative to regulation. Basel II has the potential to further improve bank risk management systems and banking supervision, and encourage greater market discipline. All of this should improve financial stability. However, particularly outside the G-10 countries, implementation and pursuit of the Basel II principles may stretch supervisory resources.

This section is intended as a brief update on some of the issues, and we intend to conduct a more thorough review in the September 2004 GFSR on the capital market implications of Basel II after the mid-2004 target date for completion of the revised framework.

Appendix I: Determinants of the Rally in Emerging Market Debt—Liquidity and Fundamentals

During the 2003 rally, spreads on emerging market bonds tightened by 347 basis points and the EMBI+ returned 28.8 percent. Improving country-specific fundamentals clearly played an important role in driving this performance. However, low mature market interest rates, buoyant global liquidity, and increased risk appetite have also strongly influenced spread movements. While improvements in fundamentals are, it is to be hoped, a secular trend, the monetary stance driving liquidity is a cyclical phenomenon, and risk appetite is subject to change. It is critical for both investors and policymakers to understand the relative roles of these factors to form a view on the sustainability of low spreads.

The academic literature on emerging market bond spreads has generally found that country-specific fundamentals (so-called "pull" factors) have played a major role in explaining differences in spreads, especially across countries at a specific point in time. The possibility that "push" factors, such as low interest rates in mature markets, could also be an important determinant of emerging market spreads has been understood for some time. Nevertheless, early empirical studies were unable to detect their influence. However, a number of recent studies have found that mature market interest rates do play the role theoretically expected of them. Furthermore, econometric investigation of the most recent data appears to point to a more important role for U.S. interest rates and risk preference than during earlier periods.

As monetary policies return to more cyclically neutral stances, the role of external drivers is likely to diminish and the role of fundamentals is likely to reassume its historical predominance. This highlights the importance of early and sustained efforts at improving creditworthiness by those countries that wish to maintain access to international capital markets at reasonable cost. This finding also underscores the importance of taking advantage of favorable external financing conditions to improve the maturity profile and composition of debt.

Global Liquidity Versus Fundamentals

Ample liquidity stemming from the looseness of monetary policy in the financial centers was a key driver of the emerging market debt rally in 2003. Negative real short-term rates in the United States catalyzed a broad search for yield that led to portfolio reallocations toward riskier assets throughout the year, including to emerging markets (Figure 2.50).

Earlier, the accelerated easing of monetary policy in the United States following the events on September 11, 2001, had spurred a rally in the emerging bond markets that began in late 2001. Falling policy rates boosted the "carry" offered by emerging bond

Figure 2.50. Cumulative Flows into U.S.-Based Mutual Funds
(In billions of U.S. dollars, cumulative since January 2002)

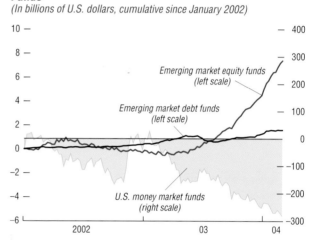

Sources: AMG Data Services; and IMF staff estimates.

Figure 2.51. Federal Funds Rate and Excess Emerging Market Bond Market Yield over Three-Month LIBOR

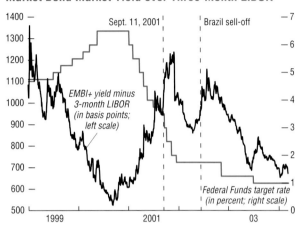

Sources: Bloomberg L.P.; and IMF staff estimates.

Figure 2.52. EMBI+ Bond Spreads and the Slope of the U.S. Yield Curve
(In basis points)

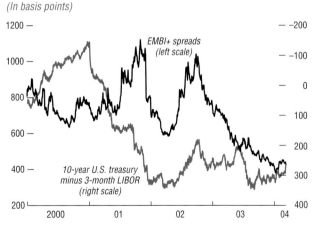

Sources: Bloomberg L.P.; J.P. Morgan Chase & Co.; and IMF staff estimates.

markets, defined as the differential of the emerging market bond index (EMBI+) yield over short-term borrowing costs (three-month LIBOR). This differential spiked in late 2001, creating incentives for leveraged positions. The ensuing rally, however, was interrupted in mid-2002 by a sell-off triggered by concerns ahead of the presidential elections in Brazil (Figure 2.51).

The emerging bond market rally resumed in late 2002 as investor concerns over the course of policy in Brazil dissipated and amid continued monetary easing in the United States. Throughout the rally, market participants commonly emphasized the risk that a sharper or earlier-than-expected rise in U.S. interest rates could trigger a de-leveraging and sell-off in the emerging debt markets. This view was given weight by the sudden reversal of net inflows to dedicated emerging market debt funds when treasury rates rose during June and July 2003. Again, the FOMC's surprise dropping of the "considerable period" language in its January 2004 statement, widely interpreted as a harbinger of eventual rate rises, sparked an immediate 25 basis point rise in emerging market debt spreads.

At the same time, a secular trend of improving domestic fundamentals in emerging market countries and firmer prospects for global growth have been posited as important drivers of the market's performance. This gives rise to the question of how much of the spread compression in emerging market debt was due to improvements in fundamentals and how much was due to low U.S. interest rates or other factors.

Prima Facie Evidence

The *prima facie* case for the importance of liquidity relative to fundamentals is illustrated by a number of developments.
- The rally in emerging market debt was preceded by an easing of monetary policy in mature markets. For example, the steepness

of the U.S. yield curve, a measure of the looseness of U.S. monetary policy, has tracked movements in emerging market spreads reasonably well since late 2001 (Figure 2.52).

- The emerging market rally also appears to coincide with indicators of reduced investor risk aversion. A widely used measure of equity market volatility is also well correlated with emerging market spreads (Figure 2.53).

- Notwithstanding the broader trend of improvements in emerging market credit-worthiness and the abatement of concerns over Brazil's policy framework following the 2002 election, the average sovereign rating of emerging market borrowers, weighted by market capitalization, has remained stable since the beginning of the emerging market rally in the fourth quarter of 2002. There have been a number of ratings upgrades during this period, notably Russia, which was upgraded to investment grade, as well as Bulgaria, Malaysia, Poland, and Turkey. At the same time, there have been some downgrades elsewhere, such as the Philippines and Venezuela, as well as an overall shift in the weight of the index toward lower-rated, higher-yielding credits, which have outperformed during the course of the rally (Figure 2.54).

- Increases in average cross-correlations and reductions in the dispersion of returns within the emerging market universe suggest investors became less discriminating, implying a relatively greater role for common factors in driving returns.

The Literature on the Determinants of Emerging Market Spreads

In the last decade, a burgeoning literature has considered the determinants of emerging market spreads. However, earlier work on balance of payments crises and the determinants of capital flows to emerging markets first shed light on many of the pertinent theoretical

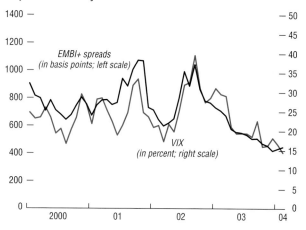

Figure 2.53. EMBI+ Bond Spreads and Equity Market Implied Volatility

Sources: Bloomberg L.P.; J.P. Morgan Chase & Co.; and IMF staff estimates.

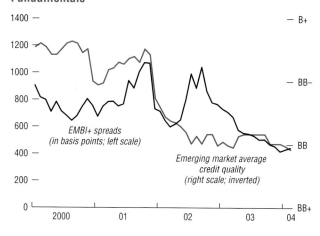

Figure 2.54. EMBI+ Bond Spreads and Credit Fundamentals

Sources: Bloomberg L.P.; J.P. Morgan Chase & Co.; Moody's; Standard & Poor's; and IMF staff estimates.

issues.[19] While much of this early literature focused on fundamentals in emerging markets as "pull" factors, Calvo, Leiderman, and Reinhart (1993) drew early attention to the potential role of "push" factors in stimulating capital flows.[20]

The literature on the determinants of emerging market bond spreads was largely stimulated by the rise of the market for Brady bonds in the early 1990s and the subsequent development of widely tracked indices of secondary market bond spreads. In particular, economists sought an explanation for the massive decline in Brady bond spreads in the three years following the Mexican crisis. During this period, spreads fell from a peak of over 1,500 basis points in March 1995 to under 400 basis points by the third quarter of 1997, when the Asian crisis began to push them up again.

On a theoretical basis, it was recognized that lower world interest rates could lower emerging market bond spreads for a number of reasons:[21]

- The possibility of non-repayment of the risky emerging market bond drives a wedge between the riskless return and the return on the emerging market bond that, in equilibrium, is positively correlated with the riskless return. Thus, arbitrage should drive spreads lower when the riskless rate falls.
- A fall in world interest rates lowers debt-servicing costs on floating rate debt, and hence improves creditworthiness of emerging markets. It also lowers the rates at which existing debts must be rolled over.
- A fall in world interest rates should increase investor risk tolerance, which should drive spreads on risky bonds lower.

Nevertheless, early empirical literature on emerging market bond spreads failed to find the predicted relationship between world interest rates and emerging market bond spreads. Studying launch spreads on emerging market bonds, Cline and Barnes (1997) and Min (1998) failed to find significant relationships between U.S. treasury yields and emerging market spreads. Using both a broader sample of launch spreads and secondary market Brady bond spreads, Kamin and von Kleist (1999) also failed to find the expected relationship, either finding no significance, or in some cases, finding that industrial country interest rates were negatively related to spreads.

Eichengreen and Mody (1998) postulated that a selectivity bias could lead to a failure to find the proposed relationship, since at a time of high interest rates, lower-quality borrowers would be unlikely to issue, biasing launch spreads down during such times. They used a two-step process to first estimate the impact of fundamentals and U.S. treasury yields on the probability that an emerging market borrower would issue, and then studied separately the impact of fundamentals and treasury yields on launch spreads. They found that higher U.S. yields did indeed significantly reduce the probability of an issue. However, they found that spreads tended to move in the opposite direction to treasury yields, so that a decrease (increase) in treasury yields actually increased (decreased) spreads. They attributed this finding to the fact that supply considerations were outweighing demand considerations. While, say, lower U.S. rates may have increased the demand for emerging market bonds, the influence of such rates in inducing emerging markets to issue additional supply more than

[19]See Kaminsky, Lizondo, and Reinhart (1998) for an overview of the theoretical and empirical literature on balance of payments crises.
[20]The authors note that "falling interest rates, a continuing recession, and balance of payments developments in the United States" were common external factors that had helped stimulate flows to a wide swathe of Latin American countries in the early 1990s.
[21]See Kamin and von Kleist (1999) for a more detailed exposition.

compensated for the additional demand, thus increasing spreads.

Most studies found statistically significant influences (and generally of the expected sign) for fundamental factors in determining spreads. For instance, Min (1998) found that improved indicators of domestic solvency and liquidity (debt/GDP, foreign exchange reserves/GDP, and debt service ratios) and better macroeconomic fundamentals (such as lower inflation rates and better terms of trade) tended to reduce spreads. Eichengreen and Mody (1998), Kamin and von Kleist (1999), and Sy (2002) all found that improved credit ratings were correlated with lower spreads.[22]

Studies however have tended to find that fundamentals are better at explaining differentials in spreads across countries at a given point in time than they are the changes in spreads over time. Eichengreen and Mody (1998) found that a significant component of spread movements over time could be explained neither by fundamentals nor external factors such as U.S. interest rates or oil prices. Thus, for example, factors that may be difficult to observe directly, such as changes in investors' risk appetite or herding behavior resulting from imperfect information, may have explained episodes of significant spread movements over time, such as the 1995–97 period when spreads fell dramatically (see, for example, Ferrucci, 2003).[23]

The existence of moral hazard has been cited as one potential explanation for spread compression not related to directly observable factors. This theory posits that investors may not need to be greatly concerned with the creditworthiness of sovereign borrowers if they believe that official lending would allow such borrowers to continue to service their debt, even though the country might be insolvent in the absence of such official support.[24] Dell'Ariccia, Schnabel, and Zettelmeyer (2002) tested this theory by trying to ascertain if emerging market spreads behaved differently after the Russian default. They interpreted that event as a largely unanticipated episode that reduced investors' expectations of future bailouts by the IMF. They found evidence of permanent and significant increases in spreads following the IMF "non-bailout," as well as a significantly higher dispersion of cross-country spreads, suggesting investors were subsequently paying closer attention to country fundamentals. At the same time, they noted that it is not possible to distinguish between the existence of moral hazard from IMF lending, and the possibility that IMF lending raises expectations for improved policy, which could lead to an improved assessment of fundamental creditworthiness.

More recent work has tended to find a greater role for industrial country interest rates in explaining emerging market spreads. Econometric work undertaken by Arora and Cerisola (2001) used a range of domestic fundamentals and U.S. interest rates on a sample period covering the second half of the 1990s.

---

[22]Eichengreen and Mody used the residual from a regression of spreads on fundamentals since they wished to avoid multicollinearity issues that would stem from including both credit ratings and fundamentals in the same regression. Kamin and von Kleist and Sy excluded such domestic fundamentals from their regressions, using ratings as a proxy for them.

[23]Calvo and Mendoza (1995) explain how costly information can lead to such behavior. If investors are highly diversified, their holdings of a given credit may be quite small, and thus it may not be worth incurring the information costs to be well informed about that credit's fundamentals. Therefore, incremental deterioration in creditworthiness may not come to the attention of such investors. But when an important piece of information does become widely known, it may trigger a large, discrete reassessment of the credit's prospects, as well as other credits with at least superficially similar characteristics (on which it is also not worth incurring the monitoring costs). This may lead to large jumps in spreads and contagion among apparently similar credits.

[24]Dell'Ariccia, Schnabel, and Zettelmeyer (2002) distinguish such "investor moral hazard" from "country moral hazard," which would refer to a deterioration of domestic policy because of the "insurance" function provided by official assistance.

Consistent with previous literature, they found an important role for country-specific fundamentals in determining spreads. However, in contrast to previous findings, notably Eichengreen and Mody, they found that U.S. interest rates and emerging market spreads were positively correlated (so that lower U.S. rates lower spreads).[25] They attribute the difference to a combination of the use of secondary market spreads, which avoid the selectivity bias problem noted above, and the fact that Eichengreen and Mody included in their sample period 1991–93 when selectivity bias may have been particularly strong due to the nascent nature of the emerging bond market.

More recent work by Ferrucci (2003) finds that while short-term U.S. treasury rates tend to be positively correlated with spreads, long-term rates (10-year treasury yields) are actually negatively correlated with spreads. Put another way, Ferrucci finds that a steeper U.S. yield curve is associated with lower emerging market spreads, a result he suggests may be attributable to the presence of leveraged investors, who borrow at short-term rates to lend at longer-term rates.[26]

Applying common factor analysis, McGuire and Schrijvers (2003) found a significant role for a single common external factor underlying the variation of spreads across the constituents of the EMBI Global index.[27] This factor accounted for about one-third of the variation of emerging bond market spreads,

with the remainder driven by factors that were unique to a country's circumstances. The authors find that the best fit for the common factor is investors' attitude toward risk as proxied by the VIX (the volatility implied by options on the S&P 500 index). Given that volatility has fallen sharply since the recovery in the equity markets that began in late 2002, this suggests at least one important factor behind the recent rally is declining risk aversion.[28]

Recent Empirical Evidence

Very recent empirical work, including some undertaken by IMF staff for this report, appears to reinforce the widespread market view that liquidity and an increase in risk appetite have become relatively more significant influences on spreads than fundamentals in the emerging market debt rally that began in late 2002. Models based purely on fundamentals have found that recent emerging market bond spreads are generally tighter than can be justified by the models (Figure 2.55).

For example, an update of Sy (2002), which reports on univariate regressions of spreads on ratings from credit agencies, finds that even after the sell-off induced by the FOMC statement of January 2004, market spreads were considerably tighter than could be justified by current ratings. In previous instances in which spreads were tighter than suggested

[25]They find this not only for three-month and 10-year treasury rates, but also for the Fed funds target rate, which they view as a more direct measure of U.S. monetary policy.

[26]Ferrucci uses secondary market spreads like Arora and Cerisola, but uses panel data over the longer period 1992–2003. Like Eichengreen and Mody, he finds that spreads in 1995–97 fell too much to be explained by measured fundamentals, thus pointing either to some degree of mispricing during that period or to the importance of unmeasured fundamentals. His work also confirms the importance of country-specific macro-fundamentals.

[27]This result is derived by applying common factor analysis and builds on earlier work by Litterman and Scheinkman (1991). Common factor analysis seeks to construct a single abstract series that explains some portion of the common factor of variations in correlated series. After identifying the abstract common factor, McGuire and Schrijvers seek economically meaningful explanations, which they do by seeing which among a range of candidate data series are best correlated with the common factor.

[28]McGuire and Schrijvers also find a significant, but smaller, correlation with 10-year U.S. treasury yields, but the correlation is negative. They suggest one possible interpretation is that a steepening yield curve is associated with expectations of future industrial country growth, which, by increasing the creditworthiness of emerging market borrowers, could reduce spreads.

by the model, Sy found that, subsequently, credit upgrades were more likely than spread widening, suggesting ratings may lag spread developments. While this may again be a possibility, almost all of the deviations of actual compared to predicted spreads were considerably larger than could be explained even by a future two-notch upgrade.[29]

Work undertaken by IMF staff for this report suggests that global liquidity has become the most important determinant of emerging market spreads following September 2001. A simple econometric model was devised with a view to identifying the drivers of the latest emerging bond market rally. Theoretical predictions suggested the model should include relevant measures of country-specific fundamentals, global liquidity as represented by mature market interest rates, the expansion of demand through the widening investor base, and risk preference.

The specific model used is described below. The main conclusions are that the variables are significant and the signs are as expected, with improved fundamentals, greater global liquidity, higher investor demand, and lower volatility all lowering spreads. However, while improving fundamentals are found to have been a significant factor driving the contraction of emerging bond market spreads, the estimation results indicate that liquidity stemming from the U.S. interest rate easing cycle has become a more important influence than fundamentals in the emerging bond market rally. While the small sample size warrants caution, this finding gives weight to the commonly expressed market view that the push factor of ample global liquidity has been a key driver of the latest emerging market rally. This result also underscores the potential vulnera-

Figure 2.55. Deviations of Actual Spreads from Ratings-Based Spreads
(In basis points, actual spreads as of February 3, 2004)

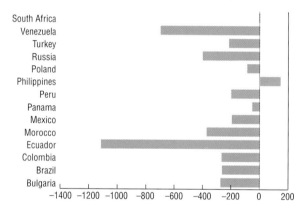

Sources: J.P. Morgan Chase & Co.; Standard & Poor's; Moody's; and IMF staff estimates.

[29]Sy found that a one-notch upgrade tended to reduce spreads by 14 percent, which for a 500 basis point spread would amount to a tightening of 70 basis points. However, most of the actual spreads in early February 2004 were more than 200 basis points tighter than suggested by the model.

bility of emerging bond markets in case of monetary tightening.

The variables considered for the model were:

- *Spreads (S):* The dependent variable, emerging bond market spreads, were captured by the spread on the EMBI index for the period 1994–97 and thereafter by the EMBI+ index.

- *Fundamentals (F):* Country-specific fundamentals were modeled using sovereign credit ratings. Although ratings are a useful general indicator of country-specific fundamentals, they are subject to the criticism that they may also be influenced by global variables such as those included in the regression, which could lead to some bias in the estimates. Nevertheless, credit ratings impact investment decisions, given that institutional investor policies are often tied to credit quality. In order to get a summary measure of ratings for the EMBI+ universe, the specific variable used was a weighted index of the average credit quality of the constituents of the EMBI/EMBI+ universe. The ratings are an average of those assigned by S&P, Moody's, and Fitch, while the country weights correspond to those in the EMBI/EMBI+.[30]

- *Global Liquidity (GL):* Interest rates provide a measure of global liquidity to the extent that they impact asset prices by catalyzing borrowing to finance investment positions. A number of interest rate variables were considered in order to capture the incentives for emerging bond market investors to undertake leveraged trades, including the level of short-term rates, the level of long-term rates, and the steepness of the yield curve as measured by the spread between short- and long-term rates. However, only the short-term interest rate was significant in the regressions. The particular short-term rate used was the three-month dollar LIBOR rate, since this interest rate serves as a benchmark in determining the costs of borrowing for investors seeking to build leveraged positions.[31]

- *Demand (D):* The secular broadening of the emerging market investor base is difficult to quantify. Data series on flows to dedicated emerging market bond mutual funds are available. However, investment flows from retail investors are likely to be a poor proxy for total flows, particularly during times when the investor base has broadened significantly. More specifically, this data would fail to capture net flows from institutional investors, trading accounts, and local investors, all of which represent important components of the changes in the investor base.[32] However, primary market issuance could provide a reasonable proxy measure for overall demand. In the process of building the order book for a new bond, underwriters go through a careful process of ascertaining demand for the new issue before deciding whether to bring it to the market. Thus, new gross supply of bonds appears likely to serve as a reasonable proxy for the changing size of the investor base, and the model uses a 12-month moving average of gross primary issuance as a proxy for this demand.[33]

---

[30]The model was also estimated for lagged ratings, but the coefficients were broadly similar to those shown below, in part reflecting the high serial correlation embedded in the ratings series.

[31]Other measures of short-term rates, such as the Fed Funds target rate or three-month treasury bill rates, are very closely correlated with the three-month LIBOR rate.

[32]Nonetheless, net inflows to dedicated emerging market funds were tested in the regression but were insignificant.

[33]One caveat to the assumed broad equilibrium of demand and supply is that there may be times of insufficient demand in which lead managers may absorb a sudden and unanticipated excess supply of bonds. However, the compression of issuance fees and a cautious approach to the deployment of capital suggests that the ability of lead managers to absorb unwanted supply is limited.

Table 2.5. Results of Estimate

(t-statistics in parentheses)

Variable	Estimation Period		
	Jan 1994–Sep. 2001	Oct. 2001–Dec. 2003	Jan. 1994–Dec. 2003
Fundamentals	−30.24 *(−0.93)*	−131.56 *(−2.98)*	−52.15 *(−1.90)*
Global liquidity	27.54 *(0.75)*	276.90 *(2.90)*	53.12 *(2.16)*
Demand	−161.11 *(−6.66)*	−29.60 *(−0.87)*	−140.60 *(−6.77)*
VIX	101.54 *(5.88)*	133.65 *(7.13)*	95.23 *(6.74)*
Crisis dummy	115.37 *(6.84)*		109.54 *(7.71)*
R^2	90%	89%	90%

Source: IMF staff estimates.

- *VIX:* The model tested two possible proxies for investors' attitude toward risk. During times of reduced risk aversion, investors are more likely to move out the credit quality spectrum. Thus, one possible measure of changing investor attitude toward risk is the spread between high-yield and high-grade corporate bonds. In addition, increased risk taking is likely to lead to less hedging against volatility. This is most commonly proxied by using the VIX. This index measures the volatility implied by options contracts on the S&P 500 index. In all specifications of the regression, the VIX proved a strong explanatory variable and was included in the final regression. However, the spread between high-yield and high-grade bond yields did not add significantly to the explanatory power of the regressions, and was dropped from the final specification.

- *Crisis dummy (CD):* The model corrects for crisis periods with spreads exceeding 1,000 basis points by introducing a dummy variable for such periods.

In a first step, the model is estimated for the period from January 1994 through December 2003 using monthly data.[34] In a second step, the model is estimated for two sub-periods: the period from 1994 to September 2001; and the period from October 2001 to end-2003 (see Table 2.5). The beginning of the latter period coincided with the onset of an emerging bond market rally, which, however, faced a temporary reversal in mid-2002.[35] All independent variables are standardized, allowing for comparisons of the relative impact of these variables on spreads.

$$S_t = \alpha_0 + \alpha_1 F_{t-1} + \alpha_2 GL_t + \alpha_3 D_t + \alpha_4 VIX_t + \alpha_5 CD_t + \varepsilon_t,$$

where $\varepsilon_t = \rho\varepsilon_{t-1} + \eta_t$.[36]

- *Fundamentals* are found to be a statistically significant driver of emerging market bond spreads for the sub-period starting October 2001 and for the entire time period of 1994 to 2003, although at a lower level of significance for the latter. However, fundamentals are not found to be statistically significant for the sub-period of 1994 to 2001. This result may in part reflect the high incidence of crises during this period as captured by the crisis dummy.

- *Global liquidity* is a statistically significant explanatory variable for the entire estimation period and for the sub-period beginning in October 2001. However, the impact of global liquidity on spreads exceeds that of any other variable since October 2001. In

[34]The analysis of the properties of the time series data and estimation results shows that the model is not subject to shortcomings associated with nonstationarity.

[35]Estimating the model since the onset of the leg of the rally that began in October 2002 would have excessively reduced the sample size.

[36]This formulation controls for possible problems associated with autocorrelated errors.

Figure 2.56. Selected Asian Countries: Outstanding Amounts of Domestic Bonds
(In billions of U.S. dollars)

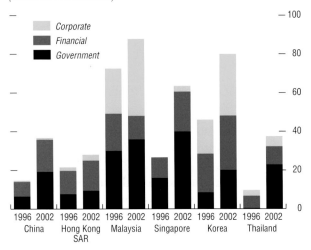

Sources: Bank for International Settlements; and IMF, *World Economic Outlook.*

contrast, global liquidity is not found to be statistically significant during the sub-period of 1994 to 2001.

- *Demand* is a statistically significant driver of spreads for the entire period. However, demand is not found to have had a statistically significant impact on spreads during the sub-period beginning in October 2001. One possible explanation is that primary issuance may not be a good proxy for the additional demand that has been generated by the secular broadening of the investor base during this period.

- *VIX* and investors' attitude toward risk is found to have been a significant driver of emerging bond market spreads during all periods, underscoring the vulnerability of the asset class to a reversal in risk tolerance.

Appendix II: Current Status of the Asian Bond Markets and Initiatives

Development of the Asian Bond Markets Since the 1998 Crisis

Local bond markets in Asia grew rapidly after the financial crisis in the late 1990s, in part reflecting a desire to develop an alternative source of financing to bank lending and foreign borrowing (Figure 2.56). Local bond markets have been viewed as mitigating the impact of lost access to international capital markets, as well as reducing the inherent currency and maturity mismatch in the borrowing of emerging market countries.

The share of Asian bonds outstanding in the total world bond market went from 2.9 percent of GDP in 1998 to 3.4 percent in 2002 (Table 2.6). Government bonds account for more than 45 percent of the total bonds outstanding in Asia.

Despite the rapid growth of its bond market, Asia remains heavily dependent on bank financing (Table 2.7). Moreover, Asian bond markets suffer from limited liquidity and depth. As a result, the authorities in a number of countries have started to take steps to

Table 2.6. Size and Structure of the Global Bond Market in 2002
(Nominal value in billions of U.S. dollars)

Country	Total Bonds Outstanding	Percent of World Bond Market	Domestic Government Billions of U.S. dollars	Government Percent of total	Financial institutions Billions of U.S. dollars	Financial institutions Percent of total	Corporate Billions of U.S. dollars	Corporate Percent of total	International[1] Billions of U.S. dollars	International[1] Percent of total
United States	19,049.3	44.5	4,530.3	23.8	9,382.2	49.3	2,418.3	12.7	2,718.5	14.3
Euro area[2]	10,199.4	23.8	3,818.7	37.4	2,269.2	22.2	548.8	5.4	3,562.7	34.9
Japan	6,914.6	16.2	4,837.5	70.0	1,145.8	16.6	683.0	9.9	248.3	3.6
Other mature markets	4,257.6	9.9	1,284.7	30.2	933.2	21.9	491.3	11.5	1,548.4	36.4
Subtotal	**40,420.9**	**94.4**	**14,471.2**	**35.8**	**13,730.4**	**34.0**	**4,141.4**	**10.2**	**8,077.9**	**20.0**
Emerging Markets										
Asia	1,448.7	3.4	645.1	44.5	387.1	26.7	262.8	18.1	153.7	10.6
Latin America	527.9	1.2	272.5	51.6	56.3	10.7	27.0	5.1	172.1	32.6
Eastern Europe, Middle East, Africa	403.5	0.9	260.4	64.5	12.7	3.1	8.0	2.0	122.4	30.3
Subtotal	**2,380.1**	**5.6**	**1,178.0**	**49.5**	**456.1**	**19.2**	**297.8**	**12.5**	**448.2**	**18.8**
Total	**42,801.0**	**100.0**	**15,649.2**	**36.6**	**14,186.5**	**33.1**	**4,439.2**	**10.4**	**8,526.1**	**19.9**

Source: Bank for International Settlements.
[1]Includes bonds issued by governments, financial institutions, and corporates in international markets.
[2]Euro area includes a total of 11 members of the euro zone, excluding Luxembourg.

strengthen both local and regional bond markets.

Regional Initiatives Promoting the Development of Local Bond Markets

A number of initiatives in various regional fora have been taken to further the development of local and regional bond markets. These include the Asian Bond Funds (ABF) and Asian Bond Market initiative (ABMI), from the Executive's Meeting of East Asia Pacific Central Banks (EMEAP), and APEC and ASEAN+3, respectively.[37]

These initiatives aim at developing both the demand and supply sides of Asian bond markets. On the demand side, the aim is to move away from both bank financing and U.S. dollar financing and to develop the local currency bond markets as an alternative source of funding. On the supply side, these initiatives seek to develop better bond market infrastructures and to synchronize rules and regulations

on cross-border flows so that local issuers can raise funds across the region. In particular, the Asian Bond Funds aim to increase the demand for Asian bonds and to facilitate the development of the regional bond market by using some foreign exchange reserves to invest in regional instruments. The ABMI focuses on addressing some of the supply-side impediments that exist in Asia and make local bond markets more accessible to Asian issuers.

Asian Bond Funds

On June 2, 2003, EMAEP announced the launch of the Asian Bond Fund I (ABFI) to "channel the resources held by Asian economies back into the region." ABFI had an initial funding of $1 billion contributed by the 11 members of the EMEAP to invest only in U.S. dollar-denominated sovereign or quasi-sovereign bonds issued by eight of the EMEAP members (excluding Japan, Australia, and New Zealand). To maintain these contributions as reserve assets, ABFI invested in bonds

[37]The 11 members of EMEAP are: Australia, China, Hong Kong SAR, Indonesia, Japan, the Republic of Korea, Malaysia, New Zealand, the Philippines, Singapore, and Thailand. ASEAN+3 refers to countries under the Association of South East Nations plus China, Japan, and Korea. More information on EMEAP can be found at http://www.emeap.org.

Table 2.7. Structure of Financing in Selected Countries

	GDP	Bank Loans	Stock Market Capitalization	Bond Market
	(In billions of U.S. dollars)			
China	1,266	1,728	463	465
Hong Kong SAR	162	242	463	68
Indonesia	173	39	30	2
Korea	477	510	216	381
Malaysia	95	101	123	83
Philippines	78	25	18	22
Singapore	87	94	102	55
Taiwan Province of China	282	354	261	141
Thailand	126	103	45	53
	(In percent of GDP)			
China		136	37	37
Hong Kong SAR		150	287	42
Indonesia		22	17	1
Korea		107	45	80
Malaysia		107	130	88
Philippines		32	23	28
Singapore		109	117	63
Taiwan Province of China		126	93	50
Thailand		81	36	42

Sources: Bank for International Settlements; IMF, *International Financial Statistics;* Hong Kong Monetary Authority; Indonesian Central Bank; The Thai Bond Dealing Centre; and World Federation of Exchanges.

with a composite investment grade rating. The fund is passively managed by the BIS according to an unpublished benchmark, and the BIS has agreed to redeem the investments at market value to the member countries at any time to safeguard their liquidity as official reserves.

Since the launch of ABFI in June 2003, discussions on ABFII have started but details are still not finalized. In contrast to ABFI, ABFII will invest in the participating countries' local currency sovereign and quasi-sovereign bonds and aims to generate more investor interest in local bond markets. Countries that are ready to open up their bond markets to foreign investment will participate, while those still facing significant hurdles in taxation, legal, and capital account restrictions will need to work to eliminate those obstacles over time to eventually allow for foreign investment in their bond markets.

In setting up ABFII, private sector participation is regarded as important both as potential future investors in the fund and as potential managers for the fund. It is likely that the private sector will be involved in structuring, marketing, and listing the fund and that the ABFII will likely be managed by the private sector (rather than the BIS as in the case of ABFI).[38]

Asian Bond Market Initiative

The Asian Bond Market Initiative (ABMI) is a broad umbrella covering many areas of bond market development. It has focused on facilitating access to bond markets, and enhancing market infrastructure for local and regional bond market development. In particular, six elements of market infrastructure are receiving particular attention: creating new securitized instruments, credit guarantee mechanisms, settlement and exchange regulations, issuance of local currency bonds by nondomestic issuers, local and regional rating agencies, and technical assistance coordination. The goal is to identify measures that can address some of the deficiencies in the current Asian bond markets, such as low liquidity, narrow investor bases, and limited high grade issuance. For example, securitization and credit guarantee will help Asian issuers with low credit ratings to issue high-grade bonds to gain access to the market. With the exception of Hong Kong SAR and Singapore, most countries do not have a settlement and clearing system conforming to international standards. Local credit rating agencies have different rating standards, and there is no regionally accepted credit rating system. Developing a settlement and clearing system consistent with international best practices and a uniform credit rating standards throughout the region would help reduce issuance costs, and improve market efficiency and liquidity.

[38]As reported in *Euroweek* (2003) and *International Financing Review* (2003).

New securitized instruments, especially asset backed securities (ABS), have been developing rapidly in Asia. In Korea, ABS issuance has risen sharply following the Asian crisis. ABS now represent almost 44 percent of corporate issuance largely reflecting securitization of nonperforming loans and credit card receivables (Figure 2.57). In Malaysia, the growth of the ABS market is expected to double from RM5.6 billion ($1.5 billion) in 2004. The strong growth has been spurred by a supportive legal environment and regulatory regime; a well functioning capital market infrastructure; and strong investor interest. Moreover, Hong Kong SAR is becoming a regional center for securitization activity in Asia.

Asian rating agencies have formed an association to enhance cooperation.[39] Most countries now have local rating agencies as well as limited participation of the international rating agencies in the local market (Table 2.8). The two regional financial centers, Hong Kong SAR and Singapore, on the other hand, do not have local rating agencies but rely on international rating agencies to rate local issues. In contrast to the international agencies, many of these regional or national rating agencies have links with their respective governments (or may have been set up as a governmental body), thus their degree of independence is open to question. Moreover, given the differences in rating culture and stage of capital market development, creating a unified credit rating system may not be feasible in the near term. Efforts are being made to raise rating standards and credit evaluation and to adopt best practices in the region.

Assessment of the Initiatives

The small size of the ABFI has limited its market impact, while its objective is well

[39]The Association of Credit Rating Agencies in Asia (ACRAA) is an association formed by Asian credit rating agencies and assisted by the Asian Development Bank.

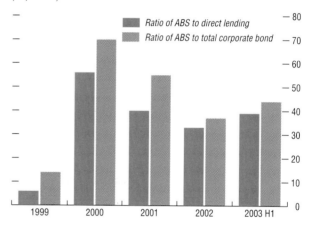

Figure 2.57. Korea: ABS Issuance and Direct Financing
(In percent)

- Ratio of ABS to direct lending
- Ratio of ABS to total corporate bond

Sources: Korea Ratings Corp.; and IMF staff estimates.

Table 2.8. Asian Rating Agencies

Country	Bond Rating Agency		Year Founded	Tie-Ups with International Rating Agencies
India	Investment Information and Credit Rating Agency of India Ltd	(ICRA)	1991	Moody's
	Credit Analysis and Research Limited	(CARE)	1993	
	Credit Rating Information Services of India Limited	(CRISIL)	1987	S&P
	Duff and Phelps India	(DCR India)	n.a.	Joint Venture with Fitch
Pakistan	JCR-VIS Credit Rating Company Limited	(JCR-VIS)	1997	Joint Venture with JCR
	Pakistan Credit Rating Agency (Private) Limited	(PACRA)	1994	Joint Venture with Fitch
Indonesia	PT Pemeringkat Efek Indonesia	(PEFINDO)	1993	S&P
	Kasnic	(KASNIC)	n.a.	Fitch
Taiwan Province of China	Taiwan Rating Corporation	(TCR)	1997	S&P
Philippines	Philippine Rating Service Corporation (PhilRatings)	(PRS)	1998	S&P
Japan	Japan Credit Rating Agency, Limited	(JCR)	1985	Independent
	Japan Rating and Investment Information Inc	(R&I)	1998[1]	Independent
Korea	Korean Investor Services	(KIS)	1985	Moody's
	Korean Management Consulting and Credit Rating Corporation	(KMCC)	1987	Fitch
	National Information and Credit Evaluation	(NICE)	1986	R&I
	Seoul Credit Rating & Information Inc.	(SCI)	1992	JCR
Malaysia	Rating Agency Malaysia	(RAM)	1990	Independent
	Malaysia Rating Corporation	(MARC)	1996	Fitch
Thailand	Thailand Rating Information Services	(TRIS)	1993	Fitch
Bangladesh	Credit Rating Information & Services	(CRIS)	2002	—
Hong Kong SAR	No local rating agencies		—	—
Singapore	No local rating agencies		—	—

Source: Japan Credit Rating Agency, Ltd.
[1]Union of NIS and JBRI in 1998.

grounded. ABFI has generated interest in Asian bond markets and paved the way for ABFII. In particular, ABFII could be an important investor in local Asian bond markets. The ABFs could have a catalytic role in encouraging countries in the region to harmonize regulatory regimes and improve legal infrastructure to allow more private sector participation in the local bond markets.

Careful consideration should be given when designing the ABFII. First, ABFI by virtue of design and the liquidity guarantee provided by BIS permits assets invested in it to be classified as reserve assets. Future funds will need to provide a similar level of liquidity if assets invested were to be counted as reserve assets. Moreover, safeguards could be useful to minimize any perception of moral hazard and governance risks. To this end, outsourcing the

management of ABFI to the BIS and inviting private sector managers for ABFII (which is likely to be designed as an indexed or passively managed fund) can ensure transparency, gain public support, and establish credibility vis-à-vis investors. It would also be desirable for the authorities to continuously disclose sufficient information to assure the public that funds are properly managed and invested.

No matter what form the ABFII fund takes, the authorities and other future investors will face the issue of whether and how to hedge the underlying credit and currency risks. This may be difficult since derivatives markets in Asia are still at an early stage of development. Moreover, if both ABF funds are buy-and-hold investors, their purchases of the bonds issued by the regional governments could even reduce the liquidity of those markets.

The ABMI could play a key role in promoting both the development of the infrastructure and access to the regional bond markets. Discussions surrounding ABMI have successfully focused the attention of policymakers in Asia on the various obstacles to developing local bond markets and generated discussions about adopting best practices in various areas of bond market development. Initiatives on providing credit enhancements to small- and medium-sized firms that otherwise are denied access to capital markets are a step forward.

However, an integrated regional bond market will clearly take time to develop. The Asian bond market, while large, remains segmented by regulatory constraints and owing to a lack of regional infrastructure. Country-specific laws, regulations, and market practices present major hurdles to cross-border issuance and investing. Clearing and settlement mechanisms vary from country to country, and there is no regional arrangement. Hedging costs remain relatively high due to illiquid derivative markets and regulatory constraints on access to both local currency funding and to onshore forward and derivatives markets by nonresidents. Taxation differs vastly and withholding tax can raise the cost of investing in local securities. Local credit rating standards vary, and there is no regional credit rating agency. Many countries in the region do not yet have a liquid benchmark yield curve. Finally, capital controls in a few countries have severely limited cross-border capital flows.

References

Arora, Vivek, and Martin Cerisola, 2001, "How Does U.S. Monetary Policy Influence Sovereign Spreads in Emerging Markets?" *IMF Staff Papers*, International Monetary Fund, Vol. 48 (November), pp. 474–98.

Asian Development Bank, 2003, "Technical Assistance for the ASEAN+3 Regional Guarantee Mechanism" (October).

Calvo, Guillermo A., Leonardo Leiderman, and Carmen Reinhart, 1993, "Capital Inflows and Real Exchange Rate Appreciation in Latin America: The Role of External Factors," *IMF Staff Papers*, International Monetary Fund, Vol. 40 (March), pp. 108–51.

Calvo, Guillermo, and Enrique Mendoza, 1995, "Mexico's Balance-of-Payments Crisis: A Chronicle of a Death Foretold," *Journal of International Economics*, Vol. 41, pp. 235–64.

Capital Markets Consultative Group (CMCG), 2003, *Foreign Direct Investment in Emerging Market Countries.*

Cline, William, and Kevin Barnes, 1997, "Spreads and Risk in Emerging Markets Lending," Working Paper 97–1 (Washington: Institute of International Finance).

Dell'Ariccia, Giovanni, Isabel Schnabel, and Jeromin Zettelmeyer, 2002, "Moral Hazard and International Crisis Lending: A Test," IMF Working Paper No. 02/181 (Washington: International Monetary Fund).

Eichengreen, Barry, and Ashoka Mody, 1998, "What Explains Changing Spreads on Emerging-Market Debt: Fundamentals or Market Sentiment?" NBER Working Paper No. 6408 (Cambridge, Mass.: National Bureau of Economic Research).

Euroweek, 2003, "Central Banks to finalize Asia Bond Fund 2 by December" (October 17).

Ferrucci, Gianluigi, 2003, "Empirical Determinants of Emerging Market Economies' Sovereign Bond Spreads," Bank of England Working Paper No. 205 (London).

Goldstein, Morris, and David Folkerts-Landau, 1994, *International Capital Markets: Developments, Prospects, and Policy Issues,* World Economic and Financial Surveys (Washington: International Monetary Fund).

International Financing Review, 2003, "Asian Bond Fund 2 Starts to Take Shape" (November 22).

Kamin, Steven B., and Karsten von Kleist, 1999, "The Evolution and Determinants of Emerging Market Credit Spreads in the 1990s," BIS Working Paper No. 68 (Basel: Bank for International Settlements).

Kaminsky, Graciela, Saul Lizondo, and Carmen M. Reinhart, 1998, "Leading Indicators of Currency Crises," *IMF Staff Papers*, International Monetary Fund, Vol. 45 (March), pp. 1–48.

Litterman, Robert, and José Scheinkman, 1991, "Common Factors Affecting Bond Returns," *Journal of Fixed Income*, pp. 54–61.

McGuire, Patrick, and Martijn A. Schrijvers, 2003, "Common Factors in Emerging Markets," *BIS Quarterly Review* (Basel: Bank for International Settlements, December).

Min, Hong G., 1998, "Determinants of Emerging Market Bond Spreads: Do Economic Fundamentals Matter?" Policy Research Paper No. 1899 (Washington: World Bank).

Sy, Amadou, 2002, "Emerging Market Bond Spreads and Sovereign Credit Ratings: Reconciling Market Views with Economic Fundamentals," *Emerging Markets Review*, Vol. 3, Issue 4, pp. 380–408.

Thailand, 2003, Ministry of Finance, "Asian Bond Market Development."

Watanabe, Hiroshi, 2003, "Asian Bond Markets Initiative (ABMI)," presentation at the Euromoney conference on "Developing Asian Bond Markets" (October), Bangkok, Thailand.

CHAPTER III

RISK TRANSFER AND THE INSURANCE INDUSTRY

The transfer of risk from banks to non-bank institutions, such as mutual funds, pension funds, insurers, and hedge funds, has been taking place for many years. Banks have generally tried to distribute the risk that they have originated—particularly concentrations of credit risk—in order to optimize the use of their balance sheets and as an integral part of their risk management practice.[1] Some nonbanks, in certain markets, have demonstrated a strong or growing appetite for credit risk exposure in various forms. These include insurers, which increasingly view credit instruments as a relatively stable investment to meet their liabilities. The development of new credit instruments, particularly derivatives, has facilitated this process.

The transfer of risk to nonbanking sectors has raised concerns about "where the risk has gone;" whether risk has been widely dispersed or concentrated; and whether the recipients of risk are able to manage such risk. As noted in previous GFSRs, most observers agree that the transfer of credit has improved the banking sector's ability to manage risks, and hence the stability of the banking system. A wide variety of nonbank institutions have taken on the risk. But the relatively less transparent nature of some nonbanking institutions, their different systems of regulation, and, in some cases, less developed risk management skills have raised questions about whether a reallocation of credit risk has *reduced* risk for the overall financial system or merely *shifted* it to less transparent sectors. In the latter case, new forms of risk and vulnerability may be introduced.

This chapter, the first of a series that will examine risk transfer, discusses the insurance sector, particularly life insurers. It expands on issues raised in previous GFSRs by asking whether financial stability has benefited or could benefit from insurers' broader participation in credit markets, including credit derivatives (see, for instance, IMF, 2002a). Life insurance companies traditionally have been viewed as long-term, savings-oriented institutions and not as a potential source of systemic risk, and as such have been seen as possibly "better" holders of credit and longer-term assets. However, in light of the increasing volume of credit being reallocated from banks to nonbanks, including certain insurance sectors and companies, and the intention among many insurers, particularly in Europe, to increase their exposure to credit, policymakers have expressed increased interest in the possible effect of risk transfer on financial stability.[2] Within the insurance sector, life insurers are the largest holders of financial assets, and their balance sheets are generally much larger than property and casualty (P&C) insurers and reinsurers.[3]

In focusing on risk reallocation, we use the term "credit risk transfer" to refer in a broad sense to all manners in which insurers have taken on credit risk (e.g., corporate bonds, loans, asset-backed securities, and credit deriv-

---

[1]International Association of Insurance Supervisors (2003), Financial Services Authority (2002), and Rule (2001b) examine the credit risk transfer between banks and nonbank financial sectors, including the insurance sector.

[2]Häusler (2004) discusses how the blurring of boundaries between insurance and other financial institutions implies heightened importance of insurers for financial stability. Das, Davies, and Podpiera (2003) also explore the potential for the insurance sector to affect the vulnerability of the financial system, focusing on the banking-type activities that life insurance companies have increasingly taken on, as well as risks stemming from the possible failure of a large reinsurer.

[3]Somewhat separate issues regarding reinsurance disclosure and risk (primarily concerning insurance liabilities) are being discussed in various fora, including an IAIS Task Force that reported to the Financial Stability Forum in March 2004. These issues are not dealt with directly in this chapter. See Swiss Re (2003b) for an overview.

atives). In so doing, we are widening the definition of credit risk transfer from its frequent use in official circles, which has focused on credit derivatives and related structured products.[4] While such products do raise important questions for policymakers, we wish to review the broader credit markets, regulatory framework, and risk management systems at insurers, taking into account all credit products, including derivatives and structured products. This chapter does not intend, however, to cover certain other issues related to the insurance industry, such as their exposure to asbestos claims and other tort liabilities, and the capital needs arising from such business risks. Our work focuses instead on the investment activities of life insurers, and how they may impact broader financial market stability.

The chapter assesses the impact on financial stability of life insurers' investment behavior and risk management in the largest mature markets (i.e., United States, United Kingdom, continental Europe, and Japan). The policy implications differ from market to market, and may offer useful lessons to emerging market countries with developing capital markets. The financial difficulties experienced by many insurance companies have eased in the last year as equity and other asset prices have risen. But, more fundamentally, they have acted as an impetus for enhancing insurers' risk management skills and for strengthening supervisory and accounting standards. These are likely to continue evolving for some time. As such, this is an appropriate time to take stock of the outstanding issues and to highlight the gaps and potential weaknesses in the framework.

Market Structure and Regulatory Framework

National insurance sectors often may hold different types of asset portfolios from each

Table 3.1. Size of Global Financial Markets, 2002
(In billions of U.S. dollars; amounts outstanding)

	United States	United Kingdom	Euro Area	Japan
Equity	11,871	2,856	3,279	2,027
Bonds[1]	14,831	2,059	7,977	7,484
Of which:[2]				
Government	9,135	441	4,122	6,028
Financial corporate debt	2,985	130	3,293	298
Nonfinancial corporate debt	2,711	370	562	1,159
Bank loans to nonfinancial corporations	1,066	692	3,117	8,824
Memorandum item:				
GDP	10,446	1,567	6,670	3,986

Sources: Board of Governors of the Federal Reserve System, *Flow of Funds;* U.K. Office of National Statistics; ECB; Bank of Japan; and IMF, *World Economic Outlook* database.
[1]For United Kingdom, the aggregates include bonds issued by nonresidents while the components are issued by residents.
[2]Following are selected components of the above aggregate.

other and show different degrees of sophistication in credit risk management. Discussions with a wide range of regulators, insurance executives, investors, and the rating agencies reveal the common view that the structure of national financial systems and capital markets and insurance regulations are very important factors explaining the observed differences. Accounting standards and rating agencies are also important influences, albeit somewhat more general, and are discussed in a later section of this chapter. The chapter will also compare the robustness of insurers' financial conditions during market downturns and will finish with certain assessments and policy conclusions on how best to ensure that credit reallocation to the insurance sector enhances financial stability.

The Structure of National and Regional Financial Markets

Insurers from different countries have evolved different investment styles. U.S. and Japanese insurers have traditionally favored

---

[4]See Committee on the Global Financial System (2003) and the Joint Forum (forthcoming) for a broad review of credit risk transfer techniques. See also Kiff (2003); Kiff, Michaud, and Mitchell (2003); IMF (2002a); and Hall and Stuart (2003) for more on credit risk transfer.

Table 3.2. United States: Financial Market Size[1]

(In billions of U.S. dollars; amounts outstanding)

	1994	1995	1996	1997	1998	1999	2000	2001	2002
Equity	6,318	8,475	10,276	13,293	15,547	19,523	17,627	15,311	11,871
Bonds	7,927	8,562	9,233	9,805	10,768	11,713	12,219	13,491	14,831
Of which:									
Treasuries	3,466	3,609	3,755	3,778	3,724	3,653	3,358	3,353	3,610
Agencies	2,199	2,405	2,635	2,848	3,321	3,912	4,345	4,971	5,525
Financial corporate debt	1,009	1,205	1,383	1,569	1,878	2,080	2,286	2,588	2,985
Nonfinancial corporate debt	1,253	1,344	1,460	1,611	1,846	2,068	2,230	2,579	2,711
Bank loans to nonfinancial corporations	681	766	836	930	1,031	1,122	1,214	1,149	1,066
Memorandum item:									
Total equity, bonds, and loans	14,926	17,804	20,345	24,028	27,346	32,357	31,060	29,950	27,768

Sources: Board of Governors of the Federal Reserve System, *Flow of Funds;* and Bond Market Association.
[1]Claims on residents.

credit instruments, U.K. insurers have preferred equity, and continental European insurers have favored a mix of government securities and equities. The structure of the underlying national and regional markets has played a major role in influencing these preferences (Table 3.1).

Differences in national financial systems and capital markets are due to a variety of factors, including stages of development, levels of financial intermediation, and regulations.[5] In a bank-based system, where banks provide the bulk of financing to corporates, capital markets for credit remain less developed. Insurance companies (and other large institutional investors) therefore have fewer opportunities to invest in credit instruments and consequently have found less reason to build up credit risk management skills. This is particularly true since, until recently, in many countries, insurance companies have been largely required to invest in domestic markets (or in instruments denominated in domestic currencies).[6] As such, their asset portfolios tend to reflect the structure of their national or regional capital markets. By contrast, in a market-based system, corporate bond markets are more well developed, and insurance companies have a longer tradition of investing in and managing credit risk.

Insurance companies, and other institutional investors, of course have an influence on the development of their national capital markets. The investment demand from insurers, in terms of the variety of credit instruments, credit quality, maturity, and other features, helps to sustain demand for corporate bonds and other assets. However, this influence is only one among many shaping the development of capital markets. For example, the European corporate bond market only took off after the introduction of the euro in 1999.

Corporate credit in the U.S. financial system operates largely through capital markets, while banks have a more prominent role in Europe and Japan. The corporate bond market is the largest source of credit for nonfinancial businesses in the United States (Table 3.2). More relationship-based systems, such as those in Europe and Japan, have

---

[5]Rajan and Zingales (2003) discuss the difference between the more market-based system in the United States and the relationship-based system in continental Europe, which remains despite Europe becoming more market-oriented and the increase in corporate bond issuance following the introduction of the euro. Hartmann, Maddaloni, and Manganelli (2003) discuss the difference between a market-based U.S. system and a bank-based Japanese system, with Europe placed somewhere between.

[6]For a more general discussion of home bias, see Ahearne, Griever, and Warnock (forthcoming).

Table 3.3. Euro Area: Financial Market Size[1]
(In billions of U.S. dollars)

	1998	1999	2000	2001	2002	2003:Q1
Equity	4,591	5,498	5,054	4,104	3,279	4,066
Bonds	6,834	6,382	6,278	6,406	7,977	9,260
Of which:						
Government bonds	3,862	3,460	3,292	3,310	4,122	4,795
Financial corporate debt	2,625	2,570	2,583	2,634	3,293	3,801
Nonfinancial corporate debt	347	353	403	462	562	664
Loans to nonfinancial corporations (NFC)	2,690	2,440	2,499	2,559	3,117	3,448
Memorandum items:						
Total equity, bonds, and loans to NFC	14,114	14,321	11,248	13,068	14,373	16,774
Asset-backed securities (issuance)[2]	. . .	68	80	80	134	. . .
Collateralized debt obligations (issuance)[3]	. . .	42	71	71	114	. . .

Sources: ECB, *Monthly Bulletin* (various issues); and Moody's.
[1]Claims on residents.
[2]For 2002, data shown as year-to-date as of September 30.
[3]For 2002, data refer to first half of 2002.

Table 3.4. Japan: Financial Market Size[1]
(In billions of U.S. dollars)

	1994	1995	1996	1997	1998	1999	2000	2001	2002
Equity	3,232	3,940	3,005	2,443	2,966	4,850	3,173	2,420	2,027
Bonds	5,478	5,755	5,526	5,147	5,919	7,096	6,770	6,257	7,484
Of which:									
Government bonds	3,490	3,771	3,704	3,585	4,262	5,225	5,121	4,896	6,028
Financial corporate debt	768	710	607	471	482	535	416	315	298
Nonfinancial corporate debt	1,220	1,275	1,215	1,091	1,175	1,336	1,233	1,045	1,159
Loans to nonfinancial corporations	11,918	11,712	10,318	9,234	10,336	11,464	9,983	8,454	8,824
Memorandum item:									
Total equity, bonds, and loans	20,629	21,407	18,848	16,824	19,222	23,410	19,926	17,131	18,335

Source: Bank of Japan, *Flow of Funds.*
[1]Claims on residents.

relatively smaller nonfinancial corporate bond markets and larger stocks of loans. However, the difference in structure between the United States and continental Europe has been narrowing since the adoption of the euro, and the euro-area corporate bond market has almost doubled in size since 1999 (Table 3.3). By contrast, the weak credit demand from the corporate sector and the prolonged period of sluggish economic activity in Japan help to account for the slow growth of Japan's nonfinancial corporate bond market (Table 3.4).

In more capital market-based systems, like the United States, life insurance companies have a wide variety of credit instruments in which they can invest. Corporate bonds represented 61 percent of the aggregate general account portfolio of U.S. life insurers at the end of 2002, well above other asset classes and much greater than their non-U.S. peer group (Figure 3.1). (Corporate bond holdings have been the largest asset class for some time, and grew further in 2002 as insurers sought to earn extra spread income from credit instruments.) U.S. insurers also hold investments in "separate accounts," relating to products such as variable annuities where, like a mutual fund, policyholders receive a return based on the assets invested (see the Glossary at the end of this report for definitions of insurance terms).[7] In 2002, 28 percent of U.S. life insurers' assets were in separate accounts, with 74 percent of separate account assets comprising equities (Table 3.5).[8] The insurance products related to separate account assets (in the United States and elsewhere) explicitly pass the investment risk to the end-consumer or policyholder, and do not represent a financial or solvency risk to the insurer.

U.S. life insurers are an important and cyclically stable source of credit to business. The amount of credit to corporates and consumers held in the bond portfolios of insurance companies has grown steadily and today exceeds the stock of such loans at banks (Figure 3.2). This contrasts with the more cyclical pattern of bank lending. U.S. insurance companies can use a range of capital market instruments to achieve targeted credit and equity exposures, as well as the desired risk/return profile. Moreover, because the U.S. capital markets are very liquid, significant trading activity by insurance companies usually has little impact on market prices or volatility. This has facilitated the ability of U.S. insurers to manage risk generally, and U.S. insurers have employed more people and systems with specific credit and risk management skills than their non-U.S. peers. However, even in the

[7]Insurance company balance sheets are divided into general and separate accounts. Separate accounts are established by insurers to legally segregate funds—for example, related to pension or variable life insurance products—where the investment risk is borne by the client, not the insurer. General accounts contain all other assets and liabilities of the insurer.

[8]Zucker and Joseph (2003). These figures are consistent with the 24 percent equity allocation of the life insurance sector reflected in U.S. flow of funds data, which comprise both general and separate accounts. Complete data on separate accounts are not available for insurance companies in other regions. Discussions with market participants suggest that equity holdings in the general account could also be somewhat lower than for the combined accounts in the euro area, the United Kingdom, and Japan, but remain well above U.S. general account levels. For example, among some of the largest life insurance companies in Japan, the differences between the equity share in the general and combined accounts is approximately one percentage point.

Figure 3.1. Asset Allocation for Life Insurance Industry, 2002
(In percent of total assets)

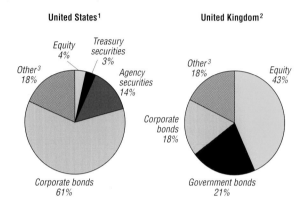

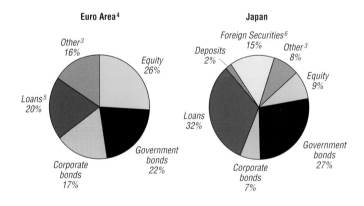

Sources: Board of Governors of the Federal Reserve System, *Flow of Funds;* U.K. Office of National Statistics; Comité Européen des Assurances; Bank of Japan, *Flow of Funds;* Fox-Pitt Kelton; and IMF staff estimates.
[1]U.S. data exclude holdings in separate accounts.
[2]U.K. data are for 2001.
[3]Unless separately shown, the "Other" investment category includes real estate (including mortgages), money market funds, deposits, and other investment assets.
[4]For the euro area, the data are for life and nonlife insurance sectors for the year 2001.
[5]Loans include medium-term notes (MTNs), such as schuldscheinforderungen, and other private placements.
[6]Discussions with major Japanese insurance companies suggest that there is wide variation in the composition of foreign securities from company to company. However, they typically include government and agency securities, but also corporate bonds and equities.

Table 3.5. United States: Asset Allocation for the Life Insurance Industry[1]
(In percent of investment assets in general accounts)

	1994–1997	1998	1999	2000	2001	2002
Equities	3.9	4.7	5.0	4.7	3.9	3.6
Bonds	70.7	71.6	71.2	71.4	72.4	79.7
Of which:[2]						
U.S. government securities	18.8	14.7	13.6	19.4	12.7	17.2
Treasuries	8.3	5.1	4.6	4.3	3.9	3.3
Agencies	10.5	9.6	9.0	15.1	8.8	13.9
Corporate bonds	41.5	47.8	49.3	50.8	53.0	60.8
Mortgages	12.8	11.5	11.9	11.8	11.3	11.2
			(In billions of U.S. dollars)			
Memorandum items:						
Total assets of life insurance	2,172	2,770	3,068	3,136	3,225	3,335
Of which:						
Amounts in separate accounts	512	906	1,129	1,129	1,058	950
Nonlife insurers' assets	758	876	873	862	858	919

Sources: Board of Governors of the Federal Reserve System, *Flow of Funds;* Fox-Pitt Kelton; and IMF staff estimates.
[1]These data (apart from memorandum items) exclude separate accounts. The table shows selected assets only, and therefore allocations do not total 100 percent.
[2]Following are selected components of the total for bonds.

United States, large life insurers have noted that their targeted investments can be large relative to the overall size of certain market segments or an individual bond issue. Needless to say, insurers' activity can have a more significant impact in the less liquid markets outside the United States.

The U.K. market structure helps to explain why U.K. insurers have historically had a high proportion of investments allocated to equities and a significantly lower allocation to government and corporate bonds (Table 3.6). The U.K. financial system has a capital market-based orientation, like the United States, but

Table 3.6. United Kingdom: Asset Allocation for the Life Insurance Industry[1]
(In percent of total investment assets)

	1997	1998	1999	2000	2001
Equities	55.8	52.1	58.2	51.9	43.4
Bonds	27.9	31.3	27.3	31.5	38.9
Of which:					
Government	18.6	20.8	16.4	16.7	17.7
Corporate	9.3	10.4	10.9	14.8	21.2
Other	16.3	16.7	14.5	16.7	17.7
		(In billions of U.S. dollars)			
Memorandum item:					
Total financial assets for life insurance industry	430	480	550	540	565

Sources: Bank of England; and Standard & Poor's.
[1]Excludes separate accounts.

continues to have a relatively small and concentrated corporate bond market. In many respects, the U.K. market structure has features similar to both the U.S. and continental European systems. The U.K. equity market is large and liquid, while U.K. bank lending to nonfinancial businesses is larger in comparison to GDP than in the United States and more in line with the euro area (Table 3.7). At the same time, the U.K. markets for government and corporate debt are relatively small compared with those in the United States, and corporate issuance is somewhat concentrated in a few sectors, such as banks and utilities. In 1999, equities represented more than 58 percent of U.K. insurers' investment portfolios. However, starting in 2000, insurers have increased their corporate bond allocations significantly, as the broader European credit markets have developed, and reduced their equity allocation.

Insurers in more relationship-based systems, such as continental Europe, have historically had a narrower range of investment options. In continental Europe, the great majority of corporate credit claims continue to be held in the banking system. While the European credit securities market has grown, it remains less developed than the U.S. market in terms of diversity of products, credit names, and maturities, and it is less liquid. Therefore, insurers in some euro area countries, such as Germany, tend to hold relatively larger amounts of government bonds and more equity securities (Table 3.8). The same is true in Switzerland. In addition, in both the corporate and government bond markets, life insurers have fewer long-duration securities available to hedge longer-term liabilities. Finally, the smaller size of these equity and credit markets also restricts large insurers. These constraints limit the capital market tools available to insurance risk managers. However, the credit market in Europe has expanded since 1999, as noted above, and the largest European insurers have increased risk management skills and systems in the last few years.[9]

Of course, the credit experience of continental European insurers is diverse, as some European insurers have operated on a global scale for some time. Several European insurers have purchased companies in the United States and Japan, and through these operations tend to manage larger credit positions. These institutions are often recognized by market observers as possibly ahead of other European insurers in their investment activities and risk management systems because of their experience in these other markets.

In Japan, insurance companies have a culture of managing credit, but in the country's relationship-based structure this has been principally through loans rather than corporate bonds. (Table 3.9). During the rapid

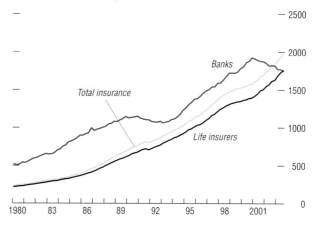

Figure 3.2. United States: Total Nonmortgage Credit to Private Nonfarm Sectors[1]
(In billions of U.S. dollars)

Source: Board of Governors of the Federal Reserve System, *Flow of Funds.*
[1]Including consumer credit, nonfinancial corporate and noncorporate sectors, and financial sector.

[9]An example of this expansion would be the growth of the asset-backed securities, mortgage-backed securities, and covered bond markets in Europe. In Germany, the "True Sale Initiative" (TSI) is aimed at developing securitizations as an additional funding source for small and medium-sized German business loans. TSI is supported by a consortium of 13 banks (Landesbanks, cooperative, savings, and commercial banks, including Citigroup) led by KfW, the German industrial development bank. A press release giving some details on TSI is available at *http://www.kfw.de/ Dateien_RSP/pdf/118_e.pdf.* See Chapter II for a broader discussion of the growth of securitization markets in Europe.

Table 3.7. United Kingdom: Financial Market Size[1]
(In billions of U.S. dollars)

	1994	1995	1996	1997	1998	1999	2000	2001	2002
Equity held	1,583	1,860	2,247	2,751	3,107	3,838	3,643	3,156	2,856
Bonds issued[2]	878	1,033	1,252	1,386	1,536	1,637	1,686	1,714	2,059
Of which:[3]									
Government	282	348	398	443	483	449	398	367	441
Financial corporate debt	54	59	74	78	89	109	111	113	130
Nonfinancial corporate debt	105	130	149	170	209	257	300	306	370
Bank loans to nonfinancial corporations	337	368	427	449	471	516	543	583	692
Memorandum item:									
Total financial assets	8,538	9,617	11,379	12,998	14,112	15,638	15,740	15,564	16,894

Source: U.K. Office of National Statistics, *Blue Book 2003.*
[1]Claims on residents.
[2]Includes bonds issued by nonresidents.
[3]Following are selected components of the above aggregate.

expansion of credit through the early 1980s, regulations granted insurance companies (together with long-term credit banks and trust banks) an exclusive privilege of providing long-term credit to the corporate sector. This policy and the culture of relationship-based lending inhibited the development of a corporate bond market. During the late 1980s, however, deregulation allowed commercial banks also to compete in long-term lending, and since the 1990s there has been weak loan demand overall and overcapacity in banking. These factors, combined with deteri-

orating loan quality, have reduced credit holdings by insurers and led them to shift their portfolios more toward government bonds, and, in some cases in recent years, to foreign securities.

Credit Derivatives

Credit derivatives remain a small but rapidly growing market and are increasingly used in both market-based and relationship-based systems. (Table 3.10 and Box 3.1 on page 90). In the early days of the credit derivative market, regulatory arbitrage (whereby banks sought to lower their capital risk weightings) was an important factor behind many transactions. However, more recently, banks have been primarily motivated by the desire to reduce credit risk concentrations and to diversify their credit exposure. This diversification has tended to occur mostly by banks (particularly larger banks) transferring risk to other banks (particularly smaller banks, such as regional European and Asian banks), allowing the latter to gain credit exposure to names they may not otherwise be able to access.[10]

Insurers have made some use of credit derivatives to gain additional credit exposure

Table 3.8. Euro Area: Asset Allocation for the Insurance Industry[1]
(In percent of total investment assets)

	1999	2000	2001
Equities	25.2	26.8	25.9
Bonds[2]	39.1	37.8	38.8
Loans[3]	21.3	20.4	19.6
Real estate	4.4	4.3	4.2
Other	9.9	10.7	11.5
	(In billions of U.S. dollars)		
Memorandum item:			
Total assets of insurance industry	2,081	2,448	2,479

Source: Comité Européen des Assurances.
[1]These data include separate and general accounts. Comparable disaggregated data for the euro area are not readily available prior to 1999.
[2]Based on IMF staff discussions with market participants and review of annual reports, approximately 60–65 percent of fixed-income holdings are often government bonds, with the remainder represented by credit securities.
[3]Loans include medium-term notes (MTNs), such as *schuldscheinforderungen*, and other private placements.

[10]Standard and Poor's (2003b) provides a review of the factors underlying banks' use of credit derivatives. See also FitchRatings (2004) for a similar study.

Table 3.9. Japan: Asset Allocation for the Life Insurance Industry[1]
(In percent of total investment assets)

	1994–1997	1998	1999	2000	2001	2002
Equity	16.1	14.0	16.4	13.6	11.8	8.8
Bonds	22.2	26.2	29.1	34.4	36.9	40.3
Of which:[2]						
Government bonds	15.2	17.7	20.0	22.7	24.6	27.3
Corporate bonds[3]	3.6	4.9	5.2	5.8	6.2	6.6
Foreign securities[4]	6.6	9.8	9.7	9.7	12.5	14.5
Loans	49.0	42.8	38.1	36.7	34.4	32.2
Other	6.1	7.2	6.7	5.6	4.3	4.2
			(In billions of U.S. dollars)			
Memorandum items:						
Total assets of life insurance	1,249	1,270	1,489	1,290	1,094	1,213
Total assets of nonlife insurance	312	291	337	267	219	227

Source: Bank of Japan, *Flow of Funds.*

[1]These data include separate and general accounts, and do not include the Japanese Postal Insurance System.

[2]Following are selected components of the above aggregate.

[3]Excludes debt of government-related enterprises.

[4]Discussions with major Japanese insurance companies suggest that there is wide variation in the composition of foreign securities from company to company. However, the foreign securities typically include government and agency securities, but also corporate bonds and equities.

Table 3.10. Credit Derivatives and Bank Credit
(In billions of U.S. dollars)

	1998	1999	2000	2001	2002	2003	2004
Credit derivatives (notional value)[1]	350	586	893	1,189	*1,952*	. . .[2]	*4,799*
(As a percent of global corporate bonds and bank loans to nonfinancial corporations)	1.5	2.4	3.8	5.2	7.7	. . .	. . .
Memorandum items:[3]							
Corporate bonds	8,650	9,308	9,563	10,042	11,507	. . .	. . .
Bank loans to nonfinancial corporations	14,528	15,541	14,238	12,745	13,698	. . .	. . .

Sources: British Bankers' Association (BBA); Board of Governors of the Federal Reserve System; U.K. Office of National Statistics; ECB; Bank of Japan; and IMF staff estimates.

[1]Credit derivatives include all forms of derivative products, including portfolio products. Numbers in italics are BBA forecasts made by the BBA in the end-2001 survey.

[2]No forecast was made for 2003.

[3]The following global aggregates are corporate bonds issued by financial and nonfinancial corporations, and bank loans taken by nonfinancial corporations in the United States, United Kingdom, the euro area, and Japan.

and to diversify credit risks. Monoline credit insurers are the largest insurance sector represented in this market, with $166 billion of net credit protection sold via credit derivatives. (Table 3.11). Primary insurance companies (life and nonlife) accounted for $105 billion and reinsurers for $32 billion of net credit protection sold, as of September 2002. The exposure taken on to date is small (relative to their total investments or capital), largely in the form of portfolio products, such as collat-

eralized debt obligations (CDOs), and generally of high credit quality.[11]

However, supervisory authorities must monitor credit derivative activity closely, because reporting of exposures is often not sufficiently disaggregated in financial or regulatory reports. A significant number of supervisors comment that a lack of information impedes their monitoring of these activities, and the current work by the Joint Forum, including its survey on credit risk transfer

[11]See Box 3.1 for a discussion of CDOs and credit quality.

Table 3.11. Global Credit Derivatives Positions by Sector, End-September 2002[1]

(In billions of U.S. dollars; notional value)

	Credit Protection Sold	Credit Protection Bought	Net Credit Protection Bought
Global banks	1,324	1,553	229
Insurance companies (including monoline credit insurers)	344	41	−303
Of which:			
Insurance companies (excluding monoline credit insurers)	152	15	−137
Monoline credit insurers	192	26	−166

Source: FitchRatings.
[1]"Credit protection sold" means that an investor has taken on credit exposure, while "credit protection bought" means that exposure has been reduced (see Box 3.1 for more details).

focusing on the credit derivative markets, is eagerly awaited.[12]

Summary

The capital market structure in the United States has facilitated corporate bond investments, while the systems in continental Europe, the United Kingdom, and Japan have led insurers to rely more on government securities, equities, and loans, respectively. As corporate bond and credit markets continue to develop outside of the United States, the broad shift in credit exposure from banks to insurers is expected to continue. Similarly, today we see relatively more credit specialists and market-oriented risk management systems at U.S. insurers; however, the trend in other markets is clear, and larger European insurers are rapidly improving their credit risk management skills.

Regulatory Framework

Regulations set a framework for insurance companies' balance sheet structures and risk management.[13] There are wide differences between regulatory regimes, with regard to both investment portfolios and insurance products. The style of regulation may also encourage or retard the development of risk management skills. Solvency regimes and regulations concerning the structure of insurance products are two important areas discussed below.

Solvency regimes vary widely between major market centers. Generally, regulators in all of the countries we reviewed intend to set capital requirements based upon overall business risk (including both insurance liabilities and investment assets). However, the existing approach varies from country to country. Approaches in the major jurisdictions generally can be split into two styles. The U.S. and Japanese regulatory systems apply a risk-based capital framework to assets, as well as a component related to insurance risks, as part of the overall solvency requirement, while the U.K. and German systems (like other EU countries) have adopted EU directives for minimum solvency standards. Swiss regulations have evolved independently; however, they have been influenced by their EU neighbors. Currently, the EU directives base the solvency calculation primarily on premiums, claims, and loss reserves, and set asset limits regarding large exposures, rather than applying a relative risk weighting or risk assessment to different asset classes. However, some European countries, such as Denmark, the Netherlands, and (under current proposals) the United Kingdom, go beyond the EU directives, incorporating elements of a risk-based system. Some countries, such as Germany and Japan, and some states in the United States also have specific

---

[12]The Joint Forum is a group of technical experts working under the umbrella of the Basel Committee on Banking Supervision, the International Organization of Securities Commissions, and the International Association of Insurance Supervisors.

[13]IMF (2002b) compared regulatory frameworks for the insurance industry across countries and discussed the additional oversight roles played by others, such as rating agencies and investors. The following section focuses on how regulation affects insurance company investment activities and risk management. The Appendix describes these regulations in greater detail.

Table 3.12. United States and Japan: Comparison of Risk-Based Capital Weightings for Life Insurance Companies[1]

	Capital weightings on assets[2] (in percent)	
	United States	Japan
Equities	22.5 to 45	10
Government bonds	0	0
Corporate bonds[3]	0.4 to 30	1 to 30
Foreign bonds	10	5
Real estate	10	5

Sources: U.S. National Association of Insurance Commissioners; and the Japanese Financial Services Agency.

[1]This table shows credit risk weightings only, and does not include other elements of the risk-based capital calculations, such as price fluctuation risk or business risk.

[2]The weightings are on a pre-tax basis.

[3]For the United States, these weightings also apply to assets synthetically replicated using credit derivatives, and to the potential counterparty credit exposure from derivatives.

limits on certain asset classes (see footnotes 19 and 33).[14]

A risk-based capital regime attributes a range of capital charges to different investment risks. The U.S. and Japanese systems have similar architectures, but assign different risk weightings to asset classes (Table 3.12).

Capital weightings for most assets are higher in the United States than in Japan, making U.S. insurers more sensitive to the relative weightings of different asset classes and thus more strongly reinforcing the incentive for them to hold corporate bonds rather than equities. The U.S. National Association of Insurance Commissioners (NAIC) adopted the risk-based capital approach in 1993, and U.S. insurers we met (even mutuals) indicated that immediately thereafter they began to restructure their portfolios to reduce equity holdings and to increase credit exposure. Japan introduced its

risk-based regime in 1996, amidst significant solvency problems in the insurance sector (described below), and therefore found it more difficult to introduce standards as strict as those in the United States. In addition to the lower capital weightings, there are differences concerning assets that may be included in solvency calculations, for example for deferred tax assets, which also render the Japanese system comparatively less demanding (Fukao, 2002).[15] These factors weaken the discipline provided by the Japanese risk-based capital regime, and the current upturn in financial market conditions provides a good opportunity for regulators to consider strengthening various risk weightings and the calculation method.

The U.S. system uses six different capital weightings for bonds according to their credit risk, and the Japanese system uses three. Credit securities are assigned a classification between one and six by the NAIC, closely following ratings published by the rating agencies, where they exist. Weightings are derived from historical default rates (Table 3.13). The U.S. system differentiates more than Japan according to credit quality, and thereby encourages holdings of single–A and higher credits. In addition, the U.S. system allows reductions in capital as the number of issuers in a portfolio increases, reflecting the benefit of a diversified portfolio.

The current EU solvency regime applies capital charges to investment risks only in limited cases and is expected to be replaced by Solvency II in 2007.[16] The EU intends to implement a Basel II-style three pillar approach, with a risk-sensitive capital criterion in Pillar I. This will bring a beneficial discipline upon companies to develop more

[14]Some U.S. states have limits relating to the credit quality of securities. For instance, New York state limits below-investment grade instruments to 20 percent of total fixed-income investments.

[15]The Japanese system allows deferred tax assets to be included in full in solvency margin calculations, while the U.S. system allows them to be included only up to a maximum of 10 percent of capital and surplus.

[16]Information from the EU Commission about the Solvency II project can be found at *http://europa.eu.int/comm/internal_market/insurance/solvency_en.htm#solvency2*. Annex 3 of Bank for International Settlements (2003) also provides a useful summary.

Table 3.13. **Risk Weights for Credit Instruments in the United States and Japan**[1]

United States			Japan		
NAIC rating	Moody's (S&P) ratings	Weight (percent)	FSA rating	Recognized ratings authorized by FSA	Weight (percent)
1	A (A) and above	0.4			
2	Baa (BBB)	1.3	1	BBB and above	1.0
3	Ba (BB)	4.6			
4	B (B)	10.0			
5	Caa (CCC)	23.0	2	Other	4.0
6	Ca (CC) and lower	30.0	3	In or near default	30.0

Sources: U.S. National Association of Insurance Commissioners; and the Japanese Financial Services Agency.
[1]The weighting are on a pre-tax basis.

sophisticated asset-liability management and risk management systems.[17] As noted above, the current EU solvency requirements for insurers are relatively unsophisticated. Likewise, the EU regulation of investment activity is also less developed and generally includes investments as assets in the solvency margin in full up to a given threshold for exposures to an individual issuer.[18] Member states are free to impose stricter investment restrictions, and some states have done so with regard to equity and derivative holdings.[19] The EU approach allows a substantial proportion of assets to be held in equities (since zero capital charge is applied up to a stated threshold or limit) and reflects an historical preference for holding equities to match longer-duration liabilities. This approach, whereby capital is not directly linked to investment risks, fails to encourage the development of risk management systems or address changes in the business environment. Solvency II would replace the existing frame-

work with a risk-based capital approach, and the United Kingdom is acting more immediately to introduce a risk-based system through its CP 195 initiative (Box 3.2).

Regulations and market practice influence life insurance products. The structure of life products in turn significantly influences insurers' investment strategy, with the effects varying from country to country. Life insurance products include both protection (death benefits) and savings features (like annuities). Returns to policyholders can be either fixed-rate, variable-rate (e.g., "with-profits" policies), or unit-linked (with returns determined by investment performance). Some products provide a guaranteed minimum return, and in several markets these guarantees have contributed to the recent financial stress of life insurance companies.

In Europe, guaranteed minimum returns arise partly from regulation and partly from competition and have recently been a source of stress. In Germany, for instance, regulations

[17]An overly prescriptive regulatory framework tends to retard these skills. This was previously seen in the U.S. savings and loan industry where, before deregulation, managers pursued a "3-6-3" risk management approach: "borrow at 3 percent, lend at 6 percent, and be on the golf course at 3 p.m." After deregulation, many thrift managers were ill-equipped to manage different or changing risk positions.

[18]EU directives require that holdings of securities by a single issuer should not be greater than 5 percent of the gross technical provisions (i.e., the net present value of future liabilities before reinsurance recoveries).

[19]German regulations, for instance, set limits for the amounts of equities and derivatives in the portfolio. The limit for equities (measured in book value terms) was 25 percent of total assets covering technical provisions until 1992; 30 percent from 1992 to 2002; and has now been raised to 35 percent. The limits for derivatives are as follows: for interest rate and currency swaps designed to increase yield, 7.5 percent of total assets; for derivatives to meet short-term cash flow needs, 7.5 percent of total assets for contracts of up to a year in length and 5 percent for contracts beyond one year; and for structured products such as asset-backed securities (ABSs) and CDOs, 7.5 percent and 5 percent of assets covering technical provisions, for investment-grade and other instruments, respectively.

effectively set guaranteed minimum returns, with competition often forcing guarantees above the regulatory minimum.[20] Moreover, in Germany guaranteed returns are supplemented by a regulation designed to return "excessive premiums" to policyholders, which in essence requires 90 percent of profits to be repaid to policyholders each year. In the United Kingdom, there are no regulatorily required minimum returns, but many insurers offer various guarantees on life and annuity products. In these two countries, as well as others, many insurers have suffered (and continue to suffer on certain in-force business) negative spreads in recent years between their investment returns and guaranteed rates. In several European countries, a trend of more unit-linked products (i.e., where the return is tied solely to investment performance) is under way (with recent sales of such products particularly large in the Netherlands and the United Kingdom), and should work to strengthen solvency positions. Of course, through such insurance products, the investment risks are being reallocated to policyholders.

Life insurance companies have historically been viewed as long-term savings institutions, but their liabilities have become shorter in duration in recent years. This has occurred in part because of increased competition from providers of other long-term savings products, such as mutual funds, which has led insurers to reduce penalties for early withdrawal and to create greater optionality in life policies, with guaranteed returns and principal protection features. The shorter duration and greater optionality require insurers to undertake more short-term trading and hedging of market risks, or to hold greater capital to address periodic investment underperformance.[21] This shift in balance sheet and risk profile is

particularly relevant to the current debate surrounding financial accounting and reporting standards.

Summary

The risk-based capital regimes in the United States and Japan encourage holdings of investment-grade credit and discourage relatively large equity holdings, while European solvency regulations focus largely on premium volumes and little on asset composition in setting minimum capital standards. Risk-based solvency standards also seem to stimulate greater development of risk management systems, relative to regulatory regimes that rely on premium volumes or apply strict limits on the investment portfolios of insurers. The liability structure, including the effect of guaranteed minimum rates, also strongly affects risk management, as discussed below.

Comparison of Different National Systems in the Recent Market Downturn

Insurers' financial performance and their vulnerability during market downturns have depended heavily on their investment and asset-liability management strategies. This section begins by discussing insurers' asset-liability management objectives. It then briefly examines the evidence on relative volatility of credit and equity investments over different periods. It also reviews how insurers in the United Kingdom, continental Europe, the United States, and Japan (starting at a much earlier date) weathered the recent market downturn; how the relevant historical and current market structure and regulatory framework contributed to the insurance sector's ability to manage risk during this period; and the lessons for policymakers and risk managers.

---

[20]The guaranteed minimum rate of return is effectively set by the technical interest rate for calculation of provisions against future liabilities.

[21]Brys and de Varenne (1995) demonstrate that guaranteed rates of return and bonus features can shorten duration considerably at relatively low interest rates, and that asset allocations may be biased toward equity investments.

Box 3.1. Credit Derivatives

A credit derivative transaction involves one party shedding credit risk (in other words, buying credit protection) and another taking on this risk (i.e., selling credit protection). Credit risk can be transferred in part or in its entirety either by buying credit risk protection to reduce credit risk exposure or by directly selling the credit-risk bearing instrument. Sellers of credit protection take on credit risk in a manner similar to purchasers of corporate bonds, loans, or other credit instruments.

Credit derivatives can be classified into two broad categories, those that transfer the credit risk relating to an individual borrower (single-name products) and those relating to a number of borrowers (portfolio products). Examples of these two categories are single-name credit default swaps (CDSs) and collateralized debt obligations (CDOs), respectively. In a CDS transaction, the protection seller agrees to pay the protection buyer if a reference entity (a company or sovereign) experiences a predefined "credit event," such as a default on a debt obligation. The protection seller receives a premium (typically paid quarterly) from the protection buyer over the lifetime of the transaction.

Typical "cash" CDOs are debt securities issued by a special purpose vehicle (SPV), collateralized by a portfolio of loans or bonds. "Synthetic" CDOs are created using portfolios of CDSs combined with highly rated debt securities (e.g., government bonds) to synthetically replicate credit securities. Investors who purchase CDOs from the SPV are selling credit protection, while the entities packaging the loans or bonds within (or entering into CDSs with) the SPV are protection buyers.

CDOs have often been sold in a number of tranches (senior, mezzanine, and equity), each with a different credit rating (or no credit rating). Tranching is achieved by issuing securities of different seniority in terms of their relative exposure to any credit losses from the underlying collateral. The credit enhancement provided by the tranching of risk, and (in many cases) by a guarantee from a monoline credit insurer, is an important feature of many CDOs, as they enhance the grade of the security for investors buying the more senior tranches.[1]

Insurers were reported to be the second largest group of credit protection sellers (after banks) in the Fitch and British Bankers' Association (BBA) surveys (see FitchRatings, 2003; and BBA, 2002). While life insurers seem to use CDOs to diversify or expand their existing credit exposure, nonlife insurance companies also may use them to acquire credit risk because it is seen as uncorrelated with the risks from their traditional P&C insurance business.

CDOs have been especially popular among insurance companies because they provide credit exposure to a diversified portfolio of credits, rather than to single names, and because CDOs allow insurance companies to fine-tune the credit quality of their investments, often by buying higher-quality tranches. The share of insurers' CDOs rated A or higher is greater than for fixed-income investments in general (see the Figures). Market participants report that insurance companies tend to purchase all tranches of CDOs, but only small amounts of the "equity" or first-loss tranche, which in some cases is retained by the issuer. It should also be noted that the credit ratings associated with CDOs differ from those of traditional fixed-income products because of diversification scoring procedures, and, being a portfolio product, CDOs can have defaults among some underlying obligors yet still make payments to holders of the senior tranches.

---

[1]Monoline credit insurance companies are financial guarantors that provide credit enhancements by guaranteeing securities. See Rule (2001b) for a more detailed discussion of monoline credit insurers.

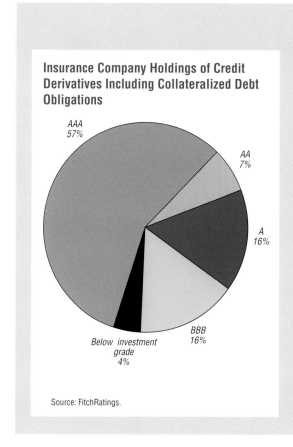

Insurance Company Holdings of Credit Derivatives Including Collateralized Debt Obligations

Source: FitchRatings.

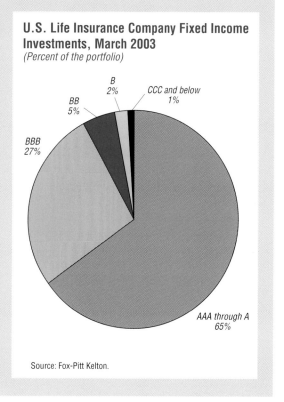

U.S. Life Insurance Company Fixed Income Investments, March 2003
(Percent of the portfolio)

Source: Fox-Pitt Kelton.

Asset-Liability Management and the Relative Risks from Credit and Equity

The liability structure of insurance companies provides further rationale for insurers to prefer credit to equity investments. Insurers manage investment portfolio risks relative to the insurance liabilities they underwrite. Key drivers of an insurer's asset strategy are the related duration, convexity, and cash flow profile of its liabilities and the need to ensure that it holds sufficient assets of appropriate term and liquidity to enable it to meet liabilities as they become due.[22] The International Association of Insurance Supervisors (IAIS) notes that an insurer's asset-liability analysis would need to include testing the resilience of the asset portfolio to a range of market scenarios and investment conditions, including examining the resulting impact on the insurer's solvency position (IAIS, 1999).

Investments need to be managed against both savings and insurance (or protection) products by life insurers, many of which pay a fixed nominal sum and, in the case of savings products, with fixed future payment dates. Other products, with variable-rate or bonus features, allow part of the risk from investments to be passed to policyholders. However, in practice insurers' flexibility is limited (competitively or regulatorily), especially where guaranteed minimum returns or similar payment features exist. Thus, a large proportion of the liabilities in life insurers' general

---

[22]Swiss Re (2000) discusses asset-liability management, including its growth in importance during the 1970s, as high and rising inflation led to an increase in the volatility of interest rates.

Box 3.2. EU Solvency II and the United Kingdom's CP 195 Initiative

EU Solvency II

The Solvency II project will further develop the capital adequacy framework for EU insurers. It aims to implement a three-pillar approach: standardized capital requirements, supervisory requirements, and risk-oriented public disclosure. It is thus a similar framework to the Basel II approach for banks. There is a great deal of agreement between member states over Pillars II and III of Solvency II, and work can now begin on drafting the framework directive. Adoption of the directive is expected by 2007.

The detailed technical work will concentrate initially on Pillar I risk-based issues of setting appropriate levels for target capital and technical reserves. The Commission has stated its aim for a higher degree of harmonization, which would reduce member states' need to set their own additional requirements. If so, it would contrast with the national flexibility shown under the existing directives and continuing under Basel II.

U.K. CP 195 Proposal

The United Kingdom is actively participating in Solvency II discussions, but it has proposed its own risk-oriented prudential approach, which anticipates or even goes beyond much of Solvency II's expected approach. The proposed U.K. system (described in a consultation paper—CP 195), which may be implemented in 2004, will introduce closer links between investment risks and the requirements for capital and reserves, especially for "with-profits" business. The required capital buffer will reflect market, credit, and persistency risks, while reserves will include an element to cover reinvestment risk. It includes stress tests designed to better reflect changing market conditions, which are described in the Table.

Market participants anticipate that CP 195 will likely be revised before adoption, with the general thrust of risk-based capital approach retained. As a result of the proposed regime,

Stress Tests Proposed Under CP 195

Risk	Proposed Stress
Equity	10 percent fall in U.K. equities or higher, contingent on index movements.
Interest rate	The more onerous of a fall or rise in yield of fixed-interest securities equivalent to a 20 percent shift in long-term gilt yields.
Real estate	10 to 20 percent decline in real estate value, depending on rate and direction of movement of an appropriate real estate index.
Credit risk	**Investment Grade Corporate Bonds** Increase in corporate bond spreads over risk-free rates, up to a maximum spread level of 90–210 basis points, depending on the rating. **Non-investment Grade Bonds** Increase in corporate bond spreads over risk-free rates, up to a maximum spread level of 525–900 basis points, depending on the rating. **Commercial Mortgages and other Nonrated Assets** If no credit rating, a 10 percent charge based on market value of the asset. **Reinsurance Concentration** Rated reinsurer—as for corporate bonds. Unrated reinsurer, 10 percent of recoverable.
Persistency rate	50 percent reduction in termination rates for each year compared with termination rates assumed in realistic liabilities.

many insurers expect with-profits business to be reduced significantly and unit-linked business to increase. Going forward, new with-profits policies are likely to have more back-loaded or terminal bonus features and/or more clearly emphasize the voluntary nature (optionality) of interim payments (a very attractive option held by insurers). Finally, many industry observers also believe that smaller insurers will suffer under the proposed system, which will require more investment in risk systems and, with potentially less product differentiation, greater emphasis on distribution. As such, this may result in some industry consolidation.

accounts are fixed in nominal terms, or have a fixed nominal guarantee.[23]

Fixed-income investments of similar duration can best match insurers' typical liability payment structures. Equities, while offering higher returns over longer periods, have unknown or less predictable future cash flows and greater risk and volatility profiles than fixed-income securities, especially during intermediate periods. As such, equities can be a less reliable cash flow source, and fixed-income instruments tend to be a better match than equities for the majority of insurers' underwriting liabilities. In Canada, for instance, companies often attempt to match assets against the individual products in their insurance business, leading them to hold equities primarily as an investment of surplus funds.[24]

The lower volatility of credit than equity implies that, even apart from the benefits of matching liabilities, an insurance sector with greater exposure to credit than equities may be more stable. As an illustration, historical comparisons for the United States suggest that, while the equity market has had a higher average return than fixed-income assets over long holding periods (e.g., 20 years), they also have a higher volatility over shorter periods. Corporate bonds, in contrast, have historically had a lower average total return than equities, but also much lower volatility.[25] The credit spread on such bonds also provides some cushion against falls in broad market prices. Between 1926 and 2002 the average return on equity shares (as represented by the S&P 500 equity index) was 10.2 percent, and corporate bonds averaged 5.9 percent. The annual standard deviation of returns on corporate bonds over this long period was 8.7 percent, com-

pared to 20.5 percent on the S&P 500 index (Ibbotson Associates, 2003).

This pattern of lower volatility and steadier returns for corporate bonds has been consistent over the years, including recent periods (Table 3.14). The volatility for corporate bonds peaked at 14.1 percent during the high inflation period of the 1980s, and has since declined to approximately half that level. By contrast, average volatility is much higher for equities than for corporate bonds, and the low point of 13.1 percent in the 1960s is only a little below the highest level of volatility for corporate bonds. Over a more recent period, 1993–2002, corporate bond returns were again much less volatile than stock returns (7.3 percent compared with 17.1 percent), and the average annual return for corporate bonds, at 8.8 percent, was only slightly below the 9.3 percent return for equities.

Recent Events in Continental Europe and the United Kingdom

Many European insurance companies increased their equity holdings during the 1990s, in the face of declining interest rates and high guarantees on in-force policies. Historically, fixed-income securities have always had a significant role in insurers' portfolios, because they fit relatively well with their liability profile. During the 1990s, disinflation and deregulation led many insurers in Europe to seek a higher return than their government bond holdings could provide, and the booming equity market, together with the limited size of the corporate bond market in many jurisdictions, led insurers to increase equity allocations. The bursting of the equity bubble, together with the growing depth and sophisti-

---

[23]Unit-linked products held in separate accounts pass the risk to policyholders, so the investments chosen to back these products have no direct balance-sheet risks for the insurer, and in many cases the investments or risk profile are selected by the policyholder.

[24]The Canadian Superintendent of Financial Institutions states that this matching approach is reinforced by the Canadian Asset Liability Method actuarial and accounting standard (Le Pan, 2003).

[25]Similar comparisons of returns and volatility in Europe and Japan over long periods are not available, as the corporate bond markets in these regions have historically been smaller and much less liquid.

Table 3.14. United States: Comparison of Bond and Equity Returns and Volatility
(In percent)

	1960s	1970s	1980s	1990s	2000s[1]	1993–2002
	Total Returns[2]					
S&P 500	7.8	5.9	17.5	18.2	−14.6	9.3
Long-term corporate bonds[3]	1.7	6.2	13.0	8.4	13.3	8.8
Long-term government bonds[4]	1.4	5.5	12.6	8.8	14.1	9.7
Intermediate-term government bonds[5]	3.5	7.0	11.9	7.2	11.0	7.3
	Volatility of Total Returns[6]					
S&P 500	13.1	17.1	19.4	15.8	16.7	17.1
Long-term corporate bonds[3]	4.9	8.7	14.1	6.9	7.5	7.3
Long-term government bonds[4]	6.0	8.7	16.0	8.9	9.9	9.3
Intermediate-term government bonds[5]	3.3	5.2	8.8	4.6	5.1	4.7

Source: Ibbotson Associates.
[1]For the period 2000–2002.
[2]Returns are calculated as compound annual rates.
[3]Salomon Brothers Long-Term, High-Grade corporate bond total return index.
[4]Twenty-year U.S. treasury bond.
[5]Five-year U.S. treasury note.
[6]Volatility is calculated as annualized monthly standard deviation.

cation of certain credit markets, has since led many insurers to reallocate holdings from equity to credit. However, there is still scope for this reallocation to go further.

European life insurers increased equity investments throughout the 1990s in part to meet guaranteed returns to policyholders,[26] particularly in Germany (but also in the United Kingdom and Switzerland).[27] Many insurers had offered high guaranteed rates on life insurance products since the 1980s. The adoption of EU directives and the easing of regulations on product terms in the early 1990s allowed insurers to compete more directly through the return offered on products. In Germany, for instance, after regulations were relaxed in 1994, increased competition led to much higher guaranteed returns. Premiums for annuities and pensions (which offered guaranteed rates) rose dramatically as a share of total premiums written by German life insurers, from around 4 percent during the 1970s and 1980s, to above 20 per-

cent by the late 1990s (Statistical Yearbook of German Insurance, 2003).

The stock market decline from 2000 onwards reduced the solvency margins of insurers with large equity exposures, triggering a solvency crisis and significant selling of equities. The FTSE index declined 50 percent from its January 2000 peak to the March 2003 trough, and the DAX fell more than 70 percent from its peak to trough.

Market commentary during this period included discussion of thresholds for the FTSE, DAX, and Swiss stock market that would trigger further forced selling by insurers. The rate of price declines often accelerated as markets approached these thresholds, at times threatening to lead to disorderly market conditions. The episode highlighted to market participants, regulators, and many insurers themselves the need to improve risk management capabilities and the need to rethink the desirable level of equity holdings. In addition, it highlighted the possible dan-

---

[26]Rule (2001b) makes a similar point that the need to pay guaranteed minimum nominal returns that were in excess of current nominal returns on government bonds was leading some insurers to take more risk.

[27]For example, in Germany, the share of equities rose to 30 percent of investment assets at the peak of the stock market in 2000, from 21 percent in 1997, as the regulatory ceiling was raised (as described earlier). Most of this increase was at the expense of their fixed-income (primarily government bond) holdings, which fell to 49 percent from 58 percent during this period. The regulatory ceiling on equities was also relaxed in Switzerland.

gers of amplified price falls caused by forced selling to protect regulatory capital ratios in the short term, but more fundamentally resulting from their existing investment strategies and risk management systems (across the entire balance sheet).

Discussions with many market participants suggested that pressure to sell equities came in part from the rating agencies, as well as from insurance companies' own internal risk models. Interestingly, in several cases, insurers indicated that the risk models were indicating a need to sell equities in earlier periods, but this analysis was not often followed by management. This probably reflects the relatively recent adoption and use of such models, and the need for greater management understanding of the risk management process. During this period, the high market volatility could have produced financial instability and, at certain points, a few insurers found themselves effectively unable to access the markets to raise additional solvency capital.

Regulatory authorities in some jurisdictions acted to reduce these market pressures and to ease the impact of declining equity prices on solvency margins. The German regulators responded in early 2002 by amending the regulations governing the valuation of equities and other assets, while leaving in place the solvency requirements. Insurers were allowed to value equities at an "estimated ultimate realizable value," above current market prices, based on an analogy to the treatment of long-term assets held in a "banking book" rather than a "trading book." This action eased stability pressures, but many observers noted that it also reduced the transparency of reported solvency margins.[28] The U.K. authorities took perhaps bolder and more transparent action in relieving the pressure on insurers. U.K. life

insurers must be able to pass solvency margin tests, including a stress test called "the resilience test" and, during this critical period, the resilience tests were softened or removed by the U.K. Financial Services Authority (FSA). To prevent this temporary forbearance from masking situations where an insurer was in need of greater supervisory action, the FSA also assessed companies on a case-by-case basis, proactively reviewed insurers' risk management systems and required specific actions of a number of individual companies. More recently, the FSA has introduced CP 195, which lays the groundwork for a risk-based capital regime, taking account more fully of credit and market risks in solvency requirements (see Box 3.2). It has also increased resources for insurance supervision, including a greater diversity of financial skills, such as banking experts.

Many large insurers in Europe have expressed an intention to expand credit holdings and have begun to upgrade risk management capabilities, including the employment of new people with greater risk management experience. In the past two years, a number of insurers have hired more experienced risk management professionals (often from the banking sector) and adopted more sophisticated risk management practices (e.g., banking models, including value-at-risk and economic capital measures). The decision to reduce equity holdings reflected, in part, significant pressure from the rating agencies as early as in 2001. By mid-2003, the equity holdings of most of the largest European insurance companies had declined considerably, from a high of above 25 percent to below 15 percent of total assets. While lower share prices contributed, portfolio sales were an important factor as well, which reduced insur-

[28]The German authorities also established in late 2002 an "insurance" scheme for policyholders, called Protektor, which could assume the portfolios of any failed life insurance company, and act to preserve market confidence. Life insurance companies were to contribute equity stakes in proportion to their liabilities, and further funds, if required, up to one percent of their investments. Protektor has assets of €5 billion, and it has taken over the portfolio of failed insurer Mannheimer Leben and is administering the portfolio as it runs off.

ers' risk profile but also crystallized the losses, limiting insurers' gains from the equity market rebound during the past year.

United States

The U.S. insurance sector has long had a strong credit culture, in contrast to European insurers. Many major U.S. insurers have a team of in-house credit analysts. As in Europe, the competition for business drives U.S. insurers to offer products with features attractive to savers, including guaranteed returns. However, the risk-based capital regime reinforces the portfolio allocations into less volatile assets, with significant capital requirements for equities (see Table 3.12).

U.S. insurers earned returns above those required by policy guarantees without taking large positions in equities. The recent low interest rate environment has resulted in some spread compression for U.S. insurers, as the average spread over fixed-annuity products decreased about 25 basis points to 175 basis points from a historical average of about 200 basis points (Moody's Investors Service, 2003). Still, insurers' ability to maintain a positive spread over liabilities allowed them to avoid the need to reach for higher returns. As a result, their balance sheets remained largely composed of corporate credit and other fixed-income risk, with a smaller exposure to equities than their European counterparts.

Comparison of European and U.S. Experience

The U.S. insurers weathered the deterioration in financial markets from 2000 to 2003 without experiencing solvency problems similar to European insurers. The more robust performance of U.S. insurers is reflected in the relative share price performance (Figure 3.3). In the United States, losses on equity positions have been small relative to insurance companies' solvency levels. While credit losses impaired insurers' current income, such losses were at a much lower level than losses on

Figure 3.3. International Insurance Sector Equity Indices
(January 3, 2000 = 100)

Sources: Bloomberg L.P., and Datastream.
[1]S&P 500 life and health insurance index.
[2]FTSE 350 life assurance index.
[3]Dow Jones STOXX excluding the U.K. insurance index.

equity holdings would have been, particularly since many U.S. insurers have a diverse and on average highly rated portfolio. For example, despite the highest corporate bond default rate in a decade, credit losses for life insurers rose to only 75 basis points of invested assets in 2002 (Moody's Investors Service, 2003). Even if further credit losses are yet to be recognized, the magnitude of the losses will not be nearly as damaging as the 25 percent or higher losses suffered in many European insurers' equity portfolios.

Finally, with solvency margins largely intact, U.S. life insurance companies continued to invest in market assets, including equities, even during the market downturn. Net purchases of equities slowed slightly from an average of $90 billion between 1997 and 1999 to $74 billion per year in the period since 2000. In no quarter, though, were there aggregate net sales. Net purchases of credit market instruments by U.S. insurers doubled in the same period, from an average of $78 billion to $157 billion. Purchases of corporate bonds and agency securities have been particularly strong in recent years.

Credit investments offer European insurers the opportunity to earn a positive spread without the exposure to potential large capital losses posed by equity investments. As discussed below, this is particularly important to those insurers that continue to suffer from high guaranteed returns and other product features on in-force business, which prevent a more regular building up of solvency capital during stable market periods. Of course, it will be important for insurance companies to implement adequate credit risk management skills and systems, especially for institutions

that have not had significant exposure to credit instruments in the past.[29]

Synthetic credit products may allow European and Japanese insurers with smaller domestic or regional corporate bond markets to achieve increased credit exposure.[30] Furthermore, it may be easier to make a meaningful investment or obtain a specifically tailored credit exposure through derivatives than through the cash market. A portfolio of CDO and credit default swap (CDS) investments may also improve geographic, maturity, sector, and ratings diversification (see Box 3.1).[31] As with increased credit risks generally, insurers need to improve risk management skills prior to increasing credit derivative activity.

Japan

The Japanese insurance sector was significantly affected by the market downturn of the early 1990s. Although the particulars of the Japanese insurance sector differ from those in Europe and the United States, some of the same fundamental forces were at work, especially the regulatory framework and national market structure. According to both official and private sector observers in Japan, deregulation combined with insurers' reach for higher returns through greater equity holdings in the 1980s (factors similar to those in Europe) weakened the Japanese insurance industry during the equity market downturn and posed a potential threat to financial stability.

In a similar manner to Europe, deregulation led insurers to shift into equities. In 1980, life insurers had 60 percent of their assets

[29]CGFS (2003) also makes these points, and indicates that it agrees with similar recommendations by the IAIS Working Group. It should, of course, be kept in mind that the degree of credit experience varies between companies and between countries, including credit products other than bonds. In the Netherlands, for instance, life insurers hold one-third of their assets in commercial and mortgage loans.

[30]Standard and Poor's (2003a) provides an overview of the synthetic credit markets by region and reviews how synthetic, structured credit products are created. See also Rule (2001a) and Appendix 2 of FitchRatings (2004) for more on synthetic credit products.

[31]The European CDO market has grown very rapidly, particularly in Germany. See Rule (2001b).

Table 3.15. Japanese Life Insurers' Investment in Equity and Loans
(In percent of total assets, selected years)

	FY1980	FY1989	FY1995	FY1999	FY2002
Equity at book value	17.2	21.8	19.0	15.0	11.5
Equity at market value	. . .	34.7	16.1	16.4	8.8
Loans	59.7	35.4	37.7	29.5	25.1

Source: Bank of Japan, *Financial and Economic Statistics* and *Flow of Funds.*

invested in loans (Table 3.15). However, financial deregulation during the 1980s allowed most commercial banks to compete in the long-term loan market, which significantly compressed credit spreads. To increase returns during the rising stock market of the late 1980s, insurers increased their holdings of equities.

Regulation and industry structure also encouraged generous bonus features in life insurance products. Regulations on insurance products discouraged Japanese life insurers from competing directly on the basis of the premium offered.[32] Meanwhile, mutual insurers, which form a significant part of the Japanese industry, competed not only through guaranteed rates of return but also on bonus payments to policyholders as a way of returning earnings to their stakeholders. Because bonuses can be paid only out of excess profits, insurers increasingly mismatched positions, mainly by holding equities, expecting to build excess gains over time.

Throughout the 1980s, virtually no countervailing forces existed to check insurers' high investment in equities. Similar to Europe, solvency regulations in Japan focused on the appropriateness of reserves against insurance obligations (measured by volume of premiums), but not on the quality or diversity of assets. Insurance regulators relied on prescrip-

tive rules, such as investment limits. Accounting rules exempted mutual companies from financial disclosures, and regulatory financial reporting was based on book values. Likewise, ratings agencies had little influence over mutual or other Japanese insurers at that time.

The severe and prolonged downturn in the Japanese equity market, however, exposed insurers to significant solvency pressure. Life insurers' equity positions (at market value) fell from 35 percent to 9 percent of total assets between 1989 and 2002, primarily due to price declines rather than asset sales.[33] Unlike European insurers, Japanese insurers did not sell equities into the falling market (many insurers were reluctant to sell shares of client companies), but the accumulated valuation losses significantly eroded their solvency margins. Older policies with high guaranteed rates of return, meanwhile, led to negative spreads in the low interest rate environment, further sapping financial strength. Life insurers now pay average guaranteed rates of approximately 3 to 4 percent, while their investments currently generate average returns of 1.5 to 2 percent.

In an effort to increase profitability and support solvency margins, many Japanese insurers took more market risks, including greater duration risks. As a result, many Japanese insurers reduced long-term domestic loans and invested in medium-term foreign sovereign bonds to benefit from steeper foreign yield curves. Between 1995 and 2002, life insurers increased foreign securities from 5.5 percent to 14.5 percent of total assets (see Table 3.9), which diversified holdings, but the foreign exchange risk is believed to be only partially hedged. In addition, many insurers have more than doubled their sol-

[32]The level of the required mortality reserves is calculated by using a conservative mortality table provided by the regulator. If life insurers wished to use more realistic mortality assumptions to set more competitive premiums, they were required to place additional reserves for the difference at a sharply higher rate.
[33]Japanese regulations place a limit of 30 percent on the amount of equity in the portfolio, but this is measured at book value.

vency margins by issuing surplus notes (a form of hybrid capital) and other subordinated debt, almost exclusively to Japanese banks. While this form of capital raising is used in other markets, regulatory and rating agency pressure elsewhere often limit such hybrid capital to 15–25 percent of an insurer's capital base.

The weakened financial strength of the insurance industry became a threat to financial stability in Japan. Confidence in the reliability of solvency margins was shaken between 1997 and 2001, when seven life and two nonlife insurers, all small- and medium-sized firms, failed due to funding crises stemming from significant policy cancellations, even though their reported solvency margins were several times the regulatory minimum. These failures contributed to liquidity strains faced by Japanese banks with sizable exposure to the insurers. The close relationship between banks and insurers in Japan underscores the need for stronger supervisory standards to avoid contagion between financial sectors.[34]

Improved risk management at some insurance companies has eased stability concerns within the Japanese insurance sector. Some of the more sophisticated insurers have reacted to these structural and regulatory changes by selectively increasing their investment in credit instruments. These insurers increased their investments in domestic corporate and municipal bonds, as well as foreign corporate bonds, in some cases exceeding 50 percent of total assets. Such companies are typically demutualized insurers, and some are foreign-owned. Importantly, they also aggressively reduced their equity holdings and the sale of policies with bonus features, reducing their overall risk profile and creating balance sheets more comparable to U.S. life insurers. Japanese insurance companies are also investing in structured credit, including CDOs, but

they have so far allocated less than 5 percent of total assets to these products, and (like U.S. and European insurers) generally purchase AA or AAA tranches. The increased focus on credit instruments and the reduced risk in product structuring are positive developments in Japan.

Financial Accounting and Rating Agencies

Reporting and disclosure standards, including proposed changes to accounting principles, have an important influence on the investment strategies and risk profile of insurance companies. The current discussion regarding appropriate financial reporting standards for insurers is assessed below, together with the influence rating agencies have on insurance companies, particularly reinsurers and monoline credit insurers.

Financial Accounting

There is currently an active debate in the industry regarding the appropriate accounting framework to reflect the business reality of insurance activities. This section outlines the historical view of insurance accounting, the "fair value" principles being proposed, and the desire to converge financial and regulatory accounting principles.

Historically, insurance companies' financial accounting reflected their longer-term focus on returns. This allowed market fluctuations in asset values to go unreported in earnings, with the intention of smoothing them over longer periods. Meanwhile, the long-term nature of liabilities (particularly for life insurers), and the difficulty in calculating reliable market values of these liabilities, argued for risks to be measured on an actuarial basis rather than at market prices, and for changes in valuation not to be recorded in profit and loss accounts.

---

[34]In 2001, the Japanese FSA improved the robustness of its regulations by revising the risk-based regime to be based more closely on market values for assets.

There is no existing international accounting standard for insurance liabilities. Historically, many national systems used "deferral and matching" accounting principles, which is an approach based on book values. This was seen as appropriate for an industry with a long-term focus. More recently, "embedded value" accounting has become increasingly used in some mature market jurisdictions, under which insurance liabilities are valued as the present value of cash flows on existing insurance contracts. "Market-consistent embedded value" goes one step further, by including in the calculation the estimated market value of the embedded options in insurance contracts.

The relatively stable results reported under historic accounting methods may mask the underlying volatility of insurers' balance sheets. For instance, valuing assets and liabilities using book values and estimated long-term rates of return can obscure underperformance for extended periods, and can mislead policyholders, investors, counterparties, regulators and even insurance firms themselves about the true risks in their balance sheets. Such accounting methods may also have led insurers to underestimate the market risks of certain investments (such as equities), or to underprice certain insurance products (especially if embedded options are not valued). With the greater recognition of the optionality of insurance products and recent asset market volatility, the justification for such longer-term horizons for accounting has been challenged.

The International Accounting Standards Board is developing a more comprehensive proposal for "fair value" accounting, aiming to incorporate more market-based valuations for both assets and liabilities. The aim is to provide observers with a clearer view of insurers'

risk profiles. The proposals for the asset side of the balance sheet seem relatively well defined, and would be similar to International Accounting Standard (IAS) 39, but the process of developing standards for liabilities is likely to be more protracted.[35]

Insurance liabilities can be some of the most complex financial instruments to value. A fair value approach to liabilities is controversial within the insurance industry because of difficulties and potential inconsistencies of applying such an approach to insurers' liabilities (e.g., embedded options related to guarantees, bonuses—periodic and terminal—and policyholder cancellation options). At present, it is contemplated that a new fair value standard for assets could be implemented as early as 2005, well before principles are developed for liabilities (not before 2007, and possibly delayed even longer). This carries the further risk of an extended period of accounting asset-liability mismatch.[36]

Insurers have a number of concerns about fair value accounting:

• Insurers are concerned that fair value accounting would lead to significantly greater volatility in reported profits. The trade associations for the U.S., German, and Japanese life insurance industries, among others, argue that the deferral and matching system is better suited to capture the interdependence of assets and liabilities over the longer periods of an insurance contract.

• Insurers believe that fair value accounting would increase their cost of capital. Assuming an increase in earnings volatility, many insurers believe (possibly correctly) that investors will require greater returns. The rating agencies, however, have indicated that such accounting or reporting changes would have no impact on pub-

---

[35]IAS 39 distinguishes between assets "held for trading" or "available for sale," which are marked to market, and those intended to be passive investments to maturity (and thus held at book or amortized value).

[36]The EU Parliament passed a resolution in 2002 requiring listed companies to use IAS for published accounts from 2005 onwards.

lished ratings, given that these ratings already reflect the risk in an insurance company's balance sheet. Of course, the greater focus on risk may benefit those insurance companies whose investments are well diversified and whose risks are well managed.

- Insurance industry concerns are exacerbated by the possible implementation of fair value principles for assets at least two years before liabilities. This could result in even greater volatility in earnings for that period, since assets will be marked to market but liabilities will continue to be reported on an accruals basis.

If fair value accounting principles (and risk-based capital standards) are adopted, insurers are likely to reduce the risk profile of their investments and products. In light of the losses incurred from equities from 2000 to early 2003, many insurers have already begun to reallocate their investment portfolios into credit instruments. The insurers we met indicated that adoption of fair value accounting principles will only serve to reinforce this trend. Some insurers also indicated that, while they have previously sought longer-duration assets, such reporting measures may lead them to hold more shorter-dated assets and to increase trading activity in the investment portfolio. Insurers are also likely to structure policies with bonus payments at later dates (i.e., back-loaded), and to pursue more unit-linked business, which essentially moves the investment risk and volatility from the insurer's earnings to the policyholder's return.

From a regulatory perspective, it would be desirable to have the regulatory and financial accounting standards as similar as possible. In that sense, regulatory accounts and measures of solvency in some mature market countries already use a degree of market valuation when calculating insurers' solvency positions. Moreover, most institutional investors, as well as research analysts, pay particular attention to the regulatory solvency of insurers, including the quality of the solvency calculations. As

such, there is a natural desire to move the regulatory and financial reporting standards closer together. In some jurisdictions (e.g., the EU's Solvency II initiative and adoption of IAS), this is the direction in which regulators are moving, including the use of insurers' own risk-based models to help set solvency requirements. However, the crux of the debate may lie in the degree to which fair value measures reflect the "business reality" of insurers, and whether such measures are equally appropriate when evaluating the solvency standards and the periodic earnings of insurers.

In any case, a focus on a wider range of financial disclosure by insurers, including fair value measures, may be more useful than overreliance on a "single-point estimate" of earnings. Any accounting measure for insurers is dependent on many assumptions, especially on the liability side of the balance sheet. Application of fair value accounting standards would increase these complexities. As such, it may be most useful to employ fair value measures as part of a wider range of financial reporting or disclosure information, rather than seeking a precise single-point measure of earnings. As noted earlier, investors, analysts, and other market participants currently seek market-based measures of insurers' solvency positions, and supplementary information incorporating fair value principles could only serve to improve observers' understanding of insurers' risk profile. To the extent the historic notion of insurers as long-term institutions is no longer accurate, fair value accounting principles may more correctly reflect the risk profile of insurance activities.

In recent years, some insurance companies have published detailed supplementary financial statements to complement their main accounts. These statements often illustrate the way insurers themselves think about risks, include fair value estimates for some balance sheet items, and are helpful for all stakeholders in understanding insurance risks. Interestingly, the insurers that provide additional disclosure regarding risk positions and risk management strategies more generally view such disclosure as providing a competitive advantage relative to industry peers that report only standard accounting information.

Rating Agencies

Rating agencies can be a more important influence on insurers than they are on many other types of business.[37] Rating agencies facilitate the analysis and dissemination of information on an insurer's financial condition and, in that sense, their role is little different than for any industry. However, insurers (like many other financial institutions) are more frequent users of institutional markets, where credit standing (including ratings) is of particular importance to counterparties. For example, changes in an insurer's credit rating may raise the cost of capital if policyholders, investors, or counterparties question an insurance company's financial strength. In considering the different insurance sectors, ratings may matter least to life insurers selling directly to individuals in the retail market, rather more to sellers of group life and health insurance and to P&C insurers operating in corporate or commercial markets, and take on the most significance to reinsurers and monoline credit insurers, for whom credit quality is often critical to their core business activities.

In the short term, the influence of rating agencies on insurance companies can accentuate selling pressure during market downturns. Rating agencies have the greatest impact during market downswings, when questions arise concerning firms' financial strength and capital adequacy. For example, the threat of downgrades during 2002 and early 2003 appears to have contributed to the significant selling of equities by some European insurers. This selling would very likely have been larger, but for the steps taken by a few regulators, such as the U.K. FSA and

BaFin in Germany. But these insurers would have benefited far more from a more active supervisory dialogue at an earlier stage regarding the potential volatility of their solvency position during a prolonged market downturn.

In situations where there are perceived gaps or weaknesses in supervision, rating agencies have been seen by some market participants as a *de facto* regulator. In recent years, rating agencies have independently applied pressure on certain insurers to take steps to bolster their financial soundness. This is particularly true of insurers participating in the wholesale markets, such as reinsurers, for whom regulation may be lighter. In addition, pressure from rating agencies in recent years has led many primary insurers (life and P&C companies) and reinsurers to improve capital standards (in terms of the amount and quality of capital), beyond that required by existing regulations. Such actions are not inappropriate, and even under Basel II most bank regulators assume banks will hold capital above that required by the new standard, based on a variety of market forces, including desired ratings.

Nevertheless, rating agencies have been criticized by some market participants for the quality of their analysis and a perceived overdependence on quantitative models. Particularly in Europe, some market participants have been critical of the influence rating agencies can have on insurers through their published ratings relative to the quality of their analysis and, in the case of one agency, the possible overreliance on very quantitative models. Finally, the quality of analysis remains inconsistent, and many insurers spoke of frequent analyst turnover at certain agencies and of the impact turnover has on the agencies' understanding of the particular business at the insurers they rate. Some of these criticisms are not new, and the major

[37]See Swiss Re (2003) for a detailed discussion of the methodology of the major rating agencies, as well as the relationship between ratings and the insurance firm's cost of funds and ability to attract business.

rating agencies have increased staff in Europe and Japan, and have improved their analysis to address regional and national differences.

Credit ratings are particularly important for the core business activities of reinsurers and monoline credit insurers. In these insurance subsectors, retaining a strong investment-grade rating is very important due to the institutional nature of their business and counterparties, particularly other financial institutions. Moreover, for monoline credit insurers, the very purpose of underwriting bond insurance is to provide credit enhancement, thus they must maintain the highest credit standards. As such, rating agencies strongly influence all aspects of a monoline insurer's activities, including its investment portfolio. The influence of rating agencies, and other market forces, on these insurance sectors most often produces solvency and other requirements above regulatory standards.

Any perceived overreliance on rating agencies to set disclosure, capital, and other standards should be addressed with improved supervision, not reduced scrutiny by rating agencies. Greater transparency of the business activities and financial positions of reinsurance companies, including in offshore centers, is being considered by official bodies, while some regulators (such as the European Union) are considering enhanced supervision, and we encourage these efforts.

Policy Conclusions

Greater portfolio allocation to credit instruments would provide a more predictable return for many life insurers and would strengthen financial stability more generally, but only if risk management and regulatory oversight are improved at the same time. Corporate bonds are a less volatile investment than equities and tend to be a better match for insurers' liabilities. Credit derivatives may play a useful role in the risk management process, particularly in areas where the market

for corporate credit is less developed. We are encouraged by the risk management programs being developed by many large insurers. Nevertheless, as the reallocation to credit instruments proceeds, it needs to be accompanied by a further upgrading of the risk management process.

The reallocation of credit risk to insurers that has already taken place, improvements in risk management, and the recovery in equity markets have reduced vulnerabilities and enhanced financial stability. Since we last reviewed the condition of the insurance sector in prior GFSRs, a number of things have changed (see IMF, 2002b; and IMF, 2003). Most notably, stronger capital markets have improved the financial condition of most insurers, and many insurance companies have raised new capital since 2002. Likewise, driven largely by the experience of 2000–03, as discussed above, many insurers have adjusted their asset portfolios and improved their risk management capabilities. As such, the insurance industry is clearly in better financial condition today. Nevertheless, some of our concerns expressed in previous issues of the GFSR remain, and we have outlined below a variety of policy issues that should be addressed in order to strengthen the insurance industry and its contribution to the stability of the broader financial framework.

Regulators should anticipate a growing appetite for credit, and should seek to support and facilitate further development of credit markets. We expect non-U.S. insurance companies to increase their credit exposures, including the use of synthetic portfolio products. In Europe, we encourage policymakers to support developments across the EU regarding mortgage-backed and other asset-backed securities, and the expansion of the Pfandbriefe, Obligations Foncières, and Cedulas markets to other European jurisdictions. Likewise, the "True Sale Initiative" in Germany is welcomed as a means to support small and medium-sized business lending and to provide a credit instrument that insurers should find attractive. In the area of credit derivatives, policy-makers should continue to encourage increased transparency and standardization through market initiatives, especially by the International Swaps and Derivatives Association. This should facilitate broader market participation and a deeper, more liquid market. Supervisors should look to improve regulatory reporting of credit risk (including the disaggregation of credit and risk exposures in order to act as an early warning indicator), and monitor closely the participation by smaller banks and insurers and those located in less developed markets. Such institutions and their participation in these markets are often not reflected in market surveys, and they may be more inclined to reach for higher returns at certain points in the economic cycle (e.g., when credit spreads are tight or local loan demand is weak). Moreover, there is some evidence that smaller institutions hold relatively larger percentages of structured credit and other risk positions compared with larger institutions.

Supervisors should implement risk-based solvency standards, which align prudential requirements more closely with insurance companies' risks and encourage improvements in risk management. We are encouraged by the more market- and risk-sensitive solvency regimes proposed under Solvency II in the European Union and CP 195 in the United Kingdom. We also recommend that Japanese insurance regulators use the opportunity of the current financial market recovery to introduce a stricter risk-based capital regime. A prerequisite to any increase in credit exposure should be a thorough review and upgrading of risk management systems. Among the larger, internationally active insurers, an increased focus on risk management is generally under way, including in the last few years a greater use of more sophisticated models. Consistent with this approach, we would encourage policymakers to consider the removal of rigid regulations related to investment strategies and product pricing (including effective guaranteed

returns). In large part, the recent financial turmoil experienced by some European insurers was due to the inability to build solvency reserves in good times because of guaranteed or otherwise regulatorily required returns to policyholders.

Supervisory resources should be enhanced in many mature market jurisdictions, with further investments in people, systems, and training required. In general, policymakers should seek to increase regulatory resources, with further investments in people, systems, and training, so as to better enable supervisors to evaluate and monitor the risk management models that increasingly will be required of insurers. Policymakers should also look to encourage and facilitate increased dialogue among mature market supervisors (and among insurance risk managers). Market participants frequently noted that, relative to the banking sector, risk managers and supervisors speak less often with their peers on a formal or informal basis. However, in the past six to 12 months an effort is under way by insurers to have a broader industry dialogue and consideration of best practices, and we welcome efforts by the IAIS, the Financial Stability Forum, and the Joint Forum in this area.

Policymakers and standard setters should ensure that the financial and regulatory accounts provide an accurate reflection of an insurance company's financial position, and they should seek to converge, wherever possible, financial and regulatory accounting standards. It would be desirable to have financial and regulatory accounting move closer together. The current financial accounting debate strives to improve the disclosure of balance sheet risks within the insurance sector, while providing an accurate and fair reflection of the business reality of insurance activities. This is a difficult balance, as the optionality embedded in many life insurance products has not been fully reflected in insurers' reports to date, and most insurers seek to manage these risks only over longer periods. In part, the accounting debate reflects the fact that the traditional view of life insurers as long-term, savings-oriented institutions may be less true today.

We encourage the participants in this accounting debate to consider enhanced disclosure standards, rather than placing undue emphasis on a single-point accounting measure. The resistance to fair value accounting proposals by some insurers and national bodies is clear, given that such measures will likely increase the volatility of insurers' financial reports. However, sophisticated investors seek to understand and monitor the solvency and other financial positions of financial institutions, including insurers, and so we would encourage standard setters to consider employing such fair value or market value principles as part of enhanced financial disclosures (e.g., as supplemental disclosures and measures, and possibly sensitivities), which should improve reporting standards and broader market understanding of insurance risks.

Rating agencies are a significant influence on reinsurance companies and monoline credit insurers, but should not be relied upon as a substitute for appropriate supervision. The influence of rating agencies in these insurance sectors reflects the essentially institutional markets in which they operate and in some cases (e.g., reinsurers) the comparatively light regulation of these insurers. However, rating agencies should not be relied upon as the primary monitor of these systemically important markets. To reduce the disproportionate reliance on rating agencies, greater supervisory oversight and transparency of the business activities of reinsurance companies in particular would seem appropriate.

Policymakers should be aware that improvements in risk management and reporting, while desirable, may have other market ramifications. Through many of the market-based measures policymakers and standard setters are now pursuing, the perceived long-term nature of the insurance business will come under increased scrutiny. As such, the insurance industry's abil-

ity to act as a shock absorber for the financial system could be reduced. We anticipate that many insurers will take steps to reduce the risk profile of both insurance products and investment portfolios. This may lead to further consolidation in mature markets, particularly as smaller insurers are likely to lack the analytical resources, distribution networks, or access to capital necessary to compete. In general, such developments may be welcomed. However, as insurance companies move to reduce balance sheet risk, some or all of the risk must again go somewhere, and it is likely that such risk will continue to be passed to less sophisticated participants, namely to policyholders and hence the household sector. This will be a topic for future issues of the GFSR, as we continue our review of the implications of risk transfer.

Appendix: Regulatory Capital Regimes

The countries mentioned in this chapter have different systems for imposing minimum regulatory capital requirements.[38] This appendix describes important features of the systems in the United States, United Kingdom, Germany, Switzerland, and Japan.

These countries have many basic features in common. They have a method of calculating the required excess of assets over liabilities (regulatory capital or solvency), and they have methods of valuing assets for the purpose of performing regulatory capital tests. The tests differ in levels of sophistication and risk sensitivity. The description is based on current regimes for life insurers, and Box 3.2 describes ongoing work to enhance these regimes for the United Kingdom, where changes are more immediate and far-reaching, and also for the EU as a whole.

The description of the regime for each country is divided into two parts: first, the calculation of the regulatory capital requirement; second, the valuation of assets.

---

[38]This appendix was prepared by the IMF's Monetary and Financial Systems Department.

United States

U.S. insurance regulation is conducted on a state by state basis. There is, however, a great deal of commonality provided through the superstructure of the National Association of Insurance Commissioners (NAIC). Reporting requirements and prudential rules are substantially the same throughout the United States.

Regulatory Capital Calculation

As mentioned in the chapter, the risk-based capital system identifies specified risk for which calculated amounts of regulatory capital are required. Base figures for specified risk are taken from the publicly available regulatory returns, and are multiplied by specified coefficients to produce the risk capital component. The individual components are combined to give the risk-based capital requirement, against which the value of the company is compared. Coefficients are monitored and updated annually to reflect changes in the risk environment.

BUSINESS RISK

Coefficients address risks in mortality and morbidity rates, and volatilities in the claims rates. In addition, there is an overarching life business risk element, which is a flat rate of life premiums.

ASSET RISK

The risk-based capital requirements are based on risk factors relating to the types of asset. Asset risk is defined as the risk of default or loss in market value, and is the largest of the four life risks. The NAIC has developed a detailed risk weighting system for life company assets, and they regularly reassess those weightings. The system for bonds and equities is as follows:

Bonds are classified into seven different categories: government and government-guaranteed securities are given a 0 percent weighting; all other bonds are classified into asset classes 1 to 6. The method of allocating a bond to a class depends on its nature, consid-ering contractual promise, rights, periodic payment, maturity/redemption, and involuntary redemption. The performance of bonds in asset classes 1 to 6 is monitored through the detailed NAIC reporting requirements. Actual performance is, therefore, used to determine risk weighting to prescribed confidence levels. Currently, the weightings are: 0.4 percent, 1.3 percent, 4.6 percent, 10.0 percent, 23.0 percent, and 30.0 percent for classes 1 to 6, respectively. The weightings are the same for long-term and short-term bonds, and portfolios are allowed a diversification credit as the number of issuers they contain increases.

An important feature of the system is the capital charge applied to equity holdings. The basic capital charge of 30 percent can be adjusted up to 45 percent or down to 22.5 percent depending on the volatility of the portfolio. Weights for bonds and equities are reviewed annually, based on updated estimates of bond defaults and secondary market volatility, respectively.

OTHER RISK

Various other charges are included to cover a range of risks. In particular, there is an element regarding off-balance-sheet liabilities.

Valuation of Assets

In general, most countries require regulatory returns to be completed using local Generally Accepted Accounting Principles (GAAP), although there may be instances of prescribed adjustments. This is not the case in the United States. Regulatory returns are completed under Statutory Accounting Principles (SAP), which are unique to U.S. regulatory reporting. While GAAP stresses the matching of revenue and expenses, SAP stresses measuring the ability of the insurer to pay claims in the future.

United Kingdom

The United Kingdom and other EU systems have a great deal in common with each other since they are based on EU directives. The method of calculating the regulatory capital requirement is the same; it is described for the United Kingdom below, and applies to Germany as well.

Regulatory Capital Calculation

BUSINESS RISK

The solvency margin for life insurance undertakings is made up of six elements that reflect the categories of products sold. The solvency margin is derived from EU directives and the major requirements are based on premiums and insurance liabilities. The Required Minimum Margin is the average of the six elements, and is subject to a *de minimis* provision of €3 million.

In the United Kingdom, life insurers were required to pass their solvency test after the imposition of a resilience test. This test involved an assumed 25 percent reduction in equity values and 3 percent rise in interest rates. In September 2001, the resilience test was relaxed to relieve pressure on solvency margins during volatile market conditions. In mid-2002, the test was changed in order to calculate the equity stress by reference to an index movement.

ASSET RISK

EU directives impose overarching principles, requiring assets that cover provisions for future insurance liabilities have suitable security, yield, marketability, and diversification. Restrictions are imposed that require no single equity holding be greater than 5 percent of such liabilities (i.e., a single entity or large exposure limit). Directives pose no restrictions on the assets held in excess of those required to cover insurance liabilities.

OTHER RISK

Not currently addressed.

Valuation of Assets

Assets are generally valued at market or realizable value. The counterparty and con-

centration thresholds apply to assets for the purposes of the solvency margin calculation. To the extent that an asset falls within its threshold, it is fully included in the asset valuation. To the extent the threshold is breached, it is attributed no value. Thus, the former attracts a zero percent capital charge, and the latter suffers 100 percent capital charge.

Germany

Regulatory Capital Calculation

BUSINESS RISK

Based on EU directives, the regulatory capital margin is the same as that described above for the United Kingdom. German authorities began imposing stress tests on insurers at the end of 2002. The test imposed two scenarios: first, 35 percent reduction in equity values, 10 percent reduction in bond values, and discounts of up to 30 percent in non-investment grade bond holdings; second, 20 percent reduction in equity values, 5 percent reduction in bond values, and discounts of up to 30 percent in non-investment grade bond holdings.

ASSET RISK

Germany follows the EU directives, as described above, but imposes restrictions on the form of certain investments, which apply only to assets that cover the insurance liabilities. This includes a restriction of equity investments (at book value) to 35 percent of insurance liabilities.

OTHER RISK

Not currently addressed.

Valuation of Assets

German Insurance Supervisory Law makes direct reference to the provisions of the EU directives as mentioned above. Historically, assets have been carried at cost. When assets had been held for many years, and the market value was greatly in excess of cost, German insurers benefited from large undisclosed "hidden reserves." The equity bear market and negative spreads on life insurance products caused the hidden reserves to be consumed, and increased pressure on solvency margins. Consequently, valuation rules were changed to allow the valuation of equities at their "estimated ultimate realizable value," even if this was above both cost and current market value. The rationale was that the investments were made for the long term, and the effect was to relieve pressure on solvency margins.

More recently, for financial reporting purposes, some of the larger German companies have made fair value disclosures.

Switzerland

Switzerland is not a part of the EU, but its regulations reflect those of its EU neighbors. The Swiss authorities are in the process of revising their insurance supervisory law and solvency margin regulations. Whereas the detail of the revisions is not yet known, the reference material for their drafting work was based on EU directives, and Solvency II and other technical background work.

Japan

Regulatory Capital Calculation

As mentioned in the chapter, Japan's risk-based capital system is similar to the U.S. system. Compared to the United States, the Japanese system uses lower risk weights and applies differing treatment in solvency margins in some respects, such as deferred tax assets.

BUSINESS RISK

Separate from the risk-based capital system, the Financial Services Agency (FSA) checks underwriting risks and the sufficiency of technical reserves.

ASSET RISK

Risk weights for assets are exhibited in Tables 3.12 and 3.13. In addition, price move-

Table 3.16. United States: Authorized Control Levels
(In percent)

	Capital to RBC[1]
No action	More than 250
Company submits plan to restore capital	Between 150 and 250
Company must comply with corrective measures	Between 70 and 150
Authority may take control	Below 100
Authority takes control	Less than 70

[1]Capital is the company valuation under SAP, and RBC is the combination of risk capital components.

ment reserves and general loan-loss reserves are included in solvency margin.

OTHER RISK

The FSA's inspection manual sets out qualitative standards for the treatment of risks relating to underwriting, investment, markets, credit, liquidity, real estate investment, operational, and information technology.

Valuation of Assets

This is described in the main text.

Overview of Supervisory Intervention

Supervisory intervention is often determined by law, and the nature and extent varies from country to country.

In the United States, certain types of intervention are required at certain risk-based capital thresholds, given in Table 3.16. However, U.S. supervisors typically discuss significant negative developments with insurers before these thresholds are breached.

Under the EU Solvency I reforms (which were essentially upgrades in advance of the more comprehensive Solvency II project), supervisors acquired the power to intervene when a company shows adverse trends, regardless of whether prescribed solvency margins have been breached.

In Japan, supervisors are required to intervene if the risk-based capital margin or liquidation value fall below certain levels. An early warning system also gives supervisors the power to take preventive actions, based on profitability, credit risk, market risk, or liquidity risk measures, even if the capital margin or liquidation value thresholds have not been breached.

Under IAIS Core Principles, supervisory authorities should have the power to take remedial action (including requiring capital to be increased) in a timely manner where problems are identified, and immediate action in the case of emergencies.

References

Ahearne, Alan, William Griever, and Frank Warnock, forthcoming, "Information Costs and Home Bias: An Analysis of U.S. Holdings of Foreign Equities," *Journal of International Economics.*

Bank for International Settlements, 2003, "Trends in Risk Integration and Aggregation," The Joint Forum, Basel Committee on Bank Supervision (Basel, August).

British Bankers' Association (BBA), 2002, *Credit Derivatives Report 2001/2002* (London).

Briys, Eric, and François de Varenne, 1995, "On the Risk of Life Insurance Liabilities: Debunking Some Common Pitfalls," Wharton Financial Institutions Center Working Paper No. 96–29 (Philadelphia: The Wharton School, University of Pennsylvania).

Committee on the Global Financial System (CGFS), 2003, "Credit Risk Transfer," Bank for International Settlements (Basel, January).

Das, Udaibir S., Nigel Davies, and Richard Podpiera, 2003, "Insurance and Issues in Financial Soundness," IMF Working Paper No. 03/138 (Washington: International Monetary Fund).

Financial Services Authority, 2002, "Cross-Sector Risk Transfers," Discussion Paper (London: May).

FitchRatings, 2003, "Global Credit Derivatives: A Qualified Success," *Fitch Ratings Special Report* (September).

———, 2004, "Securitization and Banks: A Reiteration of Fitch's View of Securitization's Effect on Bank Ratings in the New Context of Regulatory Capital and Accounting Reform" (February).

Fukao, Mitsuhiro, 2002, "Barriers to Financial Restructuring: Japanese Banking and Life-Insurance Industries" (unpublished; Tokyo: Keio University, February).

Hall, Keith, and Erin Stuart, 2003, "Credit Risk Transfer Markets: An Australian Perspective," *Reserve Bank of Australia Bulletin* (Sydney: Reserve Bank of Australia, May).

Hartmann, Philip, Angela Maddaloni, and Simone Manganelli, 2003, "The Euro Area Financial System: Structure, Integration and Policy Initiatives," ECB Working Paper No. 230 (Frankfurt: European Central Bank).

Häusler, Gerd, 2004, "The Insurance Industry, Systemic Financial Stability, and Fair Value Accounting," *The Geneva Papers on Risk and Insurance*, Vol. 29, No. 1 (January), pp. 63–70.

Ibbotson Associates, 2003, *Stocks, Bonds, Bills, and Inflation 2003 Yearbook* (Chicago).

International Association of Insurance Supervisors, 1999, *Supervisory Standard on Asset Management by Insurance Companies* (Basel, December).

———, 2003, *Credit Risk Transfer Between Insurance, Banking and Other Financial Sectors* (Basel, March).

IMF, 2002a, "How Effectively Is the Market for Credit Risk Transfer Vehicles Functioning?," *Global Financial Stability Report;* World Economic and Financial Surveys (Washington: International Monetary Fund, March), pp. 36–47.

———, 2002b, "The Financial Market Activities of Insurance and Reinsurance Companies," *Global Financial Stability Report*, World Economic and Financial Surveys (Washington: International Monetary Fund, June), pp. 30–47.

———, 2003, *Global Financial Stability Report*, World Economic and Financial Surveys (Washington: International Monetary Fund, March), pp. 22–24.

Joint Forum, forthcoming, *Credit Risk Transfers*, Joint Forum Working Group on Risk Assessment and Capital (Basel: Bank for International Settlements).

Kiff, John, 2003, "Recent Developments in Markets for Credit-Risk Transfer," *Financial System Review,* Bank of Canada (Ottawa, June).

———, Francois-Louis Michaud, and Janet Mitchell, 2003, "An Analytical Review of Credit Risk Transfer Instruments," *Financial Stability Review*, Banque de France (June).

Le Pan, Nick, 2003, "Adding Value to the Life Insurance Industry," notes for a speech to the Life Insurance Institute of Canada Annual Conference (Toronto, June 3).

Moody's Investors Service, 2003, "Moody's Views on Current Conditions in the U.S. Life Insurance Industry" (New York, December).

Rajan, Raghuram, and Luigi Zingales, 2003, "Banks and Markets: The Changing Character of European Finance," NBER Working Paper No. 9595 (Cambridge, Mass.: National Bureau of Economic Research).

Rule, David, 2001a, "The Credit Derivatives Market: Its Development and Possible Implications for Financial Stability," *Financial Stability Review* (London: Bank of England, June), pp. 117–40.

———, 2001b, "Risk Transfer Between Banks, Insurance Companies and Capital Markets: An Overview," *Financial Stability Review* (London: Bank of England, December), pp. 137–59.

Standard and Poor's, 2003a, "Structured Finance: ViewPoint on Credit Derivatives" (New York).

———, 2003b, "Demystifying Banks' Use of Credit Derivatives," *RatingsDirect* (New York, December).

Statistical Yearbook of German Insurance, 2003 (Berlin: German Insurance Association).

Swiss Re, 2000, "Asset-Liability Management for Insurers," *Sigma*, No. 6/2000.

———, 2003, "Insurance Company Ratings," *Sigma*, No. 4/2003.

Zucker, Jason, and Jonathan Joseph, 2003, "The Life Preserver," *Fox-Pitt, Kelton Insurance Industry Update* (November).

CHAPTER IV

INSTITUTIONAL INVESTORS IN EMERGING MARKETS

A key element in reducing the volatility of capital flows to emerging markets is the development of a stable investor base for emerging market securities. The prospects for developing such an investor base depend on such factors as the composition of the existing investor base, the economic and regulatory considerations influencing investors' asset allocations vis-à-vis emerging markets, the entry of new classes of investors, and the development of new instruments for transferring resources across national borders and hedging the associated risks.

As noted in the September 2003 *Global Financial Stability Report* (Chapter IV), changes in the composition of the investor base have had an important influence on the volatility of capital flows to emerging markets and on the degree of contagion experienced during crises. One key development has been the sharp drop in the participation of banks and hedge funds and an increased participation of nonbank institutional investors. Another important change in the investor base has been the relative decline in "dedicated" relative to "crossover" investors.[1] Crossover investors are more likely to make opportunistic investments and to be more influenced by developments in other asset classes. Although the increased importance of crossover investors may have increased volatility of capital flows, it has also broadened and diversified the investor base. Another development broadening the investor base has been the rapid growth of local emerging market nonbank institutional investors such as pension funds, mutual funds, and life insurance com-

panies. These investors have become an important source of demand for both local-currency- and foreign-currency-denominated emerging market assets. In particular, the steady growth of pension funds in Latin America and Central Europe are underpinning the development of local bond markets.

This chapter seeks to provide a better understanding of nonbank institutional investors' asset allocation decisions vis-à-vis emerging market securities. It examines the behavior of both mature market institutional investors that participate actively in emerging markets, and local emerging market institutional investors. For mature markets, the focus is on insurance companies, pension funds, hedge funds, and mutual funds (as well as other asset managers). The scale of assets under management is compared with the market capitalization of the local and external bonds and equities issued by emerging market entities. In addition, the chapter assesses the institutional constraints (as imposed by regulation and by investor mandates), as well as risk and return configurations, that make emerging market instruments a more or less attractive asset class to global investors. The trading and investment strategies of the various investors are also analyzed with regard to how they affect the stability of capital flows to emerging markets.

For emerging markets, the chapter examines the investment behavior of local pension funds, insurance companies, and mutual funds. For pension funds in particular, the focus is on their impact on the development of local markets, their diversification needs, and the constraints imposed by investment and mark-

---

[1]A "dedicated" investor's performance is measured against an emerging market asset benchmark, such as the EMBI or MSCI emerging market index. A "crossover" investor's performance is not measured against any emerging market benchmark.

to-market regulations. Insurance companies are examined in terms of asset and liability management and duration-seeking behavior and of regulatory constraints, including guaranteed returns and solvency/consumer protection issues. Finally, for mutual funds, the source of growth of assets under management, the principal types of funds offered in different regions, redemption policies, and market dynamics are examined.

The final section draws conclusions regarding the major trends in the institutional investor base for emerging markets and their implication for financial stability. This section also examines the key policy issues, particularly those relating to regulations that prevent diversification and/or magnify price volatility, issues of transparency in the mutual and hedge fund industries, and the establishment of a level playing field for different institutional investors offering similar products. Policies that could facilitate the further development of the institutional investor base are also discussed. In particular, steps that countries can take to make their markets more attractive to mature market institutional investors and to facilitate the development of their local institutional base are described.

Mature Market Institutional Investors

Institutional investors provide smaller individual investors with a means of pooling risk, thus providing diversification and enhanced risk-return opportunities for end investors. Their superior capacity to absorb and process information and their ability to conduct a large volume of transactions lower the cost of intermediation and benefit investors and issuers alike. In addition to providing better risk management and lower transaction costs, the long-term liabilities of pension funds and insurance companies allow them to invest in and contribute to the development and stability of longer-term securities markets. Finally, institutional investors also contribute to better transparency and governance, to the improve-

ment of market microstructure, and to the adoption of innovative financial products. However, some analysts argue that some institutional investors—pension funds in particular—tend to follow a herding behavior and magnify volatility in asset markets. Others also note that hedge funds' strategies may destabilize financial markets and increase volatility and sovereign issuance costs.

International portfolio theory suggests that institutional investors can achieve better risk-return profiles by diversifying abroad, mainly because of additional diversification of non-systematic national risks. A number of studies (e.g., Grauer and Hakansson, 1987; and Solnik, 1998) suggest that gains from international equity-portfolio diversification are large, but the "home bias" in most mature market investors' portfolios remains a puzzle. While the case for investing in emerging market securities during the 1990s was diminished by the string of crises in the second half of the decade, the recent stellar performance of the asset class seems to have solidified its role in international portfolios (Box 4.1).

Moreover, the dismal performance of mature market stocks in the aftermath of the bursting of the technology, media, and telecommunications (TMT) bubble and the low interest rate environment have increased institutional investors' interest in so-called alternative investments. Alternative investments are private equity, real estate, hedge funds, and special debt-offerings (such as credit derivatives and distressed debt), and they provide investors with new sources of excess returns as well as diversification from traditional bond and equity investments (Greenwich Associates, 2002; and Graham, 2003). Although most of the growth in alternative investments has been in private equity, institutional demand for hedge fund products has also increased more recently. And this has—indirectly and to some extent— increased interest in emerging market assets.

The most remarkable change in the institutional investor base for emerging market

Box 4.1. The Benefits of Portfolio Diversification: Do They Really Exist?

The basic tenet of portfolio theory is that diversification reduces risk. This suggests that an optimally diversified portfolio should be one that is invested across as many asset classes and markets as possible. However, ex post empirical evidence suggests that this is not necessarily the case, with distinctly concentrated portfolios outperforming diversified ones over certain holding periods on a risk-adjusted basis. Moreover, a dichotomy exists: while "concentrated" portfolios have historically been more desirable in terms of optimizing the risk-return trade-off, traditional institutional investors are—in practice—bound by investment parameters that may not necessarily allow such narrow allocations, even if they could reasonably estimate optimal portfolios ex ante. It is therefore unlikely that actual allocations would reflect optimal historical performance.

The effectiveness of any diversification strategy depends on the correlation or covariance between returns on the individual assets within a portfolio. Portfolio managers can achieve risk reduction by adding new securities to their portfolios, provided that the return on each new security added is not *perfectly positively* correlated with the returns on the existing portfolio. The increasing globalization of financial markets has clearly extended the universe of investment—and thus diversification—opportunities for international investors.

Using a mean-variance framework to construct optimal portfolios from historical returns data—including emerging and mature market equities and fixed-income securities—over the 1991 to 2002 period,[1] the following investment

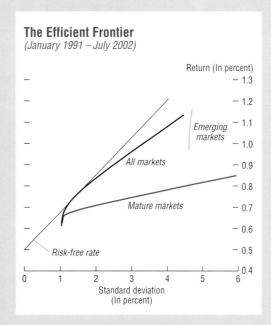

The Efficient Frontier
(January 1991 – July 2002)

strategies are separately examined: (1) mature markets only (equities and fixed income); (2) emerging markets only (equities and fixed income); and (3) all markets (mature and emerging) and asset classes (equities and fixed income).

The Figure depicts the efficient frontier for each of the three investment strategies over the January 1991 to July 2002 period.[2] Consistent with portfolio diversification theory, the global market portfolio was the most efficient, offering a higher return for any given level of risk, compared with the mature or emerging market portfolios. Not surprisingly, the results also show that emerging market assets offered diversification benefits to mature market investors over the 1991 to 2002 sample period, with returns dominating those of mature market investments, within the 4.6 to 4.7 standard deviation range.

Interestingly, however, investing in the equities asset class offered few diversification benefits, relative to fixed income assets, over this period. The

[1]The framework consists of the following categories: *Mature markets,* which includes equity indices MSCI European Union, MSCI Japan, the S&P500 and NASDAQ and the bond indices Salomon Smith Barney Investment Grade (U.S. high-grade corporates) and Merrill Lynch High Yield (U.S. high-yield corporates); *emerging markets,* which includes equity indices MSCI Total Emerging Market Free, MSCI Emerging Asia, MSCI Latin America, MSCI Europe and Middle East and the EMBI bond index; and *global markets,* which includes all of the above equity and bond indices.

[2]The EMBI series, which is available from 1991, stopped at July 2002.

Box 4.1 *(concluded)*

Portfolio Diversification: Optimal Asset Allocation (Ex Post)

Sample Period	Optimal Allocation
Jan 1991 to Dec 2002	EMBI, 19 percent; U.S. high-grade, 81 percent
Jan 1991 to Jun 1997	EMBI, 43 percent; Latin equity, 6 percent; NASDAQ, 51 percent
Jul 1997 to Jul 2002	EMBI, 22 percent; U.S. high-grade, 60 percent; U.S. high-yield, 18 percent

optimal portfolio comprised bonds allocated to the EMBI and U.S. high-grade corporate classes, with the U.S. bonds notable in their importance within the portfolio (see Table).[3] In this instance, equities-only investors would have been, on average, always worse off than their fixed income counterparts.

The sample is subsequently divided into two separate holding periods: the first holding period from January 1991 to June 1997, the second from

[3]IMF (2000) shows that emerging market equities were attractive assets in 1988–94 for mature market investors by offering higher returns with little added risk, while emerging market bonds overall added more risk to the portfolio with uncertain return benefits.

July 1997 to July 2002.[4] The results suggest that diversification across both fixed-income and equity assets, as well as across mature and emerging markets, was optimal for the investor over the 1991 to mid-1997 period. Since July 1997, however, fixed-income investments, across both mature and emerging markets, provided higher risk-adjusted returns than equities.

In conclusion, it appears that while diversification across asset classes and markets generally benefits investors, the optimal asset mix changes over time. In many instances, the concentration of the optimal allocation—which could require a significant allocation into one particular instrument or asset class—could be too extreme for the traditional institutional investor. This could partly explain the growing popularity of more "nimble" investor classes, such as hedge funds and crossover investors, which have greater flexibility in their investment mandates and are increasingly targeting absolute returns, rather than adhering to specific benchmarks.

[4]The onset of the Asian financial crisis provides a natural structural break, as this proved to be the beginning of a series of emerging market crises. The average annual risk-free rates used for these two holding periods are 6.8 percent and 5.4 percent, respectively.

instruments in the late 1990s has been the increase of crossover investors relative to both dedicated investors and hedge funds. Analysts have noted that the increase in crossover investors has increased volatility while a reduction in hedge fund activity has been associated with a drop in volatility. However, hedge funds have been growing again, and market participants expressed different views on the volatile behavior of crossover investors. In particular, while crossover investors may display more opportunistic behavior vis-à-vis the emerging

market asset class, they tend to buy and hold assets. Indeed, although there are different kinds of crossover investors, an increasing share of this investor base is ultimately pension funds and insurance companies, which are likely to be long-term, stable investors.

The 1990s have witnessed a sharp expansion of assets under management for nonbank institutional investors in mature markets (Table 4.1).[2] For the group comprising insurance companies, pension funds, and mutual funds, assets under management expanded by

[2]An unknown amount of double counting occurs when the assets under management of these institutions are added. This reflects the fact, for example, that pension funds place funds with mutual funds. An offset to this double counting is that the assets under management of hedge funds are not included.

Table 4.1. Mature Markets: Assets Under Management by Institutional Investors[1]

	1993	1994	1995	1996	1997	1998	1999	2000	2001
	(In billions of U.S. dollars)								
Institutional investors	**18,248**	**20,153**	**23,141**	**25,432**	**27,686**	**32,435**	**36,596**	**36,233**	**34,723**
Insurance companies	6,991	7,822	8,980	9,369	9,702	11,010	11,960	11,519	11,146
Pension funds	5,332	5,868	6,660	7,545	8,281	9,527	10,337	10,279	9,515
Investment companies[2]	4,050	4,478	5,309	6,200	7,293	9,201	11,168	11,293	11,091
Other institutional investors	1,876	1,986	2,192	2,318	2,409	2,697	3,132	3,143	2,971
Memo item:									
Hedge funds[3]		39	45	61	100	112	150	172	217
Mature market bank assets	**4,491**	**4,798**	**5,453**	**5,613**	**6,074**	**5,301**	**5,699**	**5,917**	**6,192**
	(In percent of institutional investors' assets)								
Mature market bank assets	**24.6**	**23.8**	**23.6**	**22.1**	**21.9**	**16.3**	**15.6**	**16.3**	**17.8**
Emerging markets	**15.5**	**15.5**	**14.3**	**15.8**	**13.8**	**11.4**	**14.5**	**13.9**	**14.4**
Stock market capitalization	**11.3**	**10.8**	**9.6**	**10.7**	**9.1**	**6.6**	**10.1**	**9.1**	**9.0**
Africa	1.0	1.1	1.2	1.0	0.9	0.6	0.8	0.6	0.5
Asia	7.8	7.3	6.5	7.2	5.0	4.2	6.6	5.9	5.8
Europe	0.2	0.2	0.2	0.4	0.8	0.3	0.7	0.4	0.5
Middle East	0.0	0.0	0.0	0.2	0.3	0.3	0.5	0.5	0.5
Western Hemisphere	2.3	2.2	1.7	1.9	2.1	1.2	1.5	1.7	1.7
Bonds oustanding	**4.2**	**4.6**	**4.8**	**5.1**	**4.7**	**4.7**	**4.4**	**4.8**	**5.4**
Asia	2.4	2.5	2.7	2.8	2.2	2.6	2.7	3.0	3.4
Western Hemisphere	0.9	1.3	1.3	1.5	1.6	1.6	1.2	1.3	1.4
Africa, Europe, and Middle East	0.8	0.8	0.8	0.8	0.8	0.6	0.5	0.5	0.6
	(In percent of mature markets GDP)								
Institutional investors	**94.7**	**97.6**	**102.0**	**111.9**	**124.2**	**143.5**	**154.4**	**151.4**	**147.2**
Insurance companies	36.3	37.9	39.6	41.2	43.5	48.7	50.5	48.1	47.3
Pension funds	27.7	28.4	29.4	33.2	37.1	42.2	43.6	43.0	40.3
Investment companies	21.0	21.7	23.4	27.3	32.7	40.7	47.1	47.2	47.0
Other institutional investors	9.7	9.6	9.7	10.2	10.8	11.9	13.2	13.1	12.6
Mature market bank assets	**23.3**	**23.2**	**24.0**	**24.7**	**27.2**	**23.5**	**24.0**	**24.7**	**26.2**

Sources: BIS; CISDM; IFS; OECD; S&P/IFC, *EMDB;* and World Federation of Exchanges.

[1] OECD countries are: Australia, Austria, Belgium, Canada, Denmark, Finland, France, Germany, Greece, Iceland, Italy, Japan, Luxembourg, Netherlands, Norway, Portugal, Spain, Sweden, Switzerland, United Kingdom, and the United States.

[2] Investment companies' include closed-end and managed investment companies, mutual funds, and unit investment trusts (see OECD, 2003).

[3] Assets under management of hedge funds are based on the information provided by CISDM (formerly MAR/Hedge), which covers mainly the U.S.-based hedge funds. Eureka/Hedge, which tracks European and Asian based hedge funds, does not provide historical assets under management.

90 percent between 1993 and 2001 and reached $34 trillion. The expansion was most rapid in the United States (113 percent) and in the countries in the European Union (111 percent). As a result of this rapid growth, assets under management for these companies rose from 95 percent of GDP at the end of 1993 to 147 percent at the end of 2001. The assets of these nonbank institutional investors also expanded much more rapidly than bank assets. Indeed, bank assets fell from the equivalent of 25 percent of nonbank institutional investors' assets under management in 1993 to 18 percent in 2001.

The assets under management of the nonbank institutional investors are very large relative to any measure of either the size of emerging markets or capital flows to these markets. To gauge comparative size, one can compare the assets under management of mature market institutional investors with the total market capitalization of emerging market bonds and equities. In addition, to examine the effects of a reallocation of institutional investors' assets under management toward emerging markets, one can consider what fraction of the assets under management would have to be shifted to emerging markets to equal the level of capital flows that actually took place during a given period. At the end of 2001, for example, the total market value of all external and domestic bonds and equities issues by emerging market residents amounted to only 14 percent of the assets under management of the mature market nonbank institutional investors. Moreover, total emerging market issuance of international bonds, equities, and syndicated lending ($135.6 billion) in 2001 was equivalent to roughly a half of 1 percent of assets under management of these institutional investors. It is evident that even a modest adjustment in the allocation of the assets under management of these institutional investors toward emerging markets can lead to substantial capital flows. Naturally, if these flows are focused on a particular region, the magnitude of the flows can be relatively more sizable. For example, Asia had the largest equity and bond market capitalization ($3.18 trillion) and received the largest capital inflows ($67.5 billion) in 2001, but these were equivalent to 9 percent and 0.2 percent, respectively, of the assets under management of the mature market nonbank institutional investors' assets under management.

The potential large-scale capital flows that could be generated by even a relatively small shift in the portfolio behavior of the mature market nonbank institutional investors raises several issues, including the extent of their holdings of claims on emerging markets, the stability of their investments, and whether there are any economic or regulatory factors that inhibit investments in emerging markets. In this chapter, these issues are addressed by examining the behavior of three types of mature market institutional investors: pension funds, life insurance companies, and asset managers (as represented by mutual funds and hedge funds). Subsequently, there is also

consideration of the behavior of local non-bank institutional investors in emerging markets.

In what follows, key features of institutional investors' asset allocation decisions vis-à-vis emerging market securities are described. Even though the risk-return configuration of emerging market securities may warrant allocations in an increasingly globalized portfolio, regulations and investors' mandates—sometimes related to risk management methods and the nature of liabilities—constitute additional constraints that could reduce institutional investors' allocation to emerging market securities.[3]

Pension Funds and Insurance Companies

Pension funds and life insurance companies are long-term investors whose investment process consists of strategic asset allocation decisions—which determine broad portfolio distributions across asset classes, such as bonds and equities—as well as tactical asset allocation that involves deviations from the basic asset categories to exploit short-term profit opportunities.[4] Finally, security selection refers to the choice of individual assets to be held within each asset class. The asset allocation decisions are driven by the preferences of the pension fund trustees or insurer's investment committees, which take into account the risk/return trade-offs of different portfolios as well as the nature of their liabilities and regulations.

The importance of liability considerations is apparent in the different asset allocation decision of defined benefit versus defined contribution pension funds. In defined benefit plans, the plan sponsor guarantees an agreed level of retirement benefits to the plan members. The plan sponsor, hence, bears the risk that the returns from the investment portfolio

---

[3]Other factors that may limit foreign investment by mature markets' institutional investors are low levels of financial transparency, corporate governance, and integrity in emerging markets.

[4]This chapter focuses on the life business and does not cover property and casualty insurance.

may not be enough to cover the pension fund liabilities, or funding gap risk. The plan sponsor can minimize this risk by choosing financial assets that match the plan's liabilities: domestic assets are better for matching domestic liabilities than foreign securities (Davis and Steil, 2001). In contrast, the retirement benefits in defined contribution plans are tied up to the pension fund portfolio performance. Regardless of whether the asset allocation is decided by the pension plan sponsor, or by the pension plan member, as is the case in the 401(k) pension plans in the United States, the investment risk is borne exclusively by the pension plan member. Therefore, the appropriate investment strategy in defined contribution plans is to maximize the expected return of the portfolio for a given level or risk, as suggested by modern portfolio theory (Davis and Steil, 2001). Some authors (Blake, 2003) argue that pension funds offering defined contribution plans would invest more in equities and in foreign securities (including emerging markets) than pension funds offering defined benefit plans.

The analysis above is supported partly by the historical evolution of asset allocation in some of the mature market pension funds. For instance, in the United States defined benefit plans covered 87 percent of pension plan participants in 1975 but only 20 percent in 1999.[5] At the same time, foreign investment in 2002 increased to more than 12 percent from less than 3 percent in 1986.[6] In the United Kingdom, in contrast, defined benefit plans covered up to 85 percent of all plan participants in 1999 (Association of British Insurers, 2000). After the release of the Myners report in 2001, stricter regulations were introduced to encourage a closer matching of assets and liabilities. Surveys by the

William Mercer Company show that pension funds met the requirements by increasing the domestic bond allocation to 12.5 percent in 2003 from 9.5 percent in 2000 while reducing their domestic equity allocation to 38 percent from 47 percent. The foreign equity allocation, however, remained steady at 25 percent.

Despite these arguments favoring diversification, current investment levels in emerging markets by pension funds are relatively small. In the United States, a survey by Greenwich Associates (2003) indicates that large public pension funds do not invest in emerging market bonds. Furthermore, these funds' allocation to emerging market equities is estimated to be around 1 percent of assets.[7] In Japan, foreign investment by the government pension fund has been limited only to mature markets. In the United Kingdom, Kimmis and others (2002) report that emerging market securities represented around 2 to 3 percent of pension assets.

Investment regulation does not appear to be a major impediment to investing in emerging market securities. A recent survey by the OECD shows that only Germany and Italy imposed tight investment limits on foreign securities (Yermo, 2003a). In Germany, pension funds only can invest up to 10 percent of assets in foreign equity and 10 percent in bonds from non-European Union countries. In Italy, the ceiling on foreign equity and bonds of non-OECD countries is 5 percent of assets. Pension funds, however, can invest up to 50 percent of assets under management in OECD emerging market countries such as Mexico, Korea, and the EU accession countries. In contrast, there are no investment limits in the United Kingdom and the United States (see the section on local pension funds). Countries that do not place invest-

[5]Hinz (2000); in terms of assets under management, each one holds about half the total.
[6]Data sources include Blake, Lehmann, and Timmermann (1999), and Greenwich and Associates (2003).
[7]The survey indicates that foreign equity holding of public pension funds in the United States amounted to 12 percent of assets under management by the end of 2002. The 1 percent weight is obtained by assuming that the relative weight of emerging markets in the portfolio is equal to the 8 percent weight of emerging markets in Morgan Stanley's All Country World Index (ACWI)—excluding the United States.

ment limits on foreign securities rely on the "prudent man rule" or prudent investor rule. The rule requires pension fund managers to make sensible investment decisions based on what is perceived as best practice among other large and prudent institutional investors.

A primary obstacle to increased asset allocation to emerging markets is the risk aversion of pension fund trustees. The repeated occurrence of financial crises in emerging markets has reduced the diversification benefits from emerging market investments and heightened the perception that emerging markets are excessively volatile. As a result, pension fund trustees have become wary of investing in emerging markets for fear of facing substantial short-term losses. In the United Kingdom, risk aversion among trustees seems to have been encouraged by regulations designed to strengthen U.K. pension funds, such as Minimum Funding Requirements and a new accounting standard, FRS17, that encourage a closer matching of assets and liabilities (Kimmis and others, 2002; and Blake, 2003). In the United States, fear of litigation over serious short-term underperformance increases the risk perception of pension fund managers.

Pension fund trustees in the United Kingdom tend to rely heavily on the advice of external consultants for selecting the fund's asset allocation and on external asset managers for security selection. Their asset allocation methods and fund management styles do not favor investment in emerging market securities. The reliance on third parties is explained partly by the fact that a substantial fraction of the funds' trustees lack investment expertise.[8] Some asset and liability management models used for asset allocation require the availability of long time series and tend to discourage asset classes that are relatively young and underresearched—such as emerg-

ing market securities. The two main styles of fund management are balanced mandates and specialists mandates. Balanced mandates measure manager performance relative to a peer group while specialists mandates use a customized benchmark, making it difficult for managers to invest in any asset class that others are not investing in or that is not included in major indices.

The increasing allocation to emerging market securities, including from pension funds in continental Europe, are reportedly outsourced to specialized asset managers—many of them in the United Kingdom. According to analysts, this delegation of asset allocation and security selection has conflicting implications: it improves the quality of the decision-making process and ensures adequate discrimination across emerging markets, but the quarterly appraisals of managers encourage a short-term focus on performance objectives, defeating to some extent the long-term horizon of pension funds.

Emerging market investment is also affected by non-economic factors. Foremost among them is the requirement that pension funds invest only in a number of "permissible countries" that satisfy "socially responsible" investment conditions. A recent study by Wilshire Associates commissioned by Calpers, the largest public pension fund in the United States, used both traditional market indicators and country factors to select permissible equity markets (Wilshire Associates, 2002). Market indicators include market liquidity and volatility, market regulation, the adequacy of the legal system, investor protection rules, capital market openness, settlement proficiency, and transaction costs. Country factors include political stability, transparency, and "productive" labor practices.[9] In 1999, Calpers's exclusion of some Asian countries

---

[8]See Myners (2001). In contrast, in the Netherlands, the pension fund board may decide the asset allocation itself, as board members are investment professionals (Davis, 2002).
[9]Socially responsible guidelines could potentially lead to the exclusion of companies that follow good labor standards but are headquartered in countries with overall weak labor standards and/or political systems.

from the list of "permissible" countries caused a brief sell-off in these countries' stock markets as investors tried to front-run a possible sell-off by pension funds. In February 2003, stock markets in Malaysia and Thailand benefited from the inclusion of these countries in the permissible country list. More recently, Argentina, Peru, and Turkey failed to meet Calpers's criteria and were excluded from the list.[10] Although another pension fund is reportedly considering the use of similar criteria to select countries to invest in, analysts do not expected the practice to spread to others. Socially responsible investment guidelines are also used in countries other than the United States. For example, in the United Kingdom, 19 percent of private sector funds and 31 percent of public sector funds reported taking into account ethical considerations in their investment decisions (Targett, 2000).

Large public pension funds approach alternative investment opportunities with caution, and, while pension funds are increasingly interested in alternative investment opportunities, actual allocations are still relatively small. A large public pension fund, for instance, has approved an allocation of up to $1 billion for hedge funds, but has managed to implement only half of that amount. The investment officers have noted that investing in hedge funds is time-consuming because of the opacity of hedge funds' investment strategies, and that the size of most hedge funds is too small for the pension fund industry asset allocations.

The asset allocation decisions of insurance companies are heavily influenced by the profile of their liabilities. As noted in Chapter III, the relative shares of equity and fixed-income allocations vary considerably among different mature market insurance sectors. However, the need to limit the mismatch that would arise from a large share of contracts that generate fixed-income-type obligations leads many insurers to make a significant portfolio allocation to bonds. Similarly, the importance of matching assets and liabilities would suggest that the insurers also tend to have lower shares of foreign assets than other institutional investors.

The strategic asset allocation of mature market insurance companies vis-à-vis emerging market securities also depends on their size and geographical presence. Global insurance companies tend to follow their insurance business—that is, issuance of local policies—and match locally the liabilities of their subsidiaries in emerging markets. That is, they invest in local securities and try to extend duration as much as possible in the local market, providing support to the development and stability of emerging market securities markets. An example of this support was provided during the recent turbulence in Hungary's local bond market. The subsidiaries of two large global insurers are the largest holders of Hungary's 10-year local bonds, and their need for duration and a buy-and-hold attitude contributed to support the market during the November 2003 sell-off by leveraged players (see Chapter II, Box 2.2).[11]

Medium- and small-sized mature market life insurers that do not distribute their insurance policies in emerging markets tend to perceive the asset class as an opportunity to diversify and enhance yields. Some of them reportedly have a higher share of their portfolio allocated to emerging market securities (5 to 10 percent of total assets, compared with around 1 to 3 percent for the large ones), and although they are of the buy-and-hold type, they are not tied to any particular emerging market by the nature of their liabilities and hence may constitute a less stable segment of the investor base. They reportedly do most of

---

[10]However, market participants reported that the exclusion did not seem to have negative effects in the respective stock markets.

[11]However, some market participants noted that the insurers' ability to lend the securities could have contributed to the sell-off.

their investment decisions in-house, but in some cases they do not have the resources to do the research needed to invest in emerging markets.

The major constraint to investing in emerging markets is the insurance companies' own ratings, which have been under pressure over the past few years.[12] In contrast, losses from emerging market investments have been small, even though insurers did not emerge totally unscathed from Argentina. Typically, equity and credit losses have been mitigated by selling other bonds whose prices have risen in a declining interest rate environment. Also, many European life insurance products offer policyholders a guaranteed minimum return and some participation in investment results above the guaranteed rate. Guaranteed returns on life policies, combined with the collapse in equity prices and the low interest rate environment, have also had a negative impact on the insurers' balance sheets (Wilson, 2003). As a result of these losses and balance sheet weaknesses, life insurance companies are operating in a risk-averse mode and are keeping their allocations to emerging markets stable.

As a result of the combined pressures from the need to enhance yields and the preservation of their own ratings, some insurance companies have invested indirectly in emerging market securities through the purchase of structured products. These include principal-protected notes with large coupons—associated sometimes with emerging market securities—securitization of emerging market future flow receivables or CDOs (collateralized debt obligations), with investment-grade ratings. They are considered promising avenues for investing in emerging markets, but actual investments are still relatively small. Moreover, market participants note that bad experiences with some CDOs in 1998–99 have made the instruments a difficult "sell" with management. Nevertheless, some asset managers consider that emerging market CDOs—backed by both sovereign and corporate bonds—can potentially widen the emerging market investor base. They noted that adequately structured CDOs, with long lock-in periods that ameliorate redemption risks, have delivered annualized returns above 20 percent over the last two years. The outstanding recent performance of some emerging market CDOs, compared to the poor performance of high-yield CDOs, has attracted the attention of European insurers and pension funds.

Mutual and Hedge Funds

Between 1993 and 2001, the assets under management of mature market investment companies increased more rapidly (174 percent) than that of any other institutional investor (Table 4.1). As a result, the proportion of total assets under management of all institutional investors held by mutual funds rose from 22 percent in 1993 to 32 percent in 2001.[13] Mutual funds are investment companies that combine the assets of investors—individual and institutional—and collectively invest those assets in equities, bonds, and money market instruments.[14] Globally, mutual funds take on a variety of structures. Mutual funds are "open-end" investment companies if they are required to redeem outstanding shares at any time, upon demand, and at a

---

[12]See Chapter III. Market participants noted that pressures on ratings came from developments both in the asset and the liability side of the balance sheet in 2002, but that in 2003 pressures derived mostly from the liability side.

[13]Mutual fund assets under management are estimated to have grown by a further 5 percent by June 2003; as a result of this growth, mature market mutual fund assets grew to 43 percent of GDP at the end of June 2003. At the end of June 2003, about 40 percent of these funds were focused on equities, 23 percent on bonds, and 37 percent on money market and other investments.

[14]Investors invest in a mutual fund by purchasing shares issued by the fund, which then uses the cash raised to invest in equities, bonds, and other securities.

price determined by the current value of the funds' net assets, known as the net asset value (NAV). In contrast, a "closed-end" mutual fund issues a fixed number of shares that trade on the stock exchange or the over-the-counter market. Unit trusts buy and hold a fixed portfolio of equities, bonds, or other securities; units in the trust are sold to investors who receive their proportionate share of dividends and interest paid by the respective investments. A unit trust has a stated date for termination, upon which investors receive their proportionate share of net assets.[15]

Mature market mutual funds have grown for a variety of reasons. In some countries, the growing importance of defined contribution pension systems has increased the placement of funds with mutual funds by both individual and institutions. Indeed, Davis and Steil (2001, p. 17) estimate that about 30 percent of mutual fund assets under management reflect placement of funds by other financial institutions, notably pension funds. Moreover, financial market deregulation and capital account liberalization have allowed foreign mutual funds to enter previously closed markets. Tax considerations have also played a role, especially in countries where retail investors have been allowed to create tax deferred retirement accounts.

The growth of mutual funds has been viewed by most analysts as a positive development because the industry has provided investors with diversified investment opportunities and professional asset management services. However, from the perspective of financial market stability, concerns have arisen at times about the ability of mutual funds to meet large scale redemptions (see Davis and

Steil, 2001, pp. 278–82). While retail investors are likely to hold more diverse views than the asset managers of a relatively small set of large institutional investors, market analysts argue that retail investors can be subject to fads (such as the TMT episode during the 1990s) and that this may lead mutual funds to focus on a single approach to investing. Since households can often switch funds at a low cost, a concern has been that a withdrawal from a favored investment style could generate large-scale redemptions, and trigger an asset sell-off.

Mutual funds can address large-scale redemptions through on-balance-sheet liquidity and/or forced sales of securities. The amount of liquidity held by a mutual fund is a portfolio decision, but holding large amounts of liquid assets will generally reduce a fund's performance.[16] As a result, large-scale redemptions have typically been met by forced sales of assets, which at times have put strong downward pressure on already declining asset prices. One means of mitigating the effects of large-scale redemption on mutual funds has been to establish a family of different funds so that investors can shift to another fund within the family (for example, from equities to a money market fund). However, some analysts argue that concerns about mass redemptions are inconsistent with the fact that, in mature markets, mass redemptions of mutual fund shares have been relatively rare.[17] For example, on October 19, 1987, when U.S. equity prices fell sharply, only 3.2 percent of equity transactions were associated with sales of equity fund shares (Davis and Steil, 2001, p. 280). In part, this reflects the fact that a significant proportion of equity mutual fund shares were held for retirement purposes. Nonetheless, the recent

[15]An exchange-traded fund (ETF) is an investment company whose shares are traded on stock exchanges at market-determined prices.
[16]Funds can also arrange backup lines of credit from banks or from within a family of funds. Only committed bank lines of credit are likely to be secure sources of funds, especially if the fund is facing heavy redemptions and will involve an up-front fee. In the United States, interfund family lending is strictly restricted.
[17]The experience with mass redemption in emerging markets is discussed on pages 140–43.

Table 4.2. U.S. International Mutual Funds: Total Net Assets
(In billions of U.S. dollars)

Investment objective	1996	1997	1998	1999	2000	2001	2002
Equity funds							
Emerging markets equities	14.0	16.0	12.7	22.1	15.4	13.7	13.7
Global equities	105.2	137.5	159.8	236.4	228.0	183.0	140.9
International equities	134.1	164.9	187.2	276.2	262.1	206.3	183.7
Regional equities	31.8	27.9	32.0	50.5	37.2	25.8	20.2
Subtotal	*285.2*	*346.4*	*391.6*	*585.3*	*542.7*	*428.8*	*358.5*
Total U.S. equity funds	**1,726.1**	**2,368.0**	**2,978.2**	**4,041.9**	**3,961.9**	**3,418.2**	**2,667.1**
Bond funds							
Global general bonds	17.5	16.1	15.9	14.9	12.7	12.4	13.2
Global short-term bonds	5.4	6.1	5.7	4.0	3.3	2.7	3.2
Global other bonds	2.8	3.8	3.3	4.0	4.0	4.0	4.7
Subtotal	*25.7*	*26.0*	*24.9*	*22.9*	*19.9*	*19.1*	*21.1*
Total U.S. bond funds	**645.4**	**724.2**	**830.6**	**812.5**	**811.2**	**925.1**	**1,125.1**

Source: Investment Company Institute.

mutual fund scandal in the United States saw relatively large redemptions from funds accused of improper trading activities. Between September and December 2003, one firm lost about 12 percent of its assets under management, mostly from institutional clients.

From the perspective of emerging markets, the categories of crossover equity investors include *global equity funds* (which invest primarily in equity securities traded worldwide, including U.S. companies) and *international equity funds* (which invest primarily in equity securities of companies located outside the United States). Dedicated equity funds include *emerging market funds* (which invest primarily in companies based in developing markets around the world). Meanwhile, *regional equity funds* (which invest in companies based in a specific part of the world, and may comprise both mature and emerging markets) could represent either dedicated or crossover accounts, albeit more benchmark indices are available for the former.[18] Within the fixed-income universe, crossover investors include *global bond funds* (which invest in debt securities worldwide, and may invest up to 25 per-

cent of assets in companies located in the United States) and *international bond funds* (which must invest at least two-thirds of the portfolio outside the United States). *Emerging market bond funds* invest primarily in the debt of less-developed regions.

Equity allocations overseas by U.S. funds—amounting to $359 billion out of $2.7 trillion total equity funds in 2002—have continued to surpass debt allocations by far (see Table 4.2). Of this amount, dedicated emerging market accounts represented $13.7 billion in 2002—or around 4 percent of total U.S. equity mutual funds—and appear relatively insignificant compared with the size of local equity funds in emerging markets. This allocation appears in line with the MSCI All Country World Index (ACWI), which has assigned a weighting of around 4 percent to emerging market equities. Moreover, total allocations by U.S. mutual funds, both dedicated and crossover, to other countries' debt—including both mature and emerging markets—in 2002 remained very small (less than $21 billion) as a proportion of total net assets of all U.S. bond funds (of $1.2 trillion). Indeed, the size of the U.S. allocation was dwarfed by the total

---

[18]For instance, the widely used Morgan Stanley Capital International (MSCI) group of regional equity indices largely comprise separate benchmarks for either mature or emerging markets.

size of local bond mutual funds in emerging markets.

The improving credit quality in emerging markets, as evidenced by the number of credit upgrades in 2003, has infused confidence in traditional high-grade crossover investors. For instance, recent institutional mandates to invest in emerging debt are widely considered a stable source of funds, as they are generally seen as longer-term, strategic allocation decisions. As more emerging market sovereigns receive an investment grade rating over time, and an increased proportion of global investment portfolios are committed to these countries and are included in core benchmarks, capital flows to these countries are expected to become less volatile. Already, more than 40 percent of the Emerging Market Bond Index Global (EMBIG) is represented by investment grade issuers (see Figure 4.1).

Among retail investors in the United States, crossover funds in both equity and debt asset classes have benefited from new net flows in 2003. On balance, equity funds have been more attractive to investors than bond funds, with international equity funds in receipt of net cash inflows of almost $14 billion for the year, while dedicated emerging market equity accounts posted net inflows of almost $5 billion.

Generally, institutional inflows are viewed as a more stable source of assets under management, compared to the retail flows that have been fuelling the growth of emerging market bond funds over the past year (see Box 4.2 for a summary of some empirical evidence on the behavior of mutual funds during crisis periods). The less sophisticated retail investors are seen to be more likely to pull out their investments quickly during a market event. For instance, analysts argue that most European institutional investors are said to prefer to follow buy-and-hold strategies unless their views on a country turn excessively negative. Additionally, the large size of some portfolios, high transaction costs, and lack of liquidity in emerging markets prevent excessive trading

Figure 4.1. Composition of Emerging Market Debt[1]
(Percent of countries)

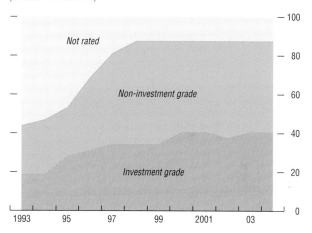

Sources: Moody's; Standard & Poor's; and J.P. Morgan Chase & Co.
[1]Based on EMBIG group of countries. Data for 2004 are as of March 2, 2004.

Box 4.2. The Behavior of Mutual Funds During Periods of Emerging Market Volatility

The increased presence of foreign investors—more specifically, mutual funds from mature markets that hold almost 95 percent of total industry net assets (or $11.7 trillion out of $12.4 trillion)—has raised concerns about their potential to destabilize emerging financial markets. The biggest concern is that these institutional investors would "herd" and pull out of emerging markets en masse during periods of financial stress and cause further disruption to already weakened markets.

Contrary to perceptions that international investors are responsible for instability and crises in emerging markets,[1] studies of the investment pattern of U.S. mutual funds in emerging markets (Rea, 1996; Rea and Marcis, 1996; and Post and Millar, 1998) suggest that neither shareholders nor portfolio managers behaved in a manner that exacerbated market volatility during emerging market crises in the 1990s.[2] The evidence indicates that shareholders in U.S. emerging market equity funds did not redeem shares in large volumes during periods of market weakness in the 1990s—any withdrawal tended to be made in modest amounts and over a period of time.[3] Similarly, portfolio managers at these mutual funds did not reallocate investments between countries in a way that would have intensified price swings. Indeed,

portfolio managers were frequently observed to have purchased shares when prices were falling and to have sold in rising markets. Overall, any liquidation of securities in falling markets was found to be small relative to the size of the positions taken in those markets. Moreover, U.S. mutual fund allocations to emerging market equities represent only a very small proportion of emerging market capitalization.[4] In contrast, Kaminsky, Lyons, and Schmukler (2001) argued that emerging market mutual fund flows around crises were unstable.

In other studies on the impact of emerging market mutual funds, Borensztein and Gelos (2003a) examined a sample consisting of 80 percent of dedicated emerging market equity funds worldwide and found herding behavior among these funds to be moderate, albeit statistically significant. However, this behavior did not appear to be more prevalent during crisis periods, and was unlikely to have been sufficiently strong enough to have accounted for instances of high volatility in international capital markets. Moreover, Borensztein and Gelos (2003b) found that open-end funds tended to sell down their holdings more than closed-end funds (which are not subject to redemptions by individual investors), implying that withdrawals by individuals, rather than fund managers, were driving the retrenchment of funds from emerging markets during crises.[5]

[1]See Aitken (1998).

[2]U.S. mutual funds held some 55 percent of worldwide industry net assets in 2003.

[3]Rea and Marcis (1996) argue that this suggests that U.S. equity fund investors are generally experienced investors with a basic understanding of investment risk and have long-term investment objectives and horizons. A 1996 survey by the Investment Company Institute shows that shareholders of international and global mutual funds, which invest in markets outside the United States, tend to be more willing to take above-average risk than those not owning such funds.

[4]In 1996, prior to the onset of the Asian financial crisis, U.S. equity mutual funds held an estimated $27.7 billion in emerging market stocks, equivalent to 1.2 percent of the $2.2 trillion in stock market capitalization of developing countries.

[5]Kim and Wei's (2002) research into transactions by portfolio investors in Korea indicated that herding behavior was more prevalent among individual investors, compared to institutional investors, and more so among non-resident investors than residents.

and practically force fund managers to adopt a buy-and-hold approach, which sometimes makes tactical asset allocations in emerging markets rather difficult.

Another type of closed-end fund that has been active in emerging markets is the hedge fund, which is typically a private unadvertised mutual fund whose investors are wealthy individuals and institutions.[19] Another major difference from conventional mutual funds is that they are allowed to take leveraged positions and are not subject to regulatory reporting requirements. Following the demise of several large macro hedge funds during 1998–2000, the hedge fund industry growth picked up again: the total assets under management of U.S.-based hedge funds almost doubled during 2001–03. The total size of the global hedge fund industry is now estimated at around $725–$750 billion compared to around $300 billion in 1997.[20] The universe of European and Asian hedge funds, though much smaller than the U.S. hedge fund industry, has been recently expanding at an even faster pace. The total assets under management of the Asia-focused hedge funds rose to $22.4 billion as of mid-2002 from about $12 billion at the end of 2000, while the assets of European hedge funds increased to $112 billion as of mid-2003 from $46 billion at the end of 2000.[21]

As with the mutual fund industry, the recent growth of the hedge fund industry has been supported by increased allocations toward hedge funds by other institutional investors (such as pension funds, endowments, and foundations). The search for "alternative" investments has reflected (1) a general dissatisfaction with traditional "benchmark-based" portfolio management amid poor performance of global markets in recent years; (2) the growing asset-liability mismatches of many institutional accounts in mature markets and, hence, the need to pick up yield; and (3) the aggressive marketing efforts of investment consultants. Indeed, many institutional investors prefer to invest in hedge funds through funds of hedge funds, because of lower monitoring costs, easier scaling of investments, and better opportunities to diversify across a larger number of styles/ managers. As a result, the number of funds of funds has continued to expand rapidly over the past two years, while their ability to allocate the growing institutional investments efficiently has not been tested yet.

The hedge funds most active in emerging markets are global funds, dedicated emerging market funds, macro funds, and event-driven funds (distressed securities and merger arbitrage).[22] Macro hedge funds are the "classic" opportunistic hedge funds that take positions whenever they see apparent macroeconomic imbalances that are not properly reflected in asset prices; they use leverage and derivatives, and their investment horizon can be either short (under one month) or long (more than 12 months). Global hedge funds typically use a top-down/bottom-up approach in that they tend to be stock-pickers in the markets that they like based on macroeconomic analysis. Dedicated emerging market hedge funds are

---

[19]Hong Kong SAR and Singapore have recently allowed hedge funds to be marketed to retail investors. In Hong Kong SAR, minimum individual subscription thresholds are: (1) single hedge fund, US$50,000; (2) fund of hedge funds, US$10,000; and (3) hedge funds with a capital guarantee feature, no minimum subscription. In Singapore, differentiated minimum subscription levels are: (1) single hedge fund, S$100,000 (US$59,000 per investor); (2) fund of hedge funds, S$20,000 (US$12,000) per investor; and (3) capital protected or capital guaranteed funds, no minimum subscription.

[20]According to Tremont TASS, one of the leading hedge fund data providers. It should also be noted that the majority of the top 100 hedge funds, which are believed to have more than $300 billion in assets under management, do not report to any data vendors. Thus, most hedge fund data providers capture at best 60 percent of the hedge fund universe and typically estimate the assets under management of other funds not included in their databases.

[21]The source for European and Asian-based hedge funds, Eureka Hedge, does not provide historical series on assets under management.

[22]Convertible arbitrage and fixed-income arbitrage funds that may occasionally invest in emerging market securities as well are typically included in the "market neutral" category. It should be noted, however, that there are significant differences between the "style" classifications used by various hedge fund data providers, and, at present, there is no single database that offers both consistent classification (by asset class/region/investment method) and comprehensive data coverage of the hedge fund universe.

similar in their investment strategies to global hedge funds, but tend to focus on specific regions. Event-driven funds try to profit on asset price movements around special events, such as mergers or acquisitions (merger arbitrage) or default (distressed securities).

In normal times, hedge funds are generally cautious about investing in locally traded assets in emerging market countries because of the relatively high cross-border risk, though they may at times do so when there is a clear trend in credit dynamics and an upside potential in local instruments is perceived to be higher than that in the foreign currency denominated bonds.[23] Indeed, the hedge funds' activities in many emerging markets are often constrained by the lack of infrastructure for borrowing/lending securities (or explicit regulatory constraints on short selling), lack of derivative instruments, thin markets, and high concentration of liquidity in a few instruments. In such markets, hedge funds often tend to have a long bias and use strategies similar to those employed by mutual funds. Although at present hedge funds' exposures to most local emerging equity and bond markets are relatively small compared to that of other institutional investors, hedge funds will likely become a bigger part of the crossover investor base for emerging market instruments going forward,[24] especially given the recent rapid expansion of the global hedge fund industry, and in particular that of dedicated emerging market hedge funds.[25]

In considering hedge fund activities in both primary and secondary markets for emerging market claims, analysts have debated the role of hedge funds as a source of either liquidity and/or potentially destabilizing trading strategies. The impact of the hedge funds' activities on price dynamics depends on the funds' strategies and investment horizon. Given that hedge funds, by nature, are more nimble than traditional "real money funds" and tend to trade more actively, they generally contribute to higher turnover and better liquidity in markets in which they participate. For example, as a result of the exit of hedge funds and proprietary trading desks of investment banks from the South African foreign exchange spot and swap markets after the tightening of capital controls in the second half of 2001, the average daily turnover fell by over 40 percent. At the same time, the bid-ask spreads widened and the implied foreign exchange rate options' volatility increased. Also, since hedge funds typically have lock-up periods and do not experience redemption pressures similar to those faced by retail mutual funds, they are better able to invest in less liquid securities and also to withstand periods of high volatility. Thus, hedge funds are less likely to be forced to sell into a falling market and can, at times, maintain contrarian positions during extended periods. All of the above suggests that hedge funds can and, in fact, do play a positive (or even stabilizing) role in various markets. However, because hedge funds have fewer investment restrictions than other insti-

[23]However, hedge funds, especially macro hedge funds, are known to punt fixed income and local currency markets in emerging market countries when there are perceived macroeconomic imbalances that are not properly reflected in asset prices (short-term directional bets) or specific misalignments in interest and exchange rates (e.g., a profitable "carry trade" opportunity).

[24]Compared to the pre-Asian crisis period, hedge funds are not nearly as important players in emerging debt markets as they used to be, mainly because they are now a smaller part of the emerging debt market investor base and also not as large (or as leveraged) as back then. Based on the information provided by a major market-maker in emerging debt markets, hedge funds now account for only 17 percent (12 percent macro hedge funds, 5 percent dedicated emerging market hedge funds) of the emerging debt market foreign institutional investor base, while in 1998, they accounted for about 30 percent (20 percent macro hedge funds, 10 percent dedicated emerging market hedge funds).

[25]According to one of the leading hedge fund data providers (CISDM/formerly MAR/Hedge), total assets under management of emerging market hedge funds have doubled during 2003, reaching over $40 billion.

tutional investors, they are perceived to have an "edge" over other investors as well as the ability to manipulate markets. Another concern is that since hedge funds use leverage, they may have to unwind positions at times of market stress, exacerbating selling pressures and volatility.

The finance literature has covered extensively the types of trading strategies that could play a role in destabilizing market dynamics. Such strategies include various momentum strategies, such as *positive-feedback trading*, which involves selling an asset after its price falls or buying an asset when its price rises, and *herding*—that is, imitating the behavior of other market participants instead of trading on one's own private information. Positive feedback trading can be a result of dynamic hedging, an application of a "stop-loss" rule (i.e., liquidating a position when investor's losses reach certain critical level), or a decision to unwind a leveraged position because of the inability or unwillingness to meet the margin calls (a shortfall in collateral on the margin account due to a decline in asset price).[26]

However, both academic and market research that analyzed the hedge funds' activities during the emerging market currency crises of 1994–98 found little evidence that hedge funds consistently used "positive-feedback" strategies (Brown, Goetzmann, and Park, 1998; Fung, Hsieh, and Tsatsaronis, 1999; Fung and Hsieh, 2000; and Eichengreen and Mathieson, 1998) or other strategies that could have had a destabilizing impact on market dynamics. In addition, these studies found no evidence that hedge funds earned abnormal profits during the Mexican or the Asian currency crises. The analysis of hedge fund positioning in several more recent emerging market currency crisis episodes yielded similar conclusions (see the Appendix to this chapter).

With regard to herding, hedge funds are generally perceived to be less likely to "herd" than other investors, such as mutual funds and pension funds, because they tend to be relatively well informed and their performance is not measured relative to any benchmark.[27] A related concern is that hedge funds and proprietary trading desks (often referred to as "smart money") are often "imitated" by other investors.[28] Although market participants may at times attempt to mimic hedge-fund strategies, hedge funds are usually reluctant to reveal their portfolio allocations because of concerns that the replication of their portfolios by other traders may erode profit margins. There are, however, circumstances when hedge funds may use trading strategies that require a coordinated effort of many market players to be successful. The most obvious example is a speculative attack against a currency peg/band. In this case, hedge funds would (if and when they initiate the attack) actually prefer to be followed by other market participants, because their actions may help to generate a critical mass that is needed to break the peg. Then, for example, the leaked information about position(s) of certain large hedge fund(s) vis-à-vis an emerging market currency may serve as a trigger for similar position-taking (or herding) by other investors, especially if hedge funds are perceived to be better informed than the rest of the market (see, for example, Corsetti and others, 2004).

As far as market manipulation is concerned, the evidence against hedge funds presented in various sources has been mainly anecdotal. For example, the Market Dynamics Study

---

[26]Various types of market manipulation, such as trade-based or information-based manipulation, may disrupt markets as well.

[27]It is often difficult to distinguish between "herding" and similar position taking based on private information by several different investors following the same or similar "investment styles."

[28]However, given the lack of high-frequency data on the hedge funds' positions and performance, it is difficult to test the hypothesis about hedge funds being "market leaders" during the episodes of market turbulence.

Group of the Financial Stability Forum, which was asked to assess concerns of authorities in Australia, Hong Kong SAR, Malaysia, New Zealand, Singapore, and South Africa about the possible destabilizing impact of highly leveraged institutions (proprietary desks and hedge funds) in the foreign exchange markets of these countries during 1998, "was unable to reach a conclusion on the extent to which manipulation and collusion might have occurred in the six economies and whether market integrity was compromised." (Financial Stability Forum, 2000, page 125).

One form of market manipulation that hedge funds have been frequently suspected of is the trade-based manipulation. For instance, speculators can establish positions in two related markets (e.g., spot and future markets or primary and secondary markets) and by aggressively selling/buying in one market (at a loss) induce the less informed players to take certain actions that would move the price in a related market in the direction that would allow speculators to more than offset their losses (see, for example, Kyle, 1984, on trade-based manipulation in spot and future markets; also, the many accounts of the Hong-Kong SAR "double play"). One of the more recent complaints about hedge funds manipulating markets by simultaneously taking positions in different market segments comes from emerging market debt fund managers. According to some market participants, after shorting some sovereign bonds in the secondary market, hedge funds would often try to induce an upward shift of the sovereign yield curve by obtaining a sizable amount of a "new" bond just issued by the sovereign in the primary market and almost immediately selling it in the secondary market (El-Erian, 2003). Such strategy could indeed be profitable, if the gains from shorting the "old" bond more than offset the losses incurred when flipping the

"new" bond (the latter can be either because of the relative sizes of the short and long positions or because of a relatively large price fall of the illiquid "old" bond).

Local Institutional Investors

The growth of institutional investors in the mature markets since the 1970s was associated with substantial growth and structural changes in capital markets, and emerging markets are following a similar path of growing institutionalization of savings and capital market development. Institutional investors' assets under management are also growing rapidly in most emerging markets, with the enactment of pension fund reforms and the growing popularity of mutual funds. Low levels of insurance penetration are also leading to relatively rapid growth in insurance companies' assets under management. The growth in assets under management is contributing to the development of local securities markets, but excessive regulation and lack of investor sophistication is creating important challenges for the efficiency and stability of local markets.

Pension Funds and Insurance Companies

A number of emerging markets have introduced pension reforms that are leading to an important increase in assets under management of private asset managers. Following the lead of Chile, which initiated the reform drive in Latin America, several other countries in Latin America and, more recently, in central and eastern Europe have adopted variants of a funded, privately managed, defined contribution personal accounts retirement system.[29] Assets under management of private pension funds in Latin America have grown from around 4 percent of GDP in 1997, to around 9 percent of GDP in 2002 (see Table 4.3).

---

[29]Most countries still saw the need to continue the pay-as-you-go (PAYG) system for older workers during a transitional period, and the compromise was to move to what the World Bank refers to as the multi-pillar framework (Holzmann, 1999).

Table 4.3. Pension Fund Assets
(In percent of GDP)

	1991	1992	1993	1994	1995	1996	1997	1998	1999	2000	2001	2002
Latin America												
Argentina	n.a.	n.a.	n.a.	0.2	1.0	2.0	3.0	3.9	5.9	7.2	7.7	11.2
Bolivia	n.a.	n.a.	n.a.	n.a.	n.a.	n.a.	0.8	2.5	4.0	5.8	6.3	7.3
Colombia	n.a.	n.a.	n.a.	0.0	0.3	0.8	1.3	2.1	3.3	4.3	5.3	6.7
Costa Rica	n.a.	n.a.	n.a.	n.a.	n.a.	n.a.	n.a.	n.a.	n.a.	n.a.	0.7	0.8
Chile	18.3	22.6	26.0	28.2	31.2	33.2	32.8	38.5	42.2	46.1	52.5	53.5
El Salvador	n.a.	n.a.	n.a.	n.a.	n.a.	n.a.	n.a.	0.4	1.7	3.7	5.8	7.6
Mexico	n.a.	n.a.	n.a.	n.a.	n.a.	n.a.	0.2	1.4	2.4	2.9	4.4	5.0
Peru	n.a.	n.a.	0.1	0.6	1.1	1.7	2.6	3.1	4.7	5.2	6.8	8.0
Uruguay	n.a.	n.a.	n.a.	n.a.	n.a.	0.2	0.9	1.7	2.8	4.0	5.6	7.2
Subtotal	1.1	1.4	1.5	1.9	3.2	3.6	4.0	5.2	6.3	7.0	8.2	9.2
Europe												
Bulgaria	n.a.	n.a.	n.a.	n.a.	n.a.	n.a.	n.a.	n.a.	n.a.	0.3	0.3	0.8
Hungary	n.a.	n.a.	n.a.	n.a.	n.a.	n.a.	n.a.	1.3	2.1	3.1	3.9	4.5
Kazakhstan	n.a.	n.a.	n.a.	n.a.	n.a.	n.a.	n.a.	1.3	2.7	4.2	5.6	6.0
Poland	n.a.	n.a.	n.a.	n.a.	n.a.	n.a.	n.a.	n.a.	n.a.	1.5	2.4	3.5
Subtotal	n.a.	n.a.	n.a.	n.a.	n.a.	n.a.	n.a.	0.4	0.6	2.0	2.9	3.8
Asia												
Hong Kong SAR	n.a.	n.a.	n.a.	n.a.	n.a.	n.a.	n.a.	n.a.	n.a.	0.4	0.4	0.4
Malaysia	38.5	40.3	41.5	42.6	43.4	45.4	45.9	51.1	53.9	52.3	55.9	56.5
Singapore	61.7	63.4	55.5	53.5	55.5	55.8	56.2	62.2	64.1	60.3	63.8	64.9
Subtotal	21.7	23.8	22.5	22.8	24.9	25.3	23.5	20.8	21.5	20.5	21.6	21.5
Total	6.3	6.9	6.7	7.1	9.6	10.2	9.8	9.8	11.0	11.4	12.6	14.2

Sources: IMF, *International Financial Statistics;* Federacion Internacional de Administradoras de Pensiones (FIAP); Central Provident Fund (Singapore); Employees Provident Fund (Malaysia); Financial Supervisory Authority (Hungary); Mandatory Provident Fund (Hong Kong SAR); and IMF staff calculations.

Chile's assets under management have reached 54 percent of GDP after 22 years of operation of the fully funded system, while the other countries are just in the early stages of asset accumulation (see Table 4.3). The growth of assets under management has been particularly rapid in Mexico, Peru, Uruguay, Hungary, and Kazakhstan.

Retirement income in Asia is provided mainly through government-sponsored national provident funds.[30] For example, in Malaysia and Singapore the government sponsors (and to a large extent also manages) a fully funded, defined-contribution system for civilian workers, and these systems have achieved a high level of assets under management (see Table 4.3). In Korea, the national pension system is fully funded but offers defined benefits and has not reached the levels of other Asian nations. National mandatory provident funds have not contributed substantially to the development of local capital markets in spite of managing sizable assets (Holzmann, MacArthur, and Sin, 2000). Fund management in these countries is very conservative, with the result that assets are heavily concentrated in government securities. In Korea, for instance, two-thirds of the assets of the National Pension Scheme are channeled to the government as direct loans, while a large share of Singapore's Central Provident Fund assets are invested in non-marketable government securities (Asher and Newman, 2001). Centralized fund management also may have held up the development of a competitive fund management industry and its

[30]The exception in the region is Hong Kong SAR, where the Mandatory Provident Fund allows citizens to select their investment plans among a large number of approved private investment funds. However, the system started operating in the year 2000 and has yet to accumulate a sizable amount of assets under management.

positive impact in local securities markets (Holzmann, MacArthur, and Sin, 2000).[31]

The rapid growth of assets managed by private pension funds in Latin America and central Europe is having a positive impact on the development of local securities markets, which has so far been concentrated in local bond markets. Pension funds have contributed to government efforts to develop liquid benchmark yield curves, especially in Hungary, Poland, and Mexico. They have also supported the growth of medium- to long-term corporate bonds.[32] A remarkable achievement in the case of Chile is the creation of a long-run market in corporate bonds. As documented in Cifuentes, Desormeaux, and Gonzalez (2002), the average maturity of bond issuance was between 10 and 15 years in the first half of the 1990s, and more recently it has been between 10 and 20 years, and even 30-year bonds have been issued. Most corporate bonds in Chile are indexed to the *Unidad de Fomento* (UF, a unit of account linked to the CPI), and analysts agree that indexed bonds have been an optimal instrument for pension funds and insurance companies. In Argentina in the second half of the 1990s and in Mexico in the last four years, the rapid growth in local corporate bond issuance has also been associated with an acceleration in the growth of pension funds' assets under management (Roldos, 2003). Pension funds have also had a significant impact in Chile's stock markets as well as in other financial markets and institutions.[33]

The growth in private pension funds' assets under management has contributed not just to the development of local securities market. It has also had a significant impact on the sovereign external debt markets. Brainard (2001) notes that local pension funds and their investment guidelines have become essential considerations for investors in external debt markets. Developing a local investor base for sovereign external debt reduces price volatility and hence market risk for foreign investors. Despite the short history of some reformed systems, the hypothesis that assets managed by local pension funds offer stability to foreign debt markets seems to have empirical backing (see Roldos, 2003).

The growth in pension funds' assets under management is likely to accelerate over the next decade or so, and it is unclear whether local securities markets will be able to respond to such growth in the demand for financial assets. Projections from Salomon Smith Barney (see Garcia-Cantera and others, 2002) suggests that by the year 2015 most systems are going to reach a level of assets under management of around 25 to 30 percent of GDP, roughly the level of the average of the Group of Seven countries in 1998. Although the institutional, demographic, and financial structures differ across both groups of countries, a comparison of both experiences (Roldos, 2003) suggests that securities markets in the pension reform countries could potentially double in size (relative to GDP) in about a

[31]Governments in Asia have started to encourage individual saving plans, adopting measures such as favorable tax treatment to individual pension plans in Korea; individual saving plans assets, however, remain small throughout the region. Singapore has also allowed members to invest a small portion of CPF savings in approved mutual funds, while Malaysia has granted permission to the EPF to invest offshore.

[32]See Mathieson and others (2004). As noted below, other institutional investors (in particular, insurance companies, see Chapter III) benefit as well with the development of an adequate volume and variety of credit products.

[33]Walker and LeFort (2000) find a statistically significant impact of pension funds' assets under management on Chile's equity prices and the cost of capital, together with a noticeable contribution to lower volatility and sensitivity to external shocks. The authors also show that in the cases of Chile, Argentina, and Peru, pension reform contributed significantly to the accumulation of "institutional capital," a combination of a better legal and regulatory framework, increased professionalism in the investment decision making process, and increased transparency and integrity. They also note that the accumulation of funds was associated with the growth of annuities, mortgage bonds, and other asset-backed securities; the creation of closed-end mutual funds and local rating companies; and the introduction of innovations in securities trading and custody (see also Yermo, 2003b).

decade. Whether these emerging markets could respond to the increased pension fund demand with a substantial volume and enough diversity of securities, as well as with the institutions to ensure financial stability, is one of the key questions for emerging markets and one of the key challenges for regulators of securities markets and the pension industry. In particular, portfolio restrictions intended to protect workers' future pension benefits and to foster the development of local securities markets may be preventing an adequate diversification of the funds' portfolios and may be distorting asset values.

Although almost no pension fund in emerging markets is allowed to follow the "prudent man" rules, four of the big countries in Table 4.4 (Argentina, Brazil, Hungary, and Poland) are allowed to invest up to half of their portfolio in stocks, and another group (Chile, Colombia, and Peru) has a ceiling of 30 to 40 percent. The exception is Mexico, which, together with a number of smaller countries in the region, does not allow pension funds to invest in equities.[34] Actual portfolio allocations do not seem to be extremely constrained by the limits, and show as much variance as in the mature markets. While in the U.S. and the U.K. pension funds hold around 60 percent of their assets in stocks, Japan's pension funds hold 28 percent and Germany's almost none. Emerging market pension funds hold smaller shares of their portfolios in stocks. In central Europe, Poland stands out with a 28 percent allocation in stocks, while Hungary holds 14 percent of its portfolio in shares and the Czech Republic holds 11 percent. In Latin America, Peru's funds hold around 31 percent of their portfolios in stocks, while Brazil's funds hold 28 percent; Argentina, Colombia, and Chile hold less than 10 percent in shares.[35]

Table 4.4. Pension Funds Portfolio Limits and Actual Asset Allocation, 2001–02
(In percent of total assets)

	Equities		Foreign Assets	
	Limit[1]	Actual[2]	Limit[1]	Actual[2]
Mature markets				
United Kingdom	P	60.9	P	22.9
United States	P	58.8	P	11.0[3]
Germany	30	0.1	30[4]	7.0[3]
Japan	30	27.7	30[5]	22.9
Canada	—	28.2	30	15.0[3]
France	—	—	—	5.0[3]
Italy	P	4.4	P[6]	0.0[3]
Emerging markets				
Argentina	49	6.6	10	8.9
Brazil	50	27.8	0	—
Chile	39	9.0	25	16.4
Colombia	30	4.3	10	—
Mexico	0	0.0	10[7]	—
Peru	35	31.3	8	7.2
Hungary	50	13.8	30	2.5
Poland	50	27.6	5[8]	0.3[3]

Sources: For mature markets, OECD (2003); Davis and Steil (2001); Davis (2002); and Yermo (2003a). For Emerging Markets, FIAP; Brainard (2001); Roldos (2003); and Garcia-Cantera and others (2002).

[1]Numbers refer to maximum allocation; P indicates that the prudent man rule applies.

[2]Data for mature markets are end of 2001 and for emerging markets are end of 2002.

[3]For 1998, see Davis (2002).

[4]In EU equity, 10 percent in foreign bonds and equities of non-EU countries. These limits are for *pensionkassen*, which are under the supervision of the insurance regulator. Other *pensionfonds* are not subject to investment limits.

[5]No investment limits for public employee funds.

[6]Securities of OECD countries not traded in regulated markets up to 50 percent; non-OECD securities traded in regulated markets limited to 5 percent (forbidden if traded in non-regulated markets).

[7]Only sovereign and investment grade Mexican corporate debt permitted in foreign limit.

[8]Polish Brady Bonds do not count against this limit.

There are a number of reasons to justify relatively large bond allocations in pension funds' portfolios, but diversification arguments suggest that equities may deserve a bigger role than they currently have in some countries. Campbell and Viceira (2002) indicate that bonds—in particular, indexed bonds—should comprise a large share of the

---

[34]Although legislation to invest in equities has already been approved, some members of the board of the regulatory agency (CONSAR) remain averse toward investment in equities due to perceived riskiness of the asset class. There is, however, also a gradual recognition that workers' savings would reap higher returns from investing in equities albeit at higher risk, especially in the current low interest rate environment and the rising stock market.

[35]In the case of Chile, the share increases to 21.8 percent if one includes holdings of equity mutual funds.

optimal portfolio of long-term investors. Besides containing the risk inherent in equities, a large allocation of government bonds helps to smooth the transition to a funded system. The recent Argentine crisis, however, has highlighted the risks involved in a concentrated exposure to the sovereign: as the government tried to decrease the cost of servicing its debt in 2001, pension fund companies and banks were forced to make asset allocation decisions that they probably would not have made in other market conditions (see Garcia-Cantera and others, 2002).[36] Thus, as noted in Box 4.1, an optimal asset allocation would include a non-negligible equity allocation. Indeed, despite the extended bear market in equities in the early 2000s, well-balanced portfolios have performed relatively well in the medium term. If local stock markets are unable to provide the needed instruments, local pension funds ought to seek international alternatives.

The limits to investments in foreign securities are stricter in emerging markets than in the mature markets (Table 4.4), but some fund managers appear to be reluctant to increase international allocations. Here, again, the experience of Chile is a good example. Only a decade after the inception of the private pension funds were they allowed to invest in foreign assets, up to 3 percent of their portfolio. The limit was then increased to 9 percent in 1995, 12 percent in 1997, 20 percent in 2001, 25 percent in June 2002, and has been at 30 percent since December 2003. Pension funds did not diversify abroad in a meaningful way in the first half of the 1990s, owing to high domestic assets returns. But following two years of large negative returns in the local stock market, a strong reallocation toward foreign assets began in 1997 and the funds currently hold around 25 percent of their assets abroad.[37] In Hungary, where the limit has been at 30 percent for several years, actual allocations are under 5 percent as a result of bad experiences with losses in the aftermath of the bursting of the TMT bubble. In Colombia, funds were allowed to invest in international equity mutual funds in April 2002, but market participants argue that allocations are under 2 percent because of a fear of not meeting required minimum returns.

The limits on international investments could distort not only portfolio allocations but also asset prices. Such limits amount to controls on capital outflows that impose a wedge, for instance, between the prices of local and foreign bonds. The case of Mexico is illustrative. In February 2003, the spread between external (swapped to pesos through cross-currency swaps) and local bonds was around 300 basis points. Analysts consider that the wide spread was caused mainly by regulations preventing some investors, especially pension funds, from arbitraging the domestic and external curves (Abdel-Motaal, 2002). The spread compressed to around 100 basis points in September 2003. The compression was arguably driven by increased arbitrage trades by institutions other than pension funds and by the gradual phasing out of these constraints by the authorities (see Box 4.3 for details). Similarly, in Peru, Brady bonds pay much higher spreads than local corporate bonds, owing to the fact that pensions can invest only up to 5 percent of their portfolio in Bradys versus 40 percent in corporate bonds.

[36]The subsequent default, devaluation, and pesificacion of deposits and local bonds have caused losses to the pension funds and have raised concerns on the increased intervention of the government in the industry. The Superintendency of Pension Funds notes, however, that the pension fund administrators have managed to prevent to a large extent the fall in asset values in real terms, even when the dollar value of assets under management declined substantially.

[37]A large share is done through global mutual funds. Mexican regulators are reluctant to follow this route as they argue that it would be difficult to monitor the funds' allocations and that pensioners would be paying management fees twice.

Box 4.3. Pension Fund Regulations and Local Yield Curves: The Case of Mexico[1]

During the past three years, it has been observed that the external U.S. dollar-denominated Mexican sovereign yield curve, when swapped into Mexican pesos using cross-currency swaps, always carries a premium (or currency swap spread) over the domestic Mexican peso-denominated sovereign yield curve. For instance, the eight-year maturity cross-currency swap spread of 300 basis points observed in February 2003 was not unusual given the historical range of 150 to 350 basis points observed for the period 2000–02 (see the Figure). Also, the currency swap spread tends to widen with maturity. It has been widely documented that domestic corporate issuers have taken advantage of this yield curve anomaly to lower their financing costs by simultaneously issuing peso-denominated bonds and swapping the peso payments into U.S. dollars (Oswald and Sekiguchi, 2002; and Kumar, 2003).

The existence of the currency swap spread creates a carry-trade arbitrage opportunity for investors. The simplest way to execute the carry-trade arbitrage is by selling short domestic sovereign bonds and using the proceeds to buy an external sovereign bond. The coupons of the external bond are then swapped into Mexican pesos using a currency swap to meet the coupon payments corresponding to the short position in the domestic bond. Because local markets in Mexico only offer floating-for-floating currency swaps, it is first necessary to swap the bonds' coupons into floating rate using fixed-for-floating interest rate swaps.

The long persistence of the carry-trade arbitrage suggests the existence of fundamental and technical factors that drive a wedge between both yield curves. The foremost fundamental factor affecting the cross-currency swap spread is default risk. The instruments underlying the domestic yield curve and the external sovereign curve are issued under different jurisdictions, and hence are subject to different legal regimes.

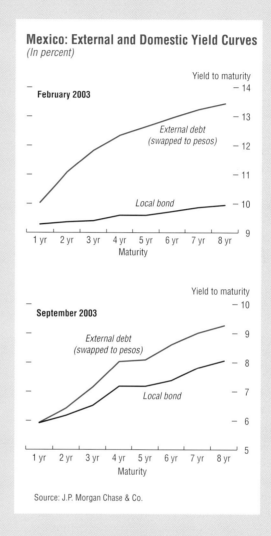

Mexico: External and Domestic Yield Curves
(In percent)

Source: J.P. Morgan Chase & Co.

Therefore, recovery rates in case of default are different for domestic and external bonds.

It can also be argued that default risk is higher for external bonds than for domestic bonds. For instance, governments can always print money to pay off the domestic debt. They can also exercise pressure on domestic investors to force a rollover of domestic debt, as was the case in Argentina in 2001.[2]

---

[1]The box is based on the analysis presented in Abdel-Motaal (2002).

[2]Notwithstanding these arguments, the Russian default on domestic debt in 1998 shows that external debt is not always riskier than domestic debt.

Box 4.3 *(concluded)*

The carry-trade arbitrage strategy is risky since the sovereign may default on the external bond. In this case, the investor cannot count on the coupons of the external bond to meet the U.S. dollar payments in the currency swap.

The arguments above suggest that the external bond must carry a premium or spread over the domestic bond to compensate investors for taking additional default risk. However, market analysts consider that the default risk premium is not large enough to account fully for the observed spreads. According to them, technical factors, most of them associated with investment restrictions that affect Mexican pension funds (AFORES), are the main drivers of the spreads (Abdel-Motaal, 2002; and Oswald and Sekiguchi, 2002). The technical factors include a lack of repo markets; regulations on pension funds' use of derivatives and investments in foreign currency instruments; and the funds' portfolio duration. These factors are explained next.

The first step in executing the carry-trade arbitrage strategy is selling short domestic bonds. This step can be executed only if there is a liquid local repo market for government bonds. In practice, this market is non-existent in Mexico, as short-selling of domestic bonds is not allowed. Investors can still take short positions using buy-sell operations. These operations, however, lack enough liquidity and are viable only for investors taking rather small positions (Abdel-Motaal, Newman, and Romo, 2003).

Before December 2003, pension fund regulations prohibited the use of derivatives, including interest rate and currency swaps. In consequence, a substantial segment of the domestic investor base is effectively barred from executing the carry-trade arbitrage strategy. Furthermore, if pension funds were fixed interest rate receivers in interest rate swaps they could exercise downward pressure on spreads even if they were not arbitraging the yield curve anomaly. Market analysts forecast that spreads will likely start compressing once pension funds are allowed to trade derivatives in early 2004.

Restrictions on foreign investment also contribute to sustain the currency swap spread. Pension funds cannot hold more than 10 percent of assets in Mexican external debt. So, even when pension funds can trade derivatives, the foreign investment restriction reduces the funds' incentives to earn the currency swap spread.

In spite of these technical factors, the Figure shows the currency swap spread compressed from February 2003 to September 2003. This compression can be attributed partly to the exploitation of the yield curve anomaly by investors other than pension funds and partly to an extension of portfolio duration following the introduction of Value-at-Risk (VaR) in December 2002.

Failure to adjust restrictions on pension funds' investment policies could increase the concentration of risk exposures and magnify price volatility. In addition to restrictions on equities and international investments, most countries have also adopted tight restrictions on the percentage of a company's capital or outstanding bonds that a pension fund can hold (Yermo, 2000). For example, in Argentina, funds can hold at most 5 percent of a company's capital and 5 percent of its bonds. When local stock markets are small (as in most emerging markets), with a limited number of qualifying companies, rapidly growing funds will quickly reach these limits, reducing their possibilities of diversification and increasing the risk of local stock market bubbles.[38] Market participants expressed fears of a market bubble in the Warsaw Stock Exchange when Polish pension funds,

[38]For example, in Chile, until 1997, only 30 stocks out of a total of 300 were eligible for pension fund investment. In Argentina, fund managers noted that there were roughly only 14–15 eligible companies listed on the stock market.

together with local and international mutual funds, shifted their portfolios away from bonds and into local equities (Kwiecinski and Wiatr, 2003). Also, as the size of funds grows relative to the local markets, individual funds are often able to move prices. This often also results in liquidity constraints for funds, since they cannot sell assets without putting downward pressure on prices. For example, when the Chilean investment regime was partially liberalized in 1985, pension funds found it difficult to close their fixed-income position and asset allocations changed only slowly in response to the liberalization (Srinivas, Whitehouse, and Yermo, 2000).

The reduction of limits on foreign investments by local pension funds amounts to a removal of capital controls on outflows, and care should be taken about the macroeconomic consequences.[39] In particular, as the Chilean and Canadian experiences have shown, a sudden shift of pension funds' allocations abroad could lead to a substantial exchange rate depreciation (Patterson and Normand, 2002; and Roldos, 2003). In Chile, the increase in the share of foreign assets, from 2 percent by end-1997 to 12 percent by end-1999, was associated with a roughly 20 percent depreciation of the peso. In Canada, an increase of the foreign investment limit from 20 percent in January 2000 to 30 percent in January 2001 contributed to a three-fold increase in capital outflows, which in turn contributed to a 10 percent depreciation of the Canadian dollar in the period January 2000 through January 2002.[40]

In central Europe and Latin America, mark-to-market and minimum return requirements have encouraged herd behavior and excessive focus on short-term returns among pension fund managers. Some countries require funds to achieve certain minimum rates of return, often calculated relative to the industry average.[41] This amounts to an extreme form of "peer-group" benchmarking that induces funds to move in herds, allocating their assets in a suboptimal manner and magnifying price fluctuations. Similarly, in several countries pension funds have to mark-to-market their portfolios on a daily basis for regulatory purposes—and on a monthly basis for investors. Increased focus on short-term results induce managers to behave like mutual fund managers, and there is excessive turnover in pension fund portfolios, as is the case in Hungary and Poland. Also, the use of risk management tools (such as Value-at-Risk in Mexico) leads pension fund managers to avoid volatile assets with favorable risk-adjusted returns since they increase the return volatility of the portfolio.

Herd behavior does not seem to be a problem for provident funds in Asia, as the national provident fund is the sole provider of pension benefits. However, there are concerns on the funds' performance and accountability. National provident funds in Asia are centrally managed and, in general, follow conservative investment strategies. Empirical studies suggest that this has resulted in poor performance in several Asian funds. For instance, provident funds in Malaysia and Singapore have performed marginally better than bank deposits. In addition, the allocation of pension funds' assets also may be excessively influenced by political interests that do not necessarily benefit contributors. For instance, pension funds in Korea were asked to contribute to a stock market stabilization plan in 2000, while in Malaysia, provident fund assets have been used to recapitalize banks and finance housing construction (*FinanceAsia,*

[39]Other things equal, this would exacerbate the position of some emerging markets as net exporters of capital (see IMF, 2003), an issue that will be taken up in future issues of the GFSR.

[40]In both cases, however, the depreciations were also associated with deteriorations in non-energy commodity prices.

[41]For an overview of regulations in Latin America, see Yermo (2000).

Table 4.5. Assets Under Management by Insurance Companies[1]
(In percent of GDP)

	1998	1999	2000	2001	2002
Asia					
Korea	25.8	29.4	30.2	34.0	35.8
Malaysia	13.6	15.1	14.9	20.5	21.0
Philippines	3.5	3.7	3.8	3.7	4.0
Singapore	18.5	23.3	24.4	34.1	37.6
Thailand	5.8	6.5	6.6	7.6	8.3
Eastern Europe, Middle East, Africa					
Hungary	3.3	3.9	4.2	4.5	3.8
Poland[2]	3.0	3.6	4.3	5.0	6.0
Turkey	1.1	1.6	1.5	1.5	n.a.
South Africa[2]				74.4	68.7
Latin America					
Argentina	1.8	2.3	2.7	3.2	4.6
Brazil	n.a.	2.1	2.6	2.6	2.8
Chile	14.4	17.1	18.6	19.2	19.9
Colombia	0.8	0.8	0.8	0.9	1.0
Mexico	1.4	1.4	1.3	1.5	1.7
Peru	na	na	na	2.0	2.2

Sources: National regulators; and IMF staff estimates.
[1]Both life and general insurers.
[2]Life insurers only.

October 2000). Some authors have also noted a number of challenges in the transparency and accountability of provident funds.[42]

In contrast to Latin America and emerging Europe, local life insurance companies are the leading institutional investors in emerging Asia. This is related in part to the Asian tradition of using insurance products as savings products.[43] Assets under management have increased very rapidly over the past five years, particularly in Korea, Malaysia, and Singapore (Table 4.5). In Latin America, however, pension funds are the more dominant institutional investors, while insurance penetration remains low. The growth of pension funds has nevertheless contributed to the expansion of the life insurance sector, in particular with a sharp rise in the sale of annuities (see Garcia-

Cantera and others, 2001). The growth of annuities markets has not been restricted to privatized systems, and Singapore has also witnessed a rapid growth in recent years, as a result of the reform of regulations governing withdrawals from the Central Provident Fund (see MacKenzie, 2002).

The investment decisions of life insurance companies operating in emerging markets depend on regulatory constraints, the development of local capital markets, and risk management guidelines. In most emerging market economies, insurers are required to maintain local assets to match local liabilities.[44] Thus most local insurance assets are invested in local capital markets. With the exception of Hong Kong SAR (which follows prudent man rules) and, to some extent, Singapore, most countries have a strong bias toward fixed-income instruments, since many regulations explicitly limit investments in equity and real estate and prohibit investment in foreign instruments.

Increasingly, insurers in emerging markets are beginning to use asset and liability management principles and risk management tools to make their strategic asset allocation decisions. However, the lack of long-term, fixed-income instruments and relative illiquidity in bond and equity markets constitutes the biggest hurdle to the management of duration gaps. In Korea, for example, a typical life insurer's liability has an average duration of 7 years, while the average duration of its assets is only 3½ years. Similar duration gaps exist in many other emerging markets. Faced with such a gap, insurers have relatively few options to increase asset duration and most strive to invest in the long-end of the local fixed-income market. As a result, insurance compa-

[42]Holzman, MacArthur, and Sin (2000); Asher (1999 and 2000); Asher and Newman (2001).

[43]In countries where insurance products are also used for savings purposes, the products tend to have a savings component in addition to the standard term life insurance.

[44]The "localization" requirement is intended for policyholder protection in cases of insurer's bankruptcy so that assets are held locally and can be used to compensate the policyholders. Hong Kong SAR is an exception. However, the Office of the Commissioner of Insurance is evaluating the current regulation on investment with a view to strengthen asset valuation and safeguard policyholder assets in the future.

nies are the largest investors in the 10-year segment of the local bond market. Also, while insurers provide a stable demand for local long bonds, their buy-and-hold behavior constrains liquidity in the secondary markets. This, in turn, makes portfolio adjustment costly and hinders asset and liability management. The paucity of interest rate derivatives and long-term swaps also constrains such activities.

Many insurers thus choose to manage duration gaps through the liability side by repricing existing products and offering new products of shorter duration. In particular, unit-linked products are gaining popularity in many emerging Asian and European markets.[45] In Hungary, for example, two-thirds of the new life insurance contracts are unit-linked products, while in Poland, one-third of life insurance products are unit-linked (Dorfman and Ennsfellner, 2002). These products usually carry a low minimum return with a "bonus" component depending on the equity market performance. The existence of the "bonus" effectively lowers the duration of the liability. By some estimates, a 20-year unit-linked life product has an effective duration of only six years. The emergence of unit-linked life products has transferred some market risk to policyholders and thus facilitates asset and liability management; however, such products pose certain competitive pressure to the mutual fund industry where traditional products carry no minimum return at all.

In a number of Latin American countries, a significant share of life insurance contracts are specified in foreign currency. This "dollarization" of liabilities is a consequence of the region's history of high inflation and exchange rate volatility. As a result, Mexican regulators, for instance, require that dollar-linked liabilities be matched with dollar-linked assets, making insurance companies one of the largest holders of sovereign dollar-denominated external debts (see Oswald and Sekiguchi, 2002). Although this offers significant support for these instruments, external diversification for the Mexican insurance industry is limited to portfolio investments in foreign-currency-denominated securities issued by Mexican entities.[46] In contrast, Colombia's regulatory framework does not have formal guidelines on asset-liability management. Nevertheless, even local insurance companies hold more than 20 percent of their assets in foreign-currency-denominated assets. Unlike the case of Mexico, Colombian insurance companies can invest in foreign currency debt instruments of any sovereign or corporate that is investment grade.

Most emerging markets have adopted solvency requirements for insurance companies that are based on or similar to those of the European Union directives (see OECD, 2001). A few economies, including Singapore, Indonesia, Malaysia, and Taiwan Province of China, have adopted risk-based capital (RBC) regimes that are similar to the U.S. and Japanese systems.[47] Under the European system, only underwriting risk is included in the calculation of the solvency requirement, while the U.S. and Japanese system explicitly accounts for investment and asset and liability mismatching risks in addition to the underwriting risk.[48] Given the growing importance of investment risks, analysts have argued that

---

[45]Unit-linked products are a form of variable life insurance products that combine insurance with an investment component. Usually the products carry a minimum return and in addition a "bonus" that varies with market movements. The appeal of this type of insurance is that the policyholders can benefit in a transparent way from the higher-than-average long-term returns on the equity markets while retaining the advantages of life insurance products.

[46]Insurance companies in Mexico are allowed to use derivatives for currency-asset-liability matching purposes, but in practice they rarely use them.

[47]See Chapter III for a broad description of the main mature market insurance regulations.

[48]The main risks insurers carry on their balance sheet can be classified as: (1) investment risks; (2) underwriting risks; and (3) asset/liability matching risks (see Babbel and Santomero, 1996; and Chapter III).

the European system does not adequately address the risks in insurance operation.[49] Under the European system, investment risks are controlled by means of investment regulations on a particular investment, asset class, or region. Consequently, regulators in many emerging market economies prescribe specific investments as well as the percentage of their assets that insurers are permitted to invest in each.

Moreover, many emerging market regulations do not provide specific guidance on asset and liability management, and this could lead to excessive risk taking. While subsidiaries of global insurance companies in emerging markets normally have to adhere to internal risk control guidelines on asset and liability management, local insurers usually lack such expertise and guidance. Therefore, some local insurers seek yield enhancement at the expense of asset and liability management. For example, in Hungary, market participants noted that during the recent turmoil in the local bond market that sent the short-term interest rates soaring, most local subsidiaries of global insurers continued to invest in the long end of the yield curve to minimize the duration gap. However, local insurers reportedly shifted their allocations to the short end of the curve to pick up yield at the expense of increasing their duration gap. When solvency requirements only account for underwriting risk, asset-liability mismatches do not cost the insurer in terms of statutory capital; market participants refer to this as "free risk." In the past, U.S. and Canadian life insurers faced similar situations, when competitive pressure drove insurance companies to incur asset and liability mismatches (and associated market and credit risks) while seeking higher returns (Briys and de Varenne, 1996). A large number of insurance companies failed in the United States in the late 1980s and early

1990s, while a few also went bankrupt in Canada in the early 1990s. These failures eventually led to changes in the U.S. and Canadian insurance regulations in the mid-1990s. (For the experience of insurance companies during recent emerging market crises, see Box 4.4.)

As in the mature markets, regulations in several emerging markets dictate minimum guaranteed returns on insurance products. However, only a few countries (including Thailand, Croatia, and Korea) reportedly have guaranteed returns that are higher than market rates. Moreover, in Thailand, policyholders are not only given guaranteed returns at maturity but they also enjoy guaranteed surrender values. During a rising interest rate environment, customers with products that are locked at guaranteed returns below the current market rate could simply cash out with the guaranteed surrender value and shop for better rates. This could force the insurers selling their bond portfolio at a loss. In a declining rate environment, many insurers have to re-calculate their liabilities on the historical products that were offered at a high guaranteed return with a lower discount rate. This re-calculation has reportedly caused many insurers to raise reserves to meet solvency requirements, which again could lead to undesirable portfolio adjustment.

Insurance regulations do not require the marking-to-market of assets on a daily basis and usually liabilities are not marked-to-market at all, thereby differentiating insurers from other institutional investors in emerging markets as well. While in most countries regulatory valuation principles prescribe for marking assets to market, the reporting for insurers is usually on quarterly basis (Dickinson, 2002). Thus, insurers can at times "sit through" short-term market turbulence, thus providing stability to the market, as long as their sol-

---

[49]A quantitative comparison of the two sets of regulations suggests that the U.S. RBC system produces higher capital requirements for U.S. insurers than under the European system (Swiss Re, 2000).

Box 4.4. The Impact of Emerging Market Crises on Insurance Companies

Financial crises worsen the operating results and balance sheets of all financial intermediaries, but the effects are particularly severe for insurance companies. A financial crisis is usually accompanied by a sharp decline in output, a massive devaluation, increasing inflation and interest rates, and a collapse in asset values. The consequences of these drastic economic changes for the insurance industry are manifold: demand for insurance products drops, resulting in lower premiums and a rise in early terminations of existing contracts; claims increase due to higher inflation and an adverse environment; insurers' assets decline in value; and rising inflation requires higher reserve on the liability side. Thus, a financial crisis poses a major threat to the solvency and liquidity of the insurance industry.

This has become rather clear after recent emerging market crises, as noted in a recent study by Swiss Re (2003). Life insurers suffered not only from a decline in new business, but also from an increase in lapses—nonpayment of premiums on existing life products. As the Table shows, new business collapsed during the year of the crisis and lapse ratios increased by almost three-fold in the year after the crisis. In Argentina, probably due to the expectation of a future crisis, the lapse ratio steadily increased beginning two years before the crisis. Savings-type policies were the most sensitive to changes in income and wealth and thus experienced the most pronounced decline in premiums. The increase in lapses was more significant in Indonesia and Argentina, where a

majority of life products were denominated in U.S. dollars. In Argentina, contracts with a savings component were mostly cancelled once the parity was broke and the majority of new products sold after the crisis were one-year local-currency-denominated pure insurance products—a major setback to a once sophisticated insurance market.

Balance sheet pressure threatened the solvency of many insurers and sometimes lead to a costly restructuring process. Virtually all local assets lost in value, and claims were higher, which required higher reserves relative to premiums. Equity relative to capital declined. Thus, solvency, measured as the capital-to-reserve and the capital-to-premium ratio, was in question. Furthermore, insufficient asset and liability management that led to large asset-liability mismatches for the life insurers and poor risk management practices have aggravated the adverse impact and resulted in a few bankruptcies, as in Korea.

The crises hit local and foreign insurers alike, but the latter were generally better equipped to withstand episodes of financial crisis. First, foreign insurers' better diversified investment portfolio and more sophisticated asset and liability management helped them to weather the financial storm. Second, they could always rely on additional capital from the parent company to shore up the balance sheet. As a result, in a few countries, such as Mexico, Indonesia, and Thailand, foreign insurers picked up market share after the crisis.

To remain liquid and solvent through a financial crisis, insurers need to protect their balance sheets and design products that can cope with a volatile environment. Proper asset and liability management is the key to maintaining a strong balance sheet, while creating a well-diversified portfolio and buying reinsurance to transfer away part of the risk are also beneficial. As the insurer's ability to conduct asset and liability management is constrained by the development of local capital markets as well as regulatory limits, a few countries recently have relaxed the investment regulations. From the liability side, insurers could move away from guaranteed benefits to unit linked products to reduce the investment risk.

Financial Crises and Emerging Market Insurers

	$T-2$	$T-1$	T	$T+1$	$T+2$
New business, percent change (year on year)					
Indonesia	25.4	21.6	−12.6	0.9	34.4
Thailand	10.1	−16.3	−29.1	37.9	40.5
Lapse ratios, in percent					
Indonesia	3.7	2.6	5.5	12.8	7.9
Thailand	3.2	3.4	5.4	9.2	8.3
Argentina	9.6	15.4	31.3		

Source: Swiss Re (2003).
T refers to the year of the financial crisis. It is 1998 for Indonesia and Thailand, and 2002 for Argentina.

vency is not threatened.[50] This perhaps makes them a more diversified and stable investor. Furthermore, most insurers are not bench-marked against any particular index, so the risk of "herding" with other investors during drastic market swings is mitigated. But most regulations only require using market value for assets but not for liabilities. The asymmetric mark-to-market requirement on the two sides of the balance sheet could have undesirable consequences. For example, in Singapore, reports indicated that during the recent equity market downturn, many insurers suffered losses on their equity holdings. While their liabilities linked to equity market performance would have been correspondingly lower, the regulation does not provide for re-calculating the liability based on the market value. Consequently, some insurers appeared to have insufficient capital due to the decline in their assets and, to meet the solvency requirements, had to sell equities in a falling market.[51,52]

Local Mutual Funds

As in the mature markets, mutual funds in emerging markets have been among the fastest-growing institutional investors (Table 4.6). Indeed, mutual fund assets under management in emerging markets grew by 96 percent between the end of 1997 and June 2003 and, as a result, rose from 8 percent of GDP to 15 percent. One key difference between mutual funds in mature and emerging markets has been the relative importance of bond and equity funds. In the mature markets, the assets under management of equity funds are often much larger than those of bond funds

(particularly in Japan, the United Kingdom, and the United States). In contrast, emerging market bond funds in a number of countries have larger assets under management than do equity funds, particularly in Brazil, Mexico, Korea, and Taiwan Province of China. In part, this reflects the difference in the relative development of the local markets in mature and emerging markets. In many emerging markets, the degree of liquidity of local government bond markets is markedly better than in local equity markets.[53] In addition, this difference reflects a search for higher yields on the part of retail investors. As nominal interest rates have declined in many emerging markets since the late 1990s, retail investors have seen extended declines in the interest earned on traditional savings instruments, such as bank time deposits. To obtain higher yields, retail investors subscribed to bond funds that invested in longer-term government and corporate bonds.

One issue that has arisen recently in a number of emerging markets is whether these local mutual funds will be a stable source of demand for local instruments. One particular concern is that retail investors may not be fully aware of the market risks associated with holding positions in longer-term bond funds. In Colombia, for example, mutual funds were at the center of a "mini-crisis" in the treasury bond (TES) market in July–September 2002. Prior to the crisis, many local mutual funds were heavily invested in long-dated (10-year) government bonds, and they had marketed their funds as savings products. Analysts noted, however, that these marketing campaigns stressed the credit ratings of the funds without

[50]Some insurers report the use of internal risk management, which requires assets to be marked-to-market on daily basis. However, as long as the valuation movement does not violate the prudential limits set internally, the need to adjust asset allocation can be avoided.

[51]While Singapore life insurers did see their asset positions deteriorate during the equity market downturn in the early part of 2003, their balance sheets improved significantly following the stock market rally in the rest of the year.

[52]In mature markets, asymmetric mark-to-market also presents similar challenges. For more discussion on appropriate accounting standards, see Chapter III.

[53]In many Asian emerging markets, however, equity markets are generally regarded as more liquid than bond markets.

Table 4.6. Emerging Market Mutual Funds: Total Net Assets[1]

	1997	1998	1999	2000	2001	2002	2003[2]
	(In billions of U. S. dollars)						
Emerging markets	**349.25**	**514.07**	**700.17**	**673.05**	**687.40**	**693.45**	**685.49**
Africa	**12.69**	**12.16**	**18.24**	**16.92**	**14.56**	**20.98**	**25.70**
South Africa	12.69	12.16	18.24	16.92	14.56	20.98	25.70
Asia	**216.50**	**370.82**	**518.63**	**463.11**	**466.82**	**501.33**	**428.01**
Hong Kong SAR	58.46	98.77	182.27	195.92	170.07	164.32	201.15
India	9.35	8.69	13.07	13.83	13.49	n.a.	n.a.
Korea	53.11	165.03	167.18	110.61	119.44	149.54	133.76
Malaysia	8.66	10.19	11.39	11.39	12.46	14.13	18.63
Philippines	n.a.	n.a.	0.12	0.11	0.21	0.47	0.63
Singapore	74.55	67.84	109.85	95.94	97.91	105.74	n.a.
Taiwan Province of China	12.37	20.31	31.15	32.07	49.74	62.15	66.83
Thailand	n.a.	n.a.	3.61	3.23	3.49	4.97	7.00
East Europe	**1.66**	**2.57**	**4.14**	**5.67**	**4.35**	**18.55**	**25.88**
Czech Republic	0.36	0.56	1.47	1.99	1.78	3.30	4.12
Hungary	0.71	1.48	1.73	1.95	2.26	3.38	4.55
Poland	0.54	0.51	0.76	1.55	n.a.	5.47	7.50
Romania	n.a.	n.a.	n.a.	0.01	0.01	0.03	0.03
Russia	0.04	0.03	0.18	0.18	0.30	0.37	0.61
Turkey	n.a.	n.a.	n.a.	n.a.	n.a.	6.00	9.07
Latin America	**118.40**	**128.53**	**159.17**	**187.34**	**201.68**	**152.58**	**205.90**
Argentina	5.25	6.93	6.99	7.43	3.75	1.02	1.32
Brazil	108.61	118.69	117.76	148.54	148.19	96.73	143.79
Chile	4.55	2.91	4.09	n.a.	5.09	6.71	6.14
Colombia	n.a.	n.a.	10.87	11.97	12.92	15.63	16.89
Costa Rica	n.a.	n.a.	n.a.	0.92	n.a.	1.74	2.17
Mexico	n.a.	n.a.	19.47	18.49	31.72	30.76	35.59
	(In percent of GDP)						
Emerging markets	**7.74**	**12.51**	**17.81**	**15.66**	**16.45**	**16.80**	**14.96**
Africa	**8.52**	**9.10**	**13.92**	**13.21**	**12.74**	**20.08**	**16.27**
South Africa	8.52	9.10	13.92	13.21	12.74	20.08	16.27
Asia	**12.18**	**24.86**	**31.42**	**26.07**	**27.34**	**27.84**	**22.26**
Hong Kong SAR	33.66	59.77	113.46	118.48	104.44	101.74	126.36
India	2.30	2.12	2.99	3.00	2.83	n.a.	n.a.
Korea	11.15	52.05	41.17	23.97	27.96	31.37	25.96
Malaysia	8.65	14.12	14.38	12.64	14.16	14.90	18.41
Philippines	n.a.	n.a.	0.15	0.14	0.29	0.61	0.77
Singapore	78.16	82.82	134.98	104.87	115.37	121.58	n.a.
Taiwan Province of China	4.25	7.60	10.82	10.36	17.69	22.07	23.14
Thailand	n.a.	n.a.	2.95	2.64	3.03	3.93	5.35
East Europe	**0.19**	**0.33**	**0.60**	**0.75**	**0.55**	**2.07**	**2.37**
Czech Republic	0.68	0.98	2.68	3.87	3.11	4.74	4.88
Hungary	1.56	3.13	3.59	4.18	4.36	5.14	5.51
Poland	0.36	0.31	0.47	0.94	n.a.	2.89	3.63
Romania	n.a.	n.a.	n.a.	0.02	0.02	0.06	0.06
Russia	0.01	0.01	0.09	0.07	0.10	0.11	0.14
Turkey	n.a.	n.a.	n.a.	n.a.	n.a.	3.37	3.83
Latin America	**6.95**	**7.57**	**10.91**	**11.46**	**12.85**	**11.49**	**14.61**
Argentina	1.79	2.32	2.47	2.61	1.40	1.10	1.03
Brazil	13.44	15.11	22.47	24.76	29.09	21.81	28.36
Chile	5.51	3.67	5.61	n.a.	7.46	10.09	8.81
Colombia	n.a.	n.a.	13.43	15.25	15.75	22.14	23.26
Costa Rica	n.a.	n.a.	n.a.	5.76	n.a.	10.27	12.19
Mexico	n.a.	n.a.	4.05	3.18	5.08	4.83	5.79

Sources: Bloomberg; Federation of Malaysian Unit Trust Managers; Investment Company Institute; Monetary Authority of Singapore; Stock Exchange of Thailand; Superintendencia Bancaria; and Superintendencia Valores Colombia.

[1] Funds of funds are not included; home-domiciled funds except for Hong Kong SAR, Korea, New Zealand, and Singapore, which include home- and foreign-domiciled funds.

[2] As of the end of June 2003.

fully indicating the market risks that were associated with their products if interest rates were to rise. When a sharp decline in interest rates occurred between February and June 2002, investors placed funds with bond funds due to the attractiveness of the 10-year bond yield and thereby took on significant duration risk. However, an increased perception of regional risk in July 2002 led to a sell-off of Colombia's Yankee bonds and a sharp increase in external debt spreads—in tandem with Brazil spreads. In addition, rising concerns about the country's fiscal situation eventually prompted investors to sell their TES holdings. After this initial sell-off, mutual funds began to experience redemptions from retail investors and were forced to liquidate their positions in a falling market, pushing bond prices down further. In the space of 10 days, the yield on the government bond maturing in 2012 went up from 12 to 20 percent. Following this episode, mutual funds shortened the duration of their fixed-income portfolios.

The experience in Thailand's bond market in 2003 also illustrates how a turn in the interest rate cycle can interact with regulatory requirements, institutional investor investment strategies, and retail investor risk aversion to induce interest rate volatility in less-than-liquid markets. Between March 2002 and July 2003, the yield on the 10-year government bond declined from 6.1 percent to 2.5 percent. As banks also reduced their deposit rates, retail investors shifted from deposits to bond mutual funds (which grew by 16 percent during this period) in search of higher yields. The investment strategies of the bond mutual fund managers were influenced by the perception that, while retail investors were searching for higher yields, they were averse to seeing higher volatility in the net asset value (NAV)

of their bond accounts. In attempting to stabilize the NAVs of the bond funds, mutual fund managers faced asymmetrical mark-to-market requirements whereby liquid assets were marked-to-market on a daily basis whereas illiquid assets were not.[54] As interest rates declined, fund managers added relatively illiquid assets (such as corporate bonds) to their portfolios both to get a higher yield and to reduce the volatility of the NAV. When the interest rate cycle reversed in mid-August 2003, with the yield on the 10-year bond rising 260 basis points by November, the NAVs of the bond funds began to decline; massive redemptions by retail investors occurred.[55] To meet these redemptions, bond mutual funds were forced to engage in large sales of bonds. This selling was seen to have increased bond market volatility and accelerated the rise in interest rates.

In Korea, the reaction of retail investors to the SK Group accounting scandal in March 2003 exposed the vulnerability of local investment trust companies (ITCs)—which typically invest in a range of corporate bonds and stocks—to developments in the corporate sector. Total redemptions from ITCs in the days following the reporting of SK Group difficulties exceeded $13 billion (out of assets of more than $140 billion), leading the ITCs to contemplate a temporary freeze on withdrawals. After liquidating most of their government debt holdings to cover the redemptions, the ITCs reportedly faced difficulties raising cash to meet further redemptions, as they could not find buyers for higher-risk corporate bonds, such as those issued by credit card firms, of which ITCs are major holders.

In contrast to Asia and Latin America, the recent turbulence in fixed-income markets in

---

[54]Requirements for mutual funds to mark-to-market on a daily basis pose a challenge in markets where assets are not frequently traded. In Thailand, "liquid" instruments are marked-to-market on a daily basis, while illiquid instruments are allowed to be marked-to-market every 15 days.

[55]Total redemptions in the three months to November amounted to an estimated 40 billion baht ($1 billion)—or 20 percent of total bond fund assets.

central Europe, while causing substantial redemption pressures on the mutual fund industry, resulted in relatively little "panic." Episodes of large sell-offs in fixed-income markets in Hungary (June 2003) and Poland (October 2003) led to redemptions amounting to more than 10 percent of assets under management for some mutual funds. However, mutual funds in Hungary are accustomed to investors shifting funds often since they do not levy up-front fees. In Poland, high levels of liquid reserves meant that funds were able to weather redemptions without huge sell-offs of their holdings.

Policy Conclusions

The increasing institutionalization of the investor base for emerging market securities has implications for both the volatility of capital flows to emerging markets and the policy measures needed to cope with such volatility and to further develop local securities markets. With regard to the volatility of capital flows, Box 4.1 notes that, in principle, the share of mature market assets under management that should be allocated to emerging market securities in an optimally diversified portfolio varies sharply over time; and, in particular, falls by half from the 1991–97 period to the 1997–2002 period. This, combined with the enormous scale of institutional investor assets under management in mature markets, suggests the potential for huge capital flow volatility even in the absence of any distortions. Moreover, many of the new crossover institutional investors have not experienced a major systemic emerging market crisis so the jury is out regarding the stability of their demand for emerging market securities dur-

ing such periods. As a result of this uncertainty and previous experiences of sudden loss of access to international markets, many emerging markets have begun to adopt policies that provide a degree of "self-insurance" against volatility in capital flows.[56] In part, these policies have included measures to improve macroeconomic performance, develop local securities markets, and strengthen domestic financial institutions— including institutional investors.

The changing composition of the investor base in mature markets has some important implications for debt management policies and practices in emerging markets. In particular, both official debt managers and market participants have argued that a number of policy measures can play an important role in broadening and diversifying both the international and domestic institutional investor bases. An important policy step is to ensure that there is transparency and adequate disclosure about both government policies and corporate developments. In particular, the official sector needs to keep investors informed about economic developments and prospects and to provide investors with a predictable schedule for local debt issues.[57] Investor relations programs can be particularly useful in this regard, as well as with gauging the potential segments of the investor base that have an interest in a particular issue.

In addition to ensuring an adequate degree of transparency, countries need to facilitate the development of market infrastructure. This would involve, for example, such steps as establishing a good clearing and settlement system potentially in conjunction with other countries (one example of recent efforts to develop bond markets infrastructure in Asia is

[56]The various policies were discussed more extensively in Chapter IV of the March 2003 GFSR.

[57]Some observers have questioned whether countries should indeed be predictable in managing the public external debt. They have argued that countries can take advantage of favorable circumstances to carry out certain operations that could lower the cost of the debt. Therefore, there might be some arguments in favor of countries not being predictable from the point of view of the *timing* of their transactions, but certainly this should not preclude countries from being predictable on their objective of net borrowing for the period or periods ahead.

described in Appendix II of Chapter II). Another important step is to help develop a liquid secondary market for debt instruments that will facilitate the management of institutional investor portfolios. Market liquidity in the government bond market can often be improved by creating benchmark issues at various maturities. Moreover, steps need to be taken to bring about the development of a market-maker system. In this context, it will be necessary to sell debt instruments to institutions, including hedge funds, that are willing to actively trade these instruments to help improve the liquidity of these instruments in the secondary market. Finally, in order to help diversify the investor base, the authorities should encourage the inclusion of a country's bonds in major bond indices, since investors that measure their performance against indices are likely to add the bonds of the countries included in the indices to their portfolios.

The rapid growth of emerging market pension funds'—and, to a lesser extent, insurance companies'—assets under management has highlighted the importance of updating and improving the regulatory framework of local institutional investors. In particular, countries need to ease limits on investments in foreign securities to achieve an appropriate degree of diversification of local institutional investors' portfolios. Despite the positive impact of institutional demand on the development of local securities markets, in many countries the growth of assets under management is outpacing the volume and variety of available local securities. Although there is room for a further loosening of restrictions on pension funds' equity allocations in some countries, it is unclear whether local markets would be able to grow accordingly. Thus, adequate diversification of pension fund portfolios requires an increase in the funds' allocations to foreign securities. Failure to open up opportunities for diversification abroad may lead to local market bubbles and to excessive exposure to sovereign risk.

The growing imbalance between local pension funds' assets under management and the available securities, and the associated risks, thus calls for a close coordination between changes in the regulatory framework for institutional investors, local capital market development, and macroeconomic policies (see Roldos, 2003, for the case of pension funds). The easing of limits on foreign investments by local pension funds amounts to a removal of capital controls on outflows, and care should be taken about the macroeconomic consequences. Experiences in mature and emerging markets show that they are usually accompanied with large exchange rate depreciations. Moreover, authorities should note that even if a gradual approach is followed, actual portfolio shifts may happen suddenly and be magnified by herding behavior.

These issues are relevant not only for local pension funds but also for insurance companies. Developing local securities markets is critical for the insurance industry to properly manage its risks and grow without threatening financial stability. The lack of long-dated bonds and derivatives presents challenges to insurers in managing the mismatch between the duration of their assets and liabilities across the emerging markets. In some countries, governments have yet to begin issuance of bonds beyond mid-range maturities. Moreover, analysts have suggested that insurance regulations should incorporate measures of investment risk and duration, or alternatively, a risk-based capital regime should be adopted with "prudent man" rules guiding investments (Kwon, 2001). With appropriate regulation that safeguards the solvency of insurers and provides enough flexibility to manage their balance sheet risks, insurance companies could become a stable long-term investor in local instruments. Moreover, as mentioned in Chapter III, life insurers can and should take advantage of a variety of credit products to match their long-term liabilities. When local markets cannot deliver these products, local insurers ought to be allowed to invest in credit products abroad, as well as have access to foreign currency derivative products to hedge the associated foreign exchange exposure.

The increasing importance of local institutional investors in both local and international markets has to be accompanied by a strengthening of risk management skills to ensure financial stability. Rapid growth of assets under management will require increasing sophistication among local institutional investors that will face increasingly more complex instruments and opportunities. At the same time, regulators will need to step up their risk management skills to be able to adjust regulations to the idiosyncrasies of rapidly growing local markets and to monitor the behavior of increasingly complex investment strategies. Active participation in international fora, to exchange experiences and lessons, would help not just in speeding up the learning process but also in harmonizing regulations across countries.

Authorities in charge of supervision and regulation of mutual funds must ensure that retail investors are fully informed and appropriately educated about the types of market risks associated with different investments. Indeed, the recent experience with runs on local bond mutual funds as the interest rate cycle reversed (with interest rates beginning to rise) has generated concerns about how well the customers of institutional investors understand the market risks they bear and how well these customers manage these risks, especially in an environment where interest rates have fallen to levels at near historical lows.[58] Market analysts have argued that retail investors often moved into bonds in search of higher yields but had the misperception that the market risks associated with these bonds were "similar" to those associated with term bank deposits. As bond prices began to fall, and investors saw the value of bond funds decline, retail investors reacted to this newly discovered market risk by quickly withdrawing from the bond funds and shifting to a "cash" (bank deposit) position. Bond funds were forced to sell assets to meet these redemptions, putting additional upward pressure on already rising interest rates.

Finally, the stability of the asset allocations of institutional investors will also be influenced by the stability of their liability structures and/or the funds placed with them. As institutional investors have come to dominate mature financial markets and have become increasingly important in emerging markets, there has also been an ongoing shift in the incidence of who ultimately bears market risk (the risks associated with fluctuations in asset prices and returns). In particular, the period since the early 1990s has witnessed a gradual shift in the incidence of market risks from the institutional investors themselves to their customers. For example, in many countries, there has been a shift from defined benefit to defined contribution pension systems, which generally shift market risk to pensioners. Similarly, life insurance companies have increasingly marketed variable rate and index-linked products as opposed to fixed guaranteed return products. Mutual funds and hedge funds by their very structure ultimately transfer market risk to their shareholders. This transfer of risk to less sophisticated

---

[58]The experience with retail investor runs on bond funds in emerging markets may have implications for mature markets. For example, some market participants have argued that retail investors in Europe and Japan, which have traditionally held emerging market bonds directly, would be better served to hold them indirectly through bond mutual funds. These retail investors have been seen as holding emerging market bonds directly in order to obtain a pickup in yields but seriously underestimating the default risk associated with these instruments. If these investors instead held these bonds indirectly through bond funds, it has been suggested that they would receive better diversification benefits and professional portfolio management services. However, it still could be the case that a bond fund with large holdings of the bonds of a country that unexpectedly defaults could face large scale redemptions. Bond fund managers would naturally have to take this risk into account when structuring their portfolios.

investors, and its potential implications for financial stability, has become apparent with the recent experience of some emerging markets and is an issue that will be taken up in future issues of the GFSR.

Appendix: Hedge Funds and Recent Emerging Market Currency Crises

This appendix presents an empirical analysis of the market positions taken by hedge funds in several recent emerging market currency crises (e.g., devaluations or the widening of currency trading bands). In particular, these episodes include the Brazilian *real* devaluation (January 13, 1999), the floatation of the Turkish lira (February 22, 2001), the Argentine peso devaluation (January 7, 2002), and the recent pressures in the Hungarian fixed-income and currency markets, which forced the central bank to lower the central Forint-Euro parity rate from 276.1 forint per euro to 282.36 forint per euro (June 4, 2003). In all these episodes, the main pre-conditions for the hedge funds' involvement—sufficiently deep and liquid local markets plus macroeconomic imbalances—were present.

One of the key problems is that information on actual hedge funds' portfolio exposures is not publicly available. Therefore, the hedge funds' positions during the crises episodes are estimated using the Sharpe investment style approach, which provides indirect estimates of their portfolio exposures. This approach assumes that the return that a hedge fund earns during any given period is a linear combination of the returns on the relevant investments and that the estimated "weights" in the linear combination are a proxy of the actual portfolio weights of the hedge fund. Thus, the estimation of the hedge fund portfolio exposures can be carried out in two steps. The first step is to estimate how sensitive the hedge funds' portfolio returns have been to changes in the local emerging market returns in each of the crisis countries, while controlling for other factors

that may have influenced the hedge fund's performance as well. The second step is to multiply these sensitivities by the hedge funds' total asset values to obtain the estimated value of the hedge funds' positions in these emerging markets. Since previous research indicated that the types of hedge funds that tend to maintain exposure to emerging market assets include the dedicated emerging market hedge funds, macro hedge funds, and event-driven hedge funds, the approach described above is applied to a sample containing these three groups of funds.

The two-step methodology used to estimate the hedge funds' exposures to local emerging markets is implemented as follows:

Step 1

For each group of hedge funds I (where I refers to macro, dedicated emerging market, or event-driven groups of funds), and for each local emerging market EM (where EM refers to local markets in Brazil, Argentina, Turkey, and Hungary), the estimates of sensitivities ($\beta_{EM,t}^I$) of the hedge fund portfolio returns to the returns on a particular local emerging market EM are obtained by estimating the following rolling regression equation (using a 20-month window):

$$R_t^I = \alpha_t^I + \beta_{EM,t}^I R_{EM,t} + \sum_{k=1}^{3} \beta_{K,t}^I R_{K,t} + \varepsilon_t^I$$

where R_t^I is the series of monthly returns on the portfolio of hedge funds in group I; $R_{EM,t}$ is the series of monthly returns on the J.P. Morgan ELMI (local market) country index. The three additional factors (the $R_{K,t}$'s) included in each regression equation—the MSCI Emerging Markets Free Index (proxy for emerging equity markets), the Merrill Lynch High Yield Corporate Bond Index (proxy for credit market), and the Federal Reserve's Trade-Weighted U.S. Dollar Index— have been shown to have high explanatory power in the previous research on hedge funds' performance. All indices are U.S. dollar denominated.

Step 2

The estimated U.S. dollar exposure of the hedge fund group I to a local market EM in period k is obtained as $E_k^{I,EM} = \beta_{EM,k}^I * A_k^I$, where A_k^I is the total asset value of hedge funds in group I and $\beta_{EM,k}^I$ is the estimated sensitivity of the returns on the portfolio of hedge funds in group I to the returns on a particular local emerging market EM.

The data sample consists of the dedicated emerging market, macro, and event-driven hedge funds that have at least $100 million in assets under management (as of end-2003), were set up on or before January 1998, and have been regularly reporting their monthly returns and assets under management either to the CISDM (formerly, MAR/Hedge) or HFR.[59] Thus, the estimated portfolio exposures based on the CISDM/HFR data should be a reasonably good proxy of the positions taken by the medium-size hedge funds that typically invest in emerging market assets. However, these exposures may not necessarily be a good proxy for the positions that could have been taken by some of the largest macro hedge funds, such as Tudor Investment Corporation or Moore Capital Management, which do not report to any hedge fund data providers, and whose assets under management are somewhere in the range of $5 billion–$10 billion, compared to only about $2.4 billion of the largest hedge fund in the CISDM/HFR sample (see footnote 20 earlier in this chapter).

The total estimated exposures of all three groups of hedge funds are presented in Figure 4.2, along with the local market indices of Argentina, Brazil, Turkey, and Hungary. The series labeled CISDM& HFR represents the estimated exposures based on betas obtained from the regression analysis that uses the average returns on the portfolios of dedicated emerging market, macro, and event-driven hedge funds from the CISDM/HFR sample described above. The series labeled CSFB are based on the regression analysis that uses the Credit Swiss First Boston (CSFB)/Tremont indices, which are asset-weighted indices of large hedge funds from the Tremont TASS database, and are more representative of the performance of larger hedge funds.[60]

The main conclusions derived from the analysis of returns and estimated exposures are as follows:

- Monthly returns provide little evidence that medium-size hedge funds (as a group) earned abnormal profits following the exchange rate adjustment in each of these episodes.
- Estimated exposures indicate that during the recent currency crises episodes hedge funds had indeed built extensive short positions vis-à-vis emerging market currencies in the run-up to the devaluations, but failed to maintain them long enough to benefit from the change in the exchange rate regime. This unwinding of the hedge funds' short positions before the devaluations may have been in part due to measures taken by the authorities of emerging market countries to discourage the shorting of local assets as they faced increasing pressures on their exchange rates (including, by raising interest rates as well as by limiting the supply of instruments that could be used for taking short positions).
- The comparison of the CISDM/HFR and CSFB exposures suggests that larger hedge funds tend to be more aggressive in shorting local markets than smaller funds, which

---

[59]CISDM (Center for International Securities and Derivatives Markets), formerly MAR/Hedge, and HFR (Hedge Fund Research) are the leading hedge fund data providers, which jointly cover a substantial part of the hedge fund universe. Our sample includes 18 macro hedge funds, 51 dedicated emerging market hedge funds and 36 event driven hedge funds. Smaller funds were dropped from the sample because their monthly returns and assets under management are often noisy or stale.

[60]Similar to other data providers' databases, the Tremont TASS database does not include most of the top 100 hedge funds.

may be due to the larger funds' "deeper pockets."

References

Abdel-Motaal, Karim, 2002, "Structural Change and Yield Curve Anomalies in the Mexican Local Market," in *Fixed Income Research, Latin America* (New York: Morgan Stanley).

———, Gray Newman, and Javier Romo, 2003, "Mexico Local Markets," in *Fixed Income Research, Latin America* (New York: Morgan Stanley).

Aitken, Brian, 1998, "Have Institutional Investors Destabilized Emerging Markets?" *Contemporary Economic Policy*, Vol. 16, pp. 173–84.

Asher, Mukul, 1999, "South East Asian Provident and Pension Funds: Investment Policies and Performance" (unpublished; Singapore: National University of Singapore).

———, 2000, "Social Security Reform Imperatives: The Southeast Asian Case" (unpublished; Singapore: National University of Singapore).

———, and David Newman, 2001, "Hong Kong and Singapore: Two Approaches to the Provision of Pensions in Asia," *Journal of Pensions Management*, Vol. 7, pp. 155–166.

Association of British Insurers, 2000, "The Pension System in the United Kingdom," in *Private Pension Systems and Policy Issues*, Private Pension Series No. 1 (Paris: OECD).

Babbel, David, and Anthony Santomero, 1996, "Risk Management by Insurers: An Analysis of the Process," The Wharton Financial Institutions Center Working Paper No. 96–16 (Philadelphia: The Wharton School, University of Pennsylvania).

Blake, David, 2003, "Financial System Require-ments for Successful Pension Reform," (unpub-lished; Pensions Institute, Birkbed College, United Kingdom).

———, Bruce N. Lehmann, and Allan Timmer-mann, 1999, "Asset Allocation Dynamics and Pension Fund Performance," *Journal of Business*, Vol. 72, pp. 429–61.

Borensztein, Eduardo, and Gaston Gelos, 2003a, "A Panic-Prone Pack? The Behavior of Emerging Market Mutual Funds," *IMF Staff Papers*, International Monetary Fund, Vol. 50, pp. 43–63.

———, 2003b, "Leaders and Followers: Emerging Market Fund Behavior During Tranquil and Turbulent Times," *Emerging Markets Review*, Vol. 4, pp. 25–38.

Figure 4.2. Estimated Portfolio Exposures of Hedge Funds and Local Emerging Markets

— ELMI *(index; right scale)*
— CSFB *(hedge fund exposures in billions of dollars; left scale)*
— CISDM and HFR *(hedge fund exposures in billions of dollars; left scale)*

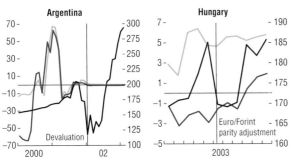

Sources: Bloomberg L.P.; CISDM; Hedge Fund Research (HFR); and IMF staff estimates.

Brainard, Larry, 2001, "Pension Reforms Altering Market Dynamics for Emerging Debt," in *Emerging Markets Research* (New York: J.P. Morgan, December).

Briys, E., and F. de Varenne, 1996, "On the Risk of Life Insurance Liabilities: Debunking Some Common Pitfalls," The Wharton Financial Institutions Center Working Paper No. 96–29 (Philadelphia: The Wharton School, University of Pennsylvania).

Brown, S., W. Goetzmann, and J. Park, 1998, "Hedge Funds and the Asian Currency Crisis of 1997," NBER Working Paper No. 6427 (Cambridge, Mass.: National Bureau of Economic Research).

Campbell, John Y., and Luis M. Viceira, 2002, *Strategic Asset Allocation: Portfolio Choice for Long-Term Investors* (New York: Oxford University Press).

Cifuentes, Rodrigo, Jorge Desormeaux, and Claudio Gonzalez, 2002, "Capital Markets in Chile: From Financial Repression to Financial Deepening," in *BIS Papers No. 11, The Development of Bond Markets in Emerging Markets* (Basel: Bank for International Settlements, June).

Corsetti G., A. Dasgupta, S. Morris, and H. S. Shin, 2004, "Does One Soros Make a Difference? The Role of a Large Trader in Currency Crises," *Review of Economic Studies*, Vol. 71, pp. 87–114.

Davis, Philip E., 2002, "Pension Fund Management and International Investment—A Global Perspective," Discussion Paper No. PI–0206 (London: The Pensions Institute, Birbeck College, London).

———, and Benn Steil, 2001, *Institutional Investors* (Cambridge, Massachusetts: MIT Press).

Dickinson, Gerry, 2002, "The Search for an International Accounting Standard for Insurance: Report to the Accounting Task Force of the Geneva Association," *The Geneva Papers on Risk and Insurance*, Vol. 28, No. 2, pp. 151–175.

Dorfman, Mark, and Karl Ennsfellner, 2002, "Insurance in Transition Economies: Poland, Czech Republic, and Hungary," International Insurance Foundation Occasional Paper No. 5 (Washington).

Eichengreen, Barry, and Donald Mathieson, 1998, "Hedge Funds and Financial Market Dynamics," Occasional Paper No. 166 (Washington: International Monetary Fund).

El-Erian, Mohamed, 2003, "The Emerging Markets Heavyweight," *Euromoney*, pp. 44–49.

Federacion Internacional de Administradoras de Fondos de Pensiones (FIAP), 2003, *Informe Semestral Numero 14* (Santiago de Chile).

FinanceAsia, 2000, "Korea Raises Money from Pensions for Market Stabilization Fund" (October).

Financial Stability Forum, 2000, *Report of the Financial Stability Forum Report Working Group on Highly Leveraged Institutions*, Annex E, "Report of the Market Dynamics Study Group" and Annex C, "Background Note on the Hedge Fund Industry" (March).

Fung, William, and David A. Hsieh, 2000, "Measuring the Market Impact of Hedge Funds," *Journal of Empirical Finance*, Vol. 7, pp. 1–36.

———, and Konstantinos Tsatsaronis, 1999, "Do Hedge Funds Disrupt Emerging Markets?" *Brookings-Wharton Papers on Financial Services*, Brookings Institution Press.

Garcia-Cantera, Jose, Steve Faucher, Flavia Montoro, and Laura Molina, 2002, "Private Pension Funds in Latin America," in *Equity Research: Latin America*, Salomon Smith Barney (December).

Garcia-Cantera, Jose, Ramon Portillo, Steve Faucher, and Laura Molina, 2001, "Latin America Insurance," in *Equity Research: Latin America*, Salomon Smith Barney (June).

Graham, Kathy, 2003, "Alternative Investments from A to Z," *Financial Engineering News*, November/December.

Grauer, Robert R., and Nils Hakansson, 1987, "Gains from International Diversification: 1968–1985 Returns on Portfolios of Stocks and Bonds," *Journal of Finance*, Vol. 42 (July), pp. 721–39.

Greenwich Associates, 2002, "Alternative Investment Becomes New Choice," Greenwich, CT.

———, 2003, *Asset Allocation: U.S. Portfolios Adjust to Difficult Markets in 2002*, Greenwich, CT.

Hinz, Richard, 2000, "Overview of the United States Pension System," in *Private Pension Systems and Policy Issues*, Private Pension Series No. 1 (Paris: OECD).

Holzmann, Robert, 1999, "The World Bank Approach to Pension Reform," Social Protection Discussion Paper Series No. 9807 (Washington: World Bank, September).

———, Ian W. MacArthur, and Yvonne Sin, 2000, "Pension Systems in East Asia and the Pacific: Challenges and Opportunities," Social

Protection Discussion Paper Series No. 0014 (Washington: World Bank).

International Monetary Fund, 2000, *International Capital Markets: Developments, Prospects, and Key Policy Issues,* World Economic and Financial Surveys (Washington).

———, 2002, *Global Financial Stability Report,* World Economic and Financial Surveys (Washington: IMF, September).

———, 2003, *Global Financial Stability Report,* World Economic and Financial Surveys, (Washington: IMF, September).

Kaminsky, Graciela, Richard Lyons, and Sergio Schmukler, 2001, "Mutual Fund Investment in Emerging Markets: An Overview," *The World Bank Economic Review,* Vol. 15, No. 2, pp. 315–40.

Kim, Woochan, and Shang-Jin Wei, 2002, "Foreign Portfolio Investors Before and During a Crisis," *Journal of International Economics,* Vol. 56, pp. 75–96.

Kimmis, Jenny, Ricardo Gottschalk, Edna Armendariz, and Stephany Griffith-Jones, 2002, "UK Pension Fund Investment and Developing Country Assets," Working Paper (Sussex: Institute of Development Studies, University of Sussex).

Kumar, Pradeep, 2003, "Mexico—Corporate Peso Issuance and Local Markets," in *Global Fixed Income Research* (New York: Citigroup).

Kwiecinski, Piotr, and Rafal Wiatr, 2003, "Poland— Pension Fund Strategy: Leading Pension Funds Increase Exposure to Stocks," Citigroup (September).

Kwon, W., 2001, "Toward Free Trade in Services: The ASEAN Insurance Market," International Insurance Foundation Occasional Paper No. 3 (Washington).

Kyle, Albert, 1984, "A Theory of Futures Market Manipulations," in *The Industrial Organization of Futures Markets,* ed. by R.W. Anderson (Lexington, MA: Heath), pp. 141–72.

Lewis, K., 1999, "Trying to Explain the Home Bias in Equities and Consumption," *Journal of Economic Literature,* Vol. 37, pp. 571–608.

MacKenzie, Sandy, 2002, "The Role of Private Sector Annuities Markets in an Individual Accounts Reform of a Public Pension Plan," IMF Working Paper No. 02/161 (Washington: International Monetary Fund).

Mathieson, Donald J., Jorge E. Roldos, Ramana Ramaswamy, and Anna Ilyina, 2004, *Emerging*

Local Securities and Derivatives Markets, World Economic and Financial Surveys (Washington: International Monetary Fund).

Merrick, J., N.Y. Naik, and P.K. Yadav, 2002, "Strategic Trading Behavior and Price Distortion in a Manipulated Market: Anatomy of a Squeeze, Working Paper, London Business School (December).

Munch Re Group, 2002, *Annual Report,* pp. 167–169.

Myners, Paul, 2001, "Institutional Investment in the United Kingdom: A Review," report prepared for HM Treasury, UK. Available on the Internet at *http://www.hm-treasury.gov.uk/media//843F0/ 31.pdf.*

OECD, 2000, "Institutional Investors in Latin America" (Paris: Organization for Economic Cooperation and Development).

———, 2001, "Insurance Regulation and Supervision in Asia and Latin America" (Paris: Organization for Economic Cooperation and Development).

———, 2003, "Institutional Investors Statistical Yearbook: 1992–2001" (Paris: Organization for Economic Cooperation and Development).

Oswald, William, and David Sekiguchi, 2002, "Mexico's Local Markets," in *Global Markets Research, Emerging Markets* (New York: Deutsche Bank).

Patterson, Rebecca, and John Normand, 2002, "Pension Fund Reform: Anticipating FX Implications," in *Global Foreign Exchange Research* (New York: J.P. Morgan, December).

Post, M. A., and K. Millar, 1998, "U.S. Emerging Market Equity Funds and the 1997 Crisis in Asian Financial Markets," Investment Company Institute, *Perspective,* Vol. 4.

Rea, John, 1996, "U.S. Emerging Market Funds: Hot Money or Stable Source of Investment Capital?" Investment Company Institute, *Perspective,* Vol. 2.

———, and Richard Marcis, 1996, "Mutual Fund Shareholder Activity During U.S. Stock Market Cycles," Investment Company Institute, *Perspective,* Vol. 2.

Roldos, Jorge, 2003, "Pension Reform and Capital Markets," paper prepared for the conference, "Results and Challenges of Pension Reform" (Mexico: Cancun, May).

Rother, P.C., M. Catenaro, and G. Schwab, 2003, "Ageing and Pensions in the Euro Area: Survey and Projection Results," Social Protection Discussion Paper Series No. 307 (Washington: World Bank).

Roy, A.D., 1952, "Safety First and the Holding of Assets," *Econometrica*, Vol. 20, pp. 431–49.

Schultes, Renee, 2003, "From the Shadows," *Global Pensions* (August).

Solnik, Bruno, 1998, "Global Asset Management," *The Journal of Portfolio Management*, Vol. 24 (summer), pp. 43–51.

Srinivas, P.S., Edward Whitehouse, and Juan Yermo, 2000, "Regulating Private Pension Fund' Structure, Performance, and Investments: Cross-Country Evidence," in *World Bank Pension Primer* (Washington: World Bank).

Superintendency of Pension Funds, 2003, "El Regimen de Capitalización: A 8 Años de la Reforma" (Argentina: Buenos Aires).

Swiss Re, 2000, "Solvency of Non-Life Insurers: Balancing Security and Profitability Expectations," Publication Brief No. 1/2000.

———, 2003, "Emerging Insurance Markets: Lessons Learned from Financial Crises," Publication Brief No. 7/2003.

Targett, Simon, 2000, "Pension Fund Industry Faces Closer Scrutiny," *Financial Times*, July 3.

Thailand, 2003, Ministry of Finance, "Asian Bond Market Development."

Walker, Eduardo, and Fernando LeFort, 2000, "Pension Reform and Capital Markets: Are There Any (Hard) Links?" (unpublished; Santiago: Universidad Católica de Chile).

Wilshire Associates, 2002, *Permissible Equity Markets: Investment Analysis and Recommendations* (Santa Monica).

Wilson, Thomas, 2003, "Is ALM at European Life Insurers Broken?" *Risk* (September).

Yermo, Juan, 2000, "Institutional Investors in Latin America: Recent Trends and Regulatory Challenges," in *Institutional Investors in Latin America* (Paris: Organization for Economic Cooperation and Development).

———, 2003a, "Survey of Investment Regulation of Pension Funds" (Paris: Organization for Economic Cooperation and Development).

———, 2003b, "Pension Reform and Capital Market Development" (unpublished; Washington: World Bank).

GLOSSARY

Annuity	A contract that provides an income for a specified period of time, such as a number of years or for life.
Asset/liability management	The management of assets to ensure that liabilities are sufficiently covered by suitable assets at all times.
Balance sheet mismatch	A balance sheet is a financial statement showing a company's assets, liabilities, and equity on a given date. Typically, a mismatch in a balance sheet implies that the maturities of the liabilities differ (are typically shorter) from those of the assets and/or that some liabilities are denominated in a foreign currency while the assets are not.
Banking soundness	The financial health of a single bank or of a country's banking system.
Benchmark issues	High-quality debt securities, typically bonds. Investors use their yield for comparison purposes and to price other bond issues.
Brady Bonds	Bonds issued by emerging market countries as part of a restructuring of defaulted commercial bank loans. These bonds are named after former U.S. Treasury Secretary Nicholas Brady and the first bonds were issued in March of 1990.
Capital account liberalization	Removal of statutory restrictions on cross-border private capital flows, an important part of financial liberalization. In particular, the relaxation of controls or prohibitions on transactions in the capital and financial accounts of the balance of payments, including the removal of foreign exchange convertibility restrictions.
Carry trade	A leveraged transaction in which borrowed funds are used to buy a security whose yield is expected to exceed the cost of the borrowed funds.
Cash securitization	The creation of securities from a pool of pre-existing assets and receivables that are placed under the legal control of investors through a special intermediary created for this purpose. This compares with a "synthetic" securitization where the generic securities are created out of derivative instruments.
Collective action clause	A clause in bond contracts that includes provisions allowing a qualified majority of lenders to amend key financial terms of the debt contract and bind a minority to accept these new terms.
Contagion	The transmission or spillover of financial shocks or crises across countries and/or across asset classes, characterized by an apparent increase in the comovement of asset prices.

Note: Insurance terms are adapted from the International Association of Insurance Supervisors (IAIS) *Glossary of Terms,* September 2003.

Convergence fund	A fund that invests in Eastern European countries' debt securities on the assumption that interest rates in these countries will converge to those in the European Union.
Convexity	A measure of the relationship between bond prices and bond yields. The more positive a bond's convexity, the less sensitive is the price of the bond to interest rate changes, other things being equal. Negative convexity implies the bond's price is more sensitive to interest rate changes, other things being equal.
Corporate governance	The governing relationships between all the stakeholders in a company—including the shareholders, directors, and management—as defined by the corporate charter, bylaws, formal policy, and rule of law.
Credit default swap	A financial contract under which an agent buys protection against credit risk for a periodic fee in return for a payment by the protection seller contingent on the occurrence of a credit/default event.
Credit insurance	A form of guarantee to manufacturers and wholesalers against loss resulting from default on the part of debtors.
Credit risk	The risk that a counterparty to the insurer is unable or unwilling to meet its obligations causing a financial loss to the insurer.
Credit spreads	The spread between sovereign benchmark securities and other debt securities that are comparable in all respects except for credit quality (e.g., the difference between yields on U.S. Treasuries and those on single A-rated corporate bonds of a certain term to maturity).
Defined benefit pensions	A retirement pension plan where the benefits that retirees receive are determined by such factors as salary history and the duration of employment. The company is typically responsible for the investment risk and portfolio management.
Defined contribution pensions	A retirement pension plan where the benefits that retirees receive are determined by the returns on the plan's investments.
Derivatives	Financial contracts whose value derives from underlying securities prices, interest rates, foreign exchange rates, market indexes, or commodity prices.
Dollarization	The widespread domestic use of another country's currency (typically the U.S. dollar) to perform the standard functions of money—that of a unit of account, medium of exchange, and store of value.
Double gearing	Situations where multiple companies use shared capital to protect against risk occurring in separate entities. For example, an insurance company may purchase shares in a bank as a reciprocal arrangement for loans. In these cases, both institutions are leveraging their exposure to risk.
Dynamic hedging	A dynamic-hedging scheme involves the periodic re-balancing of a portfolio of hedging instruments (the buying or selling of securities) in order to maintain a specific hedging level.

Eligible capital	On- or off-balance sheet element that, in accordance with domestic regulations, is suitable to cover the required solvency margin (i.e., eligible for inclusion in the calculation of available solvency or regulatory capital). As a general rule, these elements are either assets free of all foreseeable liabilities, or, if they represent liabilities, the latter should be subordinated to any other liabilities, i.e., in the event of a bankruptcy, they are to be paid only after the claims of all other creditors have been satisfied.
EMBI	The acronym for the J.P. Morgan *Emerging Market Bond Index* that tracks the total returns for traded external debt instruments in the emerging markets.
Emerging markets	Developing countries' financial markets that are less than fully developed, but are nonetheless broadly accessible to foreign investors.
Financial guarantee insurance	A form of coverage in which the insurer guarantees the payment of interest and/or principal of the insured in connection with debt instruments issued by the insured.
Foreign direct investment	The acquisition abroad (i.e., outside the home country) of physical assets, such as plant and equipment, or of a controlling stake (usually greater than 10 percent of shareholdings).
Forward price-earnings ratio	The multiple of future expected earnings at which a stock sells. It is calculated by dividing the current stock price (adjusted for stock splits) by the estimated earnings per share for a future period (typically the next 12 months).
Hedge funds	Investment pools, typically organized as private partnerships and often resident offshore for tax and regulatory purposes. These funds face few restrictions on their portfolios and transactions. Consequently, they are free to use a variety of investment techniques—including short positions, transactions in derivatives, and leverage—to raise returns and cushion risk.
Hedging	Offsetting an existing risk exposure by taking an opposite position in the same or a similar risk, for example, by buying derivatives contracts.
In-force business	In the life insurance industry, the expression refers to the stock of existing policies that have been previously written and have not yet matured or been cancelled.
Interest rate swaps	An agreement between counterparties to exchange periodic interest payments on some predetermined dollar principal, which is called the notional principal amount. For example, one party will make fixed-rate and receive variable-rate interest payments.
Intermediation	The process of transferring funds from the ultimate source to the ultimate user. A financial institution, such as a bank, intermediates credit when it obtains money from depositors and relends it to borrowers.

Investment-grade issues (Sub-investment-grade issues)	A bond that is assigned a rating in the top four categories by commercial credit rating agencies. S&P classifies investment-grade bonds as BBB or higher, and Moody's classifies investment grade bonds as Baa or higher. (Sub-investment-grade bond issues are rated bonds that are below investment-grade.)
Leverage	The proportion of debt to equity. Leverage can be built up by borrowing (on-balance-sheet leverage, commonly measured by debt-to-equity ratios) or by using off-balance-sheet transactions.
Mark-to-market	The valuation of a position or portfolio by reference to the most recent price at which a financial instrument can be bought or sold in normal volumes. The mark-to-market value might equal the current market value—as opposed to historic accounting or book value—or the present value of expected future cash flows.
Mutual insurance company	A nonprofit insurance carrier, without capital stock, that is owned by the policyholders.
Nonperforming loans	Loans that are in default or close to being in default (i.e., typically past due for 90 days or more).
Offshore instruments	Securities issued outside of national boundaries.
(Pair-wise) correlations	A statistical measure of the degree to which the movements of two variables (for example, asset returns) are related.
Pension funding gaps	The difference between the discounted value of accumulating future pension obligations and the present value of investment assets.
Policy reserves	The amounts that a life insurance company allocates specifically for the fulfillment of its policy obligations: reserves are so calculated that, together with future premiums and interest earnings, they will enable the company to pay all future claims.
Primary market	The market where a newly issued security is first offered/sold to the public.
Put (call) option	A financial contract that gives the buyer the right, but not the obligation, to sell (buy) a financial instrument at a set price on or before a given date.
Reinsurance	Insurance placed by an underwriter in another company to cut down the amount of the risk assumed under the original insurance.
Reserve	Amounts of an insurance company's funds that are set aside to meet unforeseeable liabilities (i.e., an obligation that has not yet materialized) or statutory requirements. These amounts stem either from shareholders' capital or, in the case of mutual companies, members' contributions and accumulated surplus.
Retrenchment from risk	A reduction in the purchases or holdings of risky securities.

Risk aversion	The degree to which an investor who, when faced with two investments with the same expected return but different risk, prefers the one with the lower risk. That is, it measures an investor's aversion to uncertain outcomes or payoffs.
Secondary markets	Markets in which securities are traded after they are initially offered/sold in the primary market.
Separate account	Funds held by a life insurer that are segregated from the other assets of the insured and invested for pension plans and other designated policies.
Solvency	Narrowly defined as the ability of an insurer to meet its obligations (liabilities) at any time. In order to set a practicable definition, it is necessary to clarify the type of claims covered by the assets, e.g., already written business (run-off basis, break-up basis), or would future new business (going-concern basis) also to be considered. In addition, questions regarding the volume and the nature of an insurance company's business, the appropriate time horizon to be adopted, and setting an acceptable probability of becoming insolvent are taken into consideration in assessing a company's solvency.
Solvency requirements	The statutory requirements or rules on the required solvency margin and eligible capital elements, including the performance of the solvency test, to prove compliance with these requirements.
Spread	See "credit spreads" above (the word credit is sometimes omitted). Other definitions include: (1) the gap between bid and ask prices of a financial instrument; (2) the difference between the price at which an underwriter buys an issue from the issuer and the price at which the underwriter sells it to the public.
Subordinated debt	Loans or other liabilities that rank after claims of all other creditors and to be paid, in the event of liquidation or bankruptcy, only after all other debts have been met.
Swaptions	Options on interest rate swaps.
Syndicated loans	Large loans made jointly by a group of banks to one borrower. Usually, one lead bank takes a small percentage of the loan and partitions (syndicates) the rest to other banks.
Tail events	The occurrence of large or extreme security price movements, that, in terms of their probability of occurring, lie within the tail region of the distribution of possible price movements.
Technical provision	Amount set aside to meet liabilities arising out of insurance contracts, including claims provision (whether reported or not), provision for unearned premiums, provision for unexpired risks, life assurance provision and other liabilities related to life insurance contracts (e.g., premium deposits, savings accumulated over the term of with-profit policies).

Underwriting	The process by which an insurance company determines whether or not and on what basis it will accept an application for insurance.
Unit-linked investment	An insurance policy where a portion of the premium is used to purchase insurance protection, and the balance is invested in an authorized unit trust. The return on the policy is linked to the performance of the unit trust and the risk associated with the investment is borne by the policyholder.
Variable annuity	An annuity contract under which the amount of each periodic payment fluctuates according to the investment performance of the insurer.
With-profits policies	The insurance company guarantees to pay an agreed amount at a specific time in the future, and may increase this guaranteed amount through bonus payments. In effect, the policyholders are participating in the profits of the life insurance company.
Yield curve	A chart that plots the yield to maturity at a specific point in time for debt securities having equal credit risk but different maturity dates.

The following remarks by the Acting Chair were made at the conclusion of the Executive Board's dicussion of the Global Financial Stability Report *on March 26, 2004.*

Executive Directors welcomed the continued improvement in international financial market conditions and the brighter prospects for global financial stability going forward. The improved outlook is supported by a firming of the global economic recovery, rising corporate earnings, and a strengthening of corporate balance sheets. Emerging market borrowers, many of whom have taken steps to put their public finances on a sounder footing and improved the structure of their domestic and external debt, are benefiting from higher export demand and commodity prices.

Global Financial Market Surveillance

Directors noted that, in response to this improved outlook and the exceptionally low short-term interest rates, global financial markets staged a strong, broad-based rally in 2003. While low short-term interest rates are continuing to influence investor behavior and are in some cases encouraging increased risk taking in a search for yield, most mature and emerging market indices appear recently to be pointing to a period of consolidation, with investors showing renewed caution and increased discrimination.

Directors emphasized that the improved outlook for financial stability is not without risks. These risks will require continued vigilant monitoring, not least in view of their interconnected nature. A first set of issues, discussed by Directors, arises from the environment of prolonged low interest rates and abundant liquidity. In this environment, asset

valuations may be pushed beyond levels justified by fundamental improvements. A transition to higher interest rates in mature markets will eventually need to take place. This may have broader ramifications, including increased bond market volatility if investors were to revise their interest rate outlook abruptly—as they did during the 1994 sell-off in global fixed income markets—or if asset valuations that were predicated on an unusually low level of risk-free rates were corrected abruptly. To guard against these risks, Directors encouraged policymakers to develop timely and forward-looking communication strategies that encourage investors to base their decisions on fundamentals rather than on the expectation that interest rates will be kept indefinitely at very low levels. Directors noted that the potential effects of higher interest rates on emerging market economies are being mitigated due to the progress that many of them have made in reducing vulnerabilities, while stronger world growth will also help offset the impact of higher interest rates.

Directors also discussed the potential for market instability arising from the large global external imbalances, including the possibility that adverse developments in the currency markets might spill over into other asset markets. They noted that the depreciation of the U.S. dollar against other major currencies has so far been orderly. Most Directors considered that, in view of the substantial capital flows that the U.S. economy will continue to need to attract, the risk of a pronounced currency depreciation—possibly resulting in higher U.S. dollar interest rates and a correction in asset valuations—can nevertheless not be dismissed. Directors reiterated, in this context, that a strong and sustained cooperative effort—aimed at ensuring a smooth adjustment of global imbalances over the medium term—will remain a key policy priority for the international community in the period ahead.

Directors welcomed the improved external financing environment for emerging market borrowers. They noted that the improved credit quality of many emerging market borrowers and low interest rates in the major financial centers contributed to the impressive compression of spreads on emerging market bonds last year. Directors commended the steps taken by many emerging markets in the current favorable market environment to meet a substantial part of their borrowing needs, improve their debt structures, and extend maturities. The correction of the downward exchange rate over-shooting that occurred in 2003 in many Latin American economies should further help enhance debt sustainability in these countries. Directors also welcomed the trend toward making the inclusion of collective action clauses (CACs) in sovereign bond issues an industry standard. Notwithstanding this encouraging aggregate performance, Directors noted that some countries appear to have relaxed their fiscal and structural reform efforts. Unless they take timely corrective action, these countries face a heightened risk of exposing their underlying vulnerabilities in the event of a turnaround in the current favorable external financing environment.

Directors welcomed the continued strengthening of the balance sheets of the household, corporate, and bank sectors over the course of 2003, as corporate and household sectors continued to build up liquidity and rising asset values strengthened net worth. Nevertheless, rising interest rates may increase the debt service burden, particularly in a number of European countries where debt levels of the corporate sector remain high. Directors noted

that the recent fall in long-term yields has increased refinancing activity in the U.S. mortgage market and reopened the possibility of hedging activity that might amplify yield movements. They welcomed, in this context, recent proposals to strengthen the regulation of the U.S. mortgage agencies and address the implicit government guarantee.

Directors emphasized that the relatively benign overall conditions in mature and emerging markets provide an advantageous window of opportunity to focus policy attention on several key structural reforms to underpin financial stability over the longer run. In mature markets, recent scandals in the mutual funds industry and some companies, such as Parmalat, have again underscored the need to build on ongoing efforts to improve corporate governance and strengthen market foundations. In particular, steps should be taken to strengthen scrutiny by investors and regulators of firms with complex ownership and capital structures, as well as to enhance public oversight of auditing practices. Priorities on emerging countries' agenda going forward should include further reductions in the level and vulnerability of public debt, development of local capital markets, and continued strong efforts to improve the climate for foreign direct investment, which has remained at disappointingly low levels in spite of the general rebound in capital flows.

Risk Transfer and the Insurance Industry

Directors welcomed the work being undertaken in the context of the current and forthcoming issues of the GFSR on the range of regulatory and disclosure issues raised by the transfer of risk from banking to nonbanking institutions in mature markets. A prominent example is the rapid growth of the hedge fund sector where, despite closer counterparty and investor monitoring, there appears to be a need for broader and more systematic transparency of exposures and practices. Directors noted that future staff work will focus on the hedge fund and pension fund industries.

Directors welcomed the conclusion of the staff's analysis that the reallocation of credit risk to the insurance sector, together with improvements in risk management in the sector, appears to have contributed to enhanced overall financial stability. Moreover, by allocating a greater share of their portfolio to credit instruments, many life insurers avail themselves of a more predictable return. While the investment in credit instruments by insurers deserves to be supported, Directors stressed that this will need to go hand in hand with continued efforts to improve risk management and regulatory oversight of the sector. Areas for improvement highlighted by Directors include: wider implementation of risk-based capital standards by regulators; enhancement of supervisory resources in many mature market jurisdictions; increased information sharing among supervisors; and strengthened disclosure requirements. Directors welcomed the current debate on international accounting standards for insurers, and looked forward to the development of converging standards that provide an accurate reflection of insurance companies' financial position. To be adequate, disclosure should be comprehensive, and include information on sensitivities and risks. While rating agencies play a helpful role in disseminating information on risks, Directors cautioned that they should not be relied upon as a substitute for appropriate supervision.

Institutional Investors in Emerging Markets

Directors welcomed the discussion of the institutional investor base for claims on emerging markets. They saw the development of a stable investor base as a key element in reducing the volatility of capital flows to emerging markets. While ongoing changes are contributing to a welcome broadening and diversification of the investor base, Directors observed that the decline in dedicated, relative to crossover, investors may also have increased the volatility of capital flows. Another source of potential volatility arises from the impact that even small changes in the portfolio positions of institutional investors can have on emerging markets, given the large size of the assets under management of these investors. Directors agreed that the factors influencing the changing nature of the investor base, as well as their policy implications—including for debt management policies and practices in emerging markets—will require continued careful analysis. They emphasized the importance of adequate transparency and disclosure regarding both government policies and corporate developments, with investor relations programs being a particularly useful instrument. In addition, the development of an efficient market infrastructure within emerging markets will be helpful in attracting institutional investors from both mature and domestic markets.

Directors also commented on the supervisory and regulatory implications of the expanding portfolios of nonbank institutional investors in emerging markets, in particular the rapid growth of pension funds. They noted that, in view of the growing imbalance between the assets under management of these funds and the available securities, close coordination will be required between changes in the regulatory framework, the development of local capital markets, and the gradual easing of limits on foreign investments by pension funds to increase their opportunities for portfolio diversification. Directors viewed the development of local securities markets as key to ensuring proper risk management by the insurance industry. In view of the rapid growth and increasing sophistication of the activities of local institutional investors involved in both local and international markets, it will also be important to persevere with strong efforts to enhance the risk management skills of both investors and regulators.

STATISTICAL APPENDIX

This statistical appendix presents data on financial developments in key financial centers and emerging markets. It is designed to complement the analysis in the text by providing additional data that describe key aspects of financial market developments. These data are derived from a number of sources external to the IMF, including banks, commercial data providers, and official sources, and are presented for information purposes only; the IMF does not, however, guarantee the accuracy of the data from external sources.

Presenting financial market data in one location and in a fixed set of tables and charts, in this and future issues of the GFSR, is intended to give the reader an overview of developments in global financial markets. Unless otherwise noted, the statistical appendix reflects information available up to March 2, 2004.

Mirroring the structure of the chapters of the report, the appendix presents data separately for key financial centers and emerging market countries. Specifically, it is organized into three sections:

- Figures 1–14 and Tables 1–9 contain information on market developments in key financial centers. This includes data on global capital flows, and on markets for foreign exchange, bonds, equities, and derivatives, as well as sectoral balance sheet data for the United States, Japan, and Europe.

- Figures 15 and 16 and Tables 10–21 present information on financial developments in emerging markets, including data on equity, foreign exchange, and bond markets, as well as data on emerging market financing flows.

- Tables 22–28 report key financial soundness indicators for selected countries, including bank profitability, asset quality, and capital adequacy.

List of Tables and Figures

Key Financial Centers

Figures

Tables

Emerging Markets

Figures

Tables

Financial Soundness Indicators

Figure 1. Global Capital Flows: Sources and Uses of Global Capital in 2003

Countries That Export Capital[1]

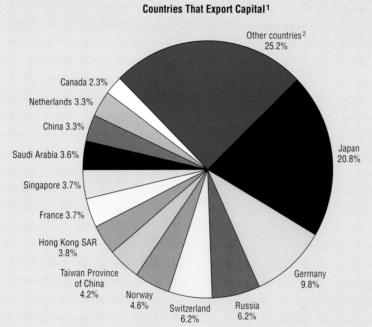

Countries That Import Capital[3]

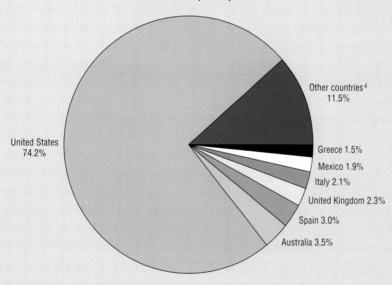

Source: International Monetary Fund, World Economic Outlook database as of March 11, 2004.
[1]As measured by countries' current (capital) account surplus (deficit).
[2]Other countries include all countries with shares of total surplus less than 2.3 percent.
[3]As measured by countries' current (capital) account deficit (surplus).
[4]Other countries include all countries with shares of total deficit less than 1.5 percent.

Figure 2. Exchange Rates: Selected Major Industrial Countries

——— Bilateral exchange rate (left scale)[1]
——— Nominal effective exchange rate (right scale)[2]

Sources: Bloomberg L.P.; and the IMF Competitive Indicators System.
Note: In each panel, the effective and bilateral exchange rates are scaled so that an upward movement implies an appreciation of the respective local currency.
[1]Local currency units per U.S. dollar except for the euro area and the United Kingdom, for which data are shown as U.S. dollars per local currency.
[2]1995 = 100; constructed using 1989–91 trade weights.

Figure 3. United States: Yields on Corporate and Treasury Bonds
(Weekly data)

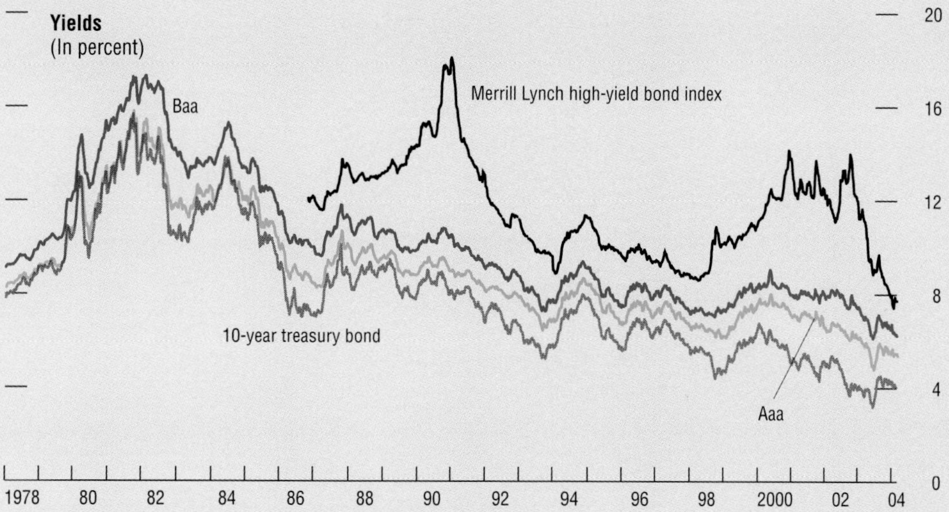

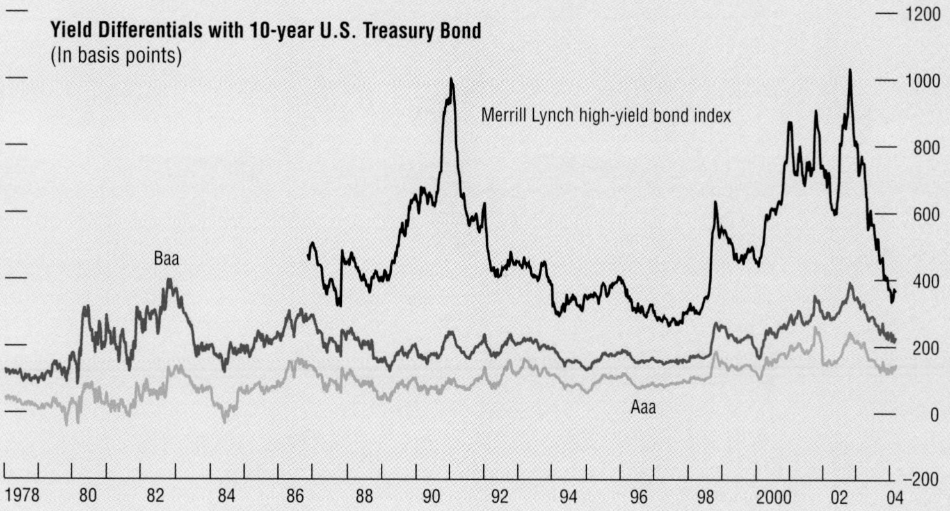

Yields
(In percent)

Baa

Merrill Lynch high-yield bond index

10-year treasury bond

Aaa

```
1978   80   82   84   86   88   90   92   94   96   98   2000   02   04
```

20
16
12
8
4
0

Yield Differentials with 10-year U.S. Treasury Bond
(In basis points)

Merrill Lynch high-yield bond index

Baa

Aaa

```
1978   80   82   84   86   88   90   92   94   96   98   2000   02   04
```

1200
1000
800
600
400
200
0
-200

Sources: Bloomberg L.P.; and Merrill Lynch.

Figure 4. Selected Spreads
(In basis points)

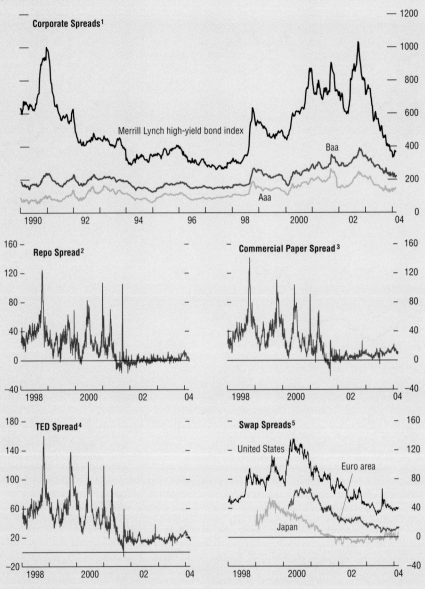

Sources: Bloomberg L.P.; and Merrill Lynch.
[1]Spreads over 10-year U.S. treasury bond; weekly data.
[2]Spread between yields on three-month U.S. treasury repo and on three-month U.S. treasury bill.
[3]Spread between yields on 90-day investment-grade commercial paper and on three-month U.S. treasury bill.
[4]Spread between three-month U.S. dollar LIBOR and yield on three-month U.S. treasury bill.
[5]Spread over 10-year government bond.

Figure 5. Nonfinancial Corporate Credit Spreads
(In basis points)

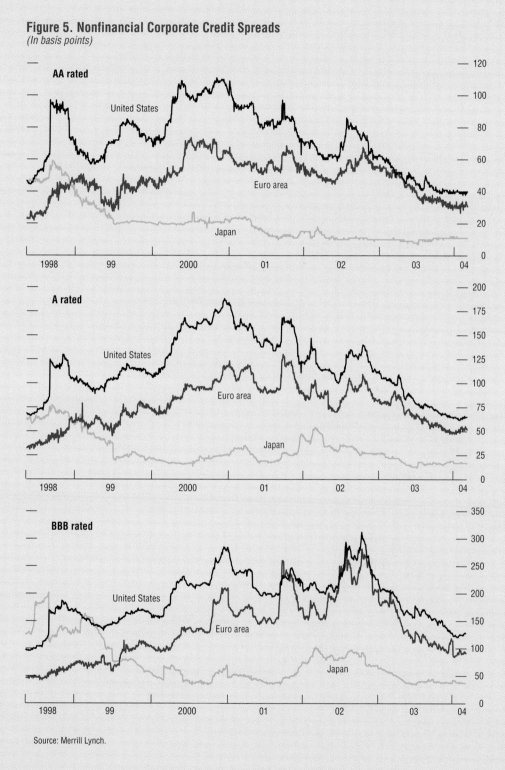

Source: Merrill Lynch.

Figure 6. Equity Markets: Price Indexes
(January 1, 1990 = 100; weekly data)

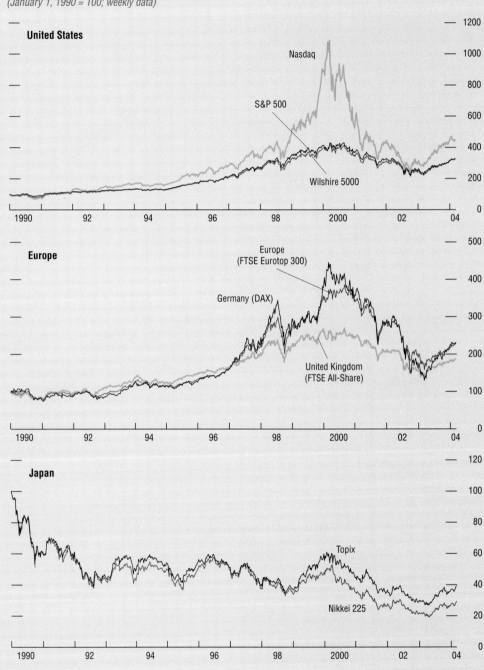

Source: Datastream.

Figure 7. Implied and Historical Volatility in Equity Markets

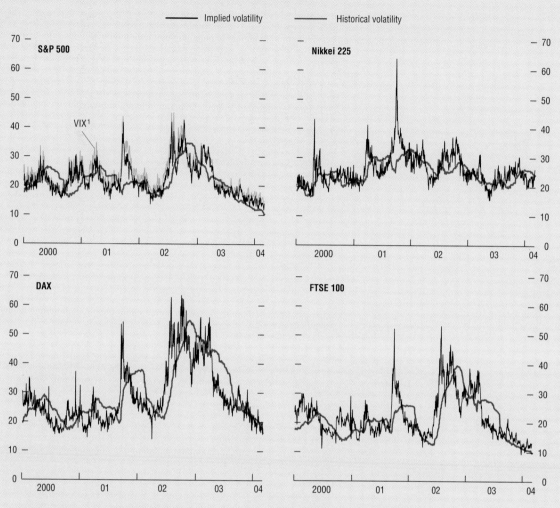

Sources: Bloomberg L.P.; and IMF staff estimates.
Note: Implied volatility is a measure of the equity price variability implied by the market prices of call options on equity futures. Historical volatility is calculated as a rolling 100-day annualized standard deviation of equity price changes. Volatilities are expressed in percent rate of change.
[1]VIX is the Chicago Board Options Exchange volatility index. This index is calculated by taking a weighted average of implied volatility for the eight S&P 500 calls and puts.

Figure 8. Historical Volatility of Government Bond Yields and Bond Returns for Selected Countries[1]

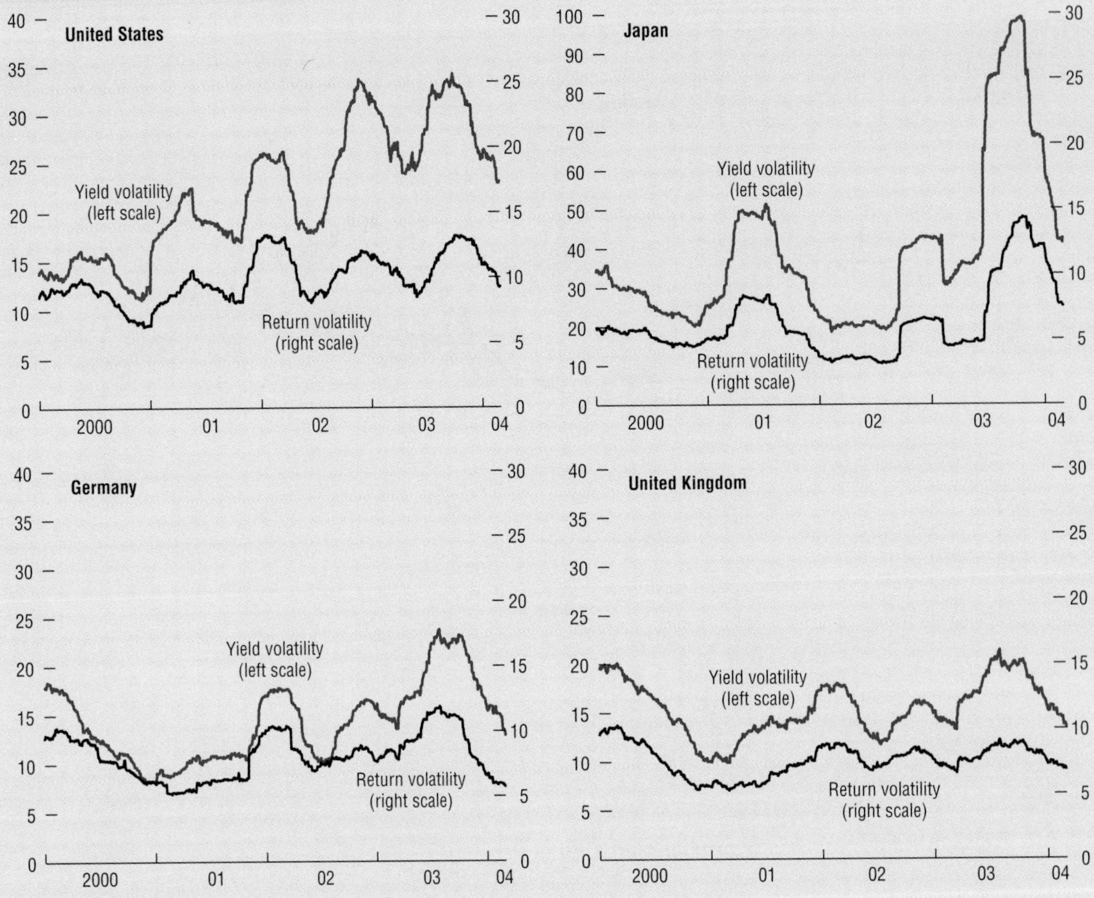

Sources: Bloomberg L.P.; and Datastream.
[1]Volatility calculated as a rolling 100-day annualized standard deviation of changes in yield and returns on 10-year government bonds. Returns are based on 10-plus year government bond indexes.

Figure 9. Twelve-Month Forward Price/Earnings Ratios

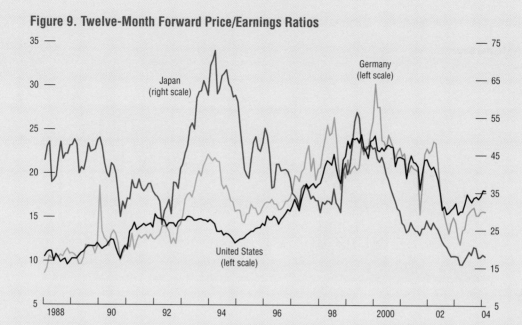

Source: I/B/E/S.

Figure 10. Flows into U.S.-Based Equity Funds

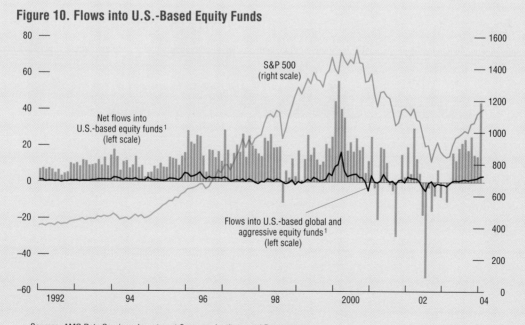

Sources: AMG Data Services; Investment Company Institute; and Datastream.
[1]In billions of U.S. dollars.

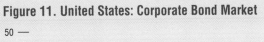

Figure 11. United States: Corporate Bond Market

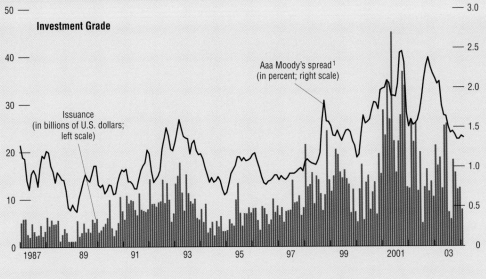

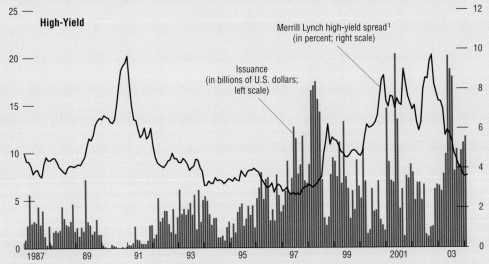

Sources: Board of Governors of the Federal Reserve System; and Bloomberg L.P.
[1]Spread against yield on 10-year U.S. government bonds.

Figure 12. Europe: Corporate Bond Market [1]

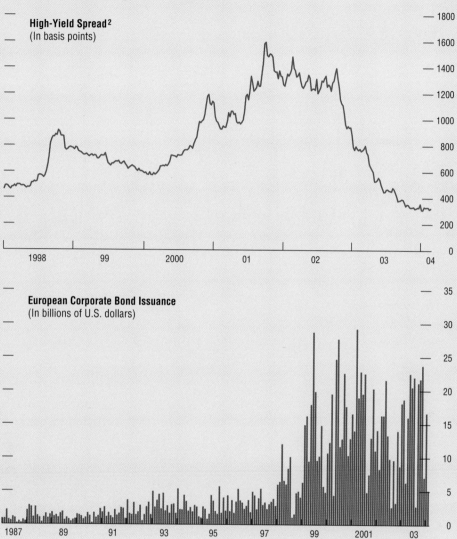

Sources: Bondware; and Datastream.
[1]Nonfinancial corporate bonds.
[2]Spread between yields on a Merrill Lynch High Yield European Issuers Index bond and a 10-year German government benchmark bond.

Figure 13. United States: Commercial Paper Market[1]

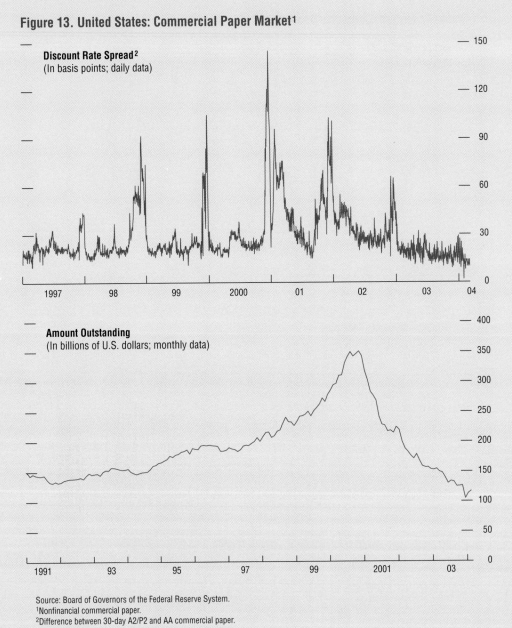

Discount Rate Spread[2]
(In basis points; daily data)

Amount Outstanding
(In billions of U.S. dollars; monthly data)

Source: Board of Governors of the Federal Reserve System.
[1]Nonfinancial commercial paper.
[2]Difference between 30-day A2/P2 and AA commercial paper.

Figure 14. United States: Asset-Backed Securities

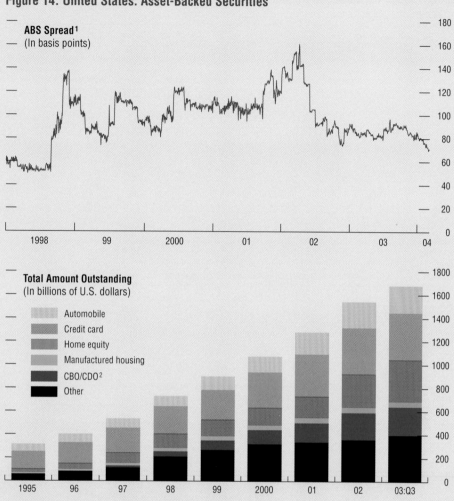

Sources: Merrill Lynch; Datastream; and the Bond Market Association.
[1]Merrill Lynch AAA Asset-Backed Master Index (fixed rate) option-adjusted spread.
[2]Collateralized bond/debt obligations.

Table 1. Global Capital Flows: Inflows and Outflows[1]

(In billions of U.S. dollars)

	Inflows										
	1992	1993	1994	1995	1996	1997	1998	1999	2000	2001	2002
United States											
Direct investment	19.8	51.4	46.1	57.8	86.5	105.6	179.0	289.4	321.3	151.6	39.6
Portfolio investment	72.0	111.0	139.4	210.4	332.8	333.1	187.6	285.6	420.0	425.1	421.4
Other investment	78.9	119.7	120.5	170.4	131.8	268.1	57.0	165.2	284.9	188.9	245.9
Reserve assets	n.a.	n.a.	n.a.	n.a.	n.a.	n.a.	n.a.	n.a.	n.a.	n.a.	n.a.
Total capital flows	170.7	282.1	306.0	438.6	551.1	706.8	423.6	740.2	1,026.1	765.5	707.0
Canada											
Direct investment	4.8	4.7	8.2	9.3	9.6	11.5	22.7	24.8	66.1	28.8	20.5
Portfolio investment	20.5	41.4	17.2	18.4	13.7	11.7	16.6	2.7	10.1	22.2	13.5
Other investment	−2.2	−6.7	16.0	−3.9	15.7	28.0	5.4	−10.8	0.6	7.4	6.0
Reserve assets	n.a.	n.a.	n.a.	n.a.	n.a.	n.a.	n.a.	n.a.	n.a.	n.a.	n.a.
Total capital flows	23.1	39.4	41.4	23.9	39.1	51.2	44.8	16.6	76.8	58.4	39.9
Japan											
Direct investment	2.8	0.1	0.9	0.0	0.2	3.2	3.3	12.3	8.2	6.2	9.1
Portfolio investment	9.6	−6.1	64.5	59.8	66.8	79.2	56.1	126.9	47.4	60.5	−20.0
Other investment	−105.2	−32.7	−5.6	97.3	31.1	68.0	−93.3	−265.1	−10.2	−17.6	26.6
Reserve assets	n.a.	n.a.	n.a.	n.a.	n.a.	n.a.	n.a.	n.a.	n.a.	n.a.	n.a.
Total capital flows	−92.9	−38.7	59.8	157.1	98.1	150.4	−34.0	−125.9	45.4	49.1	15.7
United Kingdom											
Direct investment	16.6	16.5	10.7	21.7	27.4	37.4	74.7	89.5	119.9	62.0	28.2
Portfolio investment	16.2	43.6	47.0	58.8	68.0	43.5	35.3	185.5	255.1	58.5	92.1
Other investment	96.4	191.4	−10.8	106.2	254.4	328.4	97.2	79.7	423.2	332.2	81.4
Reserve assets	n.a.	n.a.	n.a.	n.a.	n.a.	n.a.	n.a.	n.a.	n.a.	n.a.	n.a.
Total capital flows	129.1	251.6	46.9	186.7	349.7	409.2	207.2	354.8	798.3	452.7	201.7
Euro area											
Direct investment	...	...	...	...	...	...	...	212.1	403.0	181.2	132.6
Portfolio investment	...	...	...	...	...	...	...	283.4	266.3	317.2	261.9
Other investment	...	...	...	...	...	...	...	208.3	337.2	240.7	54.7
Reserve assets	n.a.	n.a.	n.a.	n.a.	n.a.	n.a.	n.a.	n.a.	n.a.	n.a.	n.a.
Total capital flows	...	...	...	...	...	...	...	703.8	1,006.5	739.1	449.3
Emerging markets and developing countries[2]											
Direct investment	48.6	71.6	97.5	128.2	147.5	184.2	177.5	209.5	204.3	221.4	172.6
Portfolio investment	52.1	93.5	93.3	35.4	106.7	81.9	40.5	127.5	81.6	4.9	−15.6
Other investment	70.5	40.5	14.3	128.1	59.0	80.0	20.8	−77.4	−51.2	−34.9	54.9
Reserve assets	n.a.	n.a.	n.a.	n.a.	n.a.	n.a.	n.a.	n.a.	n.a.	n.a.	n.a.
Total capital flows	171.3	205.6	205.0	291.6	313.1	346.1	238.9	259.6	234.7	191.5	211.9

Sources: IMF, World Economic Outlook database as of March 11, 2004; and *International Financial Statistics.*

[1]The total net capital flows are the sum of direct investment, portfolio investment, other investment flows, and reserve assets. "Other investment" includes bank loans and deposits.

[2]This aggregate comprises the group of Other Emerging Market and Developing Countries defined in the *World Economic Outlook,* together with Hong Kong SAR, Israel, Korea, Singapore, and Taiwan Province of China.

					Outflows					
1992	1993	1994	1995	1996	1997	1998	1999	2000	2001	2002
−48.3	−84.0	−80.2	−98.8	−91.9	−104.8	−142.6	−224.9	−159.2	−120.0	−137.8
−49.2	−146.2	−60.3	−122.5	−149.8	−119.0	−124.2	−116.2	−121.9	−84.6	15.8
19.1	31.0	−40.9	−121.4	−178.9	−262.8	−74.2	−171.2	−288.4	−140.4	−53.3
3.9	−1.4	5.3	−9.7	6.7	−1.0	−6.7	8.7	−0.3	−4.9	−3.7
−74.4	−200.5	−176.1	−352.4	−413.9	−487.6	−347.8	−503.7	−569.8	−350.0	−179.0
−3.5	−5.7	−9.3	−11.5	−13.1	−23.1	−34.1	−17.3	−46.4	−36.8	−28.9
−9.8	−13.8	−6.6	−5.3	−14.2	−8.6	−15.1	−15.6	−42.9	−24.4	−15.8
−3.5	−0.4	−20.4	−8.3	−21.1	−16.2	9.4	10.2	−4.2	−10.2	−6.9
4.8	−0.9	0.4	−2.7	−5.5	2.4	−5.0	−5.9	−3.7	−2.2	0.2
−12.1	−20.8	−35.9	−27.9	−53.9	−45.4	−44.8	−28.5	−97.3	−73.5	−51.4
−17.4	−13.8	−18.1	−22.5	−23.4	−26.1	−24.6	−22.3	−31.5	−38.5	−32.0
−34.0	−63.7	−92.0	−86.0	−100.6	−47.1	−95.2	−154.4	−83.4	−106.8	−85.9
46.6	15.1	−35.1	−102.2	5.2	−192.0	37.9	266.3	−4.1	46.6	36.4
−0.6	−27.5	−25.3	−58.6	−35.1	−6.6	6.2	−76.3	−49.0	−40.5	−46.1
−5.4	−90.0	−170.4	−269.4	−154.0	−271.6	−75.8	13.4	−168.0	−139.2	−127.7
−19.7	−27.3	−34.9	−45.3	−34.8	−62.4	−122.1	−201.6	−266.2	−68.2	−7.5
−49.3	−133.6	31.5	−61.7	−93.1	−85.0	−53.0	−34.2	−97.7	−124.2	2.5
−60.5	−68.5	−42.4	−74.9	−215.3	−275.9	−26.8	−94.1	−411.5	−255.1	−202.9
2.4	−1.3	−1.5	0.9	0.7	3.9	0.3	1.0	−5.3	4.5	0.6
−127.0	−230.5	−47.4	−181.0	−342.6	−419.4	−201.6	−328.8	−780.8	−443.0	−207.3
...	...	...	...	...	...	...	−338.5	−404.1	−272.7	−171.2
...	...	...	...	...	...	...	−331.1	−383.8	−258.5	−160.7
...	...	...	...	...	...	...	−34.5	−166.2	−243.5	−201.6
...	...	...	...	...	...	...	11.6	16.2	16.9	−2.6
...	...	...	...	...	...	...	−692.5	−937.9	−757.8	−536.0
−9.9	−17.9	−16.9	−26.4	−31.6	−39.2	−22.8	−29.6	−35.8	−30.1	−29.9
−2.0	2.0	−1.3	−12.4	−27.3	−28.2	−6.4	−69.1	−76.7	−104.8	−83.7
−19.2	−2.7	−38.6	−13.0	−48.0	−77.7	−82.4	−70.5	−93.3	−11.1	−38.2
−58.4	−64.0	−68.8	−131.4	−90.7	−95.7	−43.0	−94.6	−117.4	−112.5	−200.9
−89.5	−82.6	−125.5	−183.2	−197.5	−240.8	−154.7	−263.9	−323.1	−258.5	−352.7

Table 2. Global Capital Flows: Amounts Outstanding and Net Issues of International Debt Securities by Currency of Issue and Announced International Syndicated Credit Facilities by Nationality of Borrower
(In billions of U.S. dollars)

	1995	1996	1997	1998	1999	2000	2001	2002	2003 Q1	Q2	Q3
Amounts outstanding of international debt securities by currency of issue											
U.S. dollar	874.1	1,113.1	1,433.4	1,833.0	2,357.3	2,908.0	3,611.4	4,047.4	4,127.6	4,209.7	4,351.6
Japanese yen	436.0	462.9	444.4	462.6	497.5	452.5	411.5	432.9	428.6	427.8	460.6
Pound sterling	175.6	225.7	266.7	322.4	391.1	453.1	506.4	619.1	622.8	668.1	697.4
Canadian dollar	83.2	76.5	67.2	55.5	56.4	51.7	47.6	51.5	55.5	68.4	73.4
Swedish krona	5.1	5.1	4.1	7.5	7.2	7.7	8.2	11.1	12.3	13.3	14.5
Swiss franc	178.8	151.2	138.5	153.5	135.5	132.0	123.6	159.1	164.6	168.2	175.8
Euro[1]	742.9	832.7	848.9	1,133.9	1,452.9	1,770.4	2,289.9	3,283.1	3,608.0	4,010.0	4,252.2
Other	53.2	68.4	78.8	84.3	98.5	97.2	110.4	152.1	165.5	184.0	192.4
Total	2,548.9	2,935.6	3,282.0	4,052.7	4,996.4	5,872.6	7,109.0	8,756.3	9,184.9	9,749.5	10,217.9
Net issues of international debt securities by currency of issue											
U.S. dollar	65.8	238.8	320.3	399.7	399.7	524.4	550.6	435.9	80.2	82.1	141.9
Japanese yen	75.0	81.7	34.0	−33.0	−33.0	−23.5	10.9	−17.9	−3.5	−1.8	−3.1
Pound sterling	6.7	30.8	46.4	53.9	53.9	77.8	92.5	52.3	16.5	17.0	21.6
Canadian dollar	−2.2	−6.5	−6.2	−7.5	−7.5	−2.3	−2.7	3.5	0.1	8.1	4.6
Swedish krona	−0.1	0.2	−0.4	3.6	3.6	0.1	1.2	1.1	0.9	0.2	0.6
Swiss franc	−0.3	−1.3	−1.6	6.3	6.3	4.0	−0.2	8.0	1.5	4.2	3.0
Euro	72.3	140.0	130.2	214.6	214.6	508.4	423.8	493.5	194.1	223.3	158.7
Other	14.1	13.3	23.2	8.9	8.9	14.7	9.1	30.8	10.2	10.6	4.5
Total	231.3	497.0	545.9	646.5	646.5	1,103.6	1,085.2	1,007.2	300.0	343.7	331.8
Announced international syndicated credit facilities by nationality of borrower											
All countries	703.3	839.3	1,080.6	905.3	1,025.8	1,464.9	1,388.8	1,299.7	233.2	377.4	276.6
Industrial countries	610.2	732.0	903.6	819.4	960.0	1,328.6	1,276.6	1,200.7	214.1	352.5	247.5
Of which: United States	383.7	482.2	606.2	574.9	623.5	804.5	850.7	736.5	133.9	188.9	119.7
Japan	3.5	6.8	6.1	11.4	15.4	17.5	23.8	19.5	4.9	1.9	5.9
Germany	22.2	17.6	23.6	15.5	34.0	42.4	35.8	85.2	6.1	27.5	37.0
France	20.5	23.3	38.7	19.8	33.7	72.9	50.1	63.9	20.5	21.0	10.0
Italy	15.5	5.9	10.1	6.2	16.1	35.3	36.0	22.9	1.7	15.1	14.3
United Kingdom	56.8	68.4	101.3	79.8	108.5	131.2	105.7	110.4	18.0	40.7	23.0
Canada	22.4	25.7	38.2	41.4	22.8	38.4	40.6	35.1	8.3	4.9	10.7

Source: Bank for International Settlements.
[1]For 1995–98, the euro includes euro area currencies.

Table 3. Selected Indicators on the Size of the Capital Markets, 2002
(In billions of U.S. dollars unless otherwise noted)

	GDP	Total Reserves Minus Gold[1]	Stock Market Capitalization	Debt Securities Public	Debt Securities Private	Debt Securities Total	Bank Assets[2]	Bonds, Equities, and Bank Assets[3]	Bonds, Equities, and Bank Assets[3] (In percent of GDP)
World	32,197.4	2,513.9	22,809.6	16,564.8	27,005.4	43,570.2	40,063.2	106,443.0	330.8
European Union	8,656.7	289.1	5,734.3	4,930.9	7,891.4	12,822.3	17,645.9	36,202.5	418.4
Euro area	6,678.1	207.9	3,677.7	4,226.1	6,000.4	10,226.5	12,839.0	27,040.7	405.3
North America	11,216.8	104.9	11,625.8	5,033.0	14,823.3	19,856.3	6,989.6	38,471.7	344.0
Canada	736.0	37.0	570.2	499.6	307.4	807.0	1,100.2	2,477.4	336.6
United States	10,480.8	68.0	11,055.6	4,533.4	14,515.9	19,049.3	5,889.4	35,994.3	344.6
Japan	3,973.3	461.2	2,095.5	4,841.9	2,072.7	6,914.6	6,212.1	15,222.2	381.9
Memorandum items:									
EU countries									
Austria	206.1	9.7	33.6	156.3	152.6	308.9	278.8	621.3	303.5
Belgium	245.4	11.9	138.7	304.0	256.4	560.4	1,000.9	1,700.0	690.6
Denmark	172.4	27.0	76.7	100.0	238.2	338.2	425.9	840.8	486.2
Finland	131.9	9.3	138.8	82.1	52.7	134.8	297.4	571.0	435.4
France	1,438.4	28.4	1,025.6	780.7	1,151.3	1,932.0	3,161.7	6,119.3	425.7
Germany	1,992.3	51.2	686.0	860.2	2,348.0	3,208.2	2,969.6	6,863.8	344.5
Greece	133.4	8.1	66.0	161.2	11.8	173.0	175.9	414.9	311.4
Ireland	122.1	5.4	59.9	30.7	72.9	103.6	495.9	659.4	540.0
Italy	1,188.0	28.6	477.1	1,208.3	822.8	2,031.1	1,789.4	4,297.5	361.8
Luxembourg	21.1	0.2	24.6	0.0	27.0	27.0	529.4	580.9	2,820.4
Netherlands	419.8	9.6	518.6	198.4	669.3	867.7	1,345.1	2,731.4	650.7
Portugal	122.3	11.2	47.2	79.7	82.0	161.7	174.5	383.4	314.1
Spain	657.3	34.5	461.6	364.5	353.6	718.1	918.0	2,097.7	320.2
Sweden	240.6	14.9	179.1	130.7	207.2	337.9	359.4	876.5	364.7
United Kingdom	1,565.7	39.4	1,800.7	474.1	1,445.6	1,919.7	3,724.2	7,444.5	475.2
Emerging market countries	7,415.9	1,531.3	2,525.0	1,511.8	1,062.0	2,573.8	6,980.4	12,079.3	162.8
Of which:									
Asia	3,429.4	975.9	1,965.7	706.4	820.9	1,527.3	4,911.4	8,404.5	242.2
Latin America	1,658.5	161.0	308.5	464.6	178.4	643.0	773.9	1,725.4	105.2
Middle East	737.2	132.5	52.5	5.4	13.5	18.9	598.5	669.9	73.4
Africa	450.3	72.9	116.5	47.7	20.8	68.5	315.3	500.4	112.1
Europe	1,140.5	189.1	81.7	287.7	28.4	316.1	381.3	779.1	81.8

Sources: World Federation of Exchanges; Bank for International Settlements; International Monetary Fund, *International Financial Statistics* (IFS) and World Economic Outlook database as of March 11, 2004; and ©2003 Bureau van Dijk Electronic Publishing-Bankscope.
[1]Data are from IFS. For United Kingdom, excludes the assets of the Bank of England.
[2]Assets of commercial banks.
[3]Sum of the stock market capitalization, debt securities, and bank assets.

Table 4. Global Over-the-Counter Derivatives Markets: Notional Amounts and Gross Market Values of Outstanding Contracts[1]

(In billions of U.S. dollars)

	Notional Amounts					Gross Market Values				
	End-June 2001	End-Dec. 2001	End-June 2002	End-Dec. 2002	End-June 2003	End-June 2001	End-Dec. 2001	End-June 2002	End-Dec. 2002	End-June 2003
Total	**99,755**	**111,178**	**127,509**	**141,679**	**169,678**	**3,045**	**3,788**	**4,450**	**6,360**	**7,908**
Foreign exchange	**16,910**	**16,748**	**18,068**	**18,460**	**22,088**	**773**	**779**	**1,052**	**881**	**996**
Outright forwards and forex swaps	10,582	10,336	10,426	10,719	12,332	395	374	615	468	476
Currency swaps	3,832	3,942	4,215	4,503	5,159	314	335	340	337	419
Options	2,496	2,470	3,427	3,238	4,597	63	70	97	76	101
Interest rate[2]	**67,465**	**77,568**	**89,955**	**101,658**	**121,799**	**1,573**	**2,210**	**2,467**	**4,266**	**5,459**
Forward rate agreements	6,537	7,737	9,146	8,792	10,271	15	19	19	22	20
Swaps	51,407	58,897	68,234	79,120	94,583	1,404	1,969	2,213	3,864	5,004
Options	9,521	10,933	12,575	13,746	16,946	154	222	235	381	434
Equity-linked	**1,884**	**1,881**	**2,214**	**2,309**	**2,799**	**199**	**205**	**243**	**255**	**260**
Forwards and swaps	329	320	386	364	488	49	58	62	61	67
Options	1,556	1,561	1,828	1,944	2,311	150	147	181	194	193
Commodity[3]	**590**	**598**	**777**	**923**	**1,040**	**83**	**75**	**79**	**86**	**110**
Gold	203	231	279	315	304	21	20	28	28	22
Other	387	367	498	608	736	62	56	51	58	88
Forwards and swaps	229	217	290	402	458	...	...	...	...	...
Options	158	150	208	206	279	...	...	...	...	...
Other	**12,906**	**14,384**	**16,496**	**18,330**	**21,952**	**417**	**519**	**609**	**871**	**1,083**
Memorandum items:										
Gross credit exposure[4]	n.a.	n.a.	n.a.	n.a.	n.a.	1,019	1,171	1,317	1,511	1,750
Exchange-traded derivatives	16,910	16,748	18,068	18,460	22,088	...	...	...	...	...

Source: Bank for International Settlements.

[1]All figures are adjusted for double-counting. Notional amounts outstanding have been adjusted by halving positions vis-à-vis other reporting dealers. Gross market values have been calculated as the sum of the total gross positive market value of contracts and the absolute value of the gross negative market value of contracts with non-reporting counterparties.

[2]Single-currency contracts only.

[3]Adjustments for double-counting are estimated.

[4]Gross market values after taking into account legally enforceable bilateral netting agreements.

Table 5. Global Over-the-Counter Derivatives Markets: Notional Amounts and Gross Market Values of Outstanding Contracts by Counterparty, Remaining Maturity, and Currency[1]
(In billions of U.S. dollars)

	Notional Amounts					Gross Market Values				
	End-June 2001	End-Dec. 2001	End-June 2002	End-Dec. 2002	End-June 2003	End-June 2001	End-Dec. 2001	End-June 2002	End-Dec. 2002	End-June 2003
Total	**99,755**	**111,178**	**127,509**	**141,679**	**169,678**	**3,045**	**3,788**	**4,450**	**6,360**	**7,908**
Foreign exchange	**16,910**	**16,748**	**18,068**	**18,460**	**22,088**	**773**	**779**	**1,052**	**881**	**996**
By counterparty										
With other reporting dealers	5,907	5,912	6,602	6,845	7,960	229	237	372	285	284
With other financial institutions	7,287	6,755	7,210	7,602	8,955	334	319	421	377	427
With non-financial customers	3,716	4,081	4,256	4,012	5,172	210	224	259	220	286
By remaining maturity										
Up to one year[2]	13,012	13,427	14,401	14,533	17,561	...	...	...	...	...
One to five years[2]	2,833	2,340	2,537	2,719	3,128	...	...	...	...	...
Over five years[2]	1,065	981	1,130	1,208	1,399	...	...	...	...	...
By major currency										
U.S. dollar[3]	15,141	15,410	15,973	16,500	19,401	679	704	948	813	891
Euro[3]	6,425	6,368	7,297	7,818	9,914	322	266	445	429	526
Japanese yen[3]	4,254	4,178	4,454	4,791	4,907	217	313	254	189	165
Pound sterling[3]	2,472	2,315	2,522	2,462	3,093	78	69	112	98	114
Other[3]	5,528	5,225	5,890	5,349	6,861	250	206	345	233	296
Interest rate[4]	**67,465**	**77,568**	**89,955**	**101,658**	**121,799**	**1,573**	**2,210**	**2,467**	**4,266**	**5,459**
By counterparty										
With other reporting dealers	32,319	35,472	43,340	46,722	53,622	703	912	1,081	1,848	2,266
With other financial institutions	28,653	32,510	36,310	43,607	53,133	683	945	1,025	1,845	2,482
With non-financial customers	6,494	9,586	10,304	11,328	15,044	187	353	361	573	710
By remaining maturity										
Up to one year[2]	25,605	27,886	33,674	36,938	44,927	...	...	...	...	...
One to five years[2]	26,308	30,566	34,437	40,137	46,646	...	...	...	...	...
Over five years[2]	15,553	19,115	21,844	24,583	30,226	...	...	...	...	...
By major currency										
U.S. dollar	23,083	27,427	32,178	34,399	40,110	581	952	1,127	1,917	2,286
Euro	22,405	26,230	30,671	38,429	50,000	461	677	710	1,499	2,178
Japanese yen	11,278	11,799	13,433	14,650	15,270	313	304	326	378	405
Pound sterling	5,178	6,216	6,978	7,442	8,322	99	148	151	252	315
Other	5,521	5,896	6,695	6,738	8,097	119	129	153	220	275
Equity-linked	**1,884**	**1,881**	**2,214**	**2,309**	**2,799**	**199**	**205**	**243**	**255**	**260**
Commodity[5]	**590**	**598**	**777**	**923**	**1,040**	**83**	**75**	**79**	**86**	**110**
Other	**12,906**	**14,384**	**16,496**	**18,330**	**21,952**	**417**	**519**	**609**	**871**	**1,083**

Source: Bank for International Settlements.

[1]All figures are adjusted for double-counting. Notional amounts outstanding have been adjusted by halving positions vis-à-vis other reporting dealers. Gross market values have been calculated as the sum of the total gross positive market value of contracts and the absolute value of the gross negative market value of contracts with non-reporting counterparties.

[2]Residual maturity.

[3]Counting both currency sides of each foreign exchange transaction means that the currency breakdown sums to twice the aggregate.

[4]Single-currency contracts only.

[5]Adjustments for double-counting are estimated.

Table 6. Exchange-Traded Derivative Financial Instruments: Notional Principal Amounts Outstanding and Annual Turnover

	1986	1987	1988	1989	1990	1991	1992	1993	1994
	(In billions of U.S. dollars)								
Notional principal amounts outstanding									
Interest rate futures	370.0	487.7	895.4	1,201.0	1,454.8	2,157.4	2,913.1	4,960.4	5,807.6
Interest rate options	144.0	122.6	279.0	386.0	595.4	1,069.6	1,383.8	2,361.4	2,623.2
Currency futures	10.2	14.6	12.1	16.0	17.0	18.3	26.5	34.7	40.4
Currency options	39.2	59.5	48.0	50.2	56.5	62.9	71.6	75.9	55.7
Stock market index futures	13.5	17.6	27.0	41.1	69.1	76.0	79.8	110.0	127.7
Stock market index options	37.8	27.7	42.7	70.2	93.6	136.9	163.7	232.4	242.8
Total	614.8	729.7	1,304.1	1,764.5	2,286.4	3,521.2	4,638.5	7,774.9	8,897.3
North America	514.6	577.8	951.3	1,153.5	1,264.4	2,153.0	2,698.7	4,360.7	4,823.6
Europe	13.1	13.3	177.4	250.9	461.4	710.7	1,114.4	1,777.9	1,831.8
Asia-Pacific	87.0	138.5	175.5	360.1	560.5	657.0	823.5	1,606.0	2,171.8
Other	0.1	0.1	0.0	0.0	0.1	0.5	1.9	30.3	70.1
	(In millions of contracts traded)								
Annual turnover									
Interest rate futures	91.0	145.7	156.4	201.0	219.1	230.9	330.1	427.0	628.5
Interest rate options	22.2	29.3	30.5	39.5	52.0	50.8	64.8	82.9	116.6
Currency futures	19.9	21.2	22.5	28.2	29.7	30.0	31.3	39.0	69.8
Currency options	13.0	18.3	18.2	20.7	18.9	22.9	23.4	23.7	21.3
Stock market index futures	28.4	36.1	29.6	30.1	39.4	54.6	52.0	71.2	109.0
Stock market index options	140.4	139.1	79.1	101.7	119.1	121.4	133.9	144.1	197.6
Total	314.9	389.6	336.3	421.2	478.2	510.4	635.6	787.9	1,142.9
North America	288.7	318.3	252.3	288.0	312.3	302.6	341.4	382.4	513.5
Europe	10.3	35.9	40.8	64.3	83.0	110.5	185.1	263.4	398.1
Asia-Pacific	14.3	30.0	34.3	63.6	79.1	85.8	82.9	98.5	131.7
Other	1.6	5.4	8.9	5.3	3.8	11.5	26.2	43.6	99.6

Source: Bank for International Settlements.

	1995	1996	1997	1998	1999	2000	2001	2002	2003 Q1	2003 Q2	2003 Q3
(In billions of U.S. dollars)											
	5,876.2	5,979.0	7,586.7	8,031.4	7,924.8	7,907.8	9,265.3	9,950.7	11,034.1	13,448.0	13,035.8
	2,741.8	3,277.8	3,639.9	4,623.5	3,755.5	4,734.2	12,492.8	11,759.5	17,622.1	22,026.9	23,554.9
	33.8	37.7	42.3	31.7	36.7	74.4	65.6	47.0	65.9	71.6	69.8
	120.4	133.4	118.6	49.2	22.4	21.4	27.4	27.4	29.4	33.3	37.7
	172.2	195.7	211.3	291.5	340.3	371.5	333.9	325.5	366.2	410.8	433.3
	337.7	394.5	808.7	907.4	1,510.2	1,148.3	1,574.8	1,700.2	1,835.4	2,226.5	2,396.2
	9,282.0	10,017.9	12,407.5	13,934.7	13,589.9	14,257.7	23,759.9	23,810.3	30,953.1	38,217.1	39,527.7
	4,852.4	4,841.0	6,348.3	7,355.1	6,930.6	8,167.9	16,198.9	13,688.9	16,895.8	21,639.8	20,497.7
	2,241.3	2,828.1	3,587.4	4,397.1	4,008.5	4,197.4	6,141.3	8,800.4	12,787.4	15,091.2	17,284.3
	1,990.2	2,154.0	2,235.7	1,882.5	2,401.3	1,606.2	1,308.4	1,191.7	1,122.5	1,310.5	1,558.1
	198.1	194.8	236.1	300.0	249.5	286.2	111.3	129.3	147.4	175.6	187.6
(In millions of contracts traded)											
	561.0	612.2	701.6	760.0	672.7	781.2	1,057.5	1,147.9	368.5	421.9	404.8
	225.5	151.1	116.7	129.6	117.9	107.6	199.6	240.3	75.5	87.2	76.6
	99.6	73.6	73.5	54.6	37.2	43.6	49.1	42.7	13.3	15.9	14.0
	23.3	26.3	21.1	12.1	6.8	7.1	10.5	16.1	3.5	3.3	4.0
	114.8	93.9	115.9	178.0	204.8	225.2	337.1	530.2	174.1	172.0	175.9
	187.3	172.3	178.2	195.1	322.5	481.4	1,148.2	2,235.4	751.4	809.8	763.9
	1,211.6	1,129.3	1,207.2	1,329.4	1,361.9	1,646.1	2,801.9	4,212.7	1,386.3	1,510.1	1,439.3
	455.0	428.4	463.6	530.2	463.0	461.3	675.7	908.1	286.6	348.0	328.0
	354.7	391.8	482.8	525.9	604.5	718.5	957.8	1,074.8	351.7	340.1	334.1
	126.4	115.9	126.8	170.9	207.8	331.3	985.1	2,073.1	712.6	779.1	730.7
	275.5	193.2	134.0	102.4	86.6	135.0	183.3	156.7	35.4	42.9	46.5

Table 7. United States: Sectoral Balance Sheets
(In percent)

	1996	1997	1998	1999	2000	2001	2002
Corporate sector							
Debt/net worth	51.2	50.3	50.3	50.7	48.3	51.4	51.2
Short-term debt/total debt	41.0	40.5	40.1	39.0	39.8	34.6	31.8
Interest burden[1]	10.5	11.0	12.7	13.4	15.9	17.8	17.0
Household sector							
Net worth/assets	84.7	85.3	85.5	86.0	84.9	83.6	81.9
Equity/total assets	25.8	29.7	31.4	35.0	30.9	26.5	20.5
Equity/financial assets	38.1	42.8	44.9	49.2	45.0	40.1	32.8
Home mortgage debt/total assets	10.1	9.6	9.5	9.2	9.9	10.9	12.5
Consumer credit/total assets	3.6	3.4	3.3	3.1	3.5	3.8	4.0
Total debt/financial assets	22.6	21.2	20.7	19.7	22.0	24.8	29.0
Debt service burden[2]	12.0	12.2	12.2	12.5	12.8	13.3	13.3
Banking sector[3]							
Credit quality							
Nonperforming loans[4]/total loans	1.0	1.0	1.0	1.0	1.1	1.4	1.5
Net loan losses/average total loans	0.6	0.7	0.7	0.6	0.7	1.0	1.1
Loan-loss reserve/total loans	1.9	1.8	1.8	1.7	1.7	1.9	1.9
Net charge-offs/total loans	0.6	0.6	0.7	0.6	0.7	1.0	1.1
Capital ratios							
Total risk-based capital	12.5	12.2	12.2	12.2	12.1	12.7	12.8
Tier 1 risk-based capital	10.0	9.6	9.5	9.5	9.4	9.9	10.0
Equity capital/total assets	8.2	8.3	8.5	8.4	8.5	9.1	9.2
Core capital (leverage ratio)	7.6	7.6	7.5	7.8	7.7	7.8	8.0
Profitability measures							
Return on average assets (ROA)	1.2	1.3	1.3	1.3	1.2	1.2	1.4
Return on average equity (ROE)	14.8	15.6	14.8	15.7	14.8	14.2	14.9
Net interest margin	4.3	4.3	4.0	4.0	3.9	3.9	4.3
Efficiency ratio[5]	60.8	59.2	61.0	58.7	58.4	57.7	55.8

Sources: Board of Governors of the Federal Reserve System, *Flow of Funds*; Department of Commerce, Bureau of Economic Analysis; Federal Deposit Insurance Corporation; and Federal Reserve Bank of St. Louis.

[1] Ratio of net interest payments to pre-tax income.
[2] Ratio of debt payments to disposable personal income.
[3] FDIC-insured commercial banks.
[4] Loans past due 90+ days and nonaccrual.
[5] Noninterest expense less amortization of intangible assets as a percent of net interest income plus noninterest income.

Table 8. Japan: Sectoral Balance Sheets[1]
(In percent)

	FY1996	FY1997	FY1998	FY1999	FY2000	FY2001	FY2002
Corporate sector							
Debt/shareholders' equity (book value)	206.3	207.9	189.3	182.5	156.8	156.0	146.1
Short-term debt/total debt	40.5	41.8	39.0	39.4	37.7	36.8	39.0
Interest burden[2]	38.2	39.1	46.5	36.3	28.4	32.3	27.8
Debt/operating profits	1,344.7	1,498.5	1,813.8	1,472.1	1,229.3	1,480.0	1,370.0
Memorandum items:							
Total debt/GDP	106.7	106.5	106.2	107.5	102.0	100.0	98.7
Household sector							
Net worth/assets	85.5	85.3	85.1	85.5	85.4	85.1	85.1
Equity	4.7	4.3	3.1	5.6	4.9	4.5	5.0
Real estate	40.7	40.0	39.5	37.5	36.6	35.4	34.1
Interest burden[3]	5.7	5.5	5.3	5.0	5.1	5.0	4.9
Memorandum items:							
Debt/equity	307.6	345.2	477.6	259.4	299.5	333.4	298.5
Debt/real estate	35.6	36.7	37.8	38.6	40.0	41.9	43.7
Debt/net disposable income	125.3	126.1	127.0	126.7	128.5	130.4	128.7
Debt/net worth	16.9	17.2	17.5	16.9	17.2	17.4	17.5
Equity/net worth	5.5	5.0	3.7	6.5	5.7	5.2	5.9
Real estate/net worth	47.6	46.9	46.4	43.9	42.9	41.6	40.1
Total debt/GDP	75.5	75.7	76.9	77.1	76.4	76.8	76.0
Banking sector							
Credit quality							
Nonperforming loans[4]/total loans	3.9	5.5	6.2	5.9	6.3	8.4	7.4
Capital ratio							
Stockholders' equity/assets	3.3	2.7	4.2	4.5	4.5	4.0	3.4
Profitability measures							
Return on equity (ROE)	−0.7	−27.6	−18.0	−0.6	−1.2	−16.3	−19.3

Sources: Ministry of Finance, *Financial Statements of Corporations by Industries*; Cabinet Office, Economic and Social Research Institute, *Annual Report on National Accounts*; Bank of Japan, *Financial Statements of Japanese Banks*; and Financial Services Agency, *The Status of Nonperforming Loans*.
[1]Data are fiscal year beginning April 1.
[2]Interest payments as a percent of operating profits.
[3]Interest payments as a percent of income.
[4]From FY1998 onwards, nonperforming loans are based on Financial Services Agency figures reported under the Financial Reconstruction Law. Up to FY1997, they are based on loans reported by banks for risk management purposes.

Table 9. Europe: Sectoral Balance Sheets
(In percent)

	1996	1997	1998	1999	2000	2001	2002
Corporate sector[1]							
Debt/equity[2]	84.4	84.0	82.3	84.8	84.4	84.9	84.1
Short-term debt/total debt	36.5	38.1	37.3	37.7	40.0	39.0	37.6
Interest burden[3]	17.9	17.2	16.8	17.1	19.0	20.0	19.4
Debt/operating profits	262.5	263.3	258.8	288.2	315.9	326.6	337.6
Memorandum items:							
Financial assets/equity	1.6	1.7	1.8	2.1	2.0	1.9	1.6
Liquid assets/short-term debt	100.4	94.5	92.9	89.6	85.6	89.9	94.5
Household sector[1]							
Net worth/assets	85.8	86.2	86.1	86.4	86.0	85.0	83.4
Equity/net worth	12.8	14.2	15.3	17.9	17.1	16.8	14.6
Equity/net financial assets	35.9	37.8	39.8	44.0	43.3	43.1	37.7
Interest burden[4]	6.4	6.3	6.7	6.4	6.5	6.3	6.1
Memorandum items:							
Nonfinancial assets/net worth	64.3	61.2	60.6	58.5	59.8	60.7	61.7
Debt/net financial assets	49.7	45.4	44.0	41.5	43.0	45.3	51.2
Debt/income	87.2	88.6	90.9	93.8	94.8	95.0	98.8
Banking sector[5]							
Credit quality							
Nonperforming loans/total loans	...	5.0	6.1	5.6	3.1	2.6	3.1
Loan-loss reserve/nonperforming loans	...	74.3	65.9	66.3	70.9	75.7	79.3
Loan-loss reserve/total loans	...	3.7	4.0	3.7	2.2	2.0	2.5
Loan-loss provisions/total operating income[6]	...	13.2	11.7	9.1	6.7	9.4	12.3
Capital ratios							
Total risk-based capital	...	10.7	10.6	10.5	11.0	11.2	11.4
Tier 1 risk-based capital	...	7.2	7.0	7.2	7.7	7.7	8.1
Equity capital/total assets	...	3.7	3.9	3.8	4.1	4.0	4.0
Capital funds/liabilities	...	6.1	6.3	6.2	6.7	6.6	6.6
Profitability measures							
Return on assets, or ROA (after tax)	...	0.3	0.4	0.5	0.7	0.4	0.3
Return on equity, or ROE (after tax)	...	7.6	9.8	12.5	14.0	8.7	6.0
Net interest margin	...	1.9	1.7	1.4	1.5	1.4	1.6
Efficiency ratio[7]	...	69.4	68.3	68.5	69.0	70.6	71.3

Sources: ©2003 Bureau van Dijk Electronic Publishing-Bankscope; ECB *Monthly Bulletin*; and IMF staff estimates.
[1]GDP-weighted average for France, Germany, and the United Kingdom, unless otherwise noted.
[2]Corporate equity adjusted for changes in asset valuation.
[3]Interest payments as a percent of gross operating profits.
[4]Interest payments as percent of disposable income.
[5]Fifty largest euro area banks. Data availability may restrict coverage to less than 50 banks for specific indicators.
[6]Includes the write-off of goodwill in foreign subsidiaries by banks with exposure to Argentina.
[7]Cost to income ratio.

Figure 15. Emerging and Mature Market Volatilities

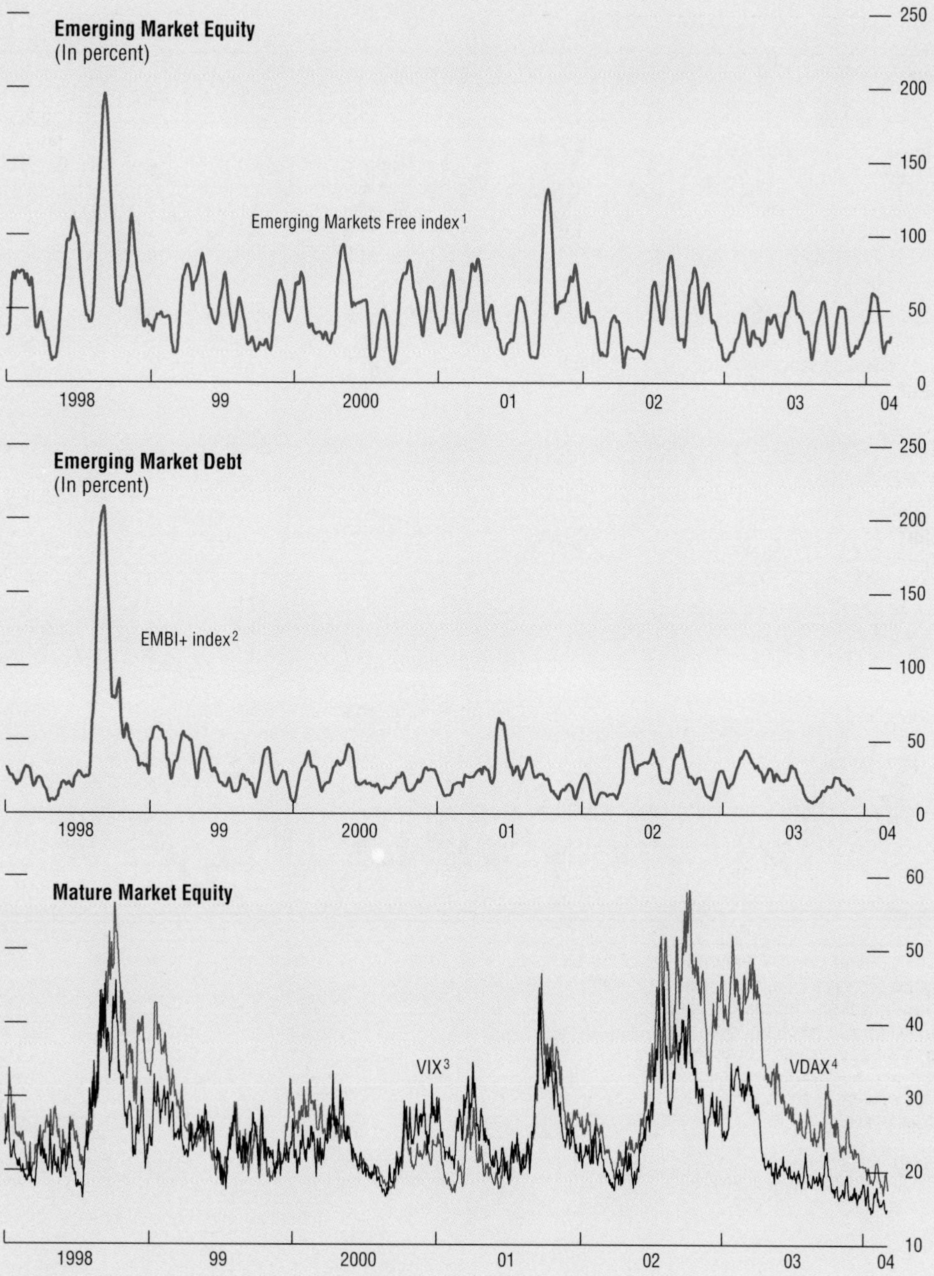
Emerging Market Equity
(In percent)
Emerging Markets Free index[1]
250
200
150
100
50
0
1998
99
2000
01
02
03
04
Emerging Market Debt
(In percent)
EMBI+ index[2]
250
200
150
100
50
0
1998
99
2000
01
02
03
04
Mature Market Equity
VIX[3]
VDAX[4]
60
50
40
30
20
10
1998
99
2000
01
02
03
04

Sources: For "Emerging Market Equity," Morgan Stanley Capital International; and IMF staff estimates. For "Emerging Market Debt," J.P. Morgan Chase & Co.; and IMF staff estimates. For "Mature Market Equity," Bloomberg L.P.

[1]Data utilize the Emerging Markets Free index in U.S. dollars to calculate 30-day rolling volatilities.

[2]Data utilize the EMBI+ total return index in U.S. dollars to calculate 30-day rolling volatilities.

[3]The VIX is a market estimate of future stock market volatility, and is based on the weighted average of the implied volatilities of 8 Chicago Board Options Exchange calls and puts (the nearest in- and out-of-the-money call and put options from the first and second month expirations).

[4]The VDAX represents the implied volatility of the German DAX assuming a constant 45 days remaining until expiration of DAX index contracts.

Figure 16. Emerging Market Debt Cross-Correlations

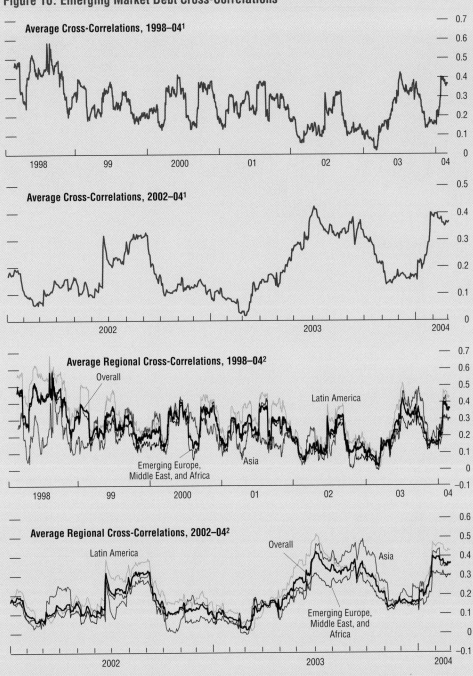

Sources: J.P. Morgan Chase & Co.; and IMF staff estimates.
[1]Thirty-day moving simple average across all pair-wise return correlations of 20 constituents included in the EMBI Global.
[2]Simple average of all pair-wise correlations of all markets in a given region with all other emerging bond markets, regardless of region.

Table 10. Emerging Market Equity Indices

| | Year to Date (as of 3/2/04) | 2003 End of Period | | | | 2000 | 2001 | 2002 | 2003 | 12-Month High | 12-Month Low | All-Time High[1] | All-Time Low[1] |
		Q1	Q2	Q3	Q4								
World	**1,074.8**	**748.6**	**871.1**	**909.6**	**1,036.3**	**1,221.3**	**1,003.5**	**792.2**	**1,036.3**	**1,078.1**	**710.8**	**1,448.8**	**423.1**
Emerging Markets													
Emerging Markets Free	**488.4**	**272.3**	**332.7**	**377.6**	**442.8**	**333.8**	**317.4**	**292.1**	**442.8**	**477.2**	**269.7**	**587.1**	**175.3**
EMF Latin America	**1,187.0**	**652.9**	**800.2**	**899.7**	**1,100.9**	**915.6**	**876.2**	**658.9**	**1,100.9**	**1,189.4**	**605.6**	**1,352.5**	**185.6**
Argentina	1,063.8	559.9	700.1	733.0	933.6	1,232.7	959.6	470.3	933.6	1,090.5	469.0	2,052.2	152.6
Brazil	816.7	410.1	503.1	593.2	802.0	763.2	597.1	395.4	802.0	875.9	352.7	1,306.4	84.1
Chile	862.3	446.0	560.4	694.7	800.6	604.7	568.7	445.5	800.6	842.2	425.0	1,119.6	178.1
Colombia	138.2	65.9	84.1	85.5	108.6	42.1	57.7	68.3	108.6	135.3	62.4	183.8	41.2
Mexico	2,187.7	1,350.9	1,637.3	1,708.0	1,873.1	1,464.9	1,698.2	1,442.8	1,873.1	2,165.7	1,302.2	2,193.1	306.7
Peru	315.2	187.1	207.8	246.1	344.1	125.0	144.1	182.7	344.1	364.2	181.4	364.2	73.5
Venezuela	119.9	67.4	125.2	145.3	103.8	106.1	95.4	77.7	103.8	175.7	56.1	278.4	56.1
EMF Asia	**228.7**	**127.2**	**154.4**	**177.5**	**206.4**	**143.6**	**149.7**	**140.4**	**206.4**	**223.0**	**126.1**	**433.0**	**104.1**
China	26.9	13.9	16.3	18.9	25.5	22.8	16.8	14.1	25.5	27.1	13.1	136.9	12.9
India	240.6	132.4	151.9	188.1	246.2	173.4	141.2	148.8	246.2	258.3	124.7	323.9	77.7
Indonesia	942.3	474.9	633.5	728.7	831.1	456.4	437.2	519.6	831.1	966.3	442.0	1,077.7	280.0
Korea	279.0	158.0	196.7	207.7	246.0	125.6	190.4	184.7	246.0	274.0	153.8	274.0	59.5
Malaysia	343.6	240.6	262.8	276.8	300.4	245.2	250.7	244.0	300.4	316.6	234.5	465.7	88.3
Pakistan	195.9	140.7	158.9	180.4	188.2	99.1	67.4	146.0	188.2	204.2	124.1	228.9	54.4
Philippines	309.6	210.6	257.0	272.6	303.7	352.6	292.2	210.1	303.7	332.2	202.2	917.3	132.6
Taiwan Province of China	299.5	184.1	210.9	250.0	259.1	222.2	255.6	189.5	259.1	279.5	177.6	483.5	103.9
Thailand	255.4	138.1	170.7	199.6	280.5	102.5	107.5	130.2	280.5	286.5	128.0	669.4	72.0
EMF Europe, Middle East, & Africa	**181.8**	**102.6**	**126.9**	**141.6**	**163.9**	**. . .**	**103.5**	**108.4**	**163.9**	**176.5**	**102.2**	**176.5**	**85.2**
Czech Republic	180.7	123.1	126.7	142.4	152.9	107.6	97.5	116.2	152.9	176.4	115.8	176.4	62.8
Egypt	269.3	114.4	158.5	195.6	234.6	154.9	101.9	97.4	234.6	293.5	97.4	293.5	89.9
Hungary	745.6	524.3	538.3	617.4	646.9	582.9	507.9	535.5	646.9	707.1	497.5	941.4	77.1
Israel	161.8	97.2	135.8	129.5	141.4	196.0	132.7	90.8	141.4	161.8	83.7	236.2	67.6
Jordan	259.6	157.6	182.3	213.8	238.3	116.1	149.5	153.5	238.3	264.0	149.1	264.0	103.1
Morocco	187.6	142.5	163.7	166.3	171.4	198.9	180.1	138.5	171.4	183.7	136.0	302.1	99.6
Poland	1,265.9	797.4	914.0	1,049.8	1,118.3	1,307.9	891.9	861.0	1,118.3	1,241.3	778.8	1,792.9	99.6
Russia	546.5	264.6	388.6	436.1	461.1	155.2	237.8	270.7	461.1	508.4	250.1	538.4	30.6
South Africa	319.3	227.6	244.3	258.5	296.8	244.8	309.3	272.7	296.8	319.7	216.1	350.5	99.7
Turkey	328,587	154,022	179,225	225,249	319,808	163,012	234,490	169,900	319,808	342,720	144,094	342,720	426
EMF Sectors													
Energy	313.8	161.7	205.8	233.5	287.4	148.5	162.1	163.1	287.4	306.7	155.4	306.7	81.7
Materials	268.4	163.5	178.1	206.1	250.1	140.8	173.9	182.8	250.1	262.6	155.0	262.6	98.5
Industrials	110.2	60.9	71.3	81.4	98.9	73.4	63.8	61.8	98.9	105.0	59.3	276.8	52.6
Consumer discretionary	248.3	130.8	166.8	188.0	233.8	126.0	130.6	138.8	233.8	243.2	126.9	243.2	74.1
Consumer staple	128.3	82.8	101.1	105.7	118.6	103.1	94.6	88.2	118.6	126.1	80.6	148.6	80.4
Healthcare	295.5	183.8	243.9	252.9	272.5	173.9	146.5	169.8	272.5	296.5	160.9	296.5	83.3
Financials	152.6	89.5	106.8	117.9	138.8	112.6	107.7	98.6	138.8	149.4	88.0	185.0	74.6
Information technology	176.7	93.5	117.2	140.7	149.6	130.9	134.2	103.9	149.6	173.5	93.4	300.0	73.1
Telecommunications	112.0	64.6	80.0	86.2	100.8	113.8	91.9	72.7	100.8	112.2	62.9	211.5	62.9
Utilities	128.9	72.7	92.8	107.8	127.2	95.7	91.5	72.4	127.2	131.3	69.9	247.8	63.1

Table 10 (continued)

	Year to Date (as of 3/2/04)	Period on Period Percent Change								12-Month High	12-Month Low	All-Time High[1]	All-Time Low[1]
		2003 End of Period				2000	2001	2002	2003				
		Q1	Q2	Q3	Q4								
World	**3.7**	**−5.5**	**16.4**	**4.4**	**13.9**	**−14.1**	**−17.8**	**−21.1**	**30.8**	...	...	...	...
Emerging Markets											...		...
Emerging Markets Free	**10.3**	**−6.8**	**22.2**	**13.5**	**17.3**	**−31.8**	**−4.9**	**−8.0**	**51.6**	...	...	...	...
EMF Latin America	**7.8**	**−0.9**	**22.6**	**12.4**	**22.4**	**−18.4**	**−4.3**	**−24.8**	**67.1**	...	...	...	...
Argentina	13.9	19.1	25.0	4.7	27.4	−26.1	−22.2	−51.0	98.5	...	...	...	...
Brazil	1.8	3.7	22.7	17.9	35.2	−14.2	−21.8	−33.8	102.9	...	...	...	...
Chile	7.7	0.1	25.7	24.0	15.2	−17.0	−6.0	−21.7	79.7	...	...	...	...
Colombia	27.3	−3.5	27.6	1.7	27.0	−41.2	37.1	18.3	59.0	...	...	...	...
Mexico	16.8	−6.4	21.2	4.3	9.7	−21.5	15.9	−15.0	29.8	...	...	...	...
Peru	−8.4	2.4	11.1	18.4	39.8	−26.7	15.3	26.8	88.4	...	...	...	...
Venezuela	15.5	−13.3	85.8	16.1	−28.5	0.8	−10.0	−18.6	33.6	...	...	...	...
EMF Asia	**10.8**	**−9.3**	**21.4**	**14.9**	**16.3**	**−42.5**	**4.2**	**−6.2**	**47.1**	...	...	...	...
China	5.6	−1.5	17.1	16.1	34.7	−32.0	−26.0	−16.0	80.3	...	...	...	...
India	−2.3	−11.0	14.7	23.8	30.9	−17.2	−18.6	5.3	65.5	...	...	...	...
Indonesia	13.4	−8.6	33.4	15.0	14.1	−49.3	−4.2	18.9	60.0	...	...	...	...
Korea	13.4	−14.4	24.5	5.6	18.4	−44.6	51.6	−3.0	33.2	...	...	...	...
Malaysia	14.4	−1.4	9.2	5.3	8.6	−17.3	2.3	−2.7	23.1	...	...	...	...
Pakistan	4.1	−3.6	12.9	13.6	4.3	−4.3	−32.0	116.7	28.9	...	...	...	...
Philippines	1.9	0.2	22.0	6.1	11.4	−32.1	−17.1	−28.1	44.5	...	...	...	...
Taiwan Province of China	15.6	−2.9	14.6	18.6	3.6	−42.3	15.0	−25.8	36.7	...	...	...	...
Thailand	−9.0	6.0	23.6	17.0	40.5	−50.0	4.9	21.1	115.4	...	...	...	...
EMF Europe, Middle East, & Africa	**10.9**	**−5.3**	**23.7**	**11.6**	**15.8**	...	...	**4.7**	**51.2**	...	...	...	...
Czech Republic	18.2	6.0	2.9	12.4	7.4	5.5	−9.4	19.2	31.6	...	...	...	...
Egypt	14.8	17.5	38.6	23.4	19.9	−38.4	−34.2	−4.4	140.8	...	...	...	...
Hungary	15.3	−2.1	2.7	14.7	4.8	−19.6	−12.9	5.4	20.8	...	...	...	...
Israel	14.4	7.0	39.7	−4.7	9.2	24.7	−32.3	−31.6	55.7	...	...	...	...
Jordan	8.9	2.7	15.6	17.3	11.4	−24.7	28.8	2.6	55.3	...	...	...	...
Morocco	9.4	2.9	14.9	1.5	3.1	−20.2	−9.5	−23.1	23.8	...	...	...	...
Poland	13.2	−7.4	14.6	14.9	6.5	−4.8	−31.8	−3.5	29.9	...	...	...	...
Russia	18.5	−2.3	46.9	12.2	5.7	−30.4	53.2	13.9	70.3	...	...	...	...
South Africa	7.6	−16.6	7.4	5.8	14.8	−1.2	26.3	−11.8	8.8	...	...	...	...
Turkey	2.7	−9.3	16.4	25.7	42.0	−33.5	43.8	−27.5	88.2	...	...	...	...
EMF Sectors													
Energy	9.2	−0.9	27.2	13.5	23.1	−24.7	9.2	0.6	76.2	...	...	...	...
Materials	7.3	−10.6	8.9	15.8	21.3	−21.0	23.5	5.2	36.8	...	...	...	...
Industrials	11.4	−1.5	17.2	14.1	21.5	−41.7	−13.1	−3.2	60.1	...	...	...	...
Consumer discretionary	6.2	−5.8	27.5	12.7	24.3	−41.6	3.6	6.3	68.4	...	...	...	...
Consumer staple	8.2	−6.1	22.1	4.5	12.2	−20.2	−8.2	−6.7	34.4	...	...	...	...
Healthcare	8.4	8.3	32.7	3.7	7.8	0.7	−15.8	15.9	60.5	...	...	...	...
Financials	9.9	−9.3	19.4	10.4	17.7	−24.3	−4.3	−8.4	40.7	...	...	...	...
Information technology	18.1	−10.0	25.3	20.1	6.3	−44.9	2.6	−22.6	43.9	...	...	...	...
Telecommunications	11.1	−11.1	23.8	7.7	17.0	−31.1	−19.2	−20.9	38.7	...	...	...	...
Utilities	1.3	0.5	27.6	16.2	17.9	−25.0	−4.4	−20.9	75.7	...	...	...	...

Table 10 *(concluded)*

	Year to Date (as of 3/2/04)	2003 End of Period				2000	2001	2002	2003	12-Month High	12-Month Low	All-Time High[1]	All-Time Low[1]
		Q1	Q2	Q3	Q4								
Developed Markets													
Australia	672.6	580.4	601.6	627.1	655.5	640.1	690.8	604.4	655.5	639.6	539.9	712.9	250.2
Austria	135.7	92.8	101.6	104.6	118.0	96.9	94.6	91.8	118.0	105.4	79.7	105.4	96.2
Belgium	66.7	44.0	52.3	55.0	60.1	85.8	78.6	55.3	60.1	65.0	38.1	53.9	51.2
Canada	1,092.4	796.3	868.0	922.4	1,019.7	1,156.4	965.8	818.3	1,019.7	886.4	705.8	1,511.4	338.3
Denmark	2,018.2	1,370.1	1,554.7	1,695.1	1,772.7	2,333.3	2,060.1	1,448.8	1,772.7	1,752.8	1,245.8	2,776.6	556.5
Finland	121.6	84.0	94.4	92.2	97.4	267.5	171.8	100.3	97.4	126.0	78.8	383.1	78.8
France	99.3	69.2	81.2	82.4	93.2	152.0	123.1	81.3	93.2	95.3	63.4	178.6	63.4
Germany	77.3	46.9	60.4	61.5	74.6	124.0	100.1	56.0	74.6	78.4	42.9	163.6	41.4
Greece	68.5	38.2	50.7	54.9	63.6	106.1	76.8	46.8	63.6	61.9	38.2	197.2	38.2
Hong Kong SAR	7,120.1	4,501.2	4,838.9	6,011.5	6,341.3	7,690.1	6,058.0	4,808.4	6,341.3	5,553.6	4,305.4	10,165.3	1,995.5
Ireland	71.1	56.8	60.7	62.0	65.9	92.1	93.1	56.8	65.9	67.1	51.9	107.3	51.9
Italy	82.7	62.6	72.2	71.3	78.1	119.9	91.2	69.6	78.1	78.4	58.7	132.1	58.7
Japan	680.7	480.4	542.9	613.4	637.3	808.2	650.3	524.3	637.3	628.7	462.1	1,655.3	462.1
Netherlands	71.6	53.4	60.3	61.9	68.4	124.5	100.4	66.0	68.4	80.9	47.4	134.9	47.4
New Zealand	108.0	88.8	101.4	102.8	107.6	83.9	94.2	90.0	107.6	101.4	86.6	141.0	56.7
Norway	1,491.7	804.4	994.1	1,041.2	1,240.9	1,458.0	1,278.4	898.3	1,240.9	1,116.3	762.2	1,599.1	455.9
Portugal	76.1	51.3	55.9	59.6	66.1	97.9	79.5	57.0	66.1	64.6	48.1	123.1	48.1
Singapore	1,069.3	725.6	831.9	932.0	1,005.1	1,173.4	936.8	764.9	1,005.1	922.1	687.3	1,624.2	508.2
Spain	96.2	67.8	79.3	77.2	89.6	107.7	99.0	69.9	89.6	81.9	61.1	133.7	27.4
Sweden	5,396.4	3,271.7	3,827.3	4,136.5	4,675.2	7,735.0	6,178.8	3,517.4	4,675.2	4,173.8	2,914.9	12,250.4	787.2
Switzerland	768.1	534.3	626.6	656.3	714.3	1,017.0	813.4	603.2	714.3	716.9	481.4	1,032.8	158.1
United Kingdom	1,366.0	1,082.4	1,215.4	1,236.1	1,348.7	1,841.4	1,586.2	1,179.2	1,348.7	1,336.7	986.4	1,974.2	585.4
United States	1,077.9	796.1	916.1	935.6	1,045.4	1,249.9	1,084.5	824.6	1,045.4	950.4	726.5	1,493.0	273.7
			Period on Period Percent Change										
Developed Markets													
Australia	2.6	−4.0	3.7	4.2	4.5	3.7	7.9	−12.5	8.5	...	...	...	...
Austria	15.0	1.1	9.5	2.9	12.8	−7.6	−2.4	−3.0	28.5	...	...	...	...
Belgium	11.0	−20.4	18.9	5.3	9.2	−13.1	−8.3	−29.7	8.7	...	...	...	...
Canada	7.1	−2.7	9.0	6.3	10.6	8.1	−16.5	−15.3	24.6	...	...	...	...
Denmark	13.9	−5.4	13.5	9.0	4.6	9.9	−11.7	−29.7	22.4	...	...	...	...
Finland	24.9	−16.2	12.4	−2.2	5.6	−8.9	−35.8	−41.6	−2.9	...	...	...	...
France	6.6	−14.9	17.3	1.5	13.1	1.4	−19.0	−34.0	14.6	...	...	...	...
Germany	3.7	−16.2	28.7	2.0	21.2	−10.8	−19.3	−44.0	33.2	...	...	...	...
Greece	7.8	−18.4	32.8	8.3	15.7	−38.6	−27.6	−39.1	35.8	...	...	...	...
Hong Kong SAR	12.3	−6.4	7.5	24.2	5.5	−16.7	−21.2	−20.6	31.9	...	...	...	...
Ireland	7.8	−0.1	7.0	2.1	6.3	−8.5	1.1	−39.0	16.0	...	...	...	...
Italy	5.9	−10.0	15.3	−1.2	9.4	3.9	−24.0	−23.6	12.2	...	...	...	...
Japan	6.8	−8.4	13.0	13.0	3.9	−20.3	−19.5	−19.4	21.6	...	...	...	...
Netherlands	4.6	−19.1	12.9	2.6	10.6	1.0	−19.4	−34.3	3.6	...	...	...	...
New Zealand	0.4	−1.4	14.2	1.4	4.7	−24.9	12.2	−4.4	19.6	...	...	...	...
Norway	20.2	−10.5	23.6	4.7	19.2	7.1	−12.3	−29.7	38.1	...	...	...	...
Portugal	15.3	−10.1	9.1	6.6	10.8	−6.2	−18.8	−28.3	15.9	...	...	...	...
Singapore	6.4	−5.1	14.6	12.0	7.8	−25.7	−20.2	−18.4	31.4	...	...	...	...
Spain	7.4	−2.9	16.8	−2.5	16.1	−11.2	−8.0	−29.5	28.3	...	...	...	...
Sweden	15.4	−7.0	17.0	8.1	13.0	−13.8	−20.1	−43.1	32.9	...	...	...	...
Switzerland	7.5	−11.4	17.3	4.7	8.8	6.2	−20.0	−25.8	18.4	...	...	...	...
United Kingdom	1.3	−8.2	12.3	1.7	9.1	−6.7	−13.9	−25.7	14.4	...	...	...	...
United States	3.1	−3.5	15.1	2.1	11.7	−13.6	−13.2	−24.0	26.8	...	...	...	...

Data are provided by Morgan Stanley Capital International. Regional and sectoral compositions conform to Morgan Stanley Capital International Definitions.
[1]From 1990 or initiation of the index.

Table 11. Foreign Exchange Rates

(Units per U.S. dollar)

	Year to Date (as of 3/2/04)	End of Period 2003				End of Period				12-Month Low	12-Month High	All-Time Low[1]	All-Time High[1]
		Q1	Q2	Q3	Q4	2000	2001	2002	2003				
Emerging Markets													
Latin America													
Argentina	2.92	2.97	2.81	2.92	2.93	1.00	1.00	3.36	2.93	3.36	2.75	3.86	0.98
Brazil	2.89	3.35	2.84	2.90	2.89	1.95	2.31	3.54	2.89	3.67	2.78	3.95	0.00
Chile	596.60	733.25	700.90	660.95	592.75	573.85	661.25	720.25	592.75	757.05	558.00	759.75	295.18
Colombia	2,662.15	2,958.00	2,817.00	2,900.80	2,780.00	2,236.00	2,277.50	2,867.00	2,780.00	2,980.00	2,724.00	2,980.00	689.21
Mexico	10.96	10.77	10.46	10.99	11.23	9.62	9.16	10.37	11.23	11.38	10.12	11.38	2.68
Peru	3.47	3.47	3.47	3.48	3.46	3.53	3.44	3.51	3.46	3.51	3.45	3.65	1.28
Venezuela	1,917.60	1,598.00	1,598.00	1,598.00	1,598.00	699.51	757.50	1,388.80	1,598.00	1,921.80	1,388.80	1,921.80	45.00
Asia													
China	8.28	8.28	8.28	8.28	8.28	8.28	8.28	8.28	8.28	8.28	8.28	8.92	5.96
India	45.25	47.47	46.49	45.76	45.63	46.68	48.25	47.98	45.63	48.01	45.19	49.05	16.89
Indonesia	8,498	8,902	8,275	8,395	8,420	9,675	10,400	8,950	8,420	9,088	8,175	16,650	1,977
Korea	1,173.50	1,254.45	1,193.05	1,150.10	1,192.100	1,265.00	1,313.50	1,185.70	1,192.10	1,257.95	1,145.75	1,962.50	681.40
Malaysia	3.80	3.80	3.80	3.80	3.80	3.80	3.80	3.80	3.80	3.80	3.80	4.71	2.44
Pakistan	57.31	58.00	57.85	57.90	57.25	57.60	59.90	58.25	57.25	58.25	57.00	64.35	21.18
Philippines	56.37	53.53	53.48	54.88	55.54	50.00	51.60	53.60	55.54	56.27	52.06	56.27	23.10
Taiwan Province of China	33.29	34.75	34.64	33.74	33.96	33.08	34.95	34.64	33.96	34.95	33.07	35.19	24.48
Thailand	39.30	42.84	42.00	40.03	39.62	43.38	44.21	43.11	39.62	43.22	38.84	55.50	23.15
Europe, Middle East, & Africa													
Czech Republic	26.90	29.37	27.51	27.36	25.71	37.28	35.60	30.07	25.71	30.22	25.37	42.17	25.37
Egypt	6.19	5.76	6.08	6.14	6.17	3.89	4.58	4.62	6.17	6.19	4.59	6.19	3.29
Hungary	209.96	227.19	231.27	218.30	208.70	282.34	274.81	224.48	208.70	238.20	204.35	317.56	90.20
Israel	4.50	4.70	4.32	4.44	4.39	4.04	4.40	4.74	4.39	4.93	4.29	5.01	1.96
Jordan	0.71	0.71	0.71	0.71	0.71	0.71	0.71	0.71	0.71	0.72	0.70	0.72	0.64
Morocco	8.99	9.85	9.45	9.33	8.80	10.56	11.59	10.18	8.80	10.28	8.64	12.06	7.75
Poland	3.97	4.10	3.90	3.95	3.73	4.13	3.96	3.83	3.73	4.10	3.64	4.71	1.72
Russia	28.54	31.39	30.37	30.59	29.24	28.16	30.51	31.96	29.24	31.96	28.44	31.96	0.98
South Africa	6.91	7.87	7.47	6.93	6.68	7.58	11.96	8.57	6.68	9.05	6.20	12.45	2.50
Turkey	1,330,500	1,714,000	1,418,500	1,391,500	1,406,500	668,500	1,450,100	1,655,100	1,406,500	1,769,000	1,309,300	1,769,000	5,036
Developed Markets													
Australia[2]	0.76	0.60	0.67	0.68	0.75	0.56	0.51	0.56	0.75	0.59	0.80	0.48	0.84
Canada	1.34	1.47	1.35	1.35	1.30	1.50	1.59	1.57	1.30	1.57	1.27	1.61	1.12
Denmark	6.10	6.80	6.45	6.37	5.91	7.92	8.35	7.08	5.91	7.17	5.81	9.00	5.34
Euro[2]	1.22	1.09	1.15	1.17	1.26	0.94	0.89	1.05	1.26	1.03	1.28	0.83	1.28
Hong Kong SAR	7.79	7.80	7.80	7.74	7.76	7.80	7.80	7.80	7.76	7.80	7.71	7.82	7.70
Japan	110.10	118.09	119.80	111.49	107.22	114.41	131.66	118.79	107.22	121.69	105.37	159.90	80.63
New Zealand[2]	0.68	0.56	0.59	0.60	0.66	0.44	0.42	0.52	0.66	0.54	0.71	0.39	0.72
Norway	7.13	7.27	7.20	7.04	6.67	8.80	8.96	6.94	6.67	7.68	6.62	9.58	5.51
Singapore	1.71	1.76	1.76	1.73	1.70	1.73	1.85	1.73	1.70	1.78	1.67	1.91	1.39
Sweden	7.58	8.45	7.99	7.75	7.19	9.42	10.48	8.69	7.19	8.81	7.11	11.03	5.09
Switzerland	1.30	1.35	1.35	1.32	1.24	1.61	1.66	1.38	1.24	1.42	1.22	1.82	1.12
United Kingdom[2]	1.84	1.58	1.65	1.66	1.79	1.49	1.45	1.61	1.79	1.55	1.90	1.37	2.01

Table 11 *(concluded)*

	Year to Date (as of 3/2/04)	Period on Period Percent Change								12-Month Low	12-Month High	All-Time Low[1]	All-Time High[1]
		End of Period 2003				End of Period							
		Q1	Q2	Q3	Q4	2000	2001	2002	2003				
Emerging Markets													
Latin America													
Argentina	0.5	13.0	5.7	−3.5	−0.5	0.2	−0.2	−70.2	14.7	...	...	...	...
Brazil	0.2	5.6	17.9	−1.9	0.3	−7.7	−15.6	−34.7	22.4	...	...	...	...
Chile	−0.6	−1.8	4.6	6.0	11.5	−7.8	−13.2	−8.2	21.5	...	...	...	...
Colombia	4.4	−3.1	5.0	−2.9	4.3	−16.3	−1.8	−20.6	3.1	...	...	...	...
Mexico	2.4	−3.7	3.0	−4.8	−2.2	−1.2	5.1	−11.7	−7.6	...	...	...	...
Peru	−0.4	1.2	0.2	−0.4	0.6	−0.5	2.4	−2.0	1.5	...	...	...	...
Venezuela	−16.7	−13.1	0.0	0.0	0.0	−7.3	−7.7	−45.5	−13.1	...	...	...	...
Asia													
China	0.0	0.0	0.0	0.0	0.0	0.0	0.0	0.0	0.0	...	...	...	...
India	0.8	1.1	2.1	1.6	0.3	−6.7	−3.3	0.6	5.2	...	...	...	...
Indonesia	−0.9	0.5	7.6	−1.4	−0.3	−26.6	−7.0	16.2	6.3	...	...	...	...
Korea	1.6	−5.5	5.1	3.7	−3.5	−9.9	−3.7	10.8	−0.5	...	...	...	...
Malaysia	0.0	0.0	0.0	0.0	0.0	0.0	0.0	0.0	0.0	...	...	...	...
Pakistan	−0.1	0.4	0.3	−0.1	1.1	−10.1	−3.8	2.8	1.7	...	...	...	...
Philippines	−1.5	0.1	0.1	−2.5	−1.2	−19.5	−3.1	−3.7	−3.5	...	...	...	...
Taiwan Province of China	2.0	−0.3	0.3	2.7	−0.7	−5.1	−5.3	0.9	2.0	...	...	...	...
Thailand	0.8	0.6	2.0	4.9	1.0	−13.6	−1.9	2.6	8.8	...	...	...	...
Europe, Middle East, & Africa													
Czech Republic	−4.4	2.4	6.8	0.5	6.4	−3.9	4.7	18.4	16.9	...	...	...	...
Egypt	−0.4	−19.8	−5.1	−1.1	−0.4	−11.5	−15.1	−0.9	−25.1	...	...	...	...
Hungary	−0.6	−1.2	−1.8	5.9	4.6	−10.6	2.7	22.4	7.6	...	...	...	...
Israel	−2.3	1.0	8.7	−2.7	1.1	2.7	−8.1	−7.3	8.0	...	...	...	...
Jordan	0.1	0.0	0.1	0.0	0.0	−0.3	0.2	−0.1	0.1	...	...	...	...
Morocco	−2.2	3.3	4.2	1.3	6.1	−4.6	−8.9	13.9	15.7	...	...	...	...
Poland	−6.0	−6.6	5.0	−1.1	5.8	0.4	4.2	3.5	2.6	...	...	...	...
Russia	2.5	1.8	3.4	−0.7	4.6	−2.2	−7.7	−4.5	9.3	...	...	...	...
South Africa	−3.3	9.0	5.3	7.8	3.7	−18.8	−36.6	39.6	28.2	...	...	...	...
Turkey	5.7	−3.4	20.8	1.9	−1.1	−18.6	−53.9	−12.4	17.7	...	...	...	...
Developed Markets													
Australia	1.6	7.6	11.4	1.0	10.6	−14.9	−8.8	10.2	33.9	...	...	...	...
Canada	−3.4	7.1	8.9	−0.4	4.2	−3.5	−5.9	1.3	21.2	...	...	...	...
Denmark	−3.1	4.1	5.4	1.3	7.7	−6.7	−5.1	17.9	19.8	...	...	...	...
Euro	−3.0	4.0	5.5	1.3	8.1	−6.3	−5.6	18.0	20.0	...	...	...	...
Hong Kong SAR	−0.3	0.0	0.0	0.7	−0.3	−0.3	0.0	0.0	0.4	...	...	...	...
Japan	−2.6	0.6	−1.4	7.5	4.0	−10.4	−13.1	10.8	10.8	...	...	...	...
New Zealand	3.8	5.8	5.9	1.3	10.2	−14.9	−6.1	25.9	25.0	...	...	...	...
Norway	−6.6	−4.6	1.0	2.3	5.7	−8.9	−1.8	29.2	4.1	...	...	...	...
Singapore	−0.5	−1.7	0.2	1.9	1.7	−4.0	−6.0	6.4	2.1	...	...	...	...
Sweden	−5.1	2.8	5.8	3.0	7.9	−9.5	−10.2	20.6	20.9	...	...	...	...
Switzerland	−4.4	2.4	0.0	2.4	6.5	−1.3	−3.0	20.0	11.7	...	...	...	...
United Kingdom	3.0	−1.7	4.5	0.4	7.5	−7.7	−2.6	10.7	10.9	...	...	...	...
United States	0.0	0.0	0.0	0.0	0.0	0.0	0.0	0.0	0.0	...	...	...	...

Source: Bloomberg L.P.

[1]From 1990 or initiation of the index.

[2]U.S. dollar per unit.

Table 12. Emerging Market Bond Index: EMBI+ Total Returns Index

	Year to Date (as of 3/2/04)	End of Period 2003				End of Period				12-Month High	12-Month Low	All-Time High	All-Time Low
		Q1	Q2	Q3	Q4	2000	2001	2002	2003				
Composite	**297**	**246**	**273**	**280**	**295**	**202**	**200**	**229**	**295**	**304**	**229**	**304**	**62**
Latin America													
Argentina	70	60	79	70	68	184	61	58	68	82	56	196	48
Brazil	377	277	322	342	388	222	238	230	388	405	230	405	67
Colombia	217	184	205	204	211	119	156	176	211	220	171	220	97
Ecuador	495	302	353	373	464	177	241	230	464	510	229	510	61
Mexico	291	261	277	279	281	190	217	252	281	288	249	288	59
Panama	460	415	437	439	451	300	354	395	451	470	395	470	56
Peru	432	378	385	420	432	244	307	340	432	449	338	449	52
Venezuela	362	260	312	339	382	221	233	276	382	392	248	392	59
Asia													
Malaysia	128	119	126	127	126	...	...	116	126	129	115	129	100
Philippines	163	145	162	164	164	98	125	143	164	168	142	168	78
Europe, Middle East, & Africa													
Bulgaria	550	511	526	527	545	356	447	494	545	551	493	551	76
Egypt	141	123	133	135	138	...	...	117	138	142	117	142	99
Morocco	264	244	254	257	263	200	223	239	263	265	239	265	73
Nigeria	417	325	369	389	396	209	256	281	396	413	281	413	61
Poland	330	313	335	325	323	246	272	308	323	344	306	344	60
Russia	346	303	335	332	337	130	203	276	337	349	276	349	24
South Africa	127	119	122	123	123	...	...	113	123	126	113	126	100
Turkey	204	137	160	179	201	105	127	154	201	207	128	207	93
Ukraine	176	165	170	173	178	...	126	152	178	180	152	180	106
Latin	253	204	229	236	253	202	174	187	253	262	185	262	62
Non-Latin	422	362	397	402	414	203	274	344	414	425	344	425	63
Period on Period Percent Change													
EMBI+	**0.8**	**7.6**	**11.0**	**2.4**	**5.3**	**15.7**	**−0.8**	**14.2**	**28.8**	...	...	...	...
Latin America													
Argentina	3.3	4.8	30.4	−11.3	−2.7	7.7	−66.8	−5.6	18.0	...	...	...	...
Brazil	−2.9	20.5	16.4	6.2	13.5	12.9	7.2	−3.3	69.0	...	...	...	...
Colombia	3.2	4.4	11.8	−0.8	3.4	2.2	30.8	12.8	19.7	...	...	...	...
Ecuador	6.8	31.2	16.9	5.9	24.1	53.9	36.1	−4.7	101.5	...	...	...	...
Mexico	3.5	3.7	6.1	0.6	0.7	17.9	14.2	16.4	11.4	...	...	...	...
Panama	1.9	4.9	5.4	0.4	2.8	8.3	17.9	11.7	14.2	...	...	...	...
Peru	0.1	11.0	2.0	9.1	2.7	0.2	26.2	10.7	26.9	...	...	...	...
Venezuela	−5.3	−6.1	20.3	8.4	12.8	15.0	5.5	18.7	38.2	...	...	...	...
Asia													
Malaysia	1.3	2.3	6.1	0.3	−0.1	...	...	...	8.7	...	...	...	...
Philippines	−0.8	0.9	11.6	1.3	0.1	−4.4	27.6	14.4	14.2	...	...	...	...
Europe, Middle East, & Africa													
Bulgaria	1.1	3.4	3.0	0.0	3.4	5.1	25.7	10.5	10.2	...	...	...	...
Egypt	2.1	5.5	8.0	1.8	1.9	...	...	...	18.2	...	...	...	...
Morocco	0.3	2.2	4.0	1.4	2.2	5.5	11.1	7.2	10.2	...	...	...	...
Nigeria	5.1	15.5	13.7	5.3	1.9	15.6	22.4	9.9	40.9	...	...	...	...
Poland	2.3	1.6	6.8	−2.9	−0.7	15.9	10.6	13.3	4.6	...	...	...	...
Russia	2.6	10.1	10.4	−1.0	1.7	54.9	55.8	35.9	22.4	...	...	...	...
South Africa	2.7	4.8	3.1	0.9	0.0	...	...	...	9.0	...	...	...	...
Turkey	1.5	−10.6	16.6	11.8	12	−1.7	21.7	20.7	30.4	...	...	...	...
Ukraine	−0.8	8.1	2.9	2.2	2.6	...	...	21.0	16.6	...	...	...	...
Latin	0.2	9.4	12.0	3.2	7.0	12.6	−13.7	7.2	35.4	...	...	...	...
Non-Latin	1.8	5.1	9.7	1.4	2.9	27.0	35.4	25.6	20.3	...	...	...	...

Source: J.P. Morgan Chase & Co.

Table 13. Emerging Market Bond Index: EMBI+ Yield Spreads

	Year to Date (as of 3/2/04)	End of Period 2003				End of Period				12-Month High	12-Month Low	All-Time High	All-Time Low
		Q1	Q2	Q3	Q4	2000	2001	2002	2003				
EMBI+	**441**	**671**	**547**	**506**	**418**	**756**	**731**	**765**	**418**	**765**	**384**	**1,697**	**384**
Latin America													
Argentina	5,795	6,165	4,554	5,484	5,632	773	4,372	6,391	5,632	7,084	4,364	7,220	383
Brazil	563	1,048	801	698	463	749	863	1,446	463	1,446	410	2,436	410
Colombia	415	602	451	478	431	755	514	645	431	722	357	1,094	357
Ecuador	746	1,372	1,178	1,121	799	1,415	1,233	1,801	799	1,801	683	4,764	630
Mexico	183	291	237	212	199	392	308	331	199	337	180	1,160	180
Panama	354	399	372	368	335	501	409	444	335	448	299	769	280
Peru	351	478	491	355	312	687	521	610	312	618	257	1,061	257
Venezuela	761	1,412	1,002	828	593	958	1,130	1,127	593	1,478	540	2,703	405
Asia													
Malaysia	84	151	98	77	71	. . .	. . .	171	71	171	67	203	67
Philippines	483	543	443	414	415	644	466	530	415	570	378	1,026	0
Europe, Middle East, & Africa													
Bulgaria	181	253	229	235	177	772	433	291	177	291	160	1,679	160
Egypt	139	307	223	178	138	. . .	. . .	358	138	358	114	561	114
Morocco	169	372	244	224	160	584	518	390	160	399	128	1,519	128
Nigeria	703	1,419	1,107	806	732	2,037	1,426	2,276	732	2,276	637	3,932	633
Poland	76	187	68	73	69	241	195	185	69	187	17	414	17
Russia	256	365	284	285	257	1,172	669	478	257	478	211	6,890	211
South Africa	128	175	180	149	141	. . .	. . .	238	141	238	115	320	115
Turkey	328	976	751	541	309	800	707	693	309	1,103	286	1,194	286
Ukraine	323	404	370	303	258	. . .	940	671	258	674	139	1,618	139
Excluding Argentina	364	577	469	418	334	752	620	670	334	670	303	921	303
				Period on Period Basis Point Change									
EMBI+	**23**	**−94**	**−124**	**−41**	**−88**	**−68**	**−25**	**34**	**−347**	. . .	. . .	. . .	. . .
Latin America													
Argentina	163	−226	−1,611	930	148	240	3,599	2,019	−759	. . .	. . .	. . .	. . .
Brazil	100	−398	−247	−103	−235	113	114	583	−983	. . .	. . .	. . .	. . .
Colombia	−16	−43	−151	27	−47	332	−241	131	−214	. . .	. . .	. . .	. . .
Ecuador	−53	−429	−194	−57	−322	−1,938	−182	568	−1,002	. . .	. . .	. . .	. . .
Mexico	−16	−40	−54	−25	−13	29	−84	23	−132	. . .	. . .	. . .	. . .
Panama	19	−45	−27	−4	−33	91	−92	35	−109	. . .	. . .	. . .	. . .
Peru	39	−132	13	−136	−43	244	−166	89	−298	. . .	. . .	. . .	. . .
Venezuela	168	285	−410	−174	−235	114	172	−3	−534	. . .	. . .	. . .	. . .
Asia													
Malaysia	13	−20	−53	−21	−6	. . .	. . .	. . .	−100	. . .	. . .	. . .	. . .
Philippines	68	13	−100	−29	1	320	−178	64	−115	. . .	. . .	. . .	. . .
Europe, Middle East, & Africa													
Bulgaria	4	−38	−24	6	−58	146	−339	−142	−114	. . .	. . .	. . .	. . .
Egypt	1	−51	−84	−45	−40	. . .	. . .	. . .	−220	. . .	. . .	. . .	. . .
Morocco	9	−18	−128	−20	−64	204	−66	−128	−230	. . .	. . .	. . .	. . .
Nigeria	−29	−857	−312	−301	−74	699	−611	850	−1,544	. . .	. . .	. . .	. . .
Poland	7	2	−119	5	−4	29	−46	−10	−116	. . .	. . .	. . .	. . .
Russia	−1	−113	−81	1	−28	−1,260	−503	−191	−221	. . .	. . .	. . .	. . .
South Africa	−13	−63	5	−31	−8	. . .	. . .	. . .	−97	. . .	. . .	. . .	. . .
Turkey	19	283	−225	−210	−232	380	−93	−14	−384	. . .	. . .	. . .	. . .
Ukraine	65	−267	−34	−67	−45	. . .	. . .	−269	−413	. . .	. . .	. . .	. . .
Excluding Argentina	30	−93	−108	−51	−84	. . .	−132	50	−336	. . .	. . .	. . .	. . .

Source: J.P. Morgan Chase & Co.

Table 14. Total Emerging Market Financing
(In millions of U.S. dollars)

	Year to Date (as of 3/2/04)	1999	2000	2001	2002	2003	2003 Q1	Q2	Q3	Q4
Total	**41,259.2**	**163,569.6**	**216,402.7**	**162,137.7**	**135,543.9**	**191,522.7**	**35,012.8**	**45,823.1**	**52,921.0**	**62,134.9**
Africa	**920.8**	**4,707.2**	**9,382.8**	**6,992.3**	**7,169.5**	**13,522.0**	**2,411.3**	**4,605.3**	**5,387.8**	**1,117.7**
Algeria	...	...	...	50.0	150.0	75.0	75.0	...	...	...
Angola	...	...	...	455.0	350.0	1,542.0	...	317.0	1,225.0	...
Botswana	...	...	...	22.5	...	...	...	...	...	...
Cameroon	...	...	...	53.8	...	100.0	...	100.0	...	...
Chad	...	...	...	400.0	...	...	...	...	...	...
Côte d'Ivoire	...	179.0	...	15.0	...	...	...	...	...	...
Ghana	...	30.0	320.0	300.0	420.0	650.0	...	...	650.0	...
Kenya	...	...	7.5	80.2	...	134.0	134.0	...	...	...
Mali	...	...	...	...	150.4	287.6	...	...	...	287.6
Mauritius	...	160.0	...	...	...	...	...	...	...	...
Morocco	...	322.2	56.4	136.1	...	474.7	...	474.7	...	...
Mozambique	...	...	...	200.0	...	35.5	35.5	...	...	...
Namibia	...	...	...	...	...	35.0	...	...	...	35.0
Niger	...	...	...	...	...	27.0	...	27.0	...	...
Nigeria	...	90.0	...	100.0	1,000.0	762.0	460.0	...	169.0	133.0
Senegal	...	...	...	...	40.0	...	...	...	...	...
Seychelles	...	...	50.0	...	150.0	...	...	...	...	...
South Africa	920.8	3,423.4	8,698.8	4,646.7	4,159.1	8,884.0	1,349.9	3,674.4	3,336.6	523.2
Tanzania	...	...	135.0	...	...	...	...	...	...	...
Tunisia	...	352.6	94.3	533.0	750.0	485.2	357.0	12.2	7.2	108.9
Zaire	...	...	20.8	...	...	...	...	...	...	...
Zambia	...	...	...	...	...	30.0	...	...	...	30.0
Zimbabwe	...	150.0	...	...	...	...	...	...	...	...
Asia	**17,523.3**	**55,958.6**	**85,881.0**	**67,483.4**	**53,900.3**	**81,796.9**	**12,937.0**	**15,639.9**	**22,914.1**	**30,641.9**
Brunei	...	...	...	...	129.0	...	...	...	...	...
China	4,782.3	3,461.8	23,063.4	5,567.3	5,051.0	10,954.9	1,269.5	1,203.7	1,761.6	7,343.3
Hong Kong SAR	429.1	11,488.3	21,046.4	18,307.3	7,014.7	7,766.3	538.5	402.5	1,849.0	4,276.3
India	1,534.5	2,376.2	2,224.2	2,382.2	1,559.6	4,017.9	382.5	650.0	1,162.2	1,823.1
Indonesia	215.0	1,465.3	1,283.1	964.9	756.0	5,109.9	2,927.5	686.7	823.7	672.1
Korea	3,362.3	13,542.3	14,230.4	17,021.0	14,546.3	17,237.0	2,384.9	6,385.3	4,774.3	3,692.6
Lao P.D.R.	...	...	...	...	30.0	...	...	...	...	...
Macao	...	...	29.5	...	...	...	...	...	...	...
Malaysia	370.0	5,177.2	4,506.4	4,432.4	5,108.9	5,621.9	1,825.9	742.7	635.9	2,524.7
Marshall Islands	...	...	...	...	34.7	...	...	...	...	...
Papua New Guinea	...	232.4	...	...	...	153.7	...	...	...	153.7
Pakistan	500.0	...	...	182.5	85.0	9.3	...	9.3	...	...
Philippines	1,370.0	7,181.7	5,021.9	3,658.8	5,797.3	5,263.5	1,699.6	247.7	1,280.0	2,036.2
Singapore	1,131.3	4,338.7	6,079.7	10,383.6	3,083.2	5,133.2	445.7	2,599.9	754.0	1,358.4
Sri Lanka	...	23.0	100.0	105.0	...	186.0	...	...	100.0	86.0
Taiwan Province of China	3,630.2	4,019.9	6,703.5	3,794.0	9,308.9	17,557.1	1,409.4	2,204.2	8,423.7	5,800.6
Thailand	198.6	2,551.7	1,572.5	684.4	1,003.1	2,735.2	53.6	462.9	1,343.7	875.0
Vietnam	...	100.0	20.0	...	392.5	51.0	...	45.0	6.0	...
Europe	**10,556.5**	**26,191.5**	**37,021.7**	**22,787.7**	**30,330.6**	**45,471.8**	**10,770.0**	**11,056.6**	**13,238.0**	**14,036.6**
Azerbaijan	...	77.2	...	16.0	...	...	...	...	...	...
Belarus	...	...	...	...	...	36.0	...	...	36.0	...
Bulgaria	...	53.9	8.9	242.3	1,260.8	381.3	...	...	6.2	375.1
Croatia	372.7	1,504.9	1,498.7	1,766.0	1,399.1	2,026.0	768.1	583.8	178.1	496.0
Cyprus	...	288.5	86.3	633.0	547.9	648.2	...	...	226.0	422.2
Czech Republic	...	540.3	127.1	564.6	463.4	1,518.8	187.7	1,284.5	2,240.4	1,331.1
Estonia	...	289.2	412.7	202.1	439.7	507.7	411.1	35.0	...	61.5

Table 14 *(concluded)*

	Year to Date (as of 3/2/04)	1999	2000	2001	2002	2003	2003 Q1	Q2	Q3	Q4
Europe *(continued)*										
Georgia	...	...	...	...	...	6.0	...	...	...	6.0
Gibraltar	...	65.0	80.0	...	...	...	...	...	...	...
Hungary	1,589.1	3,471.2	1,308.8	1,364.7	1,056.1	3,774.8	1,081.3	886.6	1,438.2	368.6
Kazakstan	...	417.0	429.6	573.5	773.5	1,535.0	30.0	50.0	730.0	725.0
Kyrgyz Republic	...	...	...	...	95.0	...	...	...	...	...
Latvia	...	288.9	23.0	212.1	74.6	70.7	...	...	70.7	...
Lithuania	754.2	959.7	683.8	247.3	374.3	431.7	431.7	...	...	...
Macedonia	10.0	...	...	...	...	47.6	...	...	...	47.6
Malta	...	57.0	...	85.0	...	114.7	...	...	114.7	...
Moldova	...	40.0	...	...	...	...	...	...	...	...
Poland	2,616.8	3,780.7	5,252.9	4,836.6	6,001.8	8,550.5	2,170.5	1,606.1	1,556.5	3,217.4
Romania	...	176.0	594.4	1,347.2	1,742.2	1,803.2	227.0	1,076.4	77.2	448.0
Russia	1,398.0	166.8	3,950.7	3,200.1	8,684.8	11,856.2	3,590.9	1,380.3	3,045.3	3,914.5
Slovak Republic	...	994.7	1,466.7	219.9	143.1	940.6	79.3	574.4	...	286.9
Slovenia	76.0	687.7	672.7	827.2	309.3	394.8	...	321.5	61.5	11.8
Turkey	3,139.7	11,900.0	20,385.4	6,405.1	6,385.5	9,408.4	1,728.6	2,412.1	3,047.2	2,225.0
Ukraine	600.0	290.7	...	15.0	514.0	1,370.0	60.0	800.0	410.0	100.0
Uzbekistan	...	142.0	40.0	30.0	46.0	38.7	3.7	35.0	...	...
Yugoslavia, FYR of	...	...	...	...	19.4	10.9	...	10.9	...	...
Middle East	**2,695.0**	**15,387.4**	**14,999.7**	**11,020.3**	**10,830.4**	**8,368.1**	**1,139.0**	**2,403.9**	**2,324.5**	**2,500.7**
Bahrain	...	361.1	1,391.0	207.0	665.0	1,800.0	500.0	1,300.0	...	...
Egypt	200.0	1,533.7	919.4	2,545.0	670.0	155.0	...	...	...	155.0
Iran, I.R. of	...	692.0	757.7	887.0	2,671.4	700.0	...	750.0	...	700.0
Israel	500.0	3,719.0	2,908.5	1,602.6	344.4	750.0	...	...	...	...
Jordan	...	...	60.0	...	80.9	...	...	...	...	...
Lebanon	...	1,421.4	1,752.4	3,300.0	990.0	160.0	...	...	160.0	...
Kuwait	...	147.5	250.0	770.0	750.0	365.0	...	...	...	365.0
Libya	...	...	50.0	...	...	...	...	...	...	...
Oman	75.0	356.8	685.0	...	2,417.0	907.8	...	...	...	907.8
Qatar	665.0	2,000.0	1,980.0	913.0	1,571.7	880.8	71.0	53.9	658.0	97.9
Saudi Arabia	230.0	4,374.8	2,200.9	275.0	300.0	569.5	400.0	...	169.5	...
United Arab Emirates	1,025.0	781.0	2,045.0	520.7	370.0	2,080.0	168.0	300.0	1,337.0	275.0
Latin America	**9,563.6**	**61,324.9**	**69,117.6**	**53,854.0**	**33,313.0**	**42,363.9**	**7,755.5**	**12,117.5**	**9,056.6**	**13,838.0**
Argentina	...	17,844.4	16,648.5	3,423.9	824.2	160.0	...	60.0	...	100.0
Bolivia	...	...	...	...	20.0	90.0	...	...	...	...
Brazil	2,905.0	12,951.9	23,238.2	19,532.9	11,032.3	11,596.2	298.0	4,298.4	3,744.8	3,660.0
Chile	600.0	8,031.7	5,782.5	3,935.3	3,011.5	4,699.0	1,150.0	730.0	1,350.0	1,469.0
Colombia	500.0	3,555.8	3,093.2	4,895.0	2,221.0	1,911.3	500.0	250.0	515.0	646.3
Costa Rica	310.0	300.0	250.0	400.0	250.0	490.0	450.0	...	...	40.0
Dominican Republic	...	...	74.0	531.1	333.0	670.4	600.0	24.4	...	46.0
Ecuador	...	73.0	...	910.0	10.0	...	...	...	...	...
El Salvador	...	316.5	160.0	488.5	1,251.5	381.0	348.5	...	...	32.5
Guadeloupe	...	...	...	...	17.4	...	...	...	...	...
Guatemala	...	222.0	505.0	325.0	44.0	300.0	...	...	300.0	...
Jamaica	247.9	...	421.0	726.5	345.0	49.6	...	48.3	1.3	...
Mexico	3,900.7	14,099.5	15,313.4	13,823.5	10,172.0	16,995.5	3,611.0	6,706.5	800.5	5,874.2
Paraguay	...	55.0	...	70.0	...	...	...	...	...	...
Peru	...	1,618.4	465.4	137.5	1,993.0	1,375.0	750.0	...	125.0	500.0
St. Lucia	...	...	...	...	...	20.0	...	...	20.0	...
Trinidad & Tobago	100.0	230.0	301.0	70.0	303.0	46.0	46.0	...	...	...
Uruguay	...	465.0	602.1	1,147.4	400.0	...	...	...	...	...
Venezuela	1,000.0	1,561.7	2,263.3	3,417.5	1,015.0	3,670.0	2.0	...	2,200.0	1,470.0

Source: Data provided by the Bond, Equity and Loan database of the International Monetary Fund sourced from Capital Data.

Table 15. Emerging Market Bond Issuance
(In millions of U.S. dollars)

	Year to Date (as of 3/2/04)	1999	2000	2001	2002	2003	2003 Q1	2003 Q2	2003 Q3	2003 Q4
Total	29,263.2	82,359.4	80,475.4	89,036.9	61,647.4	93,519.2	20,108.1	27,981.2	26,307.1	23,217.5
Africa	377.6	2,345.5	1,485.8	2,109.6	2,161.1	6,558.6	483.0	3,063.9	3,011.6	...
Mauritius	...	160.0	...	...	...	...	...	...	...	...
Morocco	...	151.5	...	...	...	464.9	...	464.9	...	...
South Africa	377.6	1,804.7	1,485.8	1,647.7	1,511.1	5,736.7	126.1	2,599.0	3,011.6	...
Tunisia	...	229.3	...	462.0	650.0	357.0	357.0	...	...	...
Asia	8,491.7	23,424.7	24,501.4	35,869.2	22,532.7	32,709.3	4,225.8	8,560.2	9,834.9	10,253.5
China	...	1,060.0	1,770.7	2,341.9	602.8	2,034.2	...	50.0	318.8	1,665.4
Hong Kong SAR	29.9	7,124.8	7,058.9	10,458.6	1,951.6	1,450.6	...	184.5	617.4	648.7
India	820.0	100.0	100.0	99.3	153.0	450.0	...	...	100.0	350.0
Indonesia	...	...	...	125.0	375.0	609.0	...	416.6	192.4	...
Korea	3,217.9	4,905.8	7,653.0	7,756.3	6,705.5	11,531.3	1,790.1	4,346.3	3,305.8	2,089.0
Malaysia	225.0	2,062.4	1,419.7	2,150.0	1,880.0	962.5	...	...	...	962.5
Pakistan	500.0									
Philippines	1,300.0	4,751.2	2,467.3	1,842.4	4,773.8	3,729.6	1,024.6	200.0	1,055.0	1,450.0
Singapore	117.9	2,147.1	2,333.8	8,664.7	562.1	2,702.4	1.7	1,404.2	617.7	678.8
Taiwan Province of China	2,281.0	475.0	1,698.0	2,152.4	5,480.8	8,939.7	1,409.4	1,658.5	3,627.8	2,409.1
Thailand	...	798.4	...	278.6	48.0	300.0	...	300.0	...	...
Europe	8,765.4	13,872.8	14,202.5	11,558.6	14,997.0	21,580.8	8,150.8	7,670.3	5,895.4	3,389.1
Bulgaria	...	53.9	...	223.4	1,247.8	...	...	...	...	...
Croatia	372.7	601.2	858.0	934.0	847.5	983.6	768.1	215.4	...	...
Cyprus	...	288.5	...	480.5	479.8	648.2	...	...	226.0	422.2
Czech Republic	...	421.7	...	50.7	428.4	337.7	187.7	1,284.5	2,240.4	150.0
Estonia	...	84.9	335.7	65.5	292.6	323.3	323.3	...	...	...
Hungary	1,239.5	2,410.5	540.8	1,247.8	70.5	2,211.4	1,081.3	...	1,130.1	...
Kazakstan	...	300.0	350.0	250.0	209.0	100.0	...	...	...	100.0
Latvia	...	236.7	...	180.8	...	...	...	...	...	...
Lithuania	754.2	531.5	376.2	222.4	355.6	431.7	431.7	...	...	...
Poland	2,210.8	1,652.6	1,553.5	2,773.7	2,679.9	4,301.2	1,622.0	1,130.2	549.0	1,000.0
Romania	...	...	259.5	908.6	1,062.2	813.6	...	813.6	...	...
Russia	820.0	...	75.0	1,352.7	3,391.5	4,005.0	2,050.0	475.0	150.0	1,330.0
Slovak Republic	...	800.2	978.3	219.9	143.1	861.3	...	574.4	...	286.9
Slovenia	...	439.1	384.7	490.0	30.2	...	...	...	...	...
Turkey	2,768.2	5,761.2	8,490.8	2,158.7	3,259.8	5,253.8	1,626.6	2,377.2	1,250.0	...
Ukraine	600.0	290.7	...	...	499.0	1,310.0	60.0	800.0	350.0	100.0
Middle East	2,065.0	4,409.8	4,670.6	5,920.7	3,706.6	1,860.0	500.0	1,000.0	160.0	200.0
Bahrain	...	209.1	188.5	...	325.0	750.0	500.0	250.0	...	...
Egypt	...	100.0	...	1,500.0	...	...	...	...	...	...
Iran, I.R. of	...	...	...	...	986.3	...	...	750.0	...	...
Israel	500.0	1,679.2	1,329.7	1,120.7	344.4	750.0	...	...	...	...
Jordan	...	...	...	...	80.9	...	...	...	...	...
Kuwait	...	...	...	...	750.0	200.0	...	...	...	200.0
Lebanon	...	1,421.4	1,752.4	3,300.0	990.0	160.0	...	...	160.0	...
Qatar	665.0	1,000.0	1,400.0	...	...	...	...	...	...	...
United Arab Emirates	900.0	...	...	...	230.0	...	...	...	...	...
Latin America	9,563.6	38,306.7	35,615.2	33,578.8	18,250.0	30,810.5	6,748.5	7,686.7	7,405.3	9,375.0
Argentina	...	14,182.8	13,024.8	1,500.5	...	100.0	...	...	...	100.0
Brazil	2,905.0	8,585.8	11,382.1	12,238.8	6,375.5	10,304.9	100.0	3,904.6	3,190.3	3,515.0
Chile	600.0	1,763.8	679.7	1,536.0	1,728.9	2,900.0	1,000.0	150.0	900.0	850.0
Colombia	500.0	1,675.6	1,547.2	4,263.3	1,000.0	1,765.0	500.0	250.0	515.0	500.0
Costa Rica	310.0	300.0	250.0	250.0	250.0	490.0	450.0	...	...	40.0
Dominican Republic	...	...	...	500.0	...	600.0	600.0	...	...	...
El Salvador	...	150.0	50.0	353.5	1,251.5	348.5	348.5	...	...	...
Grenada	...	...	...	...	100.0	...	...	...	...	...
Guatemala	...	...	...	325.0	...	300.0	...	...	300.0	...
Jamaica	247.9	...	421.0	690.7	300.0	...	...	...	...	...
Mexico	3,900.7	9,854.0	7,078.4	9,231.7	4,914.1	9,082.1	3,000.0	3,382.1	300.0	2,400.0
Peru	...	...	...	...	...	1,930.0	1,250.0	750.0	...	500.0
Trinidad & Tobago	100.0	230.0	250.0	...	...	...	...	...	...	...
Uruguay	...	350.0	442.6	1,106.1	400.0	...	...	...	...	...
Venezuela	1,000.0	1,214.7	489.4	1,583.2	...	3,670.0	...	...	2,200.0	1,470.0

Source: Data provided by the Bond, Equity and Loan database of the International Monetary Fund sourced from Capital Data.

Table 16. Emerging Market Equity Issuance
(In millions of U.S. dollars)

	Year to Date (as of 3/2/04)	1999	2000	2001	2002	2003	2003 Q1	Q2	Q3	Q4
Total	**6,231.8**	**23,187.4**	**41,772.8**	**11,245.9**	**16,359.4**	**28,047.2**	**1,210.3**	**1,994.2**	**7,092.7**	**17,871.3**
Africa	**223.3**	**658.7**	**103.3**	**150.9**	**340.5**	**977.4**	**678.8**	**75.3**	**0.0**	**223.2**
Morocco	. . .	. . .	56.4	6.8	. . .	. . .	. . .	. . .	. . .	. . .
South Africa	223.3	658.7	46.9	144.1	340.5	977.4	678.8	75.3	. . .	223.2
Asia	**5,552.4**	**18,271.8**	**31,567.7**	**9,591.5**	**12,411.4**	**24,431.1**	**517.1**	**1,711.6**	**6,906.0**	**15,417.7**
China	3,697.3	1,477.4	20,239.7	2,810.4	2,546.0	6,850.3	509.5	337.1	339.8	5,677.9
Hong Kong SAR	364.2	3,370.0	3,088.6	297.1	2,857.7	2,962.2	. . .	86.0	493.6	2,382.6
India	263.5	874.4	916.7	467.2	264.8	1,243.5	. . .	. . .	330.4	913.1
Indonesia	. . .	522.2	28.2	347.2	281.0	1,008.4	. . .	270.1	131.3	607.1
Korea	94.4	6,590.6	784.8	3,676.4	1,553.7	1,222.6	. . .	268.9	465.1	488.5
Macao	. . .	. . .	29.5			. . .	. . .	. . .	. . .	. . .
Malaysia	. . .	. . .	. . .	15.4	891.2	510.8	7.7	. . .	155.9	454.6
Papua New Guinea	. . .	232.4	. . .	. . .	. . .	153.7	. . .	. . .	. . .	153.7
Philippines	. . .	221.7	194.6	. . .	11.3	. . .	. . .	. . .	. . .	. . .
Singapore	493.4	1,725.6	2,202.2	625.8	891.6	1,168.7	. . .	481.7	123.3	563.7
Taiwan Province of China	486.2	2,500.4	3,951.5	1,126.6	3,057.9	8,272.1	. . .	267.7	4,702.8	3,301.5
Thailand	153.4	757.3	132.0	225.3	56.3	1,038.7	. . .	. . .	163.7	875.0
Europe	**456.1**	**1,411.6**	**3,339.8**	**259.4**	**1,612.4**	**1,811.3**	**14.4**	**73.5**	**33.0**	**1,690.4**
Croatia	. . .	. . .	. . .	22.3	. . .	. . .	. . .	. . .	. . .	. . .
Czech Republic	. . .	. . .	. . .	. . .	. . .	824.6	. . .	. . .	. . .	824.6
Estonia	. . .	190.3	. . .	. . .	. . .	. . .	. . .	. . .	. . .	. . .
Hungary	349.7	529.2	19.1	. . .	. . .	13.2	. . .	. . .	. . .	13.2
Latvia	. . .	. . .	. . .	. . .	22.7	. . .	. . .	. . .	. . .	. . .
Lithuania	. . .	. . .	150.5	. . .	. . .	. . .	. . .	. . .	. . .	. . .
Poland	. . .	636.3	358.9	. . .	217.3	604.9	. . .	19.7	33.0	552.1
Russia	. . .	55.8	387.7	237.1	1,301.0	368.7	14.4	53.8	. . .	300.5
Turkey	106.5	. . .	2,423.8	. . .	71.4	. . .	. . .	. . .	. . .	. . .
Middle East	**0.0**	**2,084.0**	**1,618.1**	**86.8**	**0.0**	**0.0**	**0.0**	**0.0**	**0.0**	**0.0**
Egypt	. . .	89.2	319.4	. . .	. . .	. . .	. . .	. . .	. . .	. . .
Israel	. . .	1,994.8	1,298.7	86.8	. . .	. . .	. . .	. . .	. . .	. . .
Latin America	**0.0**	**761.3**	**5,143.9**	**1,157.2**	**1,995.0**	**827.4**	**0.0**	**133.8**	**153.6**	**540.0**
Argentina	. . .	349.6	393.1	34.4	. . .	. . .	. . .	. . .	. . .	. . .
Brazil	. . .	161.4	3,102.5	1,122.9	1,148.5	287.4	. . .	133.8	153.6	. . .
Dominican Republic	. . .	. . .	74.0	. . .	. . .	. . .	. . .	. . .	. . .	. . .
Mexico	. . .	162.0	1,574.3	. . .	846.6	540.0	. . .	. . .	. . .	540.0
Peru	88.4	. . .	. . .	. . .	. . .	. . .	. . .	. . .	. . .	. . .

Source: Data provided by the Bond, Equity and Loan database of the International Monetary Fund sourced from Capital Data.

Table 17. Emerging Market Loan Syndication
(In millions of U.S. dollars)

	Year to Date (as of 3/2/04)	1999	2000	2001	2002	2003	2003 Q1	Q2	Q3	Q4
Total	**5,764.2**	**58,022.8**	**94,154.5**	**61,854.9**	**57,637.1**	**69,956.4**	**13,694.4**	**15,847.7**	**19,521.1**	**21,046.1**
Africa	**320.0**	**1,703.0**	**7,793.7**	**4,731.8**	**4,667.9**	**5,986.1**	**1,249.5**	**1,466.0**	**2,376.2**	**894.4**
Algeria	...	...	...	50.0	150.0	75.0	75.0	...	...	...
Angola	...	...	...	455.0	350.0	1,542.0	...	317.0	1,225.0	...
Botswana	...	...	...	22.5	...	...	...	...	...	...
Cameroon	...	...	...	53.8	...	100.0	...	100.0	...	...
Chad	...	...	...	400.0	...	...	...	...	...	...
Côte d'Ivoire	...	179.0	...	15.0	...	...	...	...	...	...
Ghana	...	30.0	320.0	300.0	420.0	650.0	...	...	650.0	...
Kenya	...	...	7.5	80.2	...	134.0	134.0	...	...	...
Mali	...	...	...	...	150.4	287.6	...	...	...	287.6
Morocco	...	170.6	...	129.3	...	9.8	...	9.8	...	...
Mozambique	...	...	...	200.0	...	35.5	35.5	...	...	...
Namibia	...	...	...	...	...	35.0	...	...	...	35.0
Niger	...	...	...	...	...	27.0	...	27.0	...	...
Nigeria	...	90.0	...	100.0	1,000.0	762.0	460.0	...	169.0	133.0
Senegal	...	...	...	...	40.0	...	...	...	...	...
Seychelles	...	...	50.0	...	150.0	...	...	...	...	...
South Africa	320.0	960.0	7,166.1	2,855.0	2,307.5	2,170.0	545.0	1,000.0	325.0	300.0
Tanzania	...	...	135.0	...	...	...	...	...	...	...
Tunisia	...	123.4	94.3	71.0	100.0	128.2	...	12.2	7.2	108.9
Zaire	...	...	20.8	...	...	...	...	...	...	...
Zambia	...	...	...	...	...	30.0	...	...	...	30.0
Zimbabwe	...	150.0	...	...	...	...	...	...	...	...
Asia	**3,479.2**	**14,262.0**	**29,812.0**	**22,022.7**	**18,956.2**	**24,656.4**	**8,194.0**	**5,368.2**	**6,173.2**	**4,970.7**
Brunei	...	...	...	...	129.0	...	...	...	...	...
China	1,085.0	924.4	1,053.1	415.0	1,902.2	2,070.4	760.0	816.6	1,103.0	...
Hong Kong SAR	35.0	993.5	10,898.9	7,551.6	2,205.5	3,353.5	538.5	132.0	738.0	1,245.0
India	451.0	1,401.8	1,207.6	1,815.7	1,141.8	2,324.4	382.5	650.0	731.8	560.0
Indonesia	215.0	943.1	1,254.9	492.6	100.0	3,492.5	2,927.5	...	500.0	65.0
Korea	50.0	2,046.0	5,792.6	5,588.2	6,287.1	4,483.0	594.7	1,770.0	1,003.3	1,115.0
Lao P.D.R.	...	...	...	...	30.0	...	...	...	...	...
Malaysia	145.0	3,114.8	3,086.7	2,267.0	2,337.7	4,148.6	1,818.2	742.7	480.0	1,107.6
Marshall Islands	...	...	...	...	34.7	...	...	...	...	...
Pakistan	...	...	...	182.5	85.0	9.3	...	9.3	...	...
Philippines	70.0	2,208.9	2,360.0	1,816.4	1,012.3	1,533.8	675.0	47.7	225.0	586.2
Singapore	520.0	466.0	1,543.7	1,093.2	1,629.5	1,262.2	444.0	714.0	13.0	115.9
Sri Lanka	...	23.0	100.0	105.0	...	186.0	...	...	100.0	86.0
Taiwan Province of China	863.0	1,044.5	1,054.0	515.0	770.2	345.3	...	278.0	93.0	90.0
Thailand	45.2	996.0	1,440.5	180.5	898.7	1,396.5	53.6	162.9	1,180.0	...
Vietnam	...	100.0	20.0	...	392.5	51.0	...	45.0	6.0	...
Europe	**1,335.0**	**10,907.1**	**19,479.3**	**10,969.7**	**13,721.2**	**22,079.8**	**2,604.8**	**3,312.8**	**7,309.6**	**8,957.2**
Azerbaijan	...	77.2	...	16.0	...	...	...	...	...	...
Belarus	...	...	...	...	...	36.0	...	...	36.0	...
Bulgaria	...	...	8.9	18.9	13.0	381.3	...	...	6.2	375.1
Croatia	...	903.6	640.7	809.8	551.6	1,042.5	...	368.4	178.1	496.0
Cyprus	...	...	86.3	152.5	68.1	...	...	...	...	...
Czech Republic	...	118.6	127.1	513.9	35.0	356.5	...	...	...	356.5
Estonia	...	14.0	77.0	136.6	147.1	184.3	87.8	35.0	...	61.5
Georgia	...	...	...	...	...	6.0	...	...	...	6.0

Table 17 *(concluded)*

	Year to Date (as of 3/2/04)	1999	2000	2001	2002	2003	2003 Q1	Q2	Q3	Q4
Europe *(continued)*										
Gibraltar	...	65.0	80.0	...	...	...	...	...	...	...
Hungary	...	531.6	748.9	116.9	985.6	1,550.2	...	886.6	308.2	355.4
Kazakstan	...	117.0	79.6	323.5	564.5	1,435.0	30.0	50.0	730.0	625.0
Kyrgyz Republic	...	...	...	...	95.0	...	...	...	...	...
Latvia	...	52.2	23.0	31.3	51.9	70.7	...	...	70.7	...
Lithuania	...	428.2	157.2	24.9	18.8	...	...	...	...	...
Macedonia	10.0	...	...	...	...	47.6	...	...	...	47.6
Malta	...	57.0	...	85.0	...	114.7	...	...	114.7	...
Moldova	...	40.0	...	...	...	...	...	...	...	...
Poland	406.0	1,491.9	3,340.5	2,062.9	3,104.6	3,644.4	548.5	456.1	974.5	1,665.3
Romania	...	176.0	334.9	438.6	680.0	989.6	227.0	262.8	77.2	448.0
Russia	578.0	111.0	3,488.1	1,610.3	3,992.3	7,482.5	1,526.5	851.5	2,895.3	2,284.0
Slovak Republic	...	194.5	488.3	...	...	79.3	79.3	...	...	...
Slovenia	76.0	248.6	288.0	337.2	279.0	394.8	...	321.5	61.5	11.8
Turkey	265.0	6,138.8	9,470.9	4,246.4	3,054.3	4,154.6	102.0	34.9	1,797.2	2,225.0
Ukraine	...	...	...	15.0	15.0	60.0	...	...	60.0	...
Uzbekistan	...	142.0	40.0	30.0	46.0	38.7	3.7	35.0	...	...
Yugoslavia, FYR of	...	...	...	...	19.4	10.9	...	10.9	...	...
Middle East	**630.0**	**8,893.7**	**8,711.0**	**5,012.7**	**7,123.8**	**6,508.1**	**639.0**	**1,403.9**	**2,164.5**	**2,300.7**
Bahrain	...	152.0	1,202.5	207.0	340.0	1,050.0	...	1,050.0	...	...
Egypt	200.0	1,344.5	600.0	1,045.0	670.0	155.0	...	...	...	155.0
Iran, I.R. of	...	692.0	757.7	887.0	1,685.1	700.0	...	...	...	700.0
Israel	...	45.0	280.0	395.0	...	...	...	...	...	...
Jordan	...	...	60.0	...	...	...	...	...	...	...
Kuwait	...	147.5	250.0	770.0	...	165.0	...	...	...	165.0
Libya	...	...	50.0	...	...	...	...	...	...	...
Oman	75.0	356.8	685.0	...	2,417.0	907.8	...	...	...	907.8
Qatar	...	1,000.0	580.0	913.0	1,571.7	880.8	71.0	53.9	658.0	97.9
Saudi Arabia	230.0	4,374.8	2,200.9	275.0	300.0	569.5	400.0	...	169.5	...
United Arab Emirates	125.0	781.0	2,045.0	520.7	140.0	2,080.0	168.0	300.0	1,337.0	275.0
Latin America	...	**22,257.0**	**28,358.5**	**19,118.0**	**13,167.9**	**10,726.0**	**1,007.0**	**4,296.9**	**1,497.7**	**3,923.1**
Argentina	...	3,312.1	3,230.6	1,889.0	824.2	60.0	...	60.0	...	...
Bolivia	...	...	20.0	90.0	...	...	...	...	...	...
Brazil	...	4,204.7	8,753.6	6,171.3	3,508.4	1,003.9	198.0	260.0	400.9	145.0
Chile	...	6,267.9	5,102.8	2,399.3	1,282.6	1,799.0	150.0	580.0	450.0	619.0
Colombia	...	1,880.2	1,546.0	631.7	1,221.0	146.3	...	...	...	146.3
Costa Rica	...	...	...	150.0	...	...	...	...	...	...
Dominican Republic	...	...	...	31.1	333.0	70.4	...	24.4	...	46.0
Ecuador	...	73.0	...	910.0	10.0	...	...	...	...	...
El Salvador	...	166.5	110.0	135.0	...	32.5	...	...	...	32.5
Guadeloupe	...	...	...	...	17.4	...	...	...	...	...
Guatemala	...	222.0	505.0	...	44.0	...	...	...	...	...
Jamaica	...	...	...	35.8	45.0	49.6	...	48.3	1.3	...
Mexico	...	4,083.6	6,660.7	4,591.8	4,411.4	7,373.4	611.0	3,324.3	500.5	2,934.3
Paraguay	...	55.0	...	70.0	...	...	...	...	...	...
Peru	...	1,530.0	465.4	137.5	63.0	125.0	...	...	125.0	...
St. Lucia	...	...	...	...	...	20.0	...	...	20.0	...
Trinidad & Tobago	...	...	51.0	70.0	303.0	46.0	46.0	...	...	...
Uruguay	...	115.0	159.5	41.3	...	...	...	...	...	...
Venezuela	...	347.0	1,773.9	1,834.3	1,015.0	...	2.0	...	...	...

Source: Data provided by the Bond, Equity and Loan database of the International Monetary Fund sourced from Capital Data.

Table 18. Equity Valuation Measures: Dividend-Yield Ratios

	Year to Date (as of 3/2/04)	2003				1999	2000	2001	2002	2003
		Q1	Q2	Q3	Q4					
Argentina	0.99	1.49	1.57	1.23	1.08	3.29	4.62	5.16	3.42	1.08
Brazil	3.55	5.25	5.03	4.36	3.46	2.95	3.18	4.93	5.51	3.46
Chile	1.68	2.64	1.98	1.74	1.76	1.88	2.33	2.31	2.76	1.76
China	1.91	3.52	2.92	2.96	2.19	3.14	0.95	1.95	2.41	2.19
Colombia	3.22	5.78	4.95	4.48	3.92	6.78	11.12	5.63	4.78	3.92
Czech	5.82	2.23	7.63	7.36	6.85	1.36	0.95	2.28	2.36	6.85
Egypt	4.10	6.89	5.19	4.23	4.69	3.92	5.75	6.48	7.53	4.69
Hong Kong SAR	2.65	4.15	3.93	3.20	2.82	2.31	2.58	3.25	3.85	2.82
Hungary	0.85	1.43	1.13	0.99	0.94	1.14	1.46	1.30	1.40	0.94
India	1.57	2.12	2.12	1.88	1.47	1.25	1.59	2.03	1.81	1.47
Indonesia	3.51	4.46	4.13	4.00	3.83	0.91	3.05	3.65	4.17	3.83
Israel	1.00	1.18	0.56	0.80	1.10	1.87	2.26	2.24	1.47	1.10
Jordan	2.23	3.46	3.11	2.65	2.36	4.24	4.54	3.51	3.77	2.36
Korea	1.88	2.75	2.25	2.14	1.82	0.81	2.05	1.54	1.38	1.82
Malaysia	2.15	2.52	2.44	2.49	2.38	1.15	1.70	1.87	2.04	2.38
Mexico	1.63	2.54	2.22	2.02	1.83	1.27	1.63	1.98	2.30	1.83
Morocco	3.86	4.71	4.38	4.32	4.18	2.49	3.59	3.97	4.84	4.18
Pakistan	8.33	11.30	11.07	8.78	8.63	4.00	5.12	16.01	10.95	8.63
Peru	2.01	2.43	2.34	2.31	1.75	2.86	3.38	3.16	2.37	1.75
Philippines	1.46	1.86	1.40	1.33	1.43	1.08	1.44	1.43	1.97	1.43
Poland	1.16	1.92	1.56	1.39	1.28	0.70	0.68	1.87	1.84	1.28
Russia	2.11	2.19	1.76	1.61	2.38	0.14	0.92	1.11	1.87	2.38
Singapore	1.91	2.43	2.50	2.34	2.03	0.86	1.40	1.80	2.27	2.03
South Africa	2.87	4.72	4.30	3.67	3.22	2.09	2.75	3.47	3.83	3.22
Sri Lanka	2.28	3.74	2.12	1.84	2.51	3.22	5.59	4.79	3.35	2.51
Taiwan Province of China	1.68	1.64	1.66	1.91	1.86	0.97	1.71	1.42	1.60	1.86
Thailand	1.89	3.13	2.54	2.57	1.69	0.70	2.13	2.02	2.48	1.69
Turkey	0.89	1.67	1.58	1.26	0.89	0.76	1.91	1.15	1.35	0.89
Venezuela	3.02	5.86	5.00	4.48	3.68	5.80	5.05	3.89	2.38	3.68
Emerging Markets Free	2.11	2.97	2.67	2.52	2.25	1.52	2.09	2.30	2.43	2.25
EMF Asia	1.90	2.58	2.29	2.28	1.96	1.01	1.71	1.73	1.81	1.96
EMF Latin America	2.51	3.67	3.39	3.03	2.61	2.28	2.69	3.37	3.64	2.61
EMF Europe & Middle East	1.62	1.77	1.55	1.53	1.81	1.16	1.84	1.69	1.71	1.81
ACWI Free	1.98	2.47	2.16	2.16	1.99	1.27	1.46	1.72	2.25	1.99

Note: Data are from Morgan Stanley Capital International. The countries above include the 27 constituents of the Emerging Markets Free index as well as Hong Kong SAR and Singapore. Regional breakdowns conform to Morgan Stanley Capital International conventions. All indices reflect investible opportunities for global investors by taking into account restrictions on foreign ownership. The indices attempt to achieve an 85 percent representation of freely floating stocks.

Table 19. Equity Valuation Measures: Price-to-Book Ratios

	Year to Date (as of 3/2/04)	2003 Q1	Q2	Q3	Q4	1998	1999	2000	2001	2002	2003
Argentina	1.96	1.22	1.36	1.38	1.79	1.31	1.47	1.04	0.86	1.20	1.79
Brazil	1.81	1.18	1.19	1.37	1.81	0.52	1.24	1.18	1.11	1.24	1.81
Chile	1.64	1.11	1.29	1.50	1.55	1.16	1.69	1.49	1.39	1.15	1.55
China	2.33	1.24	1.41	1.63	2.16	0.63	0.69	2.75	1.88	1.30	2.16
Colombia	1.66	1.16	1.11	1.11	1.34	0.71	0.71	0.49	0.53	1.18	1.34
Czech	1.25	0.86	0.83	0.95	1.06	0.73	0.80	1.00	0.81	0.84	1.06
Egypt	2.52	1.17	1.61	1.81	2.17	2.13	3.57	2.32	1.39	1.05	2.17
Hong Kong SAR	1.67	1.02	1.10	1.38	1.47	1.31	2.27	1.67	1.38	1.10	1.47
Hungary	2.18	1.76	1.83	1.94	1.97	3.05	3.35	2.33	2.03	1.91	1.97
India	3.61	2.07	2.47	2.88	3.79	2.00	3.55	2.71	2.13	2.15	3.79
Indonesia	2.51	1.38	1.93	2.11	2.26	1.39	2.41	1.03	2.72	2.23	2.26
Israel	3.00	1.83	2.53	2.33	2.46	1.48	2.53	3.04	2.22	1.74	2.46
Jordan	2.10	1.25	1.56	1.82	1.98	1.05	1.03	1.02	1.38	1.26	1.98
Korea	1.69	1.04	1.32	1.35	1.52	0.99	1.42	0.82	1.33	1.21	1.52
Malaysia	2.07	1.62	1.71	1.74	1.85	1.25	1.98	1.59	1.76	1.54	1.85
Mexico	2.36	1.70	1.92	2.04	2.20	1.72	2.31	1.91	1.99	1.77	2.20
Morocco	1.62	1.39	1.44	1.45	1.50	4.27	3.53	2.56	1.79	1.40	1.50
Pakistan	2.35	1.90	1.98	2.23	2.31	1.07	1.48	1.41	0.88	2.04	2.31
Peru	2.48	1.71	1.71	2.07	2.77	1.41	1.92	1.13	1.29	1.84	2.77
Philippines	1.42	0.87	1.18	1.33	1.40	1.48	1.64	1.27	1.11	0.85	1.40
Poland	1.90	1.29	1.49	1.68	1.72	1.47	2.12	2.10	1.33	1.37	1.72
Russia	1.46	1.00	1.25	1.34	1.33	0.67	2.41	0.90	1.27	1.22	1.33
Singapore	1.71	1.23	1.39	1.52	1.62	1.55	2.56	2.05	1.63	1.26	1.62
South Africa	1.97	1.47	1.66	1.70	1.95	1.52	2.75	2.68	1.81	1.72	1.95
Sri Lanka	1.60	1.04	1.83	2.02	1.52	1.15	1.00	0.60	0.83	1.22	1.52
Taiwan Province of China	2.34	1.49	1.77	2.11	2.10	2.21	3.46	1.87	1.98	1.53	2.10
Thailand	2.71	1.78	2.17	2.30	2.94	1.14	2.04	1.51	1.68	1.83	2.94
Turkey	1.95	1.43	1.31	1.49	2.02	2.55	9.21	2.72	3.80	1.76	2.02
Venezuela	1.80	0.59	1.00	1.14	1.41	0.57	0.63	0.67	0.48	0.87	1.41
Emerging Markets Free	2.03	1.33	1.54	1.67	1.90	1.21	2.12	1.64	1.59	1.45	1.90
EMF Asia	2.11	1.30	1.56	1.71	1.95	1.40	2.09	1.53	1.68	1.41	1.95
EMF Latin America	1.98	1.35	1.44	1.59	1.90	0.87	1.57	1.36	1.35	1.44	1.90
EMF Europe & Middle East	1.88	1.28	1.51	1.59	1.67	1.88	3.41	2.15	1.70	1.42	1.67
ACWI Free	2.51	1.97	2.26	2.27	2.46	3.49	4.23	3.46	2.67	2.07	2.46

Note: Data are from Morgan Stanley Capital International. The countries above include the 27 constituents of the Emerging Markets Free index as well as Hong Kong SAR and Singapore. Regional breakdowns conform to Morgan Stanley Capital International conventions. All indices reflect investible opportunities for global investors by taking into account restrictions on foreign ownership. The indices attempt to achieve an 85 percent representation of freely floating stocks.

Table 20. Equity Valuation Measures: Price-Earnings Ratios

	Year to Date (as of 3/2/04)	2003								
		Q1	Q2	Q3	Q4	1999	2000	2001	2002	2003
Argentina	14.99	−3.09	15.26	7.96	13.72	24.82	20.69	19.13	−12.86	13.72
Brazil	10.07	11.45	10.00	9.37	10.34	18.64	12.83	8.49	11.23	10.34
Chile	32.59	31.79	32.83	34.42	30.81	46.40	31.96	18.02	17.16	30.81
China	18.84	11.95	11.76	13.05	17.11	14.97	40.60	14.09	12.14	17.11
Colombia	11.06	8.85	8.79	8.57	8.94	20.30	−103.44	64.91	9.55	8.94
Czech	14.70	11.23	10.18	11.51	12.49	−42.04	16.49	9.21	10.40	12.49
Egypt	12.26	10.03	14.94	9.07	10.90	16.54	9.35	6.28	7.33	10.90
Hong Kong SAR	22.70	13.46	13.47	17.08	20.00	30.81	7.64	20.47	14.91	20.00
Hungary	14.79	10.11	10.15	11.09	13.11	18.50	14.82	19.34	10.06	13.11
India	18.07	12.46	13.25	15.97	18.96	22.84	15.61	13.84	13.56	18.96
Indonesia	11.41	5.64	7.49	8.31	10.37	−48.73	18.68	8.37	7.14	10.37
Israel	34.26	65.79	68.83	52.96	34.05	25.51	23.88	228.84	−46.62	34.05
Jordan	22.69	12.78	13.94	20.18	21.38	13.51	−107.11	15.10	12.39	21.38
Korea	15.66	8.14	8.88	11.46	13.93	23.24	8.12	15.23	11.44	13.93
Malaysia	18.68	14.49	14.78	15.37	16.33	−8.41	20.63	22.62	13.21	16.33
Mexico	16.52	13.73	17.04	14.96	15.70	14.64	13.78	14.23	14.07	15.70
Morocco	24.33	9.53	21.61	21.94	22.46	18.65	9.30	10.77	9.87	22.46
Pakistan	9.23	7.41	7.81	8.44	8.68	17.60	8.39	4.53	8.07	8.68
Peru	23.70	13.84	12.42	14.26	26.45	18.46	15.44	14.08	20.42	26.45
Philippines	19.95	17.49	19.35	20.25	20.18	142.83	−35.06	43.72	18.21	20.18
Poland	25.41	−30.30	36.79	28.67	19.50	22.33	14.30	18.32	−261.14	19.50
Russia	11.13	9.42	14.24	13.96	11.13	−126.43	5.69	5.03	7.33	11.13
Singapore	20.34	18.64	19.40	21.54	21.38	41.18	18.94	16.53	21.07	21.38
South Africa	13.85	8.71	9.44	10.93	12.75	18.73	14.87	11.30	10.50	12.75
Sri Lanka	12.18	8.67	14.77	14.83	12.69	7.59	4.24	8.53	14.35	12.69
Taiwan Province of China	28.80	61.54	37.60	36.01	25.70	38.26	14.06	21.08	73.13	25.70
Thailand	14.06	12.56	14.47	12.49	15.24	−8.94	−14.61	16.67	15.52	15.24
Turkey	9.40	−25.81	9.32	7.98	11.01	38.60	11.77	25.51	101.33	11.01
Venezuela	31.25	8.87	14.40	16.56	24.40	17.68	21.76	18.43	13.43	24.40
Emerging Markets Free	16.02	12.76	12.76	13.84	15.03	27.17	14.85	13.99	13.95	15.03
EMF Asia	18.23	12.42	12.62	14.97	16.72	40.98	15.47	16.73	14.85	16.72
EMF Latin America	13.40	15.87	13.51	12.21	13.18	18.28	14.93	11.67	13.84	13.18
EMF Europe & Middle East	14.99	19.00	17.84	16.28	14.65	37.25	14.05	13.10	16.27	14.65
ACWI Free	21.57	21.42	22.22	21.36	21.94	35.70	25.44	26.76	23.18	21.94

Note: Data are from Morgan Stanley Capital International. The countries above include the 27 constituents of the Emerging Markets Free index as well as Hong Kong SAR and Singapore. Regional breakdowns conform to Morgan Stanley Capital International conventions. All indices reflect investible opportunities for global investors by taking into account restrictions on foreign ownership. The indices attempt to achieve an 85 percent representation of freely floating stocks.

Table 21. United States Mutual Fund Flows
(In millions of U.S. dollars)

	Year to Date (as of 3/2/04)	2003				1999	2000	2001	2002	2003
		Q1	Q2	Q3	Q4					
Asia Pacific (Ex-Japan)	997	6	100	442	963	152	−1,208	−496	−43	1,511
Corporate High Yield	−1,271	7,162	9,051	310	3,739	−510	−6,162	5,938	8,082	20,262
Corporate Investment Grade	2,121	10,636	6,993	−1,722	753	7,136	4,254	21,692	32,688	16,660
Emerging Markets Debt	318	343	285	−176	437	18	−500	−448	450	889
Emerging Markets Equity	2,914	−186	539	1,645	2,676	24	−350	−1,663	−331	4,673
European Equity	365	13	−236	−2	−723	−1,665	621	−1,791	−1,045	−947
Global Equity	2,070	−1,620	−659	−437	720	4,673	12,627	−3,006	−5,152	−1,995
Growth-Aggressive	5,389	−1,895	3,419	4,654	5,287	15,248	46,610	17,883	5,612	11,465
International & Global Debt	1,784	791	1,031	−96	1,499	−1,582	−3,272	−1,602	−823	3,225
International Equity	11,374	450	1,638	4,873	7,689	2,999	13,322	−4,488	4,240	14,651
Japanese Equity	958	28	509	756	571	731	−831	−270	−82	1,863
Latin American Equity Funds	−42	−27	43	62	108	−121	−95	−147	33	186

Note: Data are provided by AMG Data Services and cover net flows of U.S.-based mutual funds. Fund categories are distinguished by a primary investment objective which signifies an investment of 65 percent or more of a fund's assets. Primary sector data are mutually exclusive, but emerging and regional sectors are all subsets of international equity.

Table 22. Bank Regulatory Capital to Risk-Weighted Assets
(In percent)

	1998	1999	2000	2001	2002	2003	Latest
Latin America							
Argentina	20.4	20.8	19.5	17.9	...	...	
Bahamas	20.0	17.5	18.8	18.5	22.9	...	
Bolivia	11.8	12.2	13.4	14.6	16.1	16.5	March
Brazil	15.6	15.5	14.3	15.3	16.5	17.2	June
Chile	12.5	13.5	13.3	12.7	14.0	14.1	November
Colombia	10.3	10.8	12.4	12.4	12.2	13.6	November
Costa Rica	14.9	17.8	16.9	15.3	15.2	...	June
Dominican Republic	...	...	...	...	...	...	
Ecuador	...	...	...	...	...	...	
Honduras	7.5	11.4	12.3	12.7	12.9	...	
Jamaica	...	...	21.9	19.7	15.5	...	
Mexico	14.4	16.2	13.8	14.7	15.5	14.4	March
Paraguay[1]	0.0	17.2	17.2	16.2	17.9	19.8	September
Peru	11.2	12.0	12.9	13.4	12.5	13.4	September
Uruguay[1,2]	25.3	22.2	17.5	17.8	14.2	...	
Venezuela	...	...	...	...	...	...	
Emerging Europe							
Armenia	29.8	27.8	25.0	13.6	30.5	34.3	September
Bulgaria	36.7	41.3	35.6	31.3	25.2	23.0	September
Croatia	12.7	20.6	21.4	18.5	17.6	17.0	September
Czech Republic	12.0	13.6	14.9	15.4	15.4	15.5	September
Estonia	17.0	16.1	13.2	14.4	15.3	14.5	December
Hungary	16.5	14.9	13.5	13.9	13.0	11.6	June
Israel	9.2	9.4	9.2	9.4	9.9	10.4	March
Kyrgyz Republic	30.9	23.9	30.5	52.2	43.4	...	June
Latvia	17.0	16.0	14.0	14.2	13.8	...	March
Lithuania	23.8	17.4	16.3	15.7	14.8	13.2	December
Macedonia	25.9	28.7	36.7	34.3	28.1	...	
Malta	...	14.3	16.0	15.9	16.0	...	
Poland	11.7	13.2	12.9	15.1	13.8	13.6	September
Russia	11.5	18.1	19.0	20.3	19.9	19.2	September
Slovak Republic	6.6	12.7	13.1	19.7	21.3	22.8	June
Slovenia	16.0	14.0	13.5	11.9	11.9	11.4	September
Turkey	...	...	17.3	15.3	25.3	31.8	September
Ukraine	...	19.6	15.5	20.7	18.6	15.3	September
Western Europe							
Austria	13.5	13.1	13.3	13.7	13.3	14.4	August
Belgium	11.3	11.9	11.9	12.9	13.1	13.0	September
Denmark	10.7	11.1	11.3	12.1	12.6	...	
Finland	11.5	11.9	11.6	10.5	11.7	17.0	June
France	...	12.7	11.9	12.1	12.3	...	
Germany	11.4	11.5	11.7	12.0	12.7	12.9	March
Greece	10.2	16.2	13.6	12.5	10.6	10.7	June
Iceland	10.4	10.6	9.7	11.3	12.3	10.6	June
Ireland	11.0	10.4	9.7	11.2	12.5	...	
Italy	11.3	10.6	10.1	10.4	11.2	...	
Luxembourg	12.6	12.9	13.1	13.7	15.0	17.2	June
Netherlands	11.4	11.2	11.3	11.4	11.9	11.7	September
Norway	12.4	12.4	12.1	12.2	12.8	...	
Portugal	11.1	10.8	9.2	9.5	9.8	9.8	June
Spain	12.9	12.6	12.5	13.0	12.2	12.2	June
Sweden	10.4	11.4	9.9	10.0	10.1	10.1	September
Switzerland	11.4	11.4	12.8	11.8	12.6	...	
United Kingdom[3]	13.2	14.0	13.0	13.2	12.2	12.4	June

Table 22 *(concluded)*

	1998	1999	2000	2001	2002	2003	Latest
Asia							
Bangladesh	7.3	7.4	6.7	6.7	7.5	...	
China	...	...	...	...	...	...	
Hong Kong SAR	18.5	18.7	17.8	16.5	15.7	15.6	September
India	11.6	11.2	11.1	11.4	11.9	12.6	March
Indonesia	−13.0	−2.4	−18.2	19.2	19.7	21.4	June
Korea	8.2	10.8	10.5	10.8	10.5	10.4	June
Malaysia	11.8	12.5	12.5	13.0	13.2	13.4	June
Mongolia	...	20.4	27.1	24.6	19.8	...	
Pakistan	10.9	10.9	9.7	8.8	8.8	9.2	June
Philippines	17.7	17.5	16.2	15.8	16.7	16.1	September
Singapore	18.1	20.6	19.6	18.1	16.9	17.8	September
Sri Lanka	10.7	10.6	8.3	7.8	8.1	7.6	December
Thailand	10.9	12.4	12.0	13.9	13.7	13.6	August
Middle East and North Africa							
Algeria	...	...	8.7	11.3	...	...	
Egypt	...	...	...	...	...	...	
Jordan	...	...	19.6	17.5	18.7	...	
Kuwait	...	23.7	22.2	22.0	19.7	...	
Lebanon	18.9	15.0	16.9	18.0	19.4	22.5	June
Morocco	12.6	12.1	12.8	12.6	12.5	...	September
Oman	...	16.5	16.5	15.6	16.9	...	
Saudi Arabia	21.2	21.2	21.0	20.3	18.7	19.0	June
Tunisia	11.7	11.6	13.3	10.6	10.6	...	
Sub-Saharan Africa							
Ghana	11.1	11.5	11.6	14.7	13.4	...	
Kenya	...	...	17.5	17.1	17.4	17.2	July
Mauritius	11.9	13.3	12.3	13.0	13.1	...	
Nigeria	12.7	19.0	17.5	16.1	...	...	
South Africa	11.5	12.6	14.5	11.4	12.6	12.8	September
Tanzania	6.5	3.8	9.6	9.6	8.6	...	
Uganda	11.0	13.6	20.5	23.1	23.7	20.5	December
Zimbabwe	...	...	44.0	44.5	30.6	28.5	September
Other							
Australia	10.3	10.1	9.8	10.5	9.9	10.6	September
Canada	10.7	11.7	11.9	12.3	12.4	12.9	September
Japan[4]	9.6	11.9	12.2	11.7	10.8	...	September
United States[5]	11.6	11.6	11.7	12.4	12.5	12.7	September

Sources: National authorities; OECD; IMF staff estimates.
[1]Private banks.
[2]For 2002 excludes suspended banks and mortgage bank.
[3]Includes mortgage banks.
[4]All internationally active banks.
[5]U.S. banks with assets greater than $1 billion.

Table 23. Bank Capital to Assets
(In percent)

	1998	1999	2000	2001	2002	2003	Latest
Latin America							
Argentina	11.3	10.6	10.1	12.5	13.1	10.6	November
Bahamas	. . .	. . .	. . .	. . .	. . .	. . .	
Bolivia	8.5	9.2	9.8	10.5	11.9	11.5	September
Brazil	10.5	11.6	12.1	13.6	13.5	16.9	October
Chile	7.5	7.7	7.5	7.2	7.2	7.5	June
Colombia	9.6	10.9	10.1	9.4	9.3	11.5	November
Costa Rica	9.8	10.9	10.8	12.9	12.6	13.4	November
Dominican Republic	. . .	. . .	9.4	10.0	10.7	7.6	October
Ecuador	14.5	12.9	12.9	8.8	10.3	10.6	September
Honduras	9.9	10.0	9.8	10.0	9.1	. . .	
Jamaica	21.5	19.6	16.2	15.5	14.2	13.9	November
Mexico	8.3	8.0	9.6	9.4	11.1	11.8	September
Paraguay	14.9	12.6	12.4	12.1	10.9	8.7	December
Peru	8.7	8.9	9.1	9.8	10.1	10.6	November
Uruguay	15.3	14.7	11.7	8.1	−2.2	7.0	October
Venezuela	14.0	13.5	12.4	14.3	16.1	14.2	November
Emerging Europe							
Armenia	11.7	11.8	12.3	13.6	15.0	13.5	November
Bulgaria	14.0	15.3	15.2	13.6	13.3	13.2	September
Croatia	18.3	15.2	11.9	10.4	9.4	9.4	September
Czech Republic	7.9	7.9	8.2	6.7	6.8	6.5	March
Estonia	20.8	19.2	15.2	15.2	13.7	12.9	November
Hungary	9.7	9.7	9.8	9.5	10.0	9.8	December
Israel	6.7	6.8	7.3	7.7	6.5	7.5	November
Kyrgyz Republic	22.1	15.5	20.5	31.5	27.7	. . .	June
Latvia	3.7	2.0	8.5	9.1	8.8	8.6	November
Lithuania	13.9	9.9	9.2	9.4	9.9	9.8	December
Macedonia	. . .	. . .	. . .	. . .	. . .	. . .	
Malta	. . .	5.7	6.5	6.7	6.6	. . .	
Poland	7.0	7.1	7.1	8.0	8.7	8.5	September
Russia	. . .	14.3	12.9	12.5	12.4	. . .	June
Slovak Republic	9.8	8.7	5.9	7.9	9.8	9.6	July
Slovenia	. . .	. . .	10.1	8.8	8.3	7.8	December
Turkey	8.7	5.2	6.1	9.6	9.7	. . .	June
Ukraine	. . .	. . .	17.5	16.6	15.5	14.6	March
Western Europe							
Austria	4.9	5.2	5.2	5.1	5.6	5.8	December
Belgium	4.0	4.1	4.6	4.4	4.7	4.3	December
Denmark	6.3	6.1	6.7	6.2	5.2	. . .	
Finland	5.9	5.6	6.3	10.2	10.1	9.6	December
France	6.4	6.8	6.7	6.7	6.7	6.6	March
Germany	4.0	4.1	4.2	4.3	4.5	4.6	March
Greece	. . .	10.1	8.9	9.2	9.4	7.6	December
Iceland	7.0	6.8	6.4	6.6	6.3	. . .	
Ireland	7.2	7.3	6.5	5.9	5.5	5.2	December
Italy	6.7	7.0	6.9	7.2	7.2	7.0	March
Luxembourg	3.5	3.8	3.9	3.9	3.7	3.8	February
Netherlands	5.0	4.8	5.1	4.8	4.7	4.3	December
Norway	6.0	6.6	6.4	6.0	5.5	5.4	May
Portugal	. . .	6.3	5.8	5.5	5.6	5.8	September
Spain	7.1	6.6	7.5	7.2	7.3	. . .	November
Sweden	5.0	5.5	5.3	5.6	5.2	. . .	
Switzerland	4.3	4.5	4.8	4.5	4.2	. . .	March
United Kingdom[1]	7.0	7.5	6.5	6.6	6.7	. . .	June

Table 23 *(concluded)*

	1998	1999	2000	2001	2002	2003	Latest
Asia							
Bangladesh	5.1	4.4	4.4	4.4	. . .	. . .	
China	. . .	5.2	5.3	5.1	4.6	. . .	
Hong Kong SAR	7.7	8.1	9.0	9.8	10.7	11.5	March
India	6.2	5.9	5.3	5.1	5.6	. . .	March
Indonesia	−12.9	−4.1	5.2	5.4	7.3	8.3	June
Korea	2.8	3.9	3.8	4.1	4.0	4.0	June
Malaysia	8.9	8.9	8.5	8.5	8.7	. . .	November
Mongolia	16.5	17.3	18.4	17.6	15.4	14.7	June
Pakistan	4.1	4.3	4.4	4.3	3.3	. . .	
Philippines	14.8	16.0	15.3	15.4	15.5	15.9	October
Singapore	7.5	7.8	7.1	9.6	8.3	8.5	March
Sri Lanka	5.9	4.3	3.7	3.8	. . .	. . .	
Thailand	4.8	5.5	4.5	5.5	5.8	6.2	August
Middle East and North Africa							
Algeria	. . .	. . .	4.5	5.6	. . .	. . .	
Egypt	5.1	5.4	5.3	4.9	4.7	5.0	September
Jordan	. . .	. . .	7.8	7.8	6.9	. . .	
Kuwait	. . .	12.6	12.4	12.2	11.1	. . .	
Lebanon	6.6	6.6	6.4	6.2	6.4	6.2	October
Morocco	9.8	9.9	9.2	9.3	8.9	8.2	November
Oman	. . .	13.0	13.0	12.6	12.5	. . .	
Saudi Arabia	10.0	9.6	9.7	9.9	10.2	10.8	June
Tunisia	. . .	. . .	. . .	. . .	. . .	. . .	
Sub-Saharan Africa							
Ghana	12.2	11.9	11.8	12.5	12.0	12.0	August
Kenya	10.7	8.9	8.7	8.8	8.0	7.9	November
Mauritius	7.1	8.1	7.8	8.4	9.3	. . .	
Nigeria	9.3	8.2	7.4	8.6	9.5	. . .	March
South Africa	8.2	8.2	8.7	7.8	8.2	7.2	March
Tanzania	6.5	3.8	9.6	9.6	8.6	. . .	
Uganda	. . .	7.0	9.8	10.0	9.5	9.9	December
Zimbabwe	8.0	9.4	9.4	9.3	9.5	9.0	September
Other							
Australia	7.6	7.3	6.9	7.1	6.3	6.1	September
Canada	4.2	4.7	4.7	4.6	4.6	4.7	November
Japan	2.4	4.6	4.8	4.2	3.0	. . .	September
United States[2]	8.2	8.1	8.2	8.9	9.0	8.9	September

Sources: National authorities; EDSS; OECD; IMF staff estimates.
[1]Data for U.K. large commercial banks (exclusive of mortgage banks and other banks).
[2]U.S. banks with assets greater than $1 billion.

Table 24. Bank Nonperforming Loans to Total Loans

(In percent)

	1998	1999	2000	2001	2002	2003	Latest
Latin America							
Argentina[1]	5.3	7.1	8.7	13.2	17.5	22.7	November
Bahamas	6.2	5.1	5.1	4.8	4.4	. . .	
Bolivia	4.6	6.6	11.6	16.2	17.6	16.7	December
Brazil***	10.2	8.7	8.4	5.7	5.3	5.7	June
Chile	1.5	1.7	1.7	1.6	1.8	1.8	September
Colombia	10.7	13.6	11.0	10.0	8.7	7.4	November
Costa Rica	3.8	2.9	3.7	2.5	2.8	. . .	June
Dominican Republic	. . .	. . .	2.6	2.6	4.9	12.0	October
Ecuador	8.1	26.0	31.0	27.8	8.5	9.6	September
Honduras	11.2	11.2	12.5	13.0	12.4	. . .	
Jamaica	. . .	. . .	9.5	6.1	3.7	. . .	
Mexico	11.3	8.9	5.8	5.1	4.6	3.7	September
Paraguay[2]	8.1	9.3	11.8	12.3	14.7	20.6	December
Peru	7.0	8.7	9.8	9.0	7.6	5.8	December
Uruguay[2,3]	. . .	8.7	8.5	9.3	13.9	. . .	
Venezuela	5.5	7.8	6.6	7.1	9.2	9.7	September
Emerging Europe							
Armenia	6.0	8.0	6.2	6.0	4.9	6.7	September
Bulgaria**	16.4	13.9	8.2	7.0	5.5	6.0	September
Croatia***	9.3	10.3	9.5	7.2	5.8	5.2	September
Czech Republic	20.3	22.0	19.9	13.7	10.6	5.3	September
Estonia	1.4	1.7	1.0	1.3	0.8	0.4	December
Hungary	4.9	4.2	3.0	2.2	2.0	1.7	September
Israel	9.9	9.0	6.7	8.1	9.9	10.2	March
Kyrgyz Republic	10.1	30.9	13.4	13.4	13.8	. . .	June
Latvia	6.0	6.0	4.6	2.8	1.9	. . .	March
Lithuania**	12.9	12.5	11.3	8.3	6.5	3.0	December
Macedonia[4]	32.9	41.3	34.8	33.7	15.9	. . .	
Malta	. . .	13.0	14.0	18.0	16.2	. . .	
Poland**	10.5	13.3	15.0	17.9	21.1	21.3	September
Russia	17.3	13.4	7.7	6.3	6.5	6.1	September
Slovak Republic	31.6	23.7	15.3	15.4	11.2	10.5	June
Slovenia	5.4	5.2	6.5	7.0	7.0	6.7	September
Turkey	6.7	9.7	9.2	29.3	17.6	14.2	September
Ukraine[5]	. . .	35.8	29.6	25.1	21.9	26.3	September
Western Europe							
Austria	2.4	2.3	2.4	2.3	2.3	. . .	
Belgium	2.7	2.7	2.7	2.9	2.9	2.8	September
Denmark	0.8	0.6	0.5	0.5	0.6	. . .	
Finland	1.2	1.0	0.6	0.6	0.5	0.5	October
France	6.3	5.7	5.0	5.0	5.0	4.9	June
Germany	4.5	4.6	5.1	4.9	5.0	. . .	
Greece	13.6	15.5	12.3	9.2	8.1	8.4	June
Iceland	2.4	2.5	2.0	2.8	3.4	3.1	December
Ireland	2.5	1.8	1.9	1.9	1.7	. . .	
Italy	9.1	8.5	7.7	6.7	6.5	. . .	
Luxembourg	0.5	0.5	0.5	0.4	0.4	0.3	June
Netherlands	2.6	2.7	2.3	2.4	. . .	. . .	
Norway	1.8	1.5	1.3	1.3	1.4	2.2	September
Portugal	3.3	2.4	2.2	2.1	2.3	2.7	September
Spain	2.0	1.5	1.2	1.2	1.1	1.0	October
Sweden	2.6	1.7	1.7	1.6	1.4	1.3	September
Switzerland	5.2	4.6	3.8	4.1	3.6	. . .	
United Kingdom[6]	3.2	3.0	2.5	2.6	2.6	2.2	June

Table 24 *(concluded)*

	1998	1999	2000	2001	2002	2003	Latest
Asia							
Bangladesh	40.7	41.1	34.9	31.5	28.0	. . .	
China[7]	. . .	28.5	22.4	29.8	25.5	22.0	June
Hong Kong SAR	5.3	7.2	6.1	5.7	4.5	4.4	June
India	14.4	14.7	12.7	11.4	10.4	8.8	March
Indonesia	48.6	32.9	18.8	11.9	5.8	. . .	
Korea	7.4	8.3	6.6	2.9	1.9	2.3	June
Malaysia	18.6	16.6	15.4	17.8	15.9	14.8	June
Mongolia	. . .	32.5	23.7	8.0	8.0	. . .	
Pakistan	23.1	25.9	23.5	23.3	23.7	20.7	June
Philippines	11.0	12.7	14.9	16.9	15.4	15.2	September
Singapore	. . .	5.3	3.4	3.6	3.4	3.5	September
Sri Lanka	16.6	16.6	15.0	16.9	15.7	13.9	December
Thailand	42.9	38.6	17.7	10.5	15.8	15.5	August
Middle East and North Africa							
Algeria	. . .	. . .	27.4	26.1	. . .	. . .	
Egypt	. . .	. . .	. . .	. . .	. . .	. . .	
Jordan	8.7	11.9	14.0	15.4	13.9	14.8	June
Kuwait	. . .	12.8	12.8	10.3	7.8	. . .	
Lebanon	12.5	14.3	19.2	22.8	27.2	31.6	June
Morocco	14.6	15.3	17.5	16.8	18.0	. . .	September
Oman	6.4	6.0	7.5	10.6	11.3	. . .	
Saudi Arabia	8.4	11.4	10.4	10.1	9.2	8.2	June
Tunisia	19.5	18.8	21.6	19.2	20.7	. . .	
Sub-Saharan Africa							
Ghana	17.2	12.8	11.9	19.6	22.7	. . .	
Kenya	. . .	. . .	32.7	29.2	28.7	27.7	July
Mauritius	9.1	8.3	7.7	8.0	8.6	. . .	
Nigeria	19.4	25.6	22.6	16.0	17.3	. . .	March
South Africa	4.1	4.9	4.3	3.3	3.3	2.9	September
Tanzania	22.9	25.2	17.3	12.0	9.2	. . .	
Uganda****	20.2	11.9	9.8	6.5	3.6	8.0	December
Zimbabwe	. . .	. . .	19.6	11.4	4.2	7.5	September
Other							
Australia	0.7	0.6	0.5	0.7	0.6	0.5	September
Canada	1.1	1.2	1.2	1.5	1.6	1.4	September
Japan	5.4	5.8	6.1	6.6	8.9	7.2	September
United States[8]	1.0	0.9	1.1	1.4	1.6	1.3	September

Sources: National authorities, EDSS, IMF staff estimates.

Notes: (*) Based on net nonperforming loans; (**) 30-day NPL classification; (***) 60-day NPL classification; and (****) 180-day NPL classification.

[1]Uncollectible credits only as a percentage of credits to the private sector.

[2]Private banks.

[3]Excluding suspended banks.

[4]Under the new methodology adopted in 2002, interbank loans are also included in total loans which results in a significant decline in the NPL ratio. Under the old methodology, the ratio remains at about one-third of all loans.

[5]The sudden increase in NPLs in 2003 reflects a revision in the official definition.

[6]Includes mortgage banks.

[7]Data for state-owned commercial banks only.

[8]U.S. Banks with assets greater than $1 billion.

Table 25. Bank Provisions to Nonperforming Loans
(In percent)

	1998	1999	2000	2001	2002	2003	Latest
Latin America							
Argentina	61.2	60.0	62.9	66.0	. . .	. . .	
Bahamas	41.0	43.1	51.5	49.8	44.8	. . .	
Bolivia	58.0	55.8	61.4	63.7	63.7	67.4	September
Brazil	110.9	125.1	82.1	126.1	143.5	139.8	September
Chile	131.4	152.9	145.5	146.5	128.1	120.8	October
Colombia	37.9	36.8	54.5	73.9	86.3	91.4	August
Costa Rica	125.6	122.4	99.8	114.0	106.6	. . .	June
Dominican Republic	. . .	. . .	. . .	. . .	. . .	. . .	
Ecuador	99.6	109.0	104.0	102.2	131.4	107.5	August
Honduras	19.3	23.1	26.7	29.5	37.4	. . .	
Jamaica	. . .	. . .	136.5	149.6	139.6	. . .	
Mexico	66.1	107.8	115.3	123.8	138.9	142.5	August
Paraguay	48.1	45.1	45.5	39.8	50.2	54.8	December
Peru	92.1	99.5	104.3	114.2	133.2	124.2	September
Uruguay	62.8	48.4	47.5	45.4	60.2	. . .	
Venezuela	123.4	101.8	93.6	92.2	97.6	102.5	September
Emerging Europe							
Armenia	27.1	81.1	65.9	. . .	. . .	. . .	
Bulgaria	75.0	71.9	79.3	74.3	74.3	53.1	September
Croatia	84.4	78.7	79.8	75.7	68.1	64.9	September
Czech Republic	54.3	52.2	55.0	59.2	74.0	77.8	March
Estonia	88.6	51.8	. . .	. . .	. . .	. . .	
Hungary	45.2	51.4	56.7	53.9	. . .	. . .	
Israel	49.5	45.7	55.8	57.1	54.7	. . .	June
Kyrgyz Republic	56.9	52.0	68.6	63.5	69.2	. . .	June
Latvia	78.0	79.3	74.1	80.4	95.5	98.5	March
Lithuania	47.5	37.5	34.6	34.2	18.6	21.6	December
Macedonia	. . .	. . .	. . .	. . .	. . .	. . .	
Malta	. . .	. . .	. . .	. . .	. . .	. . .	
Poland	. . .	. . .	46.0	48.6	48.0	47.6	September
Russia	40.1	63.4	80.1	79.3	83.7	86.0	September
Slovak Republic	. . .	42.5	61.5	70.5	72.5	73.3	September
Slovenia[1]	. . .	114.9	101.0	100.5	102.9	. . .	
Turkey	44.2	61.9	59.8	47.1	64.2	77.5	September
Ukraine	. . .	. . .	. . .	. . .	. . .	. . .	
Western Europe							
Austria	. . .	. . .	. . .	. . .	. . .	. . .	
Belgium	61.0	58.0	57.0	57.0	51.8	40.6	September
Denmark	. . .	. . .	. . .	. . .	. . .	. . .	
Finland	. . .	. . .	. . .	. . .	. . .	. . .	
France	58.5	60.7	60.8	59.9	58.4	58.3	June
Germany	73.3	76.9	81.8	85.7	. . .	. . .	
Greece	24.1	26.1	36.8	43.3	45.3	. . .	
Iceland	51.9	50.5	52.5	46.8	43.7	. . .	
Ireland	60.0	82.0	105.0	118.0	129.0	. . .	
Italy	42.8	48.1	48.6	50.0	53.6	. . .	
Luxembourg	. . .	. . .	. . .	. . .	. . .	. . .	
Netherlands	. . .	93.1	90.8	88.8	67.3	. . .	
Norway	61.0	58.0	57.0	57.0	58.0	. . .	
Portugal	. . .	. . .	66.7	66.8	62.8	. . .	
Spain	69.9	73.3	62.8	57.2	55.8	. . .	
Sweden	42.3	55.5	60.0	64.9	73.8	. . .	
Switzerland	. . .	. . .	. . .	. . .	. . .	. . .	
United Kingdom	56.0	71.2	65.0	69.5	. . .	. . .	

Table 25 *(concluded)*

	1998	1999	2000	2001	2002	2003	Latest
Asia							
Bangladesh	53.5	51.4	59.1	60.5	55.8	. . .	
China	. . .	. . .	. . .	. . .	. . .	. . .	
Hong Kong SAR	. . .	. . .	. . .	. . .	. . .	. . .	
India	. . .	. . .	. . .	. . .	. . .	46.4	March
Indonesia	28.6	77.7	59.4	97.7	125.7	152.5	March
Korea	46.2	66.6	81.8	85.2	109.4	. . .	
Malaysia	. . .	39.0	41.0	37.7	38.1	38.5	June
Mongolia	. . .	95.8	84.3	85.8	75.2	. . .	
Pakistan	58.6	48.6	55.0	56.2	58.7	58.8	August
Philippines	36.4	45.2	43.7	45.3	53.2	52.2	September
Singapore	. . .	86.2	87.2	90.1	96.7	96.6	September
Sri Lanka	. . .	. . .	. . .	40.8	46.1	51.2	December
Thailand	29.2	37.9	47.2	54.9	61.8	60.8	March
Middle East and North Africa							
Algeria	. . .	. . .	70.5	96.3	. . .	. . .	
Egypt	. . .	. . .	. . .	. . .	. . .	. . .	
Jordan	. . .	. . .	51.2	50.8	65.0	. . .	
Kuwait	. . .	. . .	. . .	. . .	. . .	. . .	
Lebanon	57.4	72.5	72.5	69.3	68.2	73.3	March
Morocco	52.6	51.8	45.7	53.0	53.8	. . .	September
Oman	70.3	75.0	71.9	68.5	79.7	. . .	
Saudi Arabia	83.0	88.0	99.0	107.0	110.4	118.9	June
Tunisia	. . .	. . .	. . .	. . .	. . .	. . .	
Sub-Saharan Africa							
Ghana	89.4	67.2	58.6	46.4	63.6	. . .	
Kenya	. . .	. . .	. . .	37.2	41.0	. . .	
Mauritius	. . .	. . .	. . .	. . .	. . .	. . .	
Nigeria	. . .	46.7	49.7	73.6	60.9	. . .	March
South Africa	41.3	41.5	43.8	36.4	42.9	50.7	September
Tanzania	. . .	. . .	. . .	. . .	. . .	. . .	
Uganda	54.2	51.9	50.5	. . .	. . .	. . .	
Zimbabwe	. . .	. . .	44.4	28.3	52.8	29.5	September
Other							
Australia	37.9	44.2	38.4	37.0	36.5	38.6	September
Canada	50.3	45.4	42.8	44.0	41.1	45.5	September
Japan	49.9	40.3	35.5	31.8	31.6	34.9	September
United States	73.7	76.1	98.2	118.2	85.6	. . .	

Sources: National authorities; and IMF staff estimates.
[1]Actual provisioning as a percentage of required provisioning.

Table 26. Bank Return on Assets

(In percent)

	1998	1999	2000	2001	2002	2003	Latest
Latin America							
Argentina	...	0.4	0.3	−0.2	−9.7	−2.5	August
Bahamas	2.9	2.5	3.5	3.3	2.7	...	
Bolivia	0.7	0.7	−0.9	−0.4	0.1	0.5	September
Brazil	0.6	1.6	1.0	0.2	1.9	1.9	June
Chile	0.9	0.7	1.0	1.3	1.1	1.3	September
Colombia	−2.2	−3.2	−2.0	0.6	1.5	2.5	November
Costa Rica	0.9	1.6	1.5	1.7	1.7	...	June
Dominican Republic	1.7	2.4	1.6	1.9	2.3	0.3	October
Ecuador	0.8	0.2	−2.8	−6.6	1.5	1.9	September
Honduras	1.7	1.2	0.8	0.8	0.7	...	
Jamaica	...	...	0.3	0.5	0.6	...	
Mexico	0.6	0.7	0.9	0.8	−1.1	1.6	September
Paraguay[1]	5.0	1.2	1.7	2.4	1.5	0.4	December
Peru	0.7	0.3	0.3	0.4	0.8	0.9	September
Uruguay[1,2]	0.9	1.3	0.9	−0.3	−4.8	...	
Venezuela	4.9	3.1	2.8	2.7	4.8	1.4	September
Emerging Europe							
Armenia	4.2	2.3	−1.9	−9.1	3.9	2.1	September
Bulgaria	1.7	2.4	2.8	2.6	2.0	2.4	September
Croatia	−2.8	0.8	1.2	1.3	1.3	1.5	September
Czech Republic	−0.2	−0.3	0.7	0.7	1.2	1.1	September
Estonia[3]	−1.2	1.4	1.1	2.5	2.6	...	
Hungary	−2.0	0.6	1.3	2.0	1.8	2.1	November
Israel	0.5	0.5	0.5	0.3	0.1	...	
Kyrgyz Republic	1.5	−8.8	−1.1	1.5	1.0	...	June
Latvia	−1.5	1.0	2.0	1.5	1.3	...	March
Lithuania	0.9	0.2	0.5	−0.1	1.0	1.4	December
Macedonia	2.0	0.8	0.8	−0.7	0.4	...	
Malta	...	0.9	0.8	0.8	0.8	...	
Poland[3]	1.8	1.6	1.5	1.3	0.8	1.2	September
Russia	−3.5	−0.3	0.9	2.4	1.7	2.3	September
Slovak Republic	−0.5	−2.3	1.4	1.0	1.2	1.3	June
Slovenia	1.2	0.8	1.1	0.5	1.1	1.2	September
Turkey	1.9	−0.4	−0.8	−5.5	1.1	1.9	September
Ukraine	...	2.0	−0.1	1.2	1.2	1.0	September
Western Europe							
Austria	0.4	0.4	0.4	0.5	0.3	0.4	September
Belgium	0.3	0.4	0.6	0.4	0.4	...	
Denmark	0.8	0.7	0.8	0.8	0.7	...	
Finland	1.2	1.0	1.2	1.2	0.7	0.8	June
France	0.3	0.4	0.5	0.4	0.5	...	
Germany	0.3	0.2	0.2	0.1	0.1	...	
Greece	0.8	2.4	1.4	1.0	0.5	0.7	September
Iceland	0.9	1.3	0.6	0.8	1.1	1.1	June
Ireland[4]	...	1.3	1.2	0.9	1.5	...	
Italy	0.5	0.6	0.8	0.6	0.5	...	
Luxembourg	0.6	0.4	0.5	0.5	0.4	...	
Netherlands	0.4	0.6	0.5	0.5	0.3	0.4	September
Norway	0.7	1.2	1.2	0.9	0.6	0.7	September
Portugal	...	0.9	0.9	0.9	0.7	0.8	September
Spain	0.9	0.9	1.0	0.9	0.8	...	
Sweden	0.7	0.7	0.9	0.8	0.6	...	
Switzerland	0.7	0.8	0.9	0.5	0.2	...	
United Kingdom[3,5]	0.8	1.0	0.9	0.5	0.9	0.5	June

Table 26 *(concluded)*

	1998	1999	2000	2001	2002	2003	Latest
Asia							
Bangladesh	0.3	0.2	0.0	0.7	0.5	. . .	
China	. . .	0.1	0.1	0.1	0.1	. . .	
Hong Kong SAR	0.4	0.4	0.8	0.8	0.8	0.8	June
India	0.8	0.5	0.7	0.5	0.8	1.0	March
Indonesia	−19.9	−9.1	0.1	0.8	1.3	. . .	
Korea	−3.2	−1.3	−0.6	0.7	0.7	0.2	March
Malaysia	. . .	0.7	1.5	1.0	1.3	. . .	
Mongolia	. . .	. . .	4.2	3.6	. . .	. . .	
Pakistan	0.5	−0.2	−0.2	−0.5	0.1	1.2	June
Philippines	0.8	0.4	0.4	0.4	0.8	1.0	September
Singapore	0.4	1.2	1.3	0.8	0.8	0.8	September
Sri Lanka	1.3	−0.2	0.8	0.8	. . .	. . .	
Thailand[3]	−5.6	−5.7	−1.7	−0.1	0.4	1.1	August
Middle East and North Africa							
Algeria	−1.1	1.5	0.6	0.8	. . .		
Egypt	0.9	0.9	0.9	0.8	0.7	0.5	September
Kuwait	. . .	1.7	2.0	2.1	1.8	. . .	
Jordan	. . .	. . .	0.3	0.7	0.6	. . .	
Lebanon	1.5	1.0	0.7	0.5	0.6	. . .	June
Morocco	0.9	0.7	0.7	0.9	0.7	. . .	September
Oman	1.9	1.6	1.3	0.1	1.4	. . .	
Saudi Arabia[3]	. . .	0.9	2.0	2.2	2.3	2.4	June
Tunisia	1.2	1.2	1.2	1.1	0.7	. . .	
Sub-Saharan Africa							
Ghana	8.8	8.5	9.8	8.7	6.7	. . .	
Kenya	0.8	0.0	0.5	2.2	2.0	. . .	
Mauritius[3]	2.4	2.2	2.3	2.2	2.3	. . .	
Nigeria	4.5	4.1	4.0	5.2	. . .	. . .	
South Africa[3]	. . .	1.4	1.5	1.1	1.0	1.4	September
Tanzania	1.9	0.1	1.3	1.2	1.3	. . .	
Uganda	. . .	3.7	4.4	4.4	3.3	3.5	December
Zimbabwe	. . .	. . .	6.0	5.1	4.0	4.7	September
Other							
Australia	1.0	1.2	1.3	1.0	1.2	. . .	
Canada	0.5	0.7	0.7	0.6	0.5	0.6	September
Japan[3]	−0.6	−0.9	0.3	0.1	0.0	. . .	September
United States[6]	1.1	1.3	1.2	1.1	1.4	1.4	September

Sources: National authorities; OECD; and IMF staff estimates.
[1]Private banks only.
[2]For 2002 ROA excludes suspended banks and mortgage bank.
[3]Before-tax.
[4]Data for 2002 corresponds to Allied Irish Bank and Bank of Ireland only.
[5]Includes mortgage banks.
[6]U.S. banks with assets greater than $1 billion.

Table 27. Bank Return on Equity
(In percent)

	1998	1999	2000	2001	2002	2003	Latest
Latin America							
Argentina	. . .	4.0	3.1	−1.5	−69.9	−20.6	August
Bahamas	35.8	27.5	34.3	29.3	23.9	. . .	
Bolivia	8.0	8.7	−8.6	−4.1	0.6	4.0	September
Brazil	7.4	18.9	11.3	2.4	20.8	21.0	June
Chile	11.5	9.4	12.7	17.7	14.4	16.4	September
Colombia	−19.2	−29.5	−17.3	5.4	13.7	21.7	November
Costa Rica	7.6	14.1	12.7	15.0	14.8	. . .	June
Dominican Republic	. . .	. . .	. . .	. . .	. . .		
Ecuador	5.3	1.3	−21.3	−36.0	15.3	18.2	September
Honduras	20.2	14.0	9.0	8.9	8.2	. . .	
Jamaica	. . .	. . .	. . .	. . .	. . .	. . .	
Mexico	6.9	5.8	10.4	8.6	−10.4	13.4	September
Paraguay[1]	. . .	20.1	12.4	21.2	9.0	4.5	December
Peru	8.4	4.0	3.1	4.5	8.4	9.0	September
Uruguay[1,2]	7.3	7.8	4.6	−18.7	. . .	. . .	
Venezuela	41.4	24.0	23.1	20.6	31.7	9.6	September
Emerging Europe							
Armenia	35.0	19.6	12.0	−6.3	. . .	. . .	
Bulgaria	21.5	20.9	22.6	19.3	14.9	17.9	September
Croatia	. . .	5.0	10.5	6.7	20.4	18.7	September
Czech Republic	−17.8	−4.3	13.1	14.4	25.4	22.7	September
Estonia[3]	−6.4	7.8	8.6	18.8	19.2*	. . .	
Hungary	−26.7	6.7	15.1	20.2	19.7	25.8	September
Israel	9.9	11.3	11.7	5.9	2.8	6.9	June
Kyrgyz Republic	6.8	−56.7	−5.3	4.8	11.9	. . .	June
Latvia	−12.9	11.0	19.0	19.0	14.7	. . .	March
Lithuania	11.9	1.3	5.0	−1.2	9.8	13.5	December
Macedonia	8.2	3.5	3.8	−3.2	2.1	. . .	
Malta	. . .	15.7	13.3	11.9	12.3	. . .	
Poland	16.1	12.9	14.5	13.1	5.2	9.5	September
Russia	−28.6	−4.0	8.0	19.4	11.8	16.0	September
Slovak Republic	−13.4	−36.5	25.2	22.7	31.1	30.5	June
Slovenia	11.3	7.8	11.4	4.8	13.3	15.7	September
Turkey	23.1	−7.2	−10.5	−69.4	9.3	13.8	September
Ukraine	. . .	8.7	−0.5	7.5	8.0	7.0	September
Western Europe							
Austria	8.7	8.4	9.9	10.7	5.4	. . .	
Belgium	11.0	17.1	20.4	13.7	11.8	. . .	
Denmark	12.9	11.8	13.5	12.6	11.7	. . .	
Finland	25.8	20.1	22.4	23.8	14.1	14.6	June
France	8.4	9.1	9.7	9.6	9.4	. . .	
Germany	8.5	5.4	5.3	4.2	2.0	. . .	
Greece	12.0	29.0	15.0	12.4	6.8	. . .	
Iceland	13.5	19.3	9.7	13.5	18.4	19.5	June
Ireland[4]	. . .	23.0	22.0	16.0	27.0	. . .	
Italy	7.2	8.7	11.2	8.6	7.0	. . .	
Luxembourg	15.6	10.1	11.1	11.6	11.3	. . .	
Netherlands	11.0	14.2	14.7	10.8	9.2	11.0	September
Norway[5]	11.4	14.7	15.1	11.4	4.8	2.5	September
Portugal	15.1	14.7	15.2	14.9	11.7	13.3	September
Spain	14.4	12.2	14.0	12.7	12.2	14.0	June
Sweden	14.2	16.0	15.7	13.0	10.1	10.1	September
Switzerland	17.1	18.8	18.2	11.2	8.6	. . .	
United Kingdom[6]	26.1	26.0	20.8	18.0	17.3	19.0	June

Table 27 *(concluded)*

	1998	1999	2000	2001	2002	2003	Latest
Asia							
Bangladesh	6.6	5.2	0.3	15.9	11.6	. . .	
China	. . .	. . .	. . .	. . .	. . .	. . .	
Hong Kong SAR	7.8	11.1	13.5	13.9	13.3	12.5	June
India	. . .	. . .	12.8	10.4	11.9	. . .	March
Indonesia	. . .	. . .	19.6	13.4	22.7	22.1	June
Korea	−52.5	−23.1	−11.9	12.9	12.1	4.8	March
Malaysia	. . .	11.5	19.6	13.3	16.7	. . .	
Mongolia	. . .	19.2	29.5	23.2	23.6	. . .	
Pakistan	9.1	−6.3	−0.3	−0.3	13.0	. . .	
Philippines	5.9	2.9	2.6	3.2	6.2	. . .	
Singapore	4.2	10.7	12.6	7.7	7.6	7.7	September
Sri Lanka	13.9	−10.1	13.1	15.5	. . .	. . .	
Thailand[3]	−38.5	−47.0	−15.9	−1.9	7.6	. . .	September
Middle East and North Africa							
Algeria	−22.0	30.6	10.5	10.9	. . .		
Egypt	. . .	14.7	16.1	13.7	12.4	8.5	September
Jordan	. . .	. . .	4.0	9.0	8.9	. . .	
Kuwait	. . .	13.7	16.6	17.1	16.3	. . .	
Lebanon	20.3	15.7	11.1	8.4	9.4	. . .	
Morocco	9.5	8.2	8.1	10.2	7.8	. . .	September
Oman	16.7	13.2	12.0	1.2	14.3	. . .	
Saudi Arabia	. . .	9.1	21.0	21.9	22.2	22.7	June
Tunisia	13.2	12.7	14.9	14.0	7.4	. . .	
Sub-Saharan Africa							
Ghana	30.8	62.8	60.8	42.3	33.8	. . .	
Kenya	8.9	0.3	5.0	16.6	. . .	. . .	
Mauritius[3]	23.9	20.7	22.1	20.6	22.0	. . .	
Nigeria	. . .	46.7	51.6	54.9	. . .	. . .	
South Africa[3]	21.7	13.3	15.3	10.8	14.8	18.8	March
Tanzania	45.6	2.1	20.5	21.4	17.6	. . .	
Uganda	. . .	56.5	53.1	45.8	33.5	. . .	June
Zimbabwe	. . .	. . .	43.2	42.7	57.7	62.8	September
Other							
Australia	15.0	18.0	19.4	15.6	18.2	. . .	
Canada	12.2	14.2	13.9	13.0	9.5	13.7	September
Japan[3]	−20.0	−25.1	6.8	1.2	0.4	. . .	September
United States[7]	13.3	15.7	14.0	12.9	15.0	15.8	September

Sources: National authorities; Bankscope (*); OECD; and IMF staff estimates
[1]Private banks only.
[2]For 2002 ROA excludes suspended banks and mortgage bank.
[3]Before-tax.
[4]Data for 2002 corresponds to Allied Irish Bank and Bank of Ireland only.
[5]Commercial banks only.
[6]U.K. large commercial banks.
[7]U.S. banks with assets greater than $1 billion.

Table 28. Moody's Weighted Average Bank Financial Strength Index[1]

	Financial Strength Index			Percent Change from Dec. 2002
	Dec. 2001	Dec. 2002	Dec. 2003	
Latin America				
Argentina	13.3	0.0	0.0	0.0
Bolivia	25.0	8.3	2.1	−74.9
Brazil	37.9	25.0	24.3	−2.8
Chile	50.6	52.5	56.5	7.6
Colombia	23.3	24.2	24.2	0.0
Ecuador	8.3	8.3	8.3	0.0
Jamaica	. . .	. . .	. . .	. . .
Mexico	36.3	39.6	39.6	0.0
Paraguay	. . .	. . .	. . .	. . .
Peru	22.9	23.3	23.3	0.0
Uruguay	31.3	0.0	0.0	0.0
Venezuela	28.8	15.4	8.3	−45.9
Emerging Europe				
Bulgaria	. . .	16.7	20.8	25.0
Croatia	33.3	33.3	33.3	0.0
Czech Republic	29.2	32.5	33.9	4.4
Estonia	38.3	46.7	46.7	0.0
Hungary	41.7	45.0	42.5	−5.6
Israel	48.3	45.8	45.8	0.0
Latvia	29.2	32.1	32.1	0.0
Lithuania	. . .	. . .	. . .	. . .
Poland	29.6	28.3	29.5	4.2
Russia	12.5	10.8	10.8	0.0
Slovak Republic	9.6	15.0	17.5	16.7
Slovenia	40.2	40.8	45.2	10.6
Turkey	30.0	20.4	20.4	0.0
Ukraine	8.3	8.3	8.3	0.0
Western Europe				
Austria	62.5	61.7	61.7	0.0
Belgium	75.0	75.0	75.0	0.0
Denmark	80.0	80.0	80.0	0.0
Finland	70.0	73.3	73.3	0.0
France	71.9	74.2	71.2	−4.0
Germany	61.7	54.2	46.7	−13.8
Greece	40.0	40.0	44.8	12.1
Ireland	69.2	70.0	71.7	2.4
Italy	64.6	63.3	63.3	0.0
Luxembourg	68.7	68.3	66.7	−2.4
Netherlands	87.5	84.2	84.2	0.0
Norway	63.3	65.0	67.5	3.8
Portugal	64.6	64.2	64.2	0.0
Spain	77.1	75.0	76.7	2.2
Sweden	72.5	73.3	75.0	2.3
Switzerland	70.8	72.1	72.1	0.0
United Kingdom	83.8	83.8	83.3	−0.5

Table 28. *(concluded)*

	Financial Strength Index			Percent Change
	Dec. 2001	Dec. 2002	Dec. 2003	from Dec. 2002
Asia				
China	10.0	10.0	10.0	0.0
Hong Kong SAR	66.6	62.3	62.3	0.0
India	25.8	27.5	27.5	0.0
Indonesia	1.7	3.0	3.0	0.0
Korea	14.2	16.7	18.3	10.0
Malaysia	30.4	31.7	33.3	5.3
Pakistan	2.1	5.0	9.6	91.7
Philippines	17.5	20.4	20.4	0.0
Singapore	75.0	74.7	74.7	0.0
Sri Lanka	. . .	. . .	. . .	. . .
Thailand	15.8	15.8	15.8	0.0
Middle East				
Egypt	22.9	22.9	22.9	0.0
Jordan[2]	25.0	19.2	19.2	0.0
Lebanon	33.3	33.3	33.3	0.0
Morocco	35.8	35.8	35.8	0.0
Oman	31.7	29.2	29.2	0.0
Saudi Arabia	43.3	43.3	43.3	0.0
Tunisia	16.7	16.7	16.7	0.0
Africa				
Ghana	. . .	. . .	. . .	. . .
Kenya	. . .	. . .	. . .	. . .
Nigeria	. . .	. . .	. . .	. . .
South Africa	53.5	49.0	50.0	2.1
Uganda	. . .	. . .	. . .	. . .
Zambia	. . .	. . .	. . .	. . .
Zimbabwe	. . .	. . .	. . .	. . .
Other				
Australia	71.7	72.5	72.5	0.0
Canada	77.1	75.0	75.0	0.0
Japan	16.7	12.9	12.0	−7.1
United States	77.1	75.0	75.0	0.0

Source: Moody's.

[1]Constructed according to a numerical scale assigned to Moody's weighted average bank ratings by country. 0 indicates the lowest possible average rating and 100 indicates the highest possible average rating.

[2]Ratings as of January 2004.

World Economic and Financial Surveys

This series (ISSN 0258-7440) contains biannual, annual, and periodic studies covering monetary and financial issues of importance to the global economy. The core elements of the series are the World Economic Outlook report, usually published in May and October, and the semiannual Global Financial Stability Report. Other studies assess international trade policy, private market and official financing for developing countries, exchange and payments systems, export credit policies, and issues discussed in the World Economic Outlook. Please consult the IMF Publications Catalog for a complete listing of currently available World Economic and Financial Surveys.

World Economic Outlook: A Survey by the Staff of the International Monetary Fund

The World Economic Outlook, published twice a year in English, French, Spanish, and Arabic, presents IMF staff economists' analyses of global economic developments during the near and medium term. Chapters give an overview of the world economy; consider issues affecting industrial countries, developing countries, and economies in transition to the market; and address topics of pressing current interest.

ISSN 0256-6877.
$49.00 (academic rate: $46.00); paper.
2003. (April). ISBN 1-58906-212-4. **Stock #WEO EA 0012003.**
2002. (Sep.). ISBN 1-58906-179-9. **Stock #WEO EA 0022002.**
2002. (April). ISBN 1-58906-107-1. **Stock #WEO EA 0012002.**

Exchange Arrangements and Foreign Exchange Markets: Developments and Issues
by a staff team led by Shogo Ishii

This study updates developments in exchange arrangements during 1998–2001. It also discusses the evolution of exchange rate regimes based on de facto policies since 1990, reviews foreign exchange market organization and regulations in a number of countries, and examines factors affecting exchange rate volatility.

ISSN 0258-7440
$42.00 (academic rate $35.00)
2003 (March) ISBN 1-58906-177-2. **Stock #WEO EA 0192003.**

Official Financing: Recent Developments and Selected Issues
by a staff team in the Policy Development and Review Department led by Martin G. Gilman and Jian-Ye Wang

This study provides information on official financing for developing countries, with the focus on low-income countries. It updates the 2001 edition and reviews developments in direct financing by official and multilateral sources.

$42.00 (academic rate: $35.00); paper.
2003. ISBN 1-58906-228-0. **Stock #WEO EA 0132003.**
2001. ISBN 1-58906-038-5. **Stock #WEO EA 0132001.**

Exchange Rate Arrangements and Currency Convertibility: Developments and Issues
by a staff team led by R. Barry Johnston

A principal force driving the growth in international trade and investment has been the liberalization of financial transactions, including the liberalization of trade and exchange controls. This study reviews the developments and issues in the exchange arrangements and currency convertibility of IMF members.

$20.00 (academic rate: $12.00); paper.
1999. ISBN 1-55775-795-X. **Stock #WEO EA 0191999.**

World Economic Outlook Supporting Studies
by the IMF's Research Department

These studies, supporting analyses and scenarios of the World Economic Outlook, provide a detailed examination of theory and evidence on major issues currently affecting the global economy.

$25.00 (academic rate: $20.00); paper.
2000. ISBN 1-55775-893-X. **Stock #WEO EA 0032000.**

Global Financial Stability Report: Market Developments and Issues

The Global Financial Stability Report, published twice a year, examines trends and issues that influence world financial markets. It replaces two IMF publications—the annual International Capital Markets report and the electronic quarterly Emerging Market Financing report. The report is designed to deepen understanding of international capital flows and explores developments that could pose a risk to international financial market stability.

$49.00 (academic rate: $46.00); paper.
September 2003 ISBN 1-58906-236-1. **Stock #GFSR EA0022003.**
March 2003 ISBN 1-58906-210-8. **Stock #GFSR EA0012003.**
December 2002 ISBN-1-58906-192-6. **Stock #GFSR EA0042002.**
September 2002 ISBN 1-58906-157-8. **Stock #GFSR EA0032002.**
June 2002 ISBN 1-58906-131-4. **Stock #GFSR EA0022002.**

International Capital Markets: Developments, Prospects, and Key Policy Issues (back issues)

$42.00 (academic rate: $35.00); paper.
2001. ISBN 1-58906-056-3. **Stock #WEO EA 0062001.**

Toward a Framework for Financial Stability
by a staff team led by David Folkerts-Landau and Carl-Johan Lindgren

This study outlines the broad principles and characteristics of stable and sound financial systems, to facilitate IMF surveillance over banking sector issues of macroeconomic significance and to contribute to the general international effort to reduce the likelihood and diminish the intensity of future financial sector crises.

$25.00 (academic rate: $20.00); paper.
1998. ISBN 1-55775-706-2. **Stock #WEO-016.**

Trade Liberalization in IMF-Supported Programs
by a staff team led by Robert Sharer

This study assesses trade liberalization in programs supported by the IMF by reviewing multiyear arrangements in the 1990s and six detailed case studies. It also discusses the main economic factors affecting trade policy targets.

$25.00 (academic rate: $20.00); paper.
1998. ISBN 1-55775-707-0. **Stock #WEO-1897.**

Available by series subscription or single title (including back issues); academic rate available only to full-time university faculty and students. For earlier editions please inquire about prices.

The IMF Catalog of Publications is available on-line at the Internet address listed below.

Please send orders and inquiries to:
International Monetary Fund, Publication Services, 700 19th Street, N.W.
Washington, D.C. 20431, U.S.A.
Tel.: (202) 623-7430   Telefax: (202) 623-7201
E-mail: publications@imf.org
Internet: http://www.imf.org